Two of the most crucial areas of education – the development of oral language and the acquisition of literacy – are examined here with an effective combination of theory and practice. The sociocultural perspective is illustrated through descriptions of learning by populations usually neglected in treatments of language and literacy – American Sign Language users, second-language speakers, and minority students. The book covers a broad range of ages, backgrounds, locations, and literacy concerns from preschool to law school. Although the populations and literacy issues are diverse, the book's unity is provided by a broadly shared theoretical framework.

Sociocultural approaches to language and literacy

Sociocultural approaches to language and literacy

An interactionist perspective

Edited by
VERA JOHN-STEINER
University of New Mexico
CAROLYN P. PANOFSKY
Rhode Island College
LARRY W. SMITH
University of New Mexico

Published by the Press Syndicate of the University of Cambridge
The Pitt Building, Trumpington Street, Cambridge CB2 1RP
40 West 20th Street, New York, NY 10011-4211, USA
10 Stamford Road, Oakleigh, Melbourne 3166, Australia

First published 1994

Printed in the United States of America

Library of Congress Cataloging-in-Publication Data
Sociocultural approaches to language and literacy: an interactionist perspective / edited by Vera John-Steiner, Carolyn P. Panofsky, Larry W. Smith.
p. cm.
Includes indexes.
ISBN 0-521-37301-8 (hc)
1. Language acquisition. 2. Literacy. 3. Interaction analysis in education. I. John-Steiner, Vera, 1930– II. Panofsky, Carolyn P, 1947–
III. Smith, Larry W., 1945–
P118.I492 1994
401′.93 – dc20 93-5495
CIP

A catalog record for this book is available from the British Library.

ISBN 0-521-37301-8 hardback

Contents

Contributors

Maria Silvia Barbieri
Department of Psychology
University of Trieste

Francine Filipek Collignon
Multifunctional Resource Center
Brown University

Pat Cordeiro
Elementary Education
Rhode Island College

Patricia A. Edwards
Teacher Education
Michigan State University

Kelly R. Ferko
Department of Psychology
University of California at Los Angeles

Georgia Earnest Garcia
Department of Curriculum and Instruction and
Center for the Study of Reading
University of Illinois, Champaign/Urbana

Vera John-Steiner
Departments of Linguistics and Education
University of New Mexico

Liliana Landolfi
Language Education
University of Naples

Karl-Erik McCullough
Department of Psychology
University of Chicago

David McNeill
Department of Psychology
University of Chicago

Michele Minnis
School of Law
University of New Mexico

Carolyn P. Panofsky
Foundations of Education
Rhode Island College

Juan Daniel Ramirez
Department of Psychology
University of Seville

Henry Shonerd
Multicultural Education Program
College of Santa Fe (at Albuquerque)

Larry W. Smith
Center for English Language and American Culture
University of New Mexico

Martha Tyrone
Department of Psychology
University of Chicago

Sherman Wilcox
Department of Linguistics
University of New Mexico

Patricia Zukow-Goldring
Department of Psychology
University of California at Irvine

1 *Introduction*

VERA JOHN-STEINER, CAROLYN P. PANOFSKY,
AND LARRY W. SMITH

In the past two decades, a shift in research perspectives has led to a transformation in how educational theorists think about language and literacy. Converging research from anthropology, linguistics, psychology, and education has given rise to new models of language and literacy development. The common element is a social and functional approach, largely replacing earlier behaviorist and nativist models.

L. S. Vygotsky's *Thought and Language* (1962) and *Mind in Society* (1978) are foundations for a new model of language and development, along with several other changes in the human sciences. We sketch some of these changes to clarify our own interactionist framework.

1.1 TENETS OF THE THEORETICAL FRAMEWORK

1. Recent studies of language and literacy use *functional* rather than structural models. Rather than regarding grammatical structure as autonomous, Fillmore (1968), Chafe (1970, 1982), Halliday (1975, 1978), and Silverstein (1976, 1985) analyze grammatical features of language in terms of their use. Particularly significant to us is the focus these scholars, and some philosophers of language (Austin, 1962; Grice, 1975; Searle, 1969), put on communicative intent and on the representational functions of language.

2. There has been increased emphasis on *social interaction* as the generative context for language mastery. Gordon Wells (1981) describes language as interaction of "people collaborating in the negotiation of meaning; talk as a form of social action; the reciprocal influence of language and context" (p. 15). Jerome Bruner (1983) refers to this interaction as "Language Acquisition Support System" (LASS).

3. Today the study of language includes *meaning and use* as well as structure (Hickman, 1987). This broadening is similar to expansions in several other disciplines. The formalism of approaches in nativist linguistics – so popular in the 1960s – corresponded to similar ap-

proaches in economics, literary criticism, and even in the philosophy of mathematics, under the strong influence of logical positivism. In the past two decades, governing paradigms have shifted. They now stress situated knowledge, constructed in particular, historical situations. Such an epistemic stance has contributed to a broader understanding of language and of the fact that its forms can be understood only in terms of context and function (Bruner, 1983; Gee, 1990).

4. Participation of anthropologists and sociologists in language study has a long history (Sapir, 1921; Whorf, 1956). Recently, their cross-cultural experience helped to study language varieties in U.S. speech communities (Heath, 1983). Ethnographic and sociological methods generated a new field, *ethnography of communication* (Gumperz & Hymes, 1972). The study of speech events, speech acts (Searle, 1969), and the effect of culture in the development of literacy (Scribner & Cole, 1981) gave a much needed interdisciplinary basis for study of language. This research has been fruitful in the areas of literacy and schooling (Cook-Gumperz, 1985; Gilmore & Glatthorn, 1982; and Schieffelin & Gilmore, 1986).

5. Sociocultural views of language development and literacy are part of a shift from the traditional focus on the individual learner. Instead, literacy events (Scribner & Cole, 1981; Goodman & Goodman, 1990), are seen as *culturally situated practices.* These theorists reject the view that Richard Shweder (1990) has called "Platonic": that the study of mind must seek central, universal, inherent mechanisms of mind and language.

6. This is replaced by a research methodology aimed at a *process approach,* which looks at "socially assembled situations," "activity-in-context," and "activity settings" (Laboratory for Comparative Human Cognition, 1983; Tharp & Gallimore, 1988). Vygotskian researchers include ethnographic methods – sustained observations in community settings. Laboratory researchers look for significant interactional and teaching strategies (Diaz, Neal, & Amaya-Williams, 1990). They look at changes over time (Berk, 1986). They rely on microgenetic approaches (Siegler & Crowley, 1991; Wertsch & Hickman, 1987). They seek to refine and extend the sociocultural theory of development (Tudge, 1990).

We review these shifts in order to situate our own approach within the contemporary reexamination of language, including altered conceptions of learning and development, and of the relationship between thinking, language, and society. The new direction denies "the fundamental dualism inherited from Descartes by both empiricist and nativist traditions. These dualisms include, among others, the separation of subject from object, knowledge from action, and the individual from the social" (Biddell, 1988).

Our work, started in 1977 (Elsasser & John-Steiner, 1977), linked Vygotsky and Freire as advancing literacy. Integrating the two traditions was a challenging task, in theory as well as in practice, since our work included teaching students from disenfranchised groups to read. John-Steiner and Tatter (1983) first described the paradigm shift in language study that gained so much momentum in the 1980s. That article articulated a model of language development that interwove philosophical and psychological assumptions of some American pragmatists with work of some European Marxists. We were influenced by American students of Vygotsky (Scribner & Cole, 1981; Wertsch, 1980; Ochs, 1987; and Rogoff, 1990, among others) and by Bruner (1975), Halliday (1975), Hymes (1972), Heath (1983), Fillmore (1968), and Snow (1983).

Why do we call our approach "interactionist"? Explanation is required because the word combines meanings on several levels of analysis and has been used by others with different meaning.

On one level, "interactionist" refers to the central role of social interaction in the development of language. Trevarthen (1974) writes that "human intelligence develops from the start as an interpersonal process" (p. 230). Gordon Wells (1981, p. 115) writes:

> Learning to communicate is a collaborative affair. Right up to the early years of schooling and beyond, the adult is the more skilled participant, with a responsibility for helping the child to develop and extend his communicative skills, at first pre-verbally, then verbally, and later in written language. But at each stage, the child also has a contribution to make, stemming from his own interests and directed at his own purposes. The sort of interaction that will be most beneficial for his development, therefore, is that which gives due weight to the contribution of *both* parties, and emphasizes mutuality and reciprocity in the meanings that are constructed and negotiated through talk.

Berko-Gleason and Weintraub (1978, p. 214) stress the child's active participation in interaction with other human beings, "who are themselves tuned to the linguistic needs of the child and whose speech is characterized by special features that mesh with those needs." More and more, language researchers take it for granted that social interaction is central to language development. Yet, some scholars in the nativist tradition still maintain that the human mind is the source of its own linguistic competence. They ignore growing evidence of fine-tuned interaction between caretakers and young speakers.

The interactionist stresses the unification of nature and culture (Toulmin, 1978), the interweaving of the biological and the social.

Bruner does not deny a possible biological substratum to language, such as Chomsky's (1965) notion of a Language Acquisition Device (LAD), but he writes: "In a word, it is the *interaction* between LAD and LASS that makes it possible for the infant to enter the linguistic community – and at the same time, the culture to which the language gives access" (Bruner, 1983, p. 19, emphasis added).

Biology and culture provide the possibilities for the growing human being. Only a subset of those possibilities can be actualized in any individual. Some possibilities are deepened, others are let go, as individuation and enculturation develop together. In viewing development as a changing system rather than as a result of polarity between genes and environment, interactionism bypasses long-standing debates. A fundamental aspect of our work is the role of dialectics. This contrasts with dualistic and reductionist approaches, which have been dominant for decades in psychology and linguistics, and which:

> depend on the separation of natural processes into isolable parts for individual study. They have provided a rich repertoire of information about the world, but they systematically ignore the aspects of reality that involve relations between the separated processes. (Biddell, 1988, p. 330)

It is rational to focus on parts or elements of a complex process. As Biddell says, doing so is often useful in scientific inquiry. But it does not fit developmental processes, which are multifaceted and which require models in which complex relationships become central. The dialectical method, with its unification of nature and culture, is not just a way to get past the endless debates between environmentalists and nativists; it is actually a more authentic account of human functioning. Its use was stressed by Vygotsky, and has also been proposed by some neo-Piagetian theorists, including Riegel (1979) and Basseches (1989), who see it as a model for open systems that undergo various transformations.

Our use of the term "interactionist" includes both the Vygotskian notion of the social sources of development and also the dialectical mode of analysis. It attempts to capture the complex, nonreductionist, and nonlinear features of our subject. At the same time, we need to distinguish our use of "interactionist" from some others. The term is used at times by researchers using an information theory perspective, particularly in discussing bottom-up and top-down processes (Stanovich, 1980).

As a consequence, some authors reject the term interactionist just because of this association with computational models. Rosenblatt (1985, p. 98) criticizes the term for "its association with the mechanistic

Newtonian model of research and the behaviorist research model patterned on it."

Shannon (1989) criticizes interactionism as a strategy-oriented approach, which ignores the *purposes* of reading or writing. He contrasts it with the "whole language approach" which he sees as focused on purposes. (See Goodman & Goodman, 1990, for some similarities and differences between these two approaches.) In our framework the strategic and the purposive are not separated, but are different aspects of one integral whole.

Although there are conflicting and alternative uses, and some have found the term "transactional" preferable (Bickhard, 1987; Rosenblatt, 1985), we are keeping the term interactionist. It expresses two essential aspects of our theory: (1) the central importance of social interaction in all forms of human communication, and (2) the necessity of addressing the complex and dialectical nature of our subject. Our use of this term fits well with the rapid development of "social interactionism" in the human sciences, particularly in language and cognitive development (Snow, 1983).

There is an influential shift toward interactionism in America and abroad. Recent collections of works with an interactionist position include Rogoff and Lave (1984); Hickman (1987); Moll (1990); and Diaz and Berk (1992). Benjamin Lee (1987, p. 104) summarizes this point of view clearly:

> Man lives in a world of meanings because of the systematicity of language. At the same time, culture is also the context for the evolution of language. The principles that guide the evolution of the mind are the product of socio-historical forces which regiment language in culturally specific ways; these ways in turn determine the development of mind in a never-ending dialectic of mind being in society.

Only a small portion of sociocultural studies, however, are devoted to education, despite the educational implications of social interactionism and of Vygotsky's work (see Moll, 1990). This is particularly true in language and literacy (with a few notable exceptions: Rivers, 1987; Cazden, 1988; Newman, Griffin, & Cole, 1989; Tharp & Gallimore, 1988; Moll, and ongoing research by Wertsch and his collaborators). The purpose of this book is to develop a coherent theoretical framework for language and literacy development that integrates some of the interdisciplinary tenets and findings just described with an expansion of Vygotskian theory. The framework should be of use to both educational theory and practice. It is based on four assumptions:

1. Language must be viewed from a social and functional perspective.

The language of the individual develops in relation to its functions in social and family life.

2. The acquisitions of language and literacy are developmental processes in which the transformation of interpersonal processes into intrapersonal functions is central. Learning and development emerge from the dynamic interaction of social and individual factors.

3. Understanding of human activity is possible only in its sociocultural context. The study of language provides a tool for understanding the culturally and historically embedded nature of human activity and knowledge.

4. Interactionist methods of investigation and analysis focus upon the processes rather than the products of learning and development. Learning and development are best examined as dynamic processes in meaningful contexts of social activity.

The social and functional perspective

Recent research on language development shows that functional concerns are the motive force in learning. Development is fostered by meaningful exchange. Learners focus first on the content, and only later on the form of their messages. Infants are "tuned" to enter the world of human action, as Bruner wrote (1983, p. 27): "Obvious though the point may seem . . . it has enormous consequences for language development." Mutuality of attention and synchronicity in movements between the language learning novice and his or her caretakers have been shown by Trevarthen (1980). In describing the process of language socialization, which is linked to the child's dependence upon others, we suggested:

> From birth the social forms of child–caretaker interactions, the tools used by humans in society to manipulate the environment, the culturally institutionalized patterns of social relations, and language, operating together as a socio-semiotic system, are used by the child in cooperation with adults to organize behavior, perception, memory, and complex mental processes. For children, the development of language is a development of social existence into individuated persons and into culture. (John-Steiner & Tatter, 1983, p. 83)

Among linguists, Michael Halliday (1978) presents the strongest statement of the primacy of function over form. He interprets social reality and culture as "an edifice of meanings." In his formulation, the lexicogrammatical system operates as a realization of the semantic system, and provides the link between meaning and structure. The relationship between "learning to mean" and "learning a language" is not seen in quite the same way by all contemporary scholars in the sociocultural tradition (see the interesting discussion of Gee [1990, pp. 73–74]). But they all emphasize the social and functional features of language acquisition.

The relationship between form, meaning, and context in language acquisition is increasingly studied by interactionists in various culture contexts. Elinor Ochs (1987) suggests that while middle-class Western mothers work hard to interpret young children's partly intelligible gestures and utterances, Samoan caretakers encourage the young speaker to improve his or her utterance without much guessing or assistance. Her comparisons highlight the importance of the broader social values and organization in which the processes of language acquisition are embedded.

Traditional approaches to language acquisition emphasize syntax and see that process in a universalist way. By focusing on structure, they ignore Bruner's (1983, p. 36) warning that "the central idea is communicative intent: we communicate with some end in mind, some function to be fulfilled." Ignoring the central role of communicative intent creates a difficult problem for educators. Focus on form at the expense of function has led to a "skills approach," stressing "phonics knowledge" in reading, or usage of grammar and spelling in written language. These methods teach students to value the form of their work at the expense of its content. It seems clear, as Barr (1991) has recently argued, that the structural element of phonics knowledge is essential in skilled reading, but that fact by no means implies that phonics or any other structural feature, such as phonological awareness, is primary in development. Nonetheless, many educational researchers continue to uphold the structuralist viewpoint (Adams, 1990; Shankweiler, 1991). In contrast, Vygotsky (1978, pp. 117–118) argued that:

> writing should be meaningful for children, that an intrinsic need should be aroused in them, and that writing should be incorporated into a task that is necessary and relevant for life. Only then can we be certain that it will develop not as a matter of hand and finger habits but as a really new and complex form of speech.

The development of speech, reading, and writing are linked to the culturally patterned ways in which children's dependence on others is realized. Barbara Rogoff (1990, p. 195) writes that:

> Human exchange is necessary for the survival of the newborn (and of the species) and continues with expanding consequences as the organism grows and becomes capable of more complex exchanges and learning.

The acquisition of language and literacy illustrates the role of interdependence in development and the way in which through words we maintain and modify relationships between individuals.

Learning and development

In Vygotsky's view learning is not equivalent to development. Rather, learning creates the possibility of development. It is linked to the child's interdependence with others and how the external process of social interaction between individuals is gradually internalized. The Estonian psychologist Jan Valsiner (1988) describes the crucial role of the concept of interdependence in Vygotsky's thinking and how it relates to the teaching/learning process. He uses a Russian term *obuchenie,* which is hard to translate. It describes an interdependent relationship between teacher and learner "in which one cannot exist without the other" (p. 162).

Vygotsky conceptualizes learning and its relationship to development by bringing together a number of ideas. He situates learning within a relationship among mutually dependent individuals, where the learner assumes an active role in the process of being taught. He considers the timing of learning to be crucial. The introduction of a new concept or strategy is effective when it is just beginning in a child, at what others have called the "teaching moment," and he specifies how the consequences of interpersonal interactions are internalized by the learner.

Vygotsky further analyzes the role of an *actual* developmental level as "a child's mental functions that have been established as a result of certain already *completed* developmental cycles" (Vygotsky, 1978, p. 85). This contrasts with *potential* development: the process of offering the child certain leading questions, or showing him or her how a problem is to be solved, an approach indicating "that what children can do with the assistance of others may be in some sense even more indicative of their mental development than what they can do alone" (p. 85). In describing this notion of the "zone of proximal development," Vygotsky emphasizes those functions that have not yet matured, functions that "could be termed the 'buds' or 'flowers' of development rather than the 'fruits' of development" (p. 86).

Lastly, Vygotsky adds the notion of the internalization of psychological functions that have first been established through interaction:

> We could formulate the general genetic law of cultural development in the following way: every function in the cultural development of the child comes on to the stage twice, in two respects; first in the

> social, later in the psychological, first in relations between people as an interpsychological category, afterwards within the child as an intrapsychological category. . . . All higher psychological functions are internalized relationships of the social kind, and constitute the social structure of personality. Their composition, genetic structure, ways of functioning, in one word all their nature is social. . . . The human being who is alone retains the function of interaction. (in Valsiner, 1987, p. 67)

In the beginning of any joint or interpsychological activity, the child depends on the adult or on more experienced peers. But over time the child takes increasing responsibility for his or her learning. Bruner (1983) dubbed this shift from dependence on another to independent functioning the "handover principle" and says "it is so ubiquitous that we hardly notice its presence" (p. 60). A similar phenomenon is described by Collins, Brown, and Newman (1990). They term it "scaffolding and fading." In her cross-cultural research Rogoff (1990) uses "guided participation" to mean both explicit and tacit efforts to guide children in development. The technique is

> embedded in the practical and routine activities of daily life that do not explicitly focus on instruction and guidance. Guided participation is jointly managed by children and their companions in ways that facilitate children's growing skills and participation in the activities of mature members of their community. (p. viii)

Some readers of Vygotsky find his emphasis on the social sources of development contradicted by the child's innovative, spontaneous activities. These views misinterpret social interaction as imitation. Sociocultural theory differs sharply from theories, such as Bandura's (1977), in which modeling and imitation are central. As Leont'ev (1981) says, "social participation leads to new understanding. It requires creative contributions, it is shaped by changing historical and technological contexts. When we discuss the relationship between learning and development from the Vygotskian point of view, we take into account the interaction of a number of variables, including individual sources (growing from both biological predispositions and family opportunities); socially patterned interactions; and culturally refined tools and practices." Vygotsky's phrase "cultural development" says that children develop linguistic and cognitive skills in cultural contexts, which are constituted of the historically provided tools, strategies, and practices of their social community. Western and Soviet researchers have paid close attention to contexts where learning and teaching take place, whether in classroom research (Davidov,

1988; Hagstrom & Wertsch, in press; Istomina, 1975) or in the field (Luria, 1976).

The sociohistorical context

"A word acquires its sense from the context in which it appears; in different contexts it changes its sense," wrote Vygotsky in *Thought and language (1962, p. 245)*. The importance of context in the study of language has been highlighted in recent research. One definition of context quoted by McLane (1987, p. 268) provides a broad description of this concept:

> Contexts are constituted by what people are doing and where and when they are doing it. As McDermott (1976) puts it succinctly, "people in interaction become environments for each other. Ultimately, social contexts consist of mutually shared and ratified definitions of situations *and* in the social actions persons take on the basis of these definitions."

In McLane's research, which compared the ways older peers versus mothers defined a task, she showed how effectively maternal strategies create a context for increasingly independent functioning by young problem-solvers. While older peers completed the same task effectively on their own, they "did not enable their tutees to build gradual control and understanding of their task" (1987, p. 283). The adults and the older children defined the situation differently, providing different contexts to the preschoolers for the acquisition of a new task.

In McLane's study, age and experiential factors contributed to the structuring of a problem-solving context within a single cultural setting. In the growing field of cultural psychology, context is a central notion in studies of language socialization (Heath, 1983, 1990; Ochs, 1990), studies of apprenticeships (Lave, 1988), and comparative studies of mathematics learning (Schoenfeld, 1988; Stigler & Perry, 1990), to name but a few areas. Intense interest in the role and meaning of context does not make it easy to define the concept of context. Griffin, Belyeava, and Soldatova (1993) write, in a chapter entitled "Creating and Reconstituting Contexts," that

> research could be designed to hold a word or concept constant while varying the context or vice versa and the interest in the issue would be exhausted. But, contemporary studies in a variety of disciplines force us to recognize that a context, too, is dynamic, fluid and complex, not given beforehand like the "backdrop" prepared for a stage play; a context emerges, being "constituted" in large measure by words used by context participants and their other actions.

In some studies our conception of context begins with verbal exchanges and dialogues, but goes beyond the "here and now" to include the origin or source of the exchange. For example, how have the participants come to interact in this way? If they are a parent and child engaged in reading a storybook, the sociocultural theorist asks how this activity has come to be routinely reenacted, how this routine expresses values of the group and relates to other cultural practices, and what part this activity plays in general patterns of the culture. In asking such questions we are inquiring about the culturally and historically provided values, tools, and practices that are formative in that particular context of social interaction. The values will include notions of appropriate roles, relationships, and activities for adults and children. The tools and practices may include specific approaches to oral reading and interpretation, such as questioning, commenting, and reciting.

It is in everyday life that culturally patterned activities affect the developing child. The notion of *activity setting* is sometimes used as a basic unit of analysis. It may be specified

> in terms of the who, what, when, where, and whys of everyday life in school, home, community, and workplace. These features of personnel, occasion, motivations and meaning, goals, places, and times are intertwined conditions that together comprise the reality of life and learning. (Gallimore, Tharp, & John-Steiner, in press)

Activity settings vary greatly both within and between cultures. In a naturalistic study of low-income Appalachian children, Berk and Garvin (1984) find that these schoolchildren developed private speech (problem-solving speech for the self) more slowly than do middle-class children. They attribute the difference to restricted adult–child verbal interaction in the Appalachian communities, "a phenomenon widely reported in anthropological literature" (Diaz & Berk, 1992, p. 27). They also find that girls use private speech more than boys, a difference they explain by the expectation in Appalachian culture that manliness requires a quiet demeanor.

The cultural context shapes the type and variety of social interactions. Elinor Ochs (1982) found interesting differences between the way in which Samoan and American parents compensate for young children's difficulties in communicating. Middle-class American mothers work hard to fill in missing information, to expand and paraphrase their children's utterances.

> Samoan children are instead socialized at a very early age into a sociocentric demeanor – to notice and to take the perspectives of others. This demeanor is tied to two basic forms of competence expected of young children by around 4–5 years of age: the show of respect to

> higher ranking persons and the care of younger siblings. By this age, Samoan children are capable of carrying out several activities at the same time – always with an eye or an ear ready to respond to a request by an elder or to notice the movements of a younger sibling. (Ochs, 1987, p. 311)

Ochs suggests that societies vary in their expectations of the "speaker-hearer" role, and in the ways in which children are helped to construct their culturally appropriate communicative competence.

The sociohistorical context provides certain patterned interactions, and at the same time these interactions provide enculturation into a particular speech community. Rogoff refers to this as "mutuality" of individual and environment. A central claim made by sociocultural scholars is that "the kinds of contexts that children spend their time in are the fundamental units out of which cognitive development is constructed" (Laboratory of Comparative Human Cognition, 1983, p. 322).

The methodological perspective

Because learning and development take place in meaningful, socially and culturally patterned contexts, they need to be studied and understood in those contexts. This rather obvious notion goes counter to well-established practice among psychologists and educational researchers, who have long favored the elimination of context as a variable. Laboratory studies and most psychometric investigations are intended to be "context free." Vygotsky saw this problem in the following way:

> The psychologist seeks to confront the subject with some kind of stimulus situation designed to influence him in a particular way, and then the psychologist examines and analyzes the response(s) elicited by that stimulating situation. After all, the very essence of experimentation is to evoke the phenomenon under study in artificial (and therefore controllable) ways and to study the variations in responses that occur in conjunction with various changes in the stimulus. (1978, p. 58)

Vygotsky suggests that while methods based on controlling the environment in which a phenomenon is studied are appropriate for very simple processes, they do not meet the requirements of complex, higher psychological functions. For the latter, exploration needs to focus on the process of change for a "developmental analysis that returns to the source and reconstructs all the points in the development of a given structure" (1978, p. 65).

Several approaches have been used to implement these methodological considerations. One of these is the microgenetic approach, which is used to sample behavior during rapid changes in acquisition. Siegler and Crowley (1991) contrast snapshots with movies, and propose "movie-like" methods where the frequency of observations is high "relative to the rate of change of the phenomenon" (p. 606). The best known microgenetic studies by sociocultural researchers are those conducted by James Wertsch and his collaborators (Hickmann, 1987; McLane, 1987; Wertsch & Minick, 1990). In these studies of dyadic interactions, the investigator examines how a skill or strategy is acquired, is first practiced interpersonally, and is eventually incorporated into the novice's repertoire. The experienced member's ability to support the learner's transition from other-regulation to self-regulation is richly documented in these studies.

An interesting modification of the microgenetic method is suggested by Rafael Diaz (1992). He finds that correlational studies between the use of private speech and task attainment yield limited results. If the relationship is studied over time, and the effect of private speech is monitored in later sessions, then a positive finding emerges. He suggests combining traditional laboratory methods with multivariate statistical techniques within a microgenetic framework.

Perhaps the most important method of investigation for sociocultural researchers is longitudinal study in natural learning contexts. In a study of the "Social Origins of Private Speech in Pretend Play," Smolucha (1992) observed very young children for 14 months. She videotaped the children's interactions with their mothers and with their peers in a semi-structured situation. She shows the first beginnings of self-regulatory speech in a 2-1/2-year-old, appropriating forms from previous interactions. Several chapters in the present book describe longitudinal approaches similar to her study, in which investigators study the acquisition of language and literacy in natural settings. The focus is on periods of rapid change. The authors use ethnographic approaches modified for psychological inquiry.

To summarize, there are several ways that Vygotsky's emphasis on context is implemented by contemporary researchers. They study social interaction, the developmental relationship between language and thought, and the shifts in mutuality and expertise over time in learning and development. Related issues, such as the role of the larger sociohistorical context and institutions, are outside the scope of this presentation of methods.

1.2 LANGUAGE AND LITERACY: EXPANSIONS OF THE FRAMEWORK

The dual functions of language

The importance of language for *communication* is taken for granted by all humans. Its second major function as a vehicle of *thought* is less widely considered. In our framework, these two functions are central: language as used for interpersonal communication and language as a means of internal representation. As a means of interpersonal communication, language is basic to social and cultural practices (Bourdieu, 1977; Lave, 1988) or what the philosopher Wittgenstein (1958) calls "forms of life." As Vygotsky (1962, p. 6) argues:

> In the absence of a system of signs, linguistic or other, only the most primitive and limited type of communication is possible. . . . Rational, intentional conveying of experience and thought to others requires a mediating system.

The development of language as communication is approached by sociocultural scholars from a functional and social perspective. Rather than isolating speech from action and from social interaction (and viewing it from an organismic point of view), Vygotsky links language, from its earliest beginnings, to the child's interdependence with others. As shown by Nelson (1989) and others, a child's first attempts at communication take place in routinized interactional contexts, where objects and the caretaker's own actions provide the learner with stability in the midst of complexity. Some of the early functions of language are interactional (maintenance of social contact); expressive (emotional release); and informational (sharing an observation with the interlocutor).

> If the emotional release and social contact functions of speech play a role in the first stages of ontogenesis, Vygotsky argued that with further development . . . new functions begin to emerge. It was in this connection that he introduced the notions of *communicative* (kommunikativnaya) and *intellectual* (intellektual'naya) functions of speech (1934, p. 11). From his discussion it is clear that these two functions represent a further specification of his notions of social and individual functions. (Wertsch, 1985, p. 93)

Although the communicative and intellectual functions of language are distinct, they are not truly separate. Their relationship interested Vygotsky:

> The initial function of speech is its communicative function. . . . this function of speech . . . has been separated from the intellectual function of speech . . . but what the relationship is between these two functions, what brings about the presence of the two functions of speech, how they develop, and how they are structurally intertwined are questions that have remained uninvestigated. (1934, p. 88)

Since Vygotsky raised these issues, a considerable amount of research has been devoted to language functions. Young children first use words in well-defined contexts. With the help of their caregivers, siblings, and peers, they generalize words across diverse situations. "The child begins to perceive the world not only through his eyes but also through his speech" (Vygotsky, 1978, p. 32). Language bridges the child's physical separateness, it aids in shared actions, and it is basic to the construction of intersubjectivity. But in addition to its communicative role, language provides a central connection between the internal and the external, between thought and communication.

The development of the intellectual function of language is central to sociocultural theory and to the analysis of literacy. In using words communicatively, the young speaker engages in certain cognitive operations. She or he singles out separate elements from an undifferentiated field, identifies specific actions (up, out, down), notices and labels recurrences and disappearances (more, all gone). These activities, even at the one-word level of development (Brown, 1973), require the child to engage in generalizations. Words are experienced as denoting some common aspect of objects and actions in more than one context. Vygotsky described this phenomenon as follows:

> Every word is a concealed *generalization*. . . . It is not difficult to see that generalization is a *verbal act of thought:* its reflection of reality differs radically from that of immediate sensation or perception. (1987, p. 47, emphasis in original)

Children do not achieve these acts of verbal thinking and generalization unassisted; their efforts to identify commonalities across situations are supported by their joint activities with caregivers (Bruner, 1975). As a consequence of these interpersonally scaffolded activities, children internalize verbal thinking and analysis. The trajectory of this process, of the transformation of interpersonal (or intermental) into intramental processes is closely linked to Vygotsky's analysis of the relationship of language and thought. He combined various aspects of his theory through the analysis of *private* (egocentric) speech: (1) its role in differentiating communicative from intellectual use of language; (2) its planning functions; (3) the transition from social, joint activity to the child's more independent use of verbal thinking.

In *Thinking and Speech* (1987, p. 259), he wrote:

> Speech for oneself has its source in a differentiation of an initially social function, a differentiation of speech for others. . . . It is not an accompaniment of the child's activity. It is an independent melody or function that facilitates intellectual orientation, conscious awareness, the overcoming of difficulties and impediments, and imagination and thinking. It is speech for oneself, a speech function that intimately serves the child's thinking.

The differentiation between speech directed to others and speech for the self takes place over several years. Preschool children are most likely to use language to help themselves solve tasks beyond their existing performance level. But the use of private speech does not disappear at age seven (as Vygotsky suggested). It is used by school-age children for difficult subjects and in certain school environments (see the overview of recent findings by Berk [1992, chap. 1]). One of the most important results from these studies is that

> private speech was largely unrelated to concurrent task performance (math achievement), yet at each grade, task-relevant private speech showed positive relationships with achievement gains over the following year. (Berk, 1992, p. 39)

In demanding situations (for instance, the acquisition of a second language), adults, too, rely upon private speech. Private speech is not only of interest to researchers on problem solving. It is also of great interest to sociocultural theorists because of its connection with inner speech. As described by Vygotsky, private speech turns gradually inward, or "goes underground" to become the basis of inner speech. The process of internalization goes through uneven periods, and is dependent on context, cultural variables, and types of schooling (to mention but a few variables recently identified by Diaz and Berk, 1992).

In inner speech, thought and language intersect and influence each other dynamically. As speech is internalized, it also is more abbreviated and predicative. In its external forms of speech and writing, language is elaborated to be effectively communicative. In inner speech, language is highly condensed. One reason that inner speech is abbreviated, and also quite rapid, is that it is embedded in an ongoing process. A particular thought is linked to what is "given" in consciousness. The given aspect (see Chafe's [1974] distinction between given and new information) is the background to what the thinker is aware of at a particular moment. The new thought is frequently saturated with "sense." The term "sense" as used by Vygotsky and by Luria (1982) means a dynamic set of possibilities that are realized in certain specific contexts:

> The sense of a word always turns out to be a dynamic, flowing, complex formation which has several zones of differential stability. Meaning is only one of the zones of the sense that a word acquires in the context of speaking. (Vygotsky, 1934, p. 305)

Some features of inner speech were identified by Vygotsky based on his study of private speech. In addition, he relied on literature (see the famous dialogue from *Anna Karenina* quoted and analyzed in *Thinking and speech,* pp. 268–269). And while he did not favor the use of introspection for theoretical analyses, some of his notions, including his description of sense, do confirm self-reports of individuals interested in their mental processes. Luria described how in preparing a lecture he would just list a number of topics. He said that the "conversion of sense to meaning is the central issue of speech production" referring to

> the transition from subjective sense, which is not yet formulated in words and is comprehensible only to the subject, to a system of meanings formulated in words and comprehensible to others. (1982, p. 152)

Inner speech serves a variety of functions: planning, reflection, and generation/creation – reordering or transforming the givens of consciousness into new perspectives or insights. It is difficult to gain access to this level of human functioning. One of the ways we have approached it is by examining the planning notes of people engaged in rapid, productive, and creative thinking (John-Steiner, 1985). Writers, scientists, musicians, and other creative thinkers often provide evidence in their notebooks of what we have come to call "inner speech" writing. This is a condensed, even cryptic form of written language, which can be important when used by "experienced thinkers" to keep abreast of rapid bursts of thought:

> These notes are jottings to the self; they assist the writer remembering an organization of important details and concepts that emerge in the sequence of her work. [See example in Figure 1.1.] Use of a telegraphic style makes it possible to gallop ahead, exploring new connections, a task which is much harder when the writer's intention is to shape connected and readable prose. (John-Steiner, 1985, p. 112)

This model of the transformations of internalized language from fully elaborated speech to private and inner speech, and the externalization of thought into communicated speech or text, is based on sociocultural theory. Our understanding of all the steps of these transformations is incomplete. Recent research on the development of private speech has contributed to a fuller picture of the various components of thought and language and the way in which they are interwoven developmentally. Wertsch's (1991) work linking Bakhtin and Vygotsky has introduced a broader concept of inner speech as linked to speech genres, dialogicality, and the institutional contexts in which language development occurs. Our own research, particularly as conducted in the Southwest (John-Steiner & Osterreich, 1975), has raised the issue of multiple modalities in internal representation (John-Steiner, 1985) and the transformations of these modes of thought into communicative forms. Language is the most powerful and flexible of "bridges" between experiences, representation, and communication. But it is not the only one. Vygotsky

EXTERNAL

Modality	Fully elaborated communicative speech	Private speech
	Functions: *Referential* *Interactional* *Evaluative* *Regulatory*	*Functions:* *Planning* *Labeling* *Problem solving*
Spoken	Ref: "This is a diagram." Int: "Why don't you join us?" Eval: "Yours is the best one here" Reg: "You shouldn't do that"	>Children's private speech: P: "I'll be better after the doctor." L: "It's ten. It's ten, the answer is ten." PS: "You . . . You . . . the yellow on that side goes . . . One yellow right next there."
Signed		>Deaf Children fingerspell to themselves while taking spelling tests.
Written		Exchange between well-acquainted individuals. "I have longed wished to ask you something." "Please do." "This," he said, and wrote the letters: Wya:icnb, dymton . . . "I understand," she said, blushing . . . She wrote the initial letters: stymfalwh . . . He seized the chalk with tense, trembling fingers, broke it, and wrote the initial letters of the following: "I have nothing to forget and forgive, I never ceased loving you." (Tolstoy, Anna Karenina; cited by Vygotsky in *Thought and Language*) >Lecture Notes (Written, embedded in lecture) "Want to capture generalization" "This is all derivational morphology" "Oh, where did I put this?"
Diagrammatic		I think
Musical Notation		

INTERNAL

→

Subvocal monologue	**Inner speech**	**Network of concepts**
Functions: *Anticipatory Rehearsal* *Verbal Planning* *Stream of Consciousness* *Intersubjectivity*	*Functions:* *Planning* *Discovery* *Rehearsal*	Hypothetical level of thought without verbal element
>"Yes. Thought so. Sloping into the Empire. Gone. Plain soda would do him good. Where Pat Kinsella had his Harp theatre before Whitbred ran the Queen's. Broth of a boy. Dion Boucicault business with his harvestmoon face in a poky bonnet. Three Purty Maids from School. How time flies, eh?" (James Joyce, *Ulysses*)		[Internal codes]
	>Journals Suppose I make a break after H's death (madness). A separate paragraph quoting what R himself said. Then a break. Then begin definitely with the first meeting. That is the first impression: a man of the world, not professor or Bohemian. Then give facts in his letters to his mother. (Virginia Woolf) (Not directly accessible. This example illustrates condensed writing reflecting the internal process as described by Vygotsky.)	[Semiotic mediation]

Figure 1.1. Internal and External Codes: Processes of Transformation.

has provided a model for the mechanisms of transformation, which we have applied to inner codes such as visualization and mathematical formulas, as well as language (John-Steiner, 1991). In Figure 1.1 both the modalities and functions of language are represented as we currently conceive of them.

Speakers and writers

In recent studies of spoken and written discourse (Chafe & Danielewicz, 1987; Collins & Gentner, 1980; Tannen, 1982, 1984; among many others) the claim is made that these two forms of language differ significantly. In face-to-face interaction, many extralinguistic devices are relied upon to maximize the chances for successful dialogue. Speakers monitor the success of their communicative efforts through eye contact, gesture, and intonation, with repairs offered for communicative gaps and failures. Speakers make rapid choices in their communicative means, and some of their interactions are characterized by pronominalization and predication that is rendered comprehensible by intonation and gesture (Chafe, 1982). Such communication is most likely to occur in the presence of friends and intimates and is reminiscent of Vygotsky's analysis of interaction where there is a common experiential context. If such speech is merely transcribed, stripped of its extralinguistic cues, it tends to be unintelligible to a third party. Words written down – untransformed to meet the needs of a reader removed in time and space – are not sufficient to communicate successfully; they resemble what Flower and Hayes (1984) have referred to as "writer-based" rather than "reader-based" text. The writing of inexperienced students frequently resembles speech written down in this sense, a transcription of one side of a dialogue between the writer and a familiar interlocutor. As such, it may have the abbreviated and highly condensed character of private speech or of a subvocal monologue, rather than being fully elaborated for an absent and unfamiliar audience.

Much recent scholarship, especially on college composition (following Moffett, 1968) has used the Piagetian notion of egocentrism to characterize this kind of student writing, which seems not to take into account the viewpoint and experience of the reader. We believe, however, that what many scholars view as egocentrism in the written language of inexperienced college writers reflects a reliance on their more developed dialogic skills, used in communicating with close associates, and not the kind of egocentrism that Piaget ascribed to preoperational thought.

When a writer's ideas are not given sufficient elaboration and contextualization to communicate with an absent, unfamiliar reader, the writer is seen, in the Piagetian view, as only looking at the material from his or her own limited perspective. The sociocultural perspective points to a different analysis of the problems faced by inexperienced writers. What is the *function* of writing for a particular individual? In many English families writing several letters a day was expected when a family member went on vacation or on a business trip.

Sustained written communication was part of family life as recalled by Margaret Drabble, and by Jessica Mitford (John-Steiner, 1985). They were part of what Gundlach (1982, p. 185) has described as a "community of writers":

> If a person participates in a community of active readers and writers, if he reads and writes regularly, and if his reading and writing put him in touch with other people, he stands a reasonably good chance of forming notions of genre and style . . . of becoming increasingly sophisticated about the act of writing itself.

The opportunity to be raised in a community of readers and writers is becoming increasingly rare, particularly in the United States, according to literacy scholars. Wolf describes contemporary family life as follows:

> The overwhelming number of children live in settings where the competing demands of several jobs, and contrasting schedules fracture family life into unrecognizable splinters. Consequently, even among the majority of middle-class families in the USA . . . the conditions that prevail for large numbers of "average" or "normal" American children are not ones which lead to early or to deep literacy. (Wolf, 1990, p. 123)

Writing and even sustained conversational interactions "have been stripped to functional leanness, bleached into a discourse about management and efficiency, or constrained into immediate and solitary entertainment" (Wolf, 1990, p. 122). For some children, preparation for literacy is linked to intimate, language-related activities (see Panofsky in this volume). Although such activities are thought to be widely practiced among parents with higher education, Wolf finds that such informal tutoring is less and less common. The lack of socialization into school literacy practices, which Heath (1983) describes in *Ways with words* among nonmainstream groups, includes increasing numbers of middle-class children raised in home settings where there is little time for word play and delight in language.

Literacy is acquired slowly; it is linked to the functions of language in children's lives, and to the particular uses of written speech. Vygotsky urged that

> writing should be meaningful for children, that an intrinsic need should be aroused in them, and that writing should be incorporated into a task

> that is necessary and relevant for life. Only then can we be certain that it will develop not as a matter of hand and finger habits but as a really new and complex form of speech. (1978, p. 118)

Several investigators have looked at home development and uses of early literacy (Bissex, 1980; John-Steiner & Roth, 1983) and of writing acquired in supportive, out-of-school situations (McLane, 1990; McNamee, 1990). In these studies writing was scaffolded to be *meaningful* to children in the relationships with others, and it also served as a form of *self-regulation.* In these contexts children were acquiring authorship as well as deep and reflective literacy (Wolf, 1990). Cultural, community, and family variations in the role of literacy are increasingly studied by ethnographers, psychologists, and linguists (Basso, 1974; Schieffelin & Ochs, 1986; Scollon & Scollon, 1981; Scribner & Cole, 1981).

Another focus of literacy studies is on the cognitive demands of writing as contrasted with speaking. A central difference between these two language processes has been mentioned – namely, the reliance on prosodic and paralinguistic devices in face-to-face communication versus the need in writing for maximally explicit prose. Vygotsky's analysis of these differences has been quite influential among contemporary students of composition. "Written speech," he wrote, "is a conversation with a white sheet of paper, with an imaginary or conceptualized interlocutor" (1987, pp. 202–203). He continues:

> The grammar of thought characteristic of inner and written speech do not coincide; . . . inner speech is maximally contracted, abbreviated and telegraphic . . . [whereas] written speech is the most expanded form of speech. . . . [It] requires a child who is capable of extremely complex operations in the voluntary construction of the fabric of meaning. (p. 203)

Rivers (1987) suggests that writers can *write* more than they realize and, in this way, can arrive at new knowledge. Writers can be *instructed by their own words.*

Recent research has described the way speakers and writers vary their language in different contexts (see Smith in this volume). For those concerned with literacy education, we think that language *functions* in varying domains and discourses should be taken as a source of the problems faced by inexperienced writers. Little ethnographic research has been devoted to the variability of writing functions. Basso (1974) develops a "partial taxonomy" of forms and functions of letter writing. He identifies nine kinds of personal letters and nine kinds of formal letters, each corresponding to "variation in the form and content of these types of messages, their immediate functions, and the kinds of social relationships that obtain among individuals who exchange them" (p. 431).

In the present book, diverse chapters deal with the development of writing among children and adults. A common theme throughout the volume is the way language mediates thinking and the acquisition of knowledge. Another shared theme is the socially constructed settings in which literacy is acquired and used.

Language and power

The acquisition and functions of language and literacy are inseparable from social contexts, roles, and institutions. As Gee (1990, pp. 61–62) writes in his recent book, *Social Linguistics and Literacies: Ideology in Discourses:* "Literacy has no effects – indeed, no meaning – apart from particular cultural contexts in which it is used, and it has different effects in different contexts." This fact is frequently ignored by those who claim universal benefits for literacy, and who think that people with "restricted literacy" have limited ability to solve problems and think powerfully (Ong, 1982). In contrast, Gee argues that claims for the generalized benefits of literacy, particularly "essay-text" literacy are ideological:

> They are part of an "armory of concepts, conventions and practices" that privilege one social formation as if it were natural, universal, or, at least, the end point of a normal developmental progression of cognitive skills (achieved only by some cultures, thanks either to their intelligence or to their technology). (Gee, 1990, p. 60)

The "academy" is a speech community with its own forms and uses of both oral and written speech. The development of "expository writing" through the schools years, and especially in high school, is preparation for writing papers in college, which is preparation for writing at the professional level. Some of the specialized writing forms practiced in the academy, for instance, in law school (see Minnis in this volume), require additional language socialization and instruction. Great importance is attached to specific genres and functions characteristic of the academic speech community. This is shown by lengthy socialization into appropriate practice to which students must submit; the existence of handbooks and manuals for experts and novices alike (the APA publication manual or MLA style guide; the numerous "rhetoric" and compositional handbooks); and the status attendant on one who has attained mastery. The benefits of mastering "essay-text literacy" for students include admission to prestigious colleges, based in part on writing samples. For faculty members, promotion and tenure depend strongly on publication in journals that require particular forms of discourse.

Although curricula for writing instruction typically purport to be teaching writing as a generic ability, the differentiation of kinds of writing in different school tracks reveals a far more ideological situation. Students in business and vocational track classes are not asked to write research papers, whereas students in private schools are given many opportunities to hone that skill, including practicing various types of term and research papers. Students seeking admission to more selective institutions are provided with the most demanding writing curriculum (Oakes, 1985). A further irony of writing instruction in schools is that college students who are not planning to go into academically oriented professions will not practice the very genre that is taught to them with such zeal (Sanborn, in preparation). They have learned a writing form that is restricted to use in school. To show how specialized school writing instruction is, a student who aspires to enter a profession devoted to writing, namely journalism, must be retrained in a genre different than that provided to college students in general. Although writing in school settings is regarded by many educators, linguists, and psychologists as the acquisition of a generic skill with universal benefits, we suggest that it is a highly specialized cultural practice, like any other. In short, it is not only that writing in academic settings is difficult for students because the addressee is removed in space and time from the writer, but also that such writing must conform to the norms of a specific speech community – its "discourses" and "literacies."

One of the most powerful expositions of the meaning of discourse in a sociocultural context is presented by Gee (1989, p. 20):

> Any discourse concerns itself with certain objects and puts forward certain concepts, viewpoints, and values at the expense of others. In doing so it will marginalize viewpoints and values central to other discourses. . . . In fact, a discourse can call for one to accept values in conflict with other discourses one is a member of. . . . Finally, discourses are intimately related to the distribution of social power and hierarchical structure in society.

The challenge of acquiring a particular way in which text and meaning are produced and interpreted in a particular speech community is movingly illustrated by Cazden (1993), who recounts the experience of a Native Alaskan student. The student, enrolled in Cazden's course on "Classroom Discourse," described her difficulty in using the word "discourse" in her own writing:

> The word felt like an intruder in my mind displacing my word "talk." I could not organize my thoughts around it. It was like a pebble thrown into a still pond disturbing the smooth water. It makes all the other words in my mind out of sync. . . . I realized that in time I will own the word and feel comfortable using it, but until that time my

> own words were legitimate. Contrary to some that exposure to the dominant culture gives one an advantage in learning, in my opinion it is *the ownership of words that gives one confidence.* I must want the word, enjoy the word to own it. When the new word becomes synonymous in my head as well as externally, then I can think with it. (emphasis added).

A different kind of struggle for "voice" is described by Sherman Wilcox (this volume) in the lives of deaf people. While most approaches to deafness are clinical, Wilcox writes of an empowering pedagogy. He quotes the character Alice in Gilbert Eastman's play *Sign Me Alice II:*

> The hearing people do not treat me right. . . . Their ideas are false. They are hypocrites. They mold deaf people's lives. Not mine. Not my soul. I won't let them reshape me. . . . Deep in my body there is a flame.

In depicting the struggle for a pedagogy and a way of life that recognizes the beauty of the native language of the deaf, American Sign Language, Wilcox incorporates some of the ideas of Bakhtin (1981), Freire (1970), Vygotsky (1962), and Gee (1990).

Gee (1990, p. 12) has suggested that these concepts of language are inherently ideological:

> They crucially involve a set of values and viewpoints about the social and political (power) relationships between people and the distribution of social goods (at the very least about who is an insider and who isn't).

Breaking the silence of powerlessness (whether that of deafness, of poverty, of marginality) has been a major goal of Paolo Freire (1970). He stresses the need for a critical pedagogy which entails a revision of both the means and ends of education:

> Literacy can only be emancipatory and critical to the extent that it is connected to the language of the people. It is through the native language that students "name their world" and begin to establish a dialectical relationship with the dominant class in the process of transforming the social and political structures that imprison them in their "culture of silence." Thus, a person is literate to the extent that he or she is able to use language for social and political reconstruction . . . literacy conducted in the dominant language is alienating to subordinant students, since it denies them the fundamental tools for reflection, critical thinking, and social interaction. Without the cultivation of their native language, and robbed of the opportunity for reflection and critical thinking, subordinant students find themselves unable to re-create their culture and history. Without the reappropriation of their cultural capital, the reconstruction of the new society . . . can hardly be a reality. (1970, p. 159)

As Freire implies in this passage, the communicative uses of speech are accessible to all individuals of normal capability but the cognitive uses of language are less accessible and harder to learn, and usually are highly developed only in the small elite portion of the population. In addition, access to the cognitive uses of language – at once more intellectually and more politically powerful – is not randomly distributed in the population. For a middle-class child of professional parents, "reproduction" (Bourdieu, 1977) is facilitated through the availability of written texts and extensive experiences with those "socially assembled situations" which allow for the explication of inner speech either in written form or in the cognitive uses of language in oral dialogue, which serve as a scaffolding for, especially, the academic forms of written language. These children may engage in the discourses of the academy and the professions around the dinner table and thus have an early and powerful introduction to these highly valued and difficult forms of communication.

In this volume the contributors have expanded and illustrated sociocultural approaches to language and literacy. Although most of the chapters are research contributions, there are clear educational implications in the authors' findings. Looking at human activity in a sociohistorical context includes examining the nature of educational practices and whether they provide appropriately for different groups. Differences in communicative competence in speech versus writing are not viewed in terms of absolute competence but as the outgrowth of differential opportunities. The "socially assembled situations" and practices that are provided in much greater number to members of privileged groups afford many more opportunities for the explication of inner speech into those complex and very difficult forms that are much less accessible in the "banking concept" forms of education. We believe that a functional-developmental theory of language understood in the sociohistorical contexts of interaction offers promise for educational practice.

REFERENCES

Adams, M. (1990). *Beginning to read: Thinking and learning about print.* Cambridge, MA: Braddford Books/MIT Press.

Austin, J. L. (1962). *How to do things with words.* Oxford: Clarendon Press.

Bakhtin, M. M. (1981). *The dialogic imagination.* M. Holquist (Ed.). C. Emerson & M. Holquist (Trans.). Austin: University of Texas Press.

Bandura, A. (1977). *Social learning theory.* Englewood Cliffs, NJ: Prentice-Hall.

Barr, R. (1991). Toward a balanced perspective on beginning reading. *Educational Researcher, 20*(4), 30–32.

Basseches, M. (1989). Intellectual development: The development of dialectical thinking. In E. Maimon, B. F. Nodine, & F. W. O'Connor (Eds.), *Thinking, reasoning, and writing* (pp. 23–45). White Plains, NY: Longman.

Basso, K. (1974). The ethnography of writing. In R. Bauman & J. Sherzer (Eds.), *Explorations in the ethnography of speaking* (pp. 425–432). Cambridge: Cambridge University Press.

Berk, L. E. (1986). Relationship of elementary school children's private speech to behavioral accompaniment to task, attention, and task performance. *Development Psychology, 22,* 671–680.

Berk, L. E. (1992). Children's private speech: An overview of theory and the status of research. In R. Diaz & L. E. Berk (Eds.), *Private speech: From social interaction to self-regulation* (pp. 17–54). Hillsdale, NJ: Lawrence Erlbaum Associates.

Berk, L. E., & Garvin, R. A. (1984). Development of private speech among low-income Appalachian children. *Developmental Psychology, 20,* 271–286.

Berko-Gleason, J., & Weintraub, S. (1978). Input language and the acquisition of communicative competence. In K. E. Nelson (Ed.), *Children's language* (Vol. 1, pp. 171–222). New York: Gardner Press.

Bickhard, M. H. (1987). The social nature of the functional nature of language. In M. Hickmann (Ed.), *Social and functional approaches to language and thought* (pp. 39–66). Orlando, FL: Academic Press.

Biddell, T. (1988). Vygotsky, Piaget and the dialectic of development. *Human Development, 31,* 329–348.

Bissex, G. L. (1980). *GNYS AT WRK: A child learns to read and write.* Cambridge, MA: Harvard University Press.

Bourdieu, P. (1977). Cultural reproduction and social reproduction. In J. Karabel & A. H. Halsey (Eds.), *Power and ideology in education* (pp. 487–511). New York: Oxford University Press.

Brown, R. (1973). *A first language: The early stages.* Cambridge, MA: Harvard University Press.

Bruner, J. (1975). From communication to language. *Cognition, 3*(3), 255–287.

Bruner, J. (1983). *Child's talk.* New York: Norton.

Cazden, C. (1988). *Classroom discourse.* Exeter, NJ: Heinemann.

Cazden, C. (1993). Vygotsky, Hymes and Bakhtin: From word to utterance and voice. In E. Forman, N. Minick, & C. A. Stone (Eds.), *Contexts for learning: Sociocultural dynamics in children's development.* London: Oxford University Press.

Chafe, W. (1970). *Meaning and the structure of language.* Chicago: University of Chicago Press.

Chafe, W. (1974). Language and Consciousness. *Language, 50,* 111–133.

Chafe, W. (1982). Integration and involvement in speaking, writing and oral literature. In D. Tannen (Ed.), *Spoken and written language: Exploring orality and literacy* (pp. 35–54). Norwood, NJ: Ablex.

Chafe, W., & Danielewicz, J. (1987). *Properties of spoken and written language* (Tech. Rep. No. 5). Berkeley and Pittsburgh: University of California and Carnegie Mellon University, Center for the Study of Writing.

Chomsky, N. (1965). *Aspects of the theory of syntax*. Cambridge, MA: MIT Press.

Collins, A., Brown, J. S., & Newman, S. E. (1990). Cognitive apprenticeship: Teaching the craft of reading, writing, and mathematics. In L. B. Resnick (Ed.), *Knowing, learning, and instruction: Essays in honor of Robert Glaser.* Hillsdale, NJ: Lawrence Erlbaum Associates.

Collins, A., & Gentner, D. (1980). A framework for a cognitive theory of writing. In L. W. Gregg & E. R. Steinberg (Eds.), *Cognitive processes in writing* (pp. 51–72). Hillsdale, NJ: Lawrence Erlbaum Associates.

Cook-Gumperz, J. (Ed.). (1985). *The social construction of literacy.* Cambridge: Cambridge University Press.

Davidov, V. V. (1988). Problems of developmental teaching: The experience of theoretical and experimental psychological research. Part 1. *Soviet Education, 3*(10).

Diaz, R. M. (1992). Methodological concerns in the study of private speech. In R. M. Diaz & L. E. Berk (Eds.), *Private speech: From social interaction to self-regulation* (pp. 55–84). Hillsdale, NJ: Lawrence Erlbaum Associates.

Diaz, R. M., & Berk, L. E. (Eds.). (1992). *Private speech: From social interaction to self-regulation.* Hillsdale, NJ: Lawrence Erlbaum Associates.

Diaz, R. M., Neal, C. J., & Amaya-Williams, M. (1990). The social origins of self-regulation. In L. C. Moll (Ed.), *Vygotsky and education: Instructional implications and applications of sociohistorical psychology* (pp. 127–154). Cambridge: Cambridge University Press.

Elsasser, N., & John-Steiner, V. (1977). Interactionist approaches to advancing literacy. *Harvard Educational Review, 47,* 355–369.

Fillmore, C. (1968). The case for case. In E. Bach & R. Harms (Eds.), *Universals in linguistic theory.* New York: Holt, Rinehart & Winston.

Flower, L., & Hayes, J. (1984). Images, plans and prose: The representation of meaning in writing. *Written Communication, 1*(1), 120–160.

Freire, P. (1970). *Pedagogy of the oppressed.* New York: Continuum.

Gallimore, R., Tharp, R. G., & John-Steiner, V. (In press). *The developmental and socio-historical foundations of mentoring.* New York: Columbia University Press and the MacArthur Foundation.

Gee, J. (1989). What is literacy? *Journal of Education, 171,* 18–25.

Gee, J. (1990). *Social linguistics and literacies: Ideology in discourses.* London: Falmer Press.

Gilmore, P., & Glatthorn, A. (1982). *Children in and out of school.* Washington, DC: Center for Applied Linguistics.

Goodman, Y. M., & Goodman, K. S. (1990). Vygotsky in a whole-language perspective. In L. C. Moll (Ed.), *Vygotsky and education: Instructional implications and applications of sociohistorical psychology* (pp. 223–250). Cambridge: Cambridge University Press.

Grice, H. P. (1975). Logic and conversation. In P. Cole & J. L. Morgan (Eds.), *Syntax and semantics: Speech acts* (pp. 41–58). New York: Academic Press.

Griffin, P., Belyeava, A. V., & Soldatova. (1993). Creating and reconstituting contexts. In E. Forman, N. Minick, & C. A. Stone (Eds.), *Contexts for learning: Sociocultural dynamics in children's development.* London: Oxford University Press.

Gumperz, J., & Hymes, D. (Eds.). (1972). *Directions in sociolinguistics.* New York: Holt, Rinehart & Winston.

Gundlach, R. (1982). Children as writers: The beginnings of learning to write. In M. Nystrand (Ed.), *What writers know: The language, process and structure of written discourse.* Orlando, FL: Academic Press.

Hagstrom, F., & Wertsch, J. V. (In press). The role of noninstructional experience statements in classroom discourse.

Halliday, M. (1975). *Learning how to mean.* London: Edward Arnold.

Halliday, M. (1978). *Language as social semiotic.* London: Edward Arnold.

Heath, S. B. (1983). *Ways with words.* Cambridge: Cambridge University Press.

Heath, S. B. (1990). The children of Trackton's children: Spoken and written language in social change. In J. W. Stigler, R. A. Shweder, & G. Herdt (Eds.), *Cultural psychology: Essays on comparative human development* (pp. 496–519). Cambridge: Cambridge University Press.

Hickmann, M. (Ed.). (1987). *Social and functional approaches to language and thought.* Orlando, FL: Academic Press.

Hymes, D. H. (1972). Models of the interaction of language and social life. In J. J. Gumperz & D. Hymes (Eds.), *Directions in sociolinguistics* (pp. 35–71). New York: Holt, Rinehart, & Winston.

Istomina, Z. M. (1975). The development of voluntary memory in preschool-age children. *Soviet Psychology, 13*(4), 5–64.

John-Steiner, V. (1985). *Notebooks of the mind.* Albuquerque: University of New Mexico Press.

John-Steiner, V. (1991). Private speech among adults. In R. Diaz & L. Berk (Eds.), *Private speech from social interaction to self regulation* (pp. 285–296). Hillsdale, NJ: Lawrence Erlbaum Associates.

John-Steiner, V., & Osterreich, H. (1975, October). *Learning styles among Pueblo children.* NIE Research Grant, Final Report, Albuquerque, University of New Mexico, Department of Educational Foundations.

John-Steiner, V., & Roth, N. (1983). A study of children's writings in noninstructional settings. In D. Rogers & J. A. Sloboda (Eds.), *The acquisition of symbolic skills* (pp. 431–443). New York: Plenum.

John-Steiner, V., & Tatter, P. (1983). An interactionist model of language development. In B. Bain (Ed.), *Sociogenesis of language and human conduct* (pp. 79–97). New York: Plenum.

Laboratory of Comparative Human Cognition. (1983). Culture and cognitive development. In W. Kessen (Ed.), *Handbook of child psychology: Volume 1.* New York: Wiley.

Lave, J. (1988). *Cognition in practice.* Cambridge: Cambridge University Press.

Lee, B. (1987). Recontextualizing Vygotsky. In M. Hickmann (Ed.), *Social and functional approaches to language and thought* (pp. 87–105). Orlando, FL: Academic Press.

Leont'ev, A. N. (1981). The problem of activity in psychology. In J. V. Wertsch (Ed.), *The concept of activity in Soviet psychology* (pp. 37–71). Armonk, NY: M. E. Sharpe.

Luria, A. R. (1976). *Cognitive development: Its cultural and social foundations.* Cambridge, MA: Harvard University Press.

Luria, A. R. (1982). *Language and cognition.* New York: Wiley.

McDermott, R. (1976). *Kids make sense: An ethnographic account of the interactional management of success and failure in one first-grade classroom.* Unpublished doctoral dissertation, Stanford University, Stanford, CA.

McLane, J. B. (1987). Interaction, context, and the zone of proximal development. In M. Hickmann (Ed.), *Social and functional approaches to language and thought* (pp. 267–286). Orlando, FL: Academic Press.

McLane, J. B. (1990). Writing as a social process. In L. C. Moll (Ed.), *Vygotsky and education* (pp. 304–318). Cambridge: Cambridge University Press.

McNamee, G. D. (1990). Learning to read and write in an inner-city setting: A longitudinal study of community change. In L. C. Moll (Ed.), *Vygotsky and education* (pp. 287–303). Cambridge: Cambridge University Press.

Moffett, J. W. (1968). *Teaching the universe of discourse.* Boston, MA: Houghton Mifflin.

Moll, L. C. (1990). *Vygotsky and education.* Cambridge: Cambridge University Press.

Nelson, K. (1989). Monologues in the crib. In K. Nelson (Ed.), *Narratives from the crib* (pp. 1–23). Cambridge, MA: Harvard University Press.

Newman, D., Griffin, P., & Cole, M. (1989). *The construction zone.* Cambridge: Cambridge University Press.

Oakes, J. (1985). *Keeping track: How schools structure inequality.* New Haven, CT: Yale University Press.

Ochs, E. (1982). Talking to children in Western Samoa. *Language in Society, 11,* 66–104.

Ochs, E. (1987). Input: A socio-cultural perspective. In M. Hickmann (Ed.), *Social and functional approaches to language and thought* (pp. 305–319). Orlando, FL: Academic Press.

Ochs, E. (1990). Indexicality and socialization. In J. W. Stigler, R. A. Shweder, & G. Herdt (Eds.), *Cultural psychology: Essays on comparative human development* (pp. 287–308). Cambridge: Cambridge University Press.

Ong. W. (1982). *Orality and literacy: The technologizing of the word.* London: Methuen.

Riegel, K. (1979). *Foundations of dialectical psychology.* New York: Academic Press.

Rivers, W. J. (1987). *Problems in composition: A Vygotskian perspective.* Unpublished doctoral dissertation, University of Delaware.

Rogoff, B. (1990). *Apprenticeship in thinking.* New York: Oxford University Press.

Rogoff, B., & Lave, J. (1984). *Everyday cognition.* Cambridge, MA: Harvard University Press.

Rosenblatt, L. M. (1985). Viewpoints: Transaction versus interaction – a terminological rescue operation. *Research in the Teaching of English, 19*(1), 96–107.

Sanborn, J. *The academic essay: A feminist view on students' voice.* Unpublished manuscript.

Sapir, E. (1921). *Language: An introduction to the study of speech.* New York: Harcourt Brace.

Schieffelin, B. B., & Gilmore, P. (1986). *The acquisition of literacy: Ethnographic perspectives.* Norwood, NJ: Ablex.

Schieffelin, B. B., & Ochs, E. (Eds.). (1986). *Language socialization across cultures.* Cambridge: Cambridge University Press.

Schoenfeld, A. H. (1988). *Mathematical problem solving.* New York: Academic Press.

Schweder, R. (1990) Cultural psychology – What is it? In J. W. Stigler, R. A. Shweder, & G. Herdt (Eds.), *Cultural psychology: Essays on comparative human development* (pp. 1–46). Cambridge: Cambridge University Press.

Scollon, R., & Scollon, S. (1981). *Narrative, literacy and face in interethnic communication.* Norwood, NJ: Ablex.

Scribner, S., & Cole, M. (1981). *The psychology of literacy.* Cambridge, MA: Harvard University Press.

Searle, J. (1969). *Speech acts.* Cambridge: Cambridge University Press.

Shankweiler, D. (1991). Starting on the right foot. *Educational Researcher, 20*(4), 33–35.

Shannon, P. (1989). *Broken promises: Reading instruction in twentieth century America.* Granby, MA: Bergin & Garvey.

Siegler, R., & Crowley, K. (1991). The microgenetic method: A direct means for studying cognitive development. *American Psychologist, 46*(6), 606–620.

Silverstein, M. (1976). Shifters, linguistic categories, and cultural descriptions. In K. H. Basso & H. A. Selby (Eds.). *Meaning in anthropology* (pp. 11–55). Albuquerque: University of New Mexico Press.

Silverstein, M. (1985). The functional stratification of language and ontogenesis. In J. V. Wertsch (Ed.), *Culture communication, and cognition: Vygotskian perspectives* (pp. 205–235). Cambridge: Cambridge University Press.

Smolucha, F. (1992). Social origins of private speech in pretend play. In R. M. Diaz & L. E. Berk (Eds.), *Private speech: From social interaction to self-regulation* (pp. 123–141). Hillsdale, NJ: Lawrence Erlbaum Associates.

Snow, C. (1983). Literacy and language: Relationships during the preschool years. *Harvard Educational Review, 53,* 165–189.

Snow, C., & Ferguson, C. (1978). *Talking to children: Language input and acquisition.* Cambridge: Cambridge University Press.

Stanovich, K. E. (1980). Toward an interactive-compensatory model of individual differences in the development of reading fluency. *Reading Research Quarterly, 16,* 32–71.

Stigler, J. W., & Perry, M. (1990). Mathematics learning in Japanese, Chinese, and American classrooms. In J. W. Stigler, R. A. Shweder, & G. Herdt (Eds.), *Cultural psychology: Essays on comparative human development* (pp. 328–353). Cambridge: Cambridge University Press.

Tannen, D. (1982). The oral/literate continuum in discourse. In D. Tannen (Ed.), *Spoken and written language: Exploring orality and literacy.* Norwood, NJ: Ablex.

Tannen, D. (1984). *Conversational style: Analyzing talk among friends.* Norwood, NJ: Ablex.

Tharp, R., & Gallimore, R. (1988). *Rousing minds to life.* Cambridge: Cambridge University Press.

Toulmin, S. (1978). The Mozart of psychology. *New York Review of Books, 25*(14), 51–57.

Trevarthen, C. (1974, May). Conversations with a two-month old. *New Scientist,* 230–235.

Trevarthen, C. (1980). The foundations of intersubjectivity: Development of interpersonal and cooperative understanding in infants. In D. R. Olson (Ed.), *The social foundations of language and thought.* New York: Norton.

Tudge, J. (1990). Vygotsky, the zone of proximal development, and peer collaboration: Implications for classroom practice. In L. C. Moll (Ed.), *Vygotsky and education* (pp. 154–174). Cambridge: Cambridge University Press.

Valsiner, J. (1987). *Culture and the development of children's action: A cultural-historical theory of development.* Chichester: Wiley.

Valsiner, J. (1988). *Developmental psychology in the Soviet Union.* Brighton: Harvester Press.

Vygotsky, L. S. (1934). *Myshlenie i rech. Psikhologicheskie issledovanija* (Thinking and Speech: Psychological Investigation). Moscow and Leningrad: Gosudartstvennoe Social'no-Ekonomicheskoe Izdatel'stvo.

Vygotsky, L. S. (1962). *Thought and language.* Cambridge, MA: MIT Press and Wiley. (Originally published in Russian, 1934)

Vygotsky, L. S. (1978). *Mind in society: The development of higher psychological processes.* M. Cole, V. John-Steiner, S. Scribner, & E. Souberman (Eds.). Cambridge, MA: Harvard University Press.

Vygotsky, L. S. (1987). *The collected works of L. S. Vygotsky, Volume I: Problems of general psychology.* R. Rieber & A. Carton (Eds.). New York: Plenum.

Wells, G. (Ed.). (1981). *Learning through interaction: The study of language development* (Vol. 1). Cambridge: Cambridge University Press.

Wertsch, J. V. (1980). The significance of dialogue in Vygotsky's account of social, egocentric, and inner speech. *Contemporary Educational Psychology, 5,* 150–162.

Wertsch, J. V. (1985). *Vygotsky and the social formation of mind.* Cambridge, MA: Harvard University Press.

Wertsch, J. V. (1991). *Voices of the mind: A sociocultural approach to mediated action.* Cambridge, MA: Harvard University Press.

Wertsch, J. V., & Hickmann, M. (1987). Problem-solving in social interaction: A microgenetic analysis. In M. Hickmann (Ed.), *Social and functional approaches to language and thought.* Orlando, FL: Academic Press.

Wertsch, J. V., & Minick, N. J. (1990). Negotiating sense in the zone of proximal development. In M. Schwebel, C. A. Maher, & N. S. Fagley (Eds.), *Promoting cognitive growth over the life span* (pp. 71–88). Hillsdale, NJ: Lawrence Erlbaum Associates.

Whorf, F. (1956). *Language, thought, and reality: Selected writings of Benjamin Lee Whorf.* J. Carroll (Ed.). Cambridge, MA: MIT Press.

Wittgenstein, L. (1958). *Philosophical investigations.* New York: Macmillan.

Wolf, D. P. (1990). For literate lives: The possibilities for elementary school. In C. Hedley, J. J. Houtz, & A. Baratta (Eds.), *Cognition, curriculum, and literacy* (pp. 121–136). Norwood, NJ: Ablex.

Part I

Context

Although Vygotsky did not write extensively specifically about the concept of context, all of his work implies the importance of context both at the level of individual speech acts (whether in inner speech or social dialogue) and at the level of historical and cultural patterns of language use. Vygotsky's work (as well as that of others) has been an impetus in the development of the recognition of the need to pay close attention to context in studies of language use. For example, an interactionist approach following Vygotsky is readily compatible with recent developments in such linguistics- and language-associated fields as sociolinguistics, discourse analysis, pragmatics, and the ethnography of communication, precisely because Vygotsky recognized the importance of both immediate contextual constraints and the wider social, historical, and cultural conditions of language use.

An integral part of an interactionist approach to language use and literacy is the recognition that context is a constitutive factor in language use, in the social construction of meaning. Actually, any of the papers collected in this volume could be used to illustrate the primary importance of the recognition of context for a study using an interactionist approach. The papers introduced in this section, then may be taken as varied examples of how the concept of context may be used in interactionist studies. One point that may be noticed about the particular three studies in this section is that they all, in one way or another, intentionally vary contexts in order to collect data and observations that can be used to compare language use in different contexts. Before introducing the studies offered in this section, we will consider in more detail what we mean by concepts of context and social construction of meaning.

What do we mean by context, and why is it considered to have elemental importance in language acts and uses? Neither of these questions can be answered by offering a facile, one- or two-sentence "definition" of the concept of context, since what we are after here is an attempt to specify how language is used in the social construction of meaning. It is hoped that the following discussion will clarify what we mean by context, how it is related to the social construction of meaning, and, therefore, why it is considered to be of central importance in an interactionist theoretical approach to meaning in language use.

If we wish to have a theory of how humans communicate, of how we mean, then we need to examine how texts are created, constructed, used by both speakers/writers and listeners/readers in an interactive process. Both interactants in the process are creating and constructing meaning. To develop a theoretical conception of how texts mean, it is necessary to examine the system of Discourse and discourses (Gee, 1990) within the social group with which we are concerned. This is another way of saying that texts are discourses created within a social group's system of Discourses. We are able to construct and understand meaning in discourses because they fit into socially patterned and sanctioned systems of Discourses. Gee (1990, p. xix) offers the following definition:

> Discourses are ways of behaving, interacting, valuing, thinking, believing, speaking, and often reading and writing that are accepted as instantiations of particular roles by specific *groups of people*. . . . They are always and everywhere *social.* Language, as well as literacy, is always and everywhere integrated with and relative to *social practices* constituting particular Discourses.

Since Discourses (and therefore discourses and texts) rely upon (actually are) social roles and practices, we can see that they are founded upon the recognition of (whether conscious or unconscious recognition of) contexts. Of course, social roles and practices are learned, developed, and used in specific contexts.

But the issue of context is even yet more fundamental and complex, on both individual and social levels. The point to be made here is that it is not possible to establish meaning outside of context because human beings cannot exist outside of a context and therefore can never be thinking or using language outside of a context. We are always in some place at some time, even if while in that place and time we may sometimes (often?) be imagining other places and times, other contexts. The human condition is to be situated and therefore to be coming from some perspective in our making of meaning.

M. M. Bakhtin in a number of writings (1981, 1986, 1990) has eloquently expressed his viewpoint of what it means for humans to be both individual and social beings. The following quotation philosophically establishes the concrete situatedness, the contexted uniqueness of the individual, and from this beginning point Bakhtin continued to develop his conception of the "dialogic" nature of language use in human interactions.

> When I contemplate a whole human being who is situated outside and over against me, our concrete, actually experienced horizons do not coincide. For each given moment, regardless of the position and the proximity to me of this other human being whom I am contemplating, I shall always see and know something that he, from his place outside and over against me, cannot see himself; parts of his body that are inaccessible to his own gaze (his head, his face and its expression), the world behind his back, and a whole series of objects and relations are accessible to me but not to him. As we gaze at each other, two different worlds are reflected in the pupils of our eyes. It is possible, upon assuming an appropriate position, to reduce this difference of horizons to a minimum, but in order to annihilate this difference completely, it would be necessary to merge into one, to become one and the same person.
>
> This ever-present *excess* of my seeing, knowing, and possessing in relation to any other human being is founded in the uniqueness and irreplaceability of my place in the world. For only I – the-one-and-only-I – occupy in a given set of circumstances this particular place at this particular time; all other human beings are situated outside of me. (Bakhtin, 1990, pp. 22–23)

If this were Bakhtin's only surviving writing, we could conceivably suspect that he might have taken the ideas in this quotation in a solipsistic direction. We know, however, from the more widely published and better known of Bakhtin's works that he instead used his understanding of the basic foundation of individual human situatedness to go on to develop his concept of the dialogic relationship between interactants in communication. Actually, in the quotation we can notice the seeds of that real subsequent direction. If it is true by nature of the human condition that we (you and I) are never exactly in the same place (and, of course, have not had exactly the same experiences), even if we are in the same social group and even if we are trying to participate in the same situation or discuss what we would agree is the same idea, then we also have a basic human social need (also built into the human condition) of each other. I need you (Other) to help define me, and you need me (Other) to help define you. And we both need each other to help define and say what we see in the world outside of each of our selves, for the self–other–world relationships are defined culturally for us by ourselves and others, through social networks.

For Bakhtin, although it is true by virtue of the human condition that we are each unique individuals, it is also true that meaning can be made only in social relationship, only in dialogic interaction. Meaning – whether within the individual (in inner speech), between individuals, between social groups, or between genres – is constructed in competing dialogic relationships that are situated in both individual and social contexts. There can never be true monologism, only at times monologies that mistakenly or naïvely refuse to acknowledge debt to the dialogic nature of the human condition. Nothing we ever say or write, even though we are truly individuals, is ever perfectly new, but is always in dialogic relationship to another's words or works that, in turn may be nested within another group's words or works, whether historically or contemporaneously.

We must depend on each other to construct meaning. All of us as individuals are members of multiple social groups in complex societies. Because of our individual contextedness, situatedness, we can never *be* the Other, but because of our social contextedness, situatedness we can use the Other(s) to help us negotiate meanings from a dialogic stance. We must be clear that individuals do not make meaning by themselves. Meaning only occurs within social groups within societies and cultures. The individual is both aided and constrained in making meaning by the sociohistorical development (within the social group and culture) of what Bakhtin (1986) calls "speech genres" and what we have earlier here called Discourses, following Gee (1990).

Discourses are the socially, culturally, historically developed frames in which the members of the group make and understand meaning. They are the commonly defined situational contexts for the group, contexts that have grown with the history of the group. Traditionally, discourses have been considered and analyzed as individual creations, and only as ways of using words. That is a shortsighted and limiting view of the power of Discourses, and of the need for discourses to fit into the pattern of Discourses. Instead, following Gee (1990), quoted earlier in this section, in an interactionist and socially constituted conception of how humans mean, the definition of Discourses is widened to acknowledge that they are ways of seeing, acting, thinking, behaving, believing, valuing, and interacting, as well as ways of speaking, reading, and writing. We can say that there is no meaning made or understood outside of a socially constituted and contexted Discourse.

Almost all of us are born into a primary social group, the family, which becomes our first Discourse group. As we grow through childhood and adulthood, we become members of many other Discourse groups, usually moving progressively away from the family. In order to be accepted into those groups, we must learn the Discourses of those groups, the ways of perceiving, thinking about, behaving in, acting in, and telling about the world that the groups use. In order to learn these things, we must be apprenticed to those groups for a period of time. If we only partially learn, or for some reason are excluded from a full apprenticeship in a certain group and cannot learn well its discourses and Discourses, we will always be considered to some extent an outsider by that group.

If the Discourse group has absolute sanctioning powers, it also potentially offers not only membership, but a place to be creative. All Discourse genres change over history, and they change by group members' creative reinterpretations of the group's knowing, acting, and saying. Discourses not only sanction and limit, they offer frames for individual creativity, and therefore change over time.

Since Discourses are the socially constituted vehicles for meaning in a society, we must be clear that meaning does not occur outside of Discourses. Of course, there are many conflicting Discourses within any society, especially so within a modern, complex, multicultural society. Again, we see a firm link here with Bakhtin's (1981) concept of the dialogic nature of language use. (See also Clark and Holquist, 1984; Morson and Emerson, 1990; and Hirschkop and Shepherd, 1989). Not only is there a basic dialogic relationship between individuals as expressed by Bakhtin, but social groups and their conflicting Discourses are in dialogic relationship. No Discourses are neutral; they are valuational, always from the perspective of the social group that sanctions the Discourse.

Of course, there are important educational implications of Discourses in dialogic relationship. The greater the differences and distances between one social group's Discourses and those of another, the greater the potential for conflict and exclusion there is between the groups. The dominant groups in a society use Discourses to run and control their institutions. Those who do not know and use those Discourses remain outsiders. Certainly a relevant question for educational institutions is how to integrate new members, how to provide apprenticeship to the Discourses that are valued by the groups of power. It should be noted that this is a question of much wider scope than the question of how to teach someone to read or write because reading and writing are done *in* Discourses that are ways of behaving, acting, seeing, knowing, *and* ways of using words. There are multiple literacies in each society.

This introductory section began by stressing the importance of an awareness of context in interactionist studies and proceeded to relate context to Discourse. At the foundation of Discourses (the socially sanctioned vehicles and frames for making meaning) are group-recognized situational contexts. Always meaning is made in context, through discourses, through Discourses. Traditionally, context has often been thought of as a side issue or an add on, coming late into the process of making meaning. Those who think of context in this way seem to hypothesize that meaning is first made in the conjunction of syntactic and semantic structures in the individual mind and then filtered into or applied to a context. This would seem to indicate that meaning is autonomous, of the language. We disagree with this conceptualization: meaning is not *in* the language, but instead is in the social group's *use* of the language. Context plays a part in the meaning from the inception of the meaning. Context is constitutive of meaning, which is why it is so important to be aware of context in development of theories, in research studies, and in practical applications.

The chapters in this section (by Smith, Shonerd, and Wilcox) examine literacy in divergent areas, concern different populations of learners, and use different methodologies. The chapter by Smith studies differences and similarities between spoken and written language in three situational domains. The data for this study were collected from a graduate student population, a population that could be expected to have expertise in the three situations examined. The evaluation of the language performance data uses a statistical methodology. The chapter by Shonerd uses an English as a second language (ESL) college-level student population to examine instances of "repair" used in different spontaneous speech situations. The data were collected in both classroom and interview situations from second language learners who have different levels of expertise and different first languages and cultural backgrounds. The analysis of data in this study also employs statistical methodology. The chapter by Wilcox is a case study of a young deaf girl. It follows her language use at home and at school and examines early literacy experiences. An ethnographic methodology is used to collect and interpret data.

Although there is a wide diversity among the three studies in populations examined, methodology used, and particular area of language use studied, each of the authors uses an interactionist approach to his material: in each study, context is recognized as a constitutive factor in language use.

In the study by Smith, situational context and audience are varied systematically to examine differences in spoken and written language use. The study by Shonerd varies context by varying audience, situation of use, and task. It also takes into consideration differences in subjects' cultural backgrounds and native languages. Using an ethnographic approach, Wilcox follows a deaf child through different language use contexts at home, with nonfamily members, and at school. As the child learns to sign, different literacy experiences occur in each of those contexts.

The reader will note, then, that in the chapters in this section context is taken into consideration and dealt with. Smith and Shonerd intentionally vary situations and contexts in their studies in order to observe what happens to the language use because of the variations. Wilcox offers an ethnographic study that directly details the contexts in which the subject of the study used language. In an interactionist study, regardless of whether the chosen methodology is qualitative or quantitative, it is important to recognize the constitutive nature of context in the social construction of meaning in language use.

REFERENCES

Bakhtin, M. M. 1981. *The Dialogic Imagination: Four Essays.* Holquist, M. (Ed.). Emerson, C., and M. Holquist (Trans.). Austin: University of Texas Press.

Bakhtin, M. M. 1986. *Speech Genres and Other Late Essays.* Emerson, C., and M. Holquist (Eds.). McGee, V. W. (Trans.). Austin: University of Texas Press.

Bakhtin, M. M. 1990. *Art and Answerability: Early Philosophical Essays.* Holquist, M., and V. Liapunov (Eds.). Liapunov, V. (Trans.). Bostrom, K. (Trans. supplement). Austin: University of Texas Press.

Clark, K., and M. Holquist, (Eds.). 1984. *Mikhail Bakhtin.* Cambridge, MA: Harvard University Press.

Gee, J. P. 1990. *Social Linguistics and Literacies: Ideology in Discourses.* London: Falmer Press.

Hirschkop, K., and D. Shepherd (Eds.). 1989. *Bakhtin and Cultural Theory.* Manchester: Manchester University Press.

Morson, G. S., and C. Emerson. 1990. *Mikhail Bakhtin: Creation of a Prosaics.* Stanford, CA: Stanford University Press.

2 *An interactionist approach to the analysis of similarities and differences between spoken and written language*

LARRY W. SMITH

2.1. INTRODUCTION

An interactionist approach to the analysis of similarities and differences between spoken and written language is a social and functionalist approach that has its basic theoretical underpinnings in L. S. Vygotsky's conception of language development. For Vygotsky, each individual's language development originates in social interaction, and then language development and social interaction continue a mutually mediating and transforming relationship within the semiotic system of the given culture. Various authors have referred to the Vygotskian approach as "sociohistorical." Ochs (1984, p. 327), as one example, has defined the sociohistorical approach to language development and use as acknowledging the need in language studies to

> examine closely the organization of language activities, including the verbal means used to achieve goals, the sequential organization of verbal means, and the contexts in which goals, means, and sequential orders are taken up by language users, and relate these organizational patterns to cognitive skills and to systems of belief and social order.

It is possible to use the term "interactionist" to refer to several different levels of analysis: (1) In its broadest sense, "interactionist" refers to the Vygotskian conception of the "unification of nature and culture in the course of ontogenetic development" (John-Steiner and Tatter, 1983, p. 95) as opposed to either nativist or behaviorist conceptions of human development. (See also Wertsch, 1985a, 1985b; and Scinto, 1986). (2) In a second sense, "interactionist" refers to the use of language as social action and the understanding of language as based in human interaction in the various contexts available in the social semiotic of a given culture. (See Halliday, 1978; Bakhtin, 1981; Hasan, 1985; and Nystrand, 1986). (3) Finally, and particularly in this chapter, "interactionist" may also refer to the influences and interactions – both historically and contemporaneously – between spoken and written language in the development of language genres that we know today, which, of course, are continuing to develop. (See Gregory and Carroll, 1978; and Bakhtin, 1986.)

One advantage of an interactionist theoretical approach, then, is that it makes possible the consideration of a wide range of relationships between spoken and written language within the semiotic system. The communicative economy (that interrelated system of possibilities and potentialities of a language that its speakers and writers use to understand, form, and re-form their culture) of a modern literate society is complex, with various complicated bridges and interrelationships between spoken and written language. Although there has been a growing research interest in differences between spoken and written language within the past decade, much of the research continues to focus on overly generalized, "universal" differences between speech and writing, at least partly because such research is atheoretical to the extent that it is not grounded in an inclusive theory of language development. This interactionist approach, on the other hand, offers a theoretical approach conducive to the consideration of differences and similarities between spoken and written language at the levels of function, process, structure, and discourse, while taking into consideration contexts of use in the social semiotic. An additional strength of the interactionist approach used here is that it is compatible with recent advances in sociolinguistic and discourse analysis methodology.

Grounded in interactionist theoretical assumptions, this chapter reports results of an empirical examination of language use in three situational domains – informal conversation, formal spoken interview, and written essay – while controlling the contextual variables of topic, subject-participants, and audience. The data collected for the three situational domains are analyzed on two different levels: the first level of analysis reports results on differences in the use of linguistic structures in the three domains; the second level of analysis reports results on how coherence is achieved differently in the three domains through differences in the management of given and new information.

The study is empirical and discourse-based in that in a controlled experimental environment it examines linguistic structures and communicative strategies that members of a defined speech community actually used in the different domains studied, and in that the total output of all subject-participants in all of the experimental conditions was examined. It is hoped that such detailed, side-by-side empirical examinations of the relationships between spoken and written languauge that look at different genres, situational domains, audience constructs, discourse strategies, and topic and context variables can help researchers move toward development of a theory of text construction and a theory of literacy.

2.2. HISTORICAL

2.2.1. Linguistic theory and differences between spoken and written language

Before discussing the study, it may be useful to briefly review both the history of previous theory and the history of some previous research studies concerning relationships between spoken and written language. As will be seen, the main limitation of theory in this area is that the field of theoretical linguistics has never shown an interest in undertaking serious comparative studies of spoken and written language, and the main limitation of many earlier empirical studies is that their comparisons remain generalized and abstract, promoting what Tannen (1982a) has called "the myth of orality and literacy."

Reasonably, one might expect numerous studies of the relationships between spoken and written language to have been conducted within the field of theoretical linguistics, given the potential of such studies to help answer such nontrivial questions as what language is, how it is learned, and how it is used. Historically, however, the study of the relationships between spoken and written language has never been a major objective in theoretical linguistics. The dominant theoretical paradigms, whether unconsciously held or consciously stated, have never been conducive to such studies. Previous to the twentieth century, linguistics was primarily concerned with philological studies that often relied upon careful examination of written texts. As a consequence of this almost exclusive consideration of written texts, there was a general acceptance of the written form of a language as the most perfected form, the "real" language. The spoken form of a language was generally considered unworthy of serious study – defective in comparison to the written form. For most of the twentieth century, however, a different situation has existed. Beginning early in the century with Saussure's studies, the field of linguistics has been redirected from its earlier approach of diachronic studies of written material to, instead, synchronic studies of spoken language. Modern theoretical linguistics has virtually ignored the study of written language.

Saussure's important influence on the development of modern linguistics is readily acknowledged in the field. One of his basic tenets, and perhaps the most influential, was his distinction between "la langue," the underlying system of rules and norms of a language, and "la parole," actual manifestations of speech acts in real time in speech and writing. He held that the linguist's real interest should be in discovering the nature of the underlying system and that the actual utterances should be studied only to the extent that they provide evidence for the underlying system.

In the subsequent development of twentieth-century linguistics, this redirection of the focus of linguistics to what de Beaugrande (1984, p. 43) has called "the virtual system over its actualizations" has influenced what linguists would consider as relevant data, and how they would collect and analyze the data. As far as dealing with speech data is concerned, one could analyze the dominant movements of structuralism, generative transformationalism, and their various offshoots as actually exhibiting a progression away from the collection of data from informants in real-life language use situations to a greater reliance upon data generated by the linguist himself or herself.

The creation of "citation" forms of data begs the question of whether there are differences between spoken and written language, since citation forms are a curious hybrid – often designed to imply spoken language but actually invented and provided in a nearly contextless written form. This type of inattention to potential major problems associated with the data base not only makes the citation form suspect as a vehicle for syntactic, semantic, and pragmatic theories, but inappropriate for use in studies attempting to focus on possible similarities or differences between spoken and written language.

By the 1970s, with the proliferation of linguist-generated citation forms as a primary data source in the field of theoretical linguistics and with the consistent conception – from Saussure through Bloomfield to Postal – of written language as a derived, secondary symbol system with no direct relationship to the world (see Householder, 1971), there was no impetus within major linguistic paradigms to study differences between spoken and written language. Within the transformational – generative paradigm, with its concepts of ideal speaker/hearer and underlying competence, any differences between speech and writing were relegated to use-performance components of the paradigm and assumed not worthy of serious investigation.

Although theoretical linguistics has shown little interest in investigating differences between spoken and written language during this century, it is also true that in various related disciplines of the humanities, such as psychology, sociology, anthropology, and education, some scholars have shown an interest in comparing written and spoken language. Often researchers in these fields have attempted to adapt various linguistic approaches to study "applied linguistics" problems in their own fields. In part because of the lack of a satisfactorily adaptable paradigm, and in part because of the diversity of these fields, the research on spoken and written language resulting from this body of work might be characterized as diverse, unsolidified, and in many cases overgeneralized. Although these studies cover a wide range and at times have variously investigated differences between spoken and written language in terms of functions, processes, and structures, the studies remain unrelated and atheoretical, unable to bring into a more complete picture the relationships between spoken and written language on all three of these levels.

2.2.2. *Studies of functional differences*

Some of those who have studied the general functional differences between spoken and written language include Vygotsky (1986), Lord (1960), McIntosh (1966), Goody and Watt (1972), Vachek (1972; 1976), Basso (1974), Goody (1977), Ong (1977), Olson (1977), Halliday (1978), Gregory and Carroll (1978), Rubin (1980), Heath (1981), Stubbs (1980; 1983), and van Dijk and Kintsch (1983). Most of these studies make the basic point that spoken and written language, in general, serve different communicative functions.

Taking the excellent work of Vygotsky and Vachek to be the best representation of this group, both make the points that the norm function for spoken language is to handle dynamic, interactive, face-to-face encounters in which participants are enclosed in situ in mutually understood, or at least immediately negotiable, concrete contexts. The primary functions for written language, on the other hand, are communication across distances to less surely known audiences and preservation of information across time. And since writing is a visual medium in which the sequential ordering is often carefully planned and revised before the final product is viewed by an audience, it is also argued that written language potentially allows and promotes increased efficiency in manipulation of complex information and ideas.

Although a general conception of the norm differences of the functions of spoken and written language is an essential foundation for studies of differences between spoken and written language, subsequent research studies have too often relied too heavily only on norm differences of functions to be explanatory and, therefore, have not explicitly defined the situational context(s) applicable in the given study. Doing so places too much faith in the concept of norm differences as an explanation of differences in linguistic uses and behaviors.

A particular, actualized use of language functions in response to (and also, at the same time, helps to create and form) a complex of issues: topic, audience, medium, participants, purpose, and specific context. To ignore description of these issues, or to imply that simply by making a choice between speaking or writing a language user has addressed and solved all of these issues, is to commit an unfortunate generalization in the analysis of differences between spoken and written language. If the researcher ignores these issues, the hidden implication is that although spoken and written language are different, all spoken language is the same and all written language is the same. Instead, the actual case is that the communicative economy of a literate society is much more diverse and rich in possibilities than what can be described adequately by a general conception of functional differences between spoken and written language.

One of the unfortunate results of an overreliance on general functional differences between spoken and written language as explanatory is the conceptualization of written language as "decontextualized." This now popular conceptualization is given its strongest statement by Olson (1977), who has been widely interpreted as saying that "in writing 'the meaning is in the text' and in speaking 'the meaning is in the context' " (in Tannen, 1982, p. 39). This is an oversimplification in that it seems to claim that readers do not use knowledge of the world that they already possess to make inferences in reading as listeners do when taking part in conversations. Although it may be true that systems for contexting meaning are different in written and spoken language (see Nystrand, 1986), it cannot be true that written language does not use context, previous knowledge, and wide-ranging inferences to help create and communicate meaning.

Bakhtin (1986) expresses the fundamental, constitutive nature of context at the level of word, utterance, and genre, whether the use is in spoken or written language:

> Neutral dictionary meanings of the words of a language ensure their common features and guarantee that all speakers of a given language will understand one another, but the use of words in live speech [language] communication is always individual and contextual in nature. (p. 88)

> However monological the utterance may be (for example, a scientific or philosophical treatise), however much it may concentrate on its own object, it cannot but be, in some measure, a response to what has already been said about the given topic, on the given issue, even though this responsiveness may not have assumed a clear-cut external expression. It will be manifested in the overtones of the style, in the finest nuances of the composition. The utterance is filled with dialogic overtones, and they must be taken into account in order to understand fully the style of the utterance. After all, our thought itself – philosophical, scientific, and artistic – is born and shaped in the process of interaction and struggle with others' thought, and this cannot but be reflected in the forms that verbally express our thought as well. (p. 92)

> An essential (constitutive) marker of the utterance is its quality of being directed to someone, its addressivity. . . . This addressee can be an immediate participant-interlocutor in an everyday dialogue, a

> differentiated collection of specialists in some particular area of cultural communication, a more or less differentiated public, ethnic group, contemporaries, like-minded people, opponents and enemies, a subordinate, a superior, someone who is lower, higher, familiar, foreign, and so forth. And it can also be an indefinite, concretized other. . . . Both the composition and, particularly, the style of the utterance depend on those to whom the utterance is addressed, how the speaker (or writer) senses and imagines his addressees, and the force of their effect on the utterance. Each speech [language] genre in each area of speech [language] communication has its own typical conception of the addressee and this defines it as a genre. (p. 95)

The challenge for those studying differences between spoken and written language is not to figure out how written language could operate as a "decontextualized" language form, but instead to identify how word choice, semantic fields, syntactic forms, metalinguistic forms, punctuation, and genre awareness, as well as other possible factors, may help to portray context in the different genres of written language.

A generalized conception of the functional differences between speech and writing is an essential theoretical foundation for studies of differences between spoken and written language, but it is actually only a first step. Those theoretical studies and speculations that have relied on abstract and generalized conceptions and that have not proceeded to empirical examinations of language use in context have led to monolithic, dichotomized conceptions of the differences between spoken and written language.

2.2.3. Studies of differences in production processes

With the exception of some recent studies, very little research specifically comparing the production processes of spoken and written language exists. First, as has been mentioned earlier, a theoretical linguistics paradigm that would allow or foster such comparative research has not existed until recent advances in discourse analysis theory. Second, language production processes have been considered to be more difficult to examine than have comprehension processes. Traditionally (see Clark and Clark, 1977), as well as currently in a discourse paradigm (van Dijk & Kintsch, 1983), psycholinguists have studied comprehension processes more than production processes because they have felt that comprehension is easier to test objectively. Third, processes involved in the production of written language were traditionally ignored in favor of a three-stage product-oriented model of production. Only recently has there been a focus on the processes involved in writing, represented in such work as de Beaugrande (1979a, 1979b, 1980, 1982, 1984), Flower and Hayes (1980a, 1980b, 1981a, 1981b, 1981c), and Matsuhashi (1981, 1982).

Because the necessary paradigms and assumptions are still being developed, a comparison of the production processes of spoken and written language is difficult. An important issue yet to be determined is to what extent "the flow of thought and the flow of language" (Chafe, 1979) must be handled differently in the production of spoken versus written language. De Beaugrande (1982), Chafe (1980, 1982, 1985, 1986), and Tannen (1979, 1980) are among those who have directly addressed this question.

It is interesting to note that two independently developed language production models, the van Dijk and Kintsch (1983) discourse strategies model for speech production processes and the Flower and Hayes (1981b) model for writing processes, are actually quite similar in several ways: both discuss language production in terms of dynamic interaction of processes; both recognize the importance of processing constraints; and both discuss the back-and-forth movement between local and global strategies for planning, formulating, and executing language production. A shortcoming of both models, however, is that they do not recognize and address the issue of context for specific language tasks. As Nystrand (1986) points out, how the speaker/writer handles providing context for specific spoken or written tasks may be a fruitful area of investigation of differences between production processes in spoken and written language. The similarities between the two independently developed models, as well as the problems that remain to be worked out, suggest that the best way to study the relationships between the production processes of spoken and written language would be within a more fully developed discourse strategies paradigm. The most fruitful investigations of how "the flow of thought and the flow of language" may differ in the production processes of spoken and written language will be done in an interactionist discourse paradigm that (1) analyzes naturally occurring language, whether in case study or in experimentally controlled observations, rather than data contrived by the linguist or experimenter; (2) analyzes text development of extended segments of language use rather than being restricted to the sentence level; (3) includes analysis of nonlinguistic factors of the context of language use; and (4) explicitly compares spoken and written language in side-by-side empirical analysis. Unless the study of relationships between production processes in spoken and written language is based in these four assumptions, it will be generalized and abstract and will not contribute notably to our knowledge of how language is produced and used in social interaction.

2.2.4 Studies of form–structure differences

Form–structure differences between spoken and written language exist at the grapheme-sound, lexical, syntactic, semantic, discourse, and genre levels. Concerning these levels, while it is generally true that whatever can be discussed in spoken language can also be written about (and vice versa), it is also true that there are genre, register, and stylistic tendencies that differ between spoken and written language. This means that the basic (or underlying) knowledge of a language that a language user has must be employed in different ways in writing as compared with speaking situations in order to be efficient, coherent, and maximally communicative. The interactionist theoretical position proposed here holds that different stylistic tendencies are not merely surface manifestations tracked onto basic underlying structures, but that context and situation are constitutive of the language act from its inception. Language acts have specific purposes in specific contexts and therefore specific styles and uses are created to meet needs through manipulations and choices of potential structures.

The interrelationship of spoken and written language across a wide range of styles, genres, situations, and considerations of formality–informality leads to a complex communicative economy in a literate society. It is according to the relative mastery of such a communicative economy that we make judgments concerning an individual's communicative competence (Hymes, 1972), the ability to appropriately choose and use the existing and potential resources of the language. It is clear that one of the crucial components of communicative competence in a literate society is an understanding of the interrelationships of various genres of spoken and written language, not only in terms of the different functions of the genres within the given society but also in terms of the differences in the structures of respective genres.

As Tannen (1982a) points out, the field of discourse analysis would be benefited by a taxonomy of discourse types and ways of distinguishing among them. Many earlier attempts at empirical studies of form–structure differences between spoken and written language that might have contributed to the development of such a discourse typology have not been greatly successful. Many earlier form–structure difference studies tend to oversimplify the effects of the complexity of language styles, registers, and situational-contextual variables within the communicative economy. Consequently, many earlier studies make conflicting general claims about universal differences between spoken and written language.

Previous studies have variously examined the differences between spoken and written language in terms of such structural categories as types of clauses, length of T-units (an independent clause, plus any dependent clause attached to it), finite and nonfinite verb structures, self-reference terms, quantifiers, qualifying terms, length of "thought units," adjectival elaboration, passive constructions, repetitive vocabulary, average sentence length, and definite article use. In terms of the structures observed, the list is extensive, but in terms of conclusions concerning universal differences between spoken and written language that many researchers have tried to draw from their data, there are problems, as Schafer (1981, p. 12) points out in a review of previous studies:

> Many studies have been conducted, often with conflicting results. Researchers have isolated various features . . . and then, after analyzing their data, have concluded that one mode [spoken or written language] has fewer of these units, or shorter units, than the other mode. Other researchers, however, studying the same features, come up with contradictory results. . . . A frustrating aspect of these studies is that while they are based on texts produced in particular circumstances by only a few subjects . . . speaking and writing in only one situation, this doesn't prevent researchers from offering their results as accurate generalizations of universal differences between speaking and writing.

Earlier studies of form–structure differences between spoken and written language are often flawed for several reasons: (1) different researchers define key terms or categories of structures to be investigated in different ways, or in some cases not precisely enough as linguistic structures; (2) the research methodologies (especially for analysis of data) vary greatly – for example, instead of analyzing entire discourses, several of the studies analyze only certain parts of either the speech or writing in their samples, and none of the earlier studies adequately faces the difficult problem of how to define "sentence" in spoken language since none of them deals with intonation, pausing, repairs, restarts, and conversational interaction; and (3) the studies do not adequately address or control for contextual variables such as purpose, topic, audience, subject-participants, and time constraints. These methodological problems not only make most previous studies of form–structure differences between spoken and written language difficult to compare with each other, but they make suspect the various claims of general, universal differences between the two modes made by many researchers.

Actually, Biber's (1986) factor analysis study of the differences between many genres of spoken and written language is able, because of the comprehensive and careful nature of its methodology, to alleviate many of the apparent contradictions concerning individual findings about form–structure and text-type differences in the earlier studies.

But even though Biber is able to somewhat blunt Schafer's criticisms of contradictory findings in earlier studies, Biber still also finds, as has been proposed in this study, that the monolithic, global conclusions positing general universal differences between spoken and written language in those earlier studies "have been in error" (p. 410) for both theoretical and methodological reasons.

2.2.5. Conclusion

This short review of past studies of differences between spoken and written language shows that there have been both theoretical and methodological problems associated with the studies. The lack of a theoretical paradigm has made it difficult for studies to integrate considerations of differences between functions, processes, and structures. The interactionist paradigm, which is based in a conception of language development and language use as contexted social interaction, when combined with a discourse analysis methodology that allows for recognition of contextual variables, can provide the necessary theoretical and methodological approach. With this approach, it is possible to go beyond past assertions of general, universal, dichotomous differences between speech and writing toward, instead, a discourse typology arranged along a continuum. Certainly, before any such discourse typology could be firmly established, many studies comparing spoken and written language while varying topic, audience, participants, and genre would need to be done. The following is one such study.

2.3. A STUDY OF FORM–STRUCTURE DIFFERENCES BETWEEN SPOKEN AND WRITTEN LANGUAGE

2.3.1. Introduction

The present study was originally designed, in part, as a replication and extension of Chafe's (1982) study of differences between spoken and written language. In that study Chafe used a four-term theoretical construct that characterizes spoken language as exhibiting "fragmentation" and "involvement" and written language, on the other hand, as exhibiting "integration" and "detachment." For extended definitions of these terms, see Chafe (1982, 1985). Basic definitions are as follows: (1) "fragmentation" refers to the fact that spontaneous spoken language is usually produced in "spurts" of "idea units" that are bounded by pauses showing coherent intonation structure, and the idea units are often strung together by a "small set" of syntactic structures; (2) "integration" refers to that characteristic of written language in which syntactic structures seldom used in speech are used to create more complex idea units and sentences, and which condense more information into idea units; (3) "involvement" of spoken language refers to the speaker's potential in face-to-face encounters to monitor the effect of what he or she is saying and also to be more concerned with experiential details that identify personal involvement in what is being talked about; (4) "detachment" refers to those structures used in written language to make it available to a wider audience at different times and places.

Chafe (1982) uses this four-term theoretical construct to analyze the comparative percentage of instances of seventeen syntactic and linguistic categories in samples of spoken and written language, reasoning that certain linguistic structures function to promote involvement or fragmentation, whereas others promote integration or detachment. (See Biber, 1986, for extended and clear justifications of the relationships between linguistic structures and textual functions.) For example, the use of nominalizations is felt to promote both integration of idea units and detachment from or reification of the situation or concept being described; nominalizations are, therefore, more often found in written language than in spoken language according to Chafe's hypothesis.

It should be noted that Chafe's four-term theoretical construct actually takes into consideration both the general functional differences between spoken and written language discussed earlier in this chapter, as well as "real-time" language production constraints that differ between spoken and written language. For these reasons Chafe's framework is a marked advance over previous studies of differences between spoken and written language and already has become, and rightly so, a classic of the literature on differences between spoken and written language. It is, however, the point of view of the present study that Chafe's study can be extended and improved through stricter control of contextual variables.

2.3.2. Methodology

The study investigated the question, What are the differences and similarities between spoken and written language across the domains of informal conversation, formal spoken interview, and written essay when topic and participants are held constant? Data for each domain were collected over a two-week period from each of ten subject-participants, all of whom were graduate students at a large American university. The same topic, "The Pressures and Problems Faced by Graduate Students," was used in each domain, and the order of participation of each subject in each domain was also consistent: (1) informal conversation, (2) formal interview, (3) written essay.

Following Chafe's (1982) original study, the basic hypothesis of the present study was that *in an examination of the use of 22 categories of linguistic structures, there would be a higher incidence of linguistic structures which exhibit "fragmentation" and "involvement" used in spoken language, while there would be a higher incidence of linguistic structures which exhibit "integration" and "detachment" used in written language.* A secondary hypothesis was also proposed: *that the speech used in formal interviews would be structurally closer to the language used in written essays than to the speech used in formal conversations.*

Although developing the basic hypothesis from Chafe's 1982 study, and using Chafe's theoretical constructs discussed previously, the present study differs from Chafe's in two basic ways. First, it examines use in a different, additional domain, formal spoken interview, as well as examining language use in the two domains reported in Chafe's study, informal spoken conversation and formal written essay. Second, it offers strict control of such contextual variables as subject-participants, topic, and situation-domain.

In this study, both topic and subject-participants are held constant throughout the experiment while only the situation-domain (informal conversation, formal interview, or written essay) is permitted to vary at any given time. In Chafe's study (as well as in many other previous spoken–written language comparison studies), topic is not strictly controlled by having each subject deal with a consistently given topic. This introduces the potentially important bias that different topics might be best discussed or written about by using different syntactic structures or different combinations of them. Also, it is unclear in the Chafe study whether each subject has taken part in each situational domain. This introduces the potential bias of contamination of data because of differences between individuals. For these reasons it is impossible to statistically attribute differences in the data to the mode (spoken or written language) used in a given domain. This is realized by Chafe, who reports his findings in terms of percentages rather than in terms of inferential statistics. Because of the stricter control of contextual variables, the findings of the present study can be reported in terms of inferential statistics.

In addition to control of the main experimental variables, this study also carefully controlled several other conditional issues in the design of the study in order to ensure reliability in collection and analysis of the data: selection of topic, selection of participants, order of tasks, time constraints for tasks, transcription of spoken language data (intonation, pauses, restarts, overlapping utterances, sentence boundaries, etc.), and careful categorization by linguistic definition of the structures examined. Control of contextual variables is considered necessary because, within an interactionist framework, it is acknowledged that contextual factors are important constitutive elements in language acts and therefore must be accounted for and dealt with in the design of research.

Finally, in order to delineate the informal conversation domain more carefully from the formal interview domain, the informal conversation data were collected in five cells of conversations between two mutual friends who had known each other at least a year. The same ten subjects subsequently individually participated in the formal interview domain, which was conducted by an experienced interviewer who was previously unknown to any of the subject-participants. Because the subject-participants were being asked to consider the same topic ("The Pressures and Problems Faced by Graduate Students") in each domain, in order to further separate the three domains the participants were provided with the following audience constructs: (1) for the informal conversation, participants were asked to have a conversation with their friend concerning the particular topic as they would at home or in the student union; (2) for the formal interview, participants were asked to conduct themselves in the interview as if they were being taped for an FM radio program to be broadcast on the university's public radio station; (3) for the written essay, the participants were asked to provide an essay for a university committee made up of administrators, faculty, and graduate students who were considering the topic in question. The total number of words generated in the three domains was 43,825, all of which were included in the discourse analysis of the data.

2.3.3. Results and discussion

The basic hypothesis of the study was that an examination of the use of 22 categories of linguistic structures (some of the same structures investigated in Chafe, 1982, others developed specifically for this study) would show the same relationships between spoken and written language as was shown in data reported by Chafe: that there is a higher incidence of linguistic structures that exhibit "fragmentation" and "involvement" used in spoken language, while there is a higher incidence of linguistic structures that exhibit "integration" and "detachment" used in written language. See Table 2.1 for a list of the categories of structures examined and the predicted trends of use in the three domains studied.

The basic hypothesis of the study was confirmed, both in terms of strong directional trends for all but one of the 22 structural categories observed, and in terms of statistical significance at the $p < .01$ or $p < .05$ level for several of the categories, according to the results of ANOVA (repeated measures) and Post-Hoc Scheffe tests to locate significant differences between means. See Tables 2.2 and 2.3 for statistical results of differences in mean use of the structures in the three situational domains.

Table 2.1. *Categories of structures*

A. Structures that promote fragmentation	
1. And+	Speech->Interview->Writing
2. Repairs, restarts, repetitions	Speech->Interview->Writing
B. Structures that promote integration	
3. Nominalization	Writing->Interview->Speech
4. Prepositional phrase	Writing->Interview->Speech
5. Participle	Writing->Interview->Speech
6. Attributive adjective	Writing->Interview->Speech
7. Conjoined phrases	Writing->Interview->Speech
8. Series	Writing->Interview->Speech
9. Sequence of prepositional phrases	Writing->Interview->Speech
10. Complement clause	Writing->Interview->Speech
11. Relative clause	Writing->Interview->Speech
12. Complex subject nominalization	Writing->Interview->Speech
13. Adverb subordinate clause	Writing->Interview->Speech
14. Introductory phrase or clause	Writing->Interview->Speech
C. Structures that promote involvement	
15. 1st pers pronoun, vague 2nd, 3rd pers pronouns	Speech->Interview->Writing
16. Monitor info flow; emphatic particle	Speech->Interview->Writing
17. Fuzzy vocabulary	Speech->Interview->Writing
18. Direct quotation	Speech->Interview->Writing
19. Cleft; pseudo-cleft	Speech->Interview->Writing
20. Fillers	Interview->Speech->Writing
21. Feedback signals	Speech->Interview
D. Structures that promote detachment	
22. Passive voice constructions	Writing->Interview->Speech

Evaluation of the statistical data shows that of a possible 64 relationships of significant differences between mean use of 22 structures in conversational speech, formal interview, and written essay domains, 41 relationships show statistical significance in the predicted trends of use. Furthermore, of the 64 relationships, 63 of them followed the predicted trends of use. The interpretation of this evidence (moderately strong statistical significance, and almost perfect directional trend) is that the basic hypothesis of the study was confirmed and that Chafe's four-term theoretical construct, when combined with a more extensive control of contextual variables in an interactionist paradigm, is a productive way to

Table 2.2. *Actual mean use of structures per 100 words*

Structure	Speech	Interview	Writing
1. And+	3.98	3.51	0.86
2. Repairs, restarts, repetitions	3.35	3.22	1.67
3. Nominalization	3.53	5.06	9.57
4. Prepositional phrase	5.80	6.81	9.05
5. Participle	0.87	1.05	2.20
6. Attributive adjective	1.82	2.23	6.18
7. Conjoined phrases	0.45	0.65	2.00
8. Series	0.21	0.25	0.58
9. Sequence of prepositional phrases	0.56	0.86	1.38
10. Complement clause	2.14	2.75	3.94
11. Relative clause	1.27	1.57	1.50
12. Complex subject nominalization	0.02	0.05	0.35
13. Adverb subordinate clause	1.51	1.57	1.67
14. Introductory phrase or clause	2.29	3.50	4.92
15. 1st pers pronoun, vague 2nd, 3rd pers pronouns	11.98	10.44	5.20
16. Monitor info flow; emphatic particle	10.25	7.89	3.69
17. Fuzzy vocabulary	5.42	4.49	3.13
18. Direct quotation	0.52	0.27	0.07
19. Cleft; pseudo-cleft	1.19	1.09	0.53
20. Fillers	1.25	2.43	–
21. Feedback signals	4.43	1.12	–
22. Passive voice constructions	0.47	0.56	1.29

examine structural differences and similarities between conversational speech, formal spoken interview, and written essay. As a useful comparative study, the reader is also directed to Biber's (1986) comprehensive factor analysis study of differences between spoken and written language in which he finds strong evidence for at least three functionally motivated underlying textual dimensions that discriminate typologically between spoken and written language: (1) "Interactive vs. Edited Text," (2) "Abstract vs. Situated Content," and (3) "Reported vs. Immediate Style," rather than the two functionally motivated spoken–written discriminators posited by Chafe and examined here, (1) "Fragmentation vs. Integration" and (2) "Involvement vs. Detachment."

As a part of the current study on the differences between uses of structures in the three domains, a secondary hypothesis was also proposed: that the speech used in formal interviews would be structurally closer to the language used in written essays than to the speech used in

Table 2.3. *Results of Post-Hoc Scheffe Tests used for locating significant differences between means*

Structure	Speech–interview	Interview–writing	Speech–writing
1. And+	Ns	$p < .01$	$p < .01$
2. Repairs, restarts, repetitions	Ns	$p < .01$	$p < .01$
3. Nominalization	$p < .05$	$p < .01$	$p < .01$
4. Prepositional phrase	Ns	$p < .01$	$p < .01$
5. Participle	$p < .05$	$p < .01$	$p < .01$
6. Attributive adjective	$p < .05$	$p < .01$	$p < .01$
7. Conjoined phrases	Ns	$p < .01$	$p < .01$
8. Series	Ns	$p < .05$	$p < .01$
9. Sequence of prepositional phrases	Ns	Ns	$p < .01$
10. Complement clause	Ns	Ns	Ns
11. Relative clause	–	–	–
12. Complex subject nominalization	Ns	$p < .01$	$p < .01$
13. Adverb subordinate clause	–	–	–
14. Introductory phrase or clause	$p < .01$	$p < .01$	$p < .01$
15. 1st pers pronoun, vague 2nd, 3rd pers pronouns	Ns	$p < .01$	$p < .01$
16. Monitor info flow; emphatic particle	$p < .01$	$p < .01$	$p < .01$
17. Fuzzy vocabulary	Ns	$p < .01$	$p < .01$
18. Direct quotation	$p < .05$	$p < .05$	$p < .01$
19. Cleft; pseudo-cleft	Ns	$p < .01$	$p < .01$
20. Passive voice constructions	Ns	$p < .01$	$p < .01$
Results of t-tests for significant differences between means			
21. Fillers	$p < .01$		
22. Feedback signals	$p < .001$		

informal conversations. This hypothesis was developed to test whether the expected increase in formality of the interview as compared with the conversation would offset the production constraints of the mode (both conversation and interview being examples of the spoken language mode). It was felt that this hypothesis could test whether formality or mode was operating as the more dominant constraint in the interview situation.

The secondary hypothesis was not confirmed. Instead, analysis of the data shows that speech used in formal interviews was actually closer to conversational speech than it was to the language used in written essays. The interpretation is that the movement to more formality in the interview situation (as compared with conversation) did not overcome what appear to be the more dominant production constraints of spoken language.

As shown in Table 2.3, the highest number of statistically significant relationships exists between conversational speech and written essay. Of a possible 20 relationships, 17 are significant at the $p < .01$ level. The second highest number of relationships showing significant differences (14 at the $p < .01$ level and 2 at the $p < .05$ level) involves those between interview and written essay. The comparative category with the least number of statistically significant differences is conversation–interview. Of the 22 possible significant relationships in this category, there are 1 at the $p < .001$ level, 3 at the $p < .01$ level, and 4 at the $p < .05$ level. The remaining 14 relationships are statistically nonsignificant. The interpretation is, then, that the structures of the language used in the conversational speech and interview situations exhibit less differences (or more similarities) than the structures of the language used in the interview–written essay category or in the conversation–written essay category.

Simply because there are fewer statistically significant differences between the language structures used in the conversational speech and interview situations does not mean, however, that there is little difference in the language used in the two situations. The analysis of the data of the 22 structural categories observed shows that the expected trend in the conversational speech–interview comparison is followed in all 22 categories. This perfect directional trend indicates that there is a consistent pattern of differences between the language used in the speech and interview situations, even though in several categories of structures the differences may not be great enough to be picked up by the statistical procedures used.

All of the evidence indicates that, although there are fewer statistical differences between the language used in conversational speech and that used in interviews, and that although interview spoken language is closer to conversational spoken language than it is to written essay language in this study, the subject-participants definitely do speak differently (use different language structures) in different spoken language use situations. It is just that the differences between the spoken and written language modes are greater, and therefore more capable of being picked up by statistical methods. Many of the earlier studies of differences between speech and writing were misleading because they examined only the two most likely differing extremes of the spoken-written language continuum – informal conversational speech and formal written language.

Finally, the discussion of the first level of this study will be concluded with a caution. It is hoped that this section of the study will not be interpreted as yet another claim of universal differences between spoken and written language. As has been asserted earlier here, many studies that vary topic, audience, participants, and discourse types will have to be done in order to establish a discourse typology by which we could have a firmer idea of how spoken and written language may differ along a continuum. One such example of an excellent recent study is Biber (1986; 1988), which uses a different methodology than the one used here, a computer-programmed linguistic analysis and then computer-assisted factor analysis of the data. With his methodological approach, Biber is able to examine a great many more discourse text types at the same time than is possible in the more micro-analytical approach of the present study. It is interesting to note, however, that both the macro- and micro-methodologies of these two studies offer data and conclusions supporting a discourse continuum conception of the relationships between spoken and written language, rather than the traditional conception of universal differences.

The current study clearly shows, by developing a methodology within an interactionist paradigm that can more carefully notice and control contextual variables, that the subject participants used three distinctly, statistically different language styles while talking and writing about the same topic in the three situational domains. Not only does the interactionist approach allow us to confirm that conversational speech and written essay are different in the language structures used, but also that there are clear differences between the two domains of spoken language studied here.

2.4. STUDY OF COHERENCE IN THE THREE SITUATIONAL DOMAINS

2.4.1. Introduction

Since the methodology for the first part of the study had provided a great quantity of data and clearly delineated between three contextual domains, it was decided that a second empirical study using the same data from the same three situational domains could be conducted to extend the study into an additional area. The purpose of the second level of analysis was to examine the same data on a more macro-analytical discourse level to see whether there were differences between the spoken and written language used in the three domains not only on a micro-structural level, but also on the macro-discourse level. This second level of analysis examined how coherence was achieved in the three situational domains through the specific analysis of how given and new information were handled differently in the three domains.

A basic assumption of this section of the study is that the management of given and new information is the primary vehicle for the establishment of coherence. The reasons for and the importance of this assumption will be discussed in detail. It must be pointed out at the outset, however, that working with coherence and given and new information presents thorny conceptual and methodological problems. One reason for these problems is that although the concepts have been widely used, often they have been taken for granted and not clearly defined. Realizing these potential difficulties, this study relates and operationalizes the concepts of relevance, coherence, and given and new information within an interactionist paradigm.

First we must clarify the concept of coherence. Coherence is the object of this second level of analysis of the study because it is the most overarching and encompassing principle of textuality. It is only by virtue of its having coherence that a text is perceived as a text. Coherence, then, is the fundamental property of textuality, both a necessary and sufficient condition for the recognition of text as text.

Coherence is defined here (following Werth, 1984) as the semantics of discourse connectivity and involves both connections between pieces of information within the text, and between the text and the context. Coherence is the vehicle through which the relevance of what the speaker/writer has to say becomes clear to the listener/reader. Coherence, thus, is partly "in" the text and partly "outside" the text in that it consists of relationships between propositions within the text, as well as inferences interpreted and constructed by the listener/reader from the text and from his or her world knowledge.

According to the way coherence is being defined here, a native speaker should be able to decide whether a text is coherent or not. If it is processible, then it is coherent. If it is not processible, then it is not even a text. This is not to say, however, that the coherence of every text we encounter is equally satisfying or equally easily processible for every listener/reader. Texts are not determinate; they are interpretable (and reinterpretable). The crucial questions become informativity and relevance – how well a listener/reader is able to follow and understand what he or she perceives to be the intent of the speaker/writer.

In attempting to deal with questions concerning the coherence of texts, it is not very helpful simply to assert that one text is more coherent than another. What is needed is a principled operational method for examining how coherence is achieved. One way to investigate how coherence is achieved is by examining how given and new information are related and connected within the text and context. Once a speaker/writer decides that certain information is relevant for his or her purpose within a communicative context, then a decision must be made as to what the audience most likely already understands about this information, what it does not need to know, and what it needs to know in what specific way, considering the communicative context. Decisions concerning how much, what type, at what time, and in what words to present new information and how to relate it to given information are constantly being made by any speaker/writer and constantly being predicted, attuned to, and interpreted by the listener/reader.

The basis of coherence, then, is the reciprocal recognition of relevance within context. (See Nystrand, 1986, on "reciprocity" in communication.) And the vehicle of coherence is the selection and interpretation of given and new information. Such decisions and interpretations are basically semantic/pragmatic (structured in specific syntactic ways) and function to help the speaker/writer to achieve his or her purposes of reaching a given audience in a given situation, whether spoken or written language is the medium of communication.

Since three different language use situations were being investigated in this study while topic and participants were being held constant, it was hypothesized that *the patterns of distribution of given and new information (and thus coherence) would be different in the three samples of language: conversational speech, formal spoken interview, and written essay.* This hypothesis was confirmed.

2.4.2. Methodology

In order to examine coherence and given and new information as constitutive elements of discourse, it is necessary to develop methodology to operationalize the two concepts. The development of new methodology is necessary because, although these two concepts have a relatively long history of use in language study associated literature, there has been some confusion concerning precise definitions of these important concepts.

In the case of coherence, for example, it would be possible to trace the history of the concept over the past 100 years from when it was first used as a vague term analogous to "fluidity" in written language to be achieved mainly through the use of transition devices and logical connectors, to its confusion with syntactic well-formedness in the early text linguistics movement, to its more recent confusion with cohesive devices within the text. What has been lacking in a definition of coherence is a conceptualization and investigative methodology that could examine semantic/pragmatic connectivity by linking the purposes of the text producer, the situational context, the text, and the purposes of the text user or apprehender.

In the case of problems with a lack of clear conceptualizations of given and new information, Prince (1979, p. 267) expresses the problem the following way:

> This intuitively appealing notion [given/new] has never received a satisfactory characterization that would enable a working linguist to not only invoke it but to actually put it to use. In fact, if one considers the definitions that have been presented, one discovers that there is not one notion involved, but several.

Here, Prince is expressing the confusion and lack of precision in the definition of given/new that have made it difficult to conduct a principled, empirical study using the concept. (See also Vande Kopple, 1986, for a historical analysis of given/new conceptualizations.)

Recent work of Werth (1984) and Prince (1981) on given and new have been attempts to define more precisely and operationalize these concepts. The present study combines the work of both Werth and Prince, builds on this combination, and further develops that methodology within an interactionist approach in order to examine the three situational domains studied here. Although it is not possible because of space limitations to offer a detailed review of the Werth (1984) and Prince (1981) systems of analysis here, brief reviews of these systems are provided in the following. One of the major breakthroughs of both systems of analysis is that they provide more complex conceptualizations of given/new distinctions than had previously strictly binary systems of analysis.

Key concepts in Werth's (1984) system of analysis are (1) *relevance,* (2) *common ground,* (3) *text world,* (4) *coherence,* (5) *emphasis.* Part of Werth's discussion of these concepts consists of the following:

> The process of discourse consists of the establishment of a common ground, against which each new utterance is assessed for relevance (by means of the coherence constraint) and if adjudged sufficiently relevant, is added to the common ground. . . . An utterance is relevant to the common ground either if it brings new information which is related to information already present, or else if it brings further information about items already present. (p. 186)

> We shall assume that coherence, then, is a matter of semantic relationship, and . . . that there is a requirement on all propositions forming the semantic structure of a text that they must be semantically related to another proposition in the same text (or, more accurately in the common ground of the text). . . . To put this another way, we can say

> that for two items to cohere, they must allude to the same text world, in terms of a set or field or frame or scene – but in any case more or less defined in the common ground. (pp. 186–187)

> The common ground functions both on the intensional propositional information provided by the text, and on the extensional information provided by scenes and knowledge frames of various levels of complexity ranging from community knowledge to limited shared experiences of many kinds. Within this welter of potentially and actually relevant information, a text-world gradually gets built up, and it is through this text-world that all textual operations are filtered. This is an extremely important point: not only do reference acts take place within the domain of the text world (or worlds), but all of our emphatic relationships operate in respect of it too (via their adherence to the coherence constraint). (p. 146)

In this system, anything introduced into a text-world must, in order to be considered appropriate, observe the coherence constraint. The coherence constraint operates in a particular text-world (or worlds, depending on the complexity of the discourse) both to allow for potential inclusion of anything from the common ground (contextual background), and to constrain inclusion of potentially related but extraneous material from the common ground that may not be relevant or needed at the particular point reached in the construction of the text-world. The text-world is reciprocally constructed or negotiated by speaker/listeners and writer/readers. The text world is directly related to the concept of relevance through the mechanism of the coherence constraint on the common ground.

How does this theoretical system actually become operationalized in the text of a discourse? The two operationalizing functions are the *coherence constraint* and the system of *emphasis*. The coherence constraint may be thought of as a scanner that has the function of constraining the possible combinations of sentences to ensure that a given sequence of sentences is not "randomly generated" but constitutes a semantically connected succession. It scans the semantic structures of underlying propositions for various kinds of logical or pragmatic relationships that could range from the strictly logical, to the semantically or pragmatically inferential, to examples of what has been called "fuzzy logic." It is important to realize that the coherence constraint operates both on the utterances in the text and in the common ground so that it is not concerned only with relationships "in" the text. And finally, because propositions may be linked in a number of ways including identity, partial identity, implication, and antonymy, the coherence constraint is capable of specifying positive, negative, and implicit connections and distinguishing negative and nonexistent connections.

The final component of Werth's system is *emphasis*. The operations of the coherence constraint are realized and can be identified in the text through the deployment of the systematic patterns of emphasis. Werth uses the term "emphasis" to mean "semantically or pragmatically prominent." The emphasis system is itself most readily recognizable in the intonational system of prominence and nonprominence in spoken language. The fact that the emphasis system is most readily recognizable in spoken language does not mean, however, that it is not fully operational in written language.

Recall that the coherence constraint scans both utterances and the common ground on the underlying semantic level. In all examples of coherent discourse (whether spoken or written), semantic connections occur at an underlying level between the "separate bits of message information" (Werth, 1984, p. 8). It is the emphasis system that is the mechanism that "feeds the contextual factors into the sequence of linguistic forms making up the linguistic utterances" (p. 8) and at the same time "ensures" the realization of connectivity.

In spoken language, the apprehension of underlying semantic and pragmatic emphasis is more straightforward in that the intonation system overtly signals the operation of the coherence constraint in the surface structure of the utterance. Phonological emphasis in spoken language is a surface indicator of information structure, of the underlying semantic and pragmatic connections. Of course, underlying semantic and pragmatic connections are present in written language, but because of the absence of a sound system in written language, the underlying emphasis system must be shown on the surface in other ways. In written language, because the emphasis is arguably less readily apparent or noticeable in that it must be carried by punctuation, phrasing, sentence structure variations, and of course also underlying semantic connections, it may therefore be more indeterminate, more open to reader interpretation. The point is that the emphasis system, although perhaps more noticeable in spoken language, is part of the underlying, overall semantic system and therefore in operation in both spoken and written language. Werth's conception of the coherence-emphasis system is illustrated in Appendix A.

Prince's (1979, 1981) system for analysis of given and new distinctions makes no reference to analysis of phonological emphasis in spoken language but has been used in Prince (1981) to analyze both spoken and written language and also relies (as does Werth's system) on analysis of underlying semantic and pragmatic structures. Prince's system sets up a "Taxonomy of Assumed Familiarity" (1981, p. 233) to analyze the use of given and new information in a discourse according to three classifications, "New," "Inferrable," and "Evoked," rather than just according to the traditional binary categories, "given" and "new." As shown in Appendix B, each of the three main classifications can be further broken down into several other categories, all of which allow finer distinctions to be drawn than were possible in other systems, including within Werth's system for analysis of coherence.

Besides allowing for analysis of finer distinctions in all categories, Prince's most significant break with past analyses is her inclusion of the Inferrable classification. Many of the entities classified Inferrable by Prince would probably be classified as New Information in Halliday's (1967) influential system for analysis of given and new information because those entities would probably receive phonological prominence. On the other hand, some more recent psycholinguistic research would tend to classify many of the same Inferrables as Given. For Prince, the best way to handle this disagreement is to give Inferrables a classification of their own and work under a semantic/pragmatic system to show relationships. This makes the newly created system more readily adaptable to the analysis of both written and spoken language. It may be true that Prince's system is not as elegant as Halliday's, but as Werth mentions, Halliday's system ignores the distinction between Contrast and New at an underlying semantic level since both Contrast and New would receive phonological prominence in spoken language. Brown (1983, p. 68) suggests that rather than consider phonological prominence strictly as a signal of new information, it would be better to consider such prominence as a more generalized "attention marker" or "watch it" marker for the listener.

If we are willing to accept the somewhat ambiguous "watch it" marker for Contrast/New, we should be willing to acccept the same "watch it" principle for Inferrables. By using phonological prominence for many Inferrables a speaker may be communicating something like, "What I am saying is closely related to what I have been talking about, but not in an explicit way, so watch it." Correspondingly, Inferrables may be somewhat ambiguous in written language: for a reader whose knowledge of the writer's subject area is more comprehensive, or for a reader more versed in a certain genre, an Inferrable might tend to be processed as a Given, whereas a reader with less knowledge of the author's subject area might tend to process the same Inferrable as New. There is no essential reason why Inferrables must be classified as *either* Given or New, especially if we admit that human language in use in social systems does not operate in terms of a strictly binary logical system. By accepting this not unreasonable amount of ambiguity, which in actuality is nothing more than part of the natural indeterminancy of interactive communication between human beings, we gain a three part system that can be readily applied to analysis of either spoken or written language.

Table 2.4. *A sample coded selection from one participant's written essay*

QU BNR BNR SC ES EV BNR BNR

Every graduate student that I know faces financial

BNR C IC E SC E I

difficulties throughout the period of his or her studies.

E EV C INT BNA BN IC I

It is not merely a question of meeting the costs associated

BN BN BN BN SC BN DC

with tuition, fees, supplies, books and xeroxing. As the

U U EV U E E

cost of living continues to rise, graduate students are

EV ES C BNV BNA BNA BN

finding it harder to obtain adequate affordable housing, to

BNV BNA BNR BN BNV BNR

afford a nutritionally adequate diet, to cover the cost of

C BN SC BNA BN SC BNV

necessary utilities and telephone bills, and to take care

BNA BNA BNA BN SC

of the expenses generated by personal needs such as

BNA BNA SC BNA BNA I

clothing, household items, and medical and dental care. In

I SC E EV BNA C C

situations in which the student has dependents other than

E SC E E E E EV

him or herself, these financial difficulties are

BNA

compounded.

QU I I E E

In some academic departments, graduate students are

EV BNV E BNA I SC

able to avail themselves of opportunities for teaching and

I I SC C I

research assistantships, and sometimes fellowships as

E DC E EV C C BN SC QU

well. However, this is not true university wide, as many

E E BNV BN E E

academic disciplines are losing funding. Graduate students

INT EV BNA BNA I BNR

often have to seek out alternative sources of financial

Table 2.4 (*cont.*)

BN SC BNA BN SC BNA BN
support such as help from relatives or financial loans. In
QU I E BNV BNV BNA
some cases, students are compelled to secure full- or
BNA BN SC BNV E E
part-time employment in order to finance their education.
E BNV BNR BN SC BNA BN
This presents problems with time and schedule conflicts.

Although Prince's system has these significant advantages, it also has some disadvantages. An important disadvantage is that it makes no provision to consider Contrast, a major anaphoric relationship that is considered in Werth's system. A second disadvantage is that it codes only entities and their attributes (and only attributes that are directly, sequentially linked to entities). Verbs, adjectives, and adverbs, for example, receive no unique coding, an obvious drawback if an entire discourse rather than just parts of it is to be analyzed. As Vande Kopple (1986) suggests, there is a challenge to create a more complete system for analysis, one that can show more clearly how the given/new distinction operates differently in spoken and written language, one that is more attuned to differences in social and cultural contexts.

Such a more extensive system was developed in the interactionist approach used for analysis of data collected in the three domains of this study. The Werth and Prince systems of analysis were expanded and additional categories were developed to examine given and new information and coherence. Appendix C lists the categories of analysis developed for this study, and Table 2.4 shows one sample of the use of the coding system developed and used for the study.

2.4.3. Results and discussion

The second part of this study examined the same data collected from the same ten subject-participants discussed in the first part of the study, which examined form–structure differences, except that in this second part of the study the data are analyzed in terms of the use of given and new information in the three domains. As an example of this

Table 2.5. *Results of given/new analysis for participant G*

		Conversation		Interview		Writing	
		No. used	% of use	No. used	% of use	No. used	% of use
(New)	BN	9	3.36	9	2.73	19	13.01
	BNA	8	2.97	6	1.82	21	14.38
	BNR	2	.74	7	2.12	9	6.12
	BNV	2	.74	5	1.52	11	7.53
	U	5	1.86	4	1.21	3	2.05
	Total	26	9.67%	31	9.40%	63	43.09%
(Evok Giv)	E	19	7.06	27	8.18	24	16.44
	ES	47	17.47	41	12.42	2	1.37
	EV	36	13.38	47	14.24	9	6.12
	Total	102	37.91%	115	34.84%	35	23.93%
(Cont)	C	63	23.42%	83	25.15%	9	6.12%
	Total C + E	165	61.33%	198	59.99%	44	30.05%
(Infer)	I	12	4.46	17	5.15	12	8.22
	IC	1	.37	4	1.21	2	1.37
	Total	13	4.83%	21	6.36%	14	9.59%
(Null)	P	18	6.69	13	3.94	0	0.00
	INT	9	3.36	16	4.85	2	1.37
	SC	25	9.29	33	10.00	17	11.64
	DC	4	1.49	12	3.64	2	1.37
	Q	5	1.86	0	0.00	0	0.00
	QU	1	.37	2	.61	4	2.74
	F	3	1.12	4	1.21	0	0.00
	Total	65	24.18%	80	24.75%	25	17.12%
	Total	269		330		146	

type of analysis, Tables 2.5 and 2.6 report the results of the analysis of the data for two of the ten participants (Participant G and Participant C), showing that the hypothesis is confirmed in that the patterns of distribution of given and new information are different in the three domains, indicating that coherence is being established differently in the three domains. Although because of space limitations it is not possible to offer complete analysis of the data for all ten subject-participants here, the distributions of given and new information throughout the five categories for the ten participants in the three domains follow the same

Table 2.6. *Results of given/new analysis for Participant C*

		Conversation		Interview		Writing	
		No. used	% of use	No. used	% of use	No. used	% of use
(*New*)	BN	10	2.82	23	5.01	11	10.48
	BNA	6	1.69	10	2.18	6	5.71
	BNR	6	1.69	22	4.79	5	4.76
	BNV	5	1.41	9	1.96	6	5.71
	U	2	.56	4	.87	2	1.90
	Total	29	8.17%	68	14.81%	30	28.56%
(*Evok Giv*)	E	39	11.02	37	8.06	11	10.48
	ES	48	13.56	45	9.80	7	6.67
	EV	43	12.15	56	12.20	14	13.33
	Total	130	36.73%	138	30.06%	32	30.48%
(*Cont*)	C	84	23.73%	101	22.00%	12	11.43%
	Total C + E	214	59.96%	239	52.06%	44	41.91%
(*Infer*)	I	27	7.63	42	9.15	8	7.62
	IC	2	.56	11	2.40	1	.95
	Total	29	8.17%	53	11.55%	9	8.57%
(*Null*)	P	12	3.39	12	2.61	2	1.90
	INT	22	6.21	15	3.27	1	.95
	SC	31	8.76	53	11.55	16	15.24
	DC	5	1.41	14	3.05	2	1.90
	Q	2	.56	1	.22	0	0.00
	QU	0	0.00	1	.22	1	.95
	F	10	2.82	3	.65	0	0.00
	Total	82	23.15%	99	21.57%	22	20.94%
	Total	354		459		105	

general pattern. The sample data of Participants G and C representatively illustrate that pattern.

According to Tables 2.5 and 2.6, both participants show a marked increase in the use of New information in the Written domain as compared to the use of New information in the two spoken language domains. For Participant G, the total percentages of use of New information are quite similar in the Conversation and Interview domains, but approximately 4.5 times greater in the Written domain. For Participant C, the increase in the use of New information is approximately

1.75 times greater in the Interview as compared with the Conversation, and approximately 4 times greater in the Written domain than in the Conversation.

In the Evoked classification of Given information, Participant G shows more of a distinction between the three domains than does Participant C. Participant G shows a consistent decrease in total use of Evoked forms from Conversation through Interview to Writing, whereas Participant C uses approximately the same percentage of Evoked forms as in Conversation. In the specific categories of the classification, Participant G shows especially marked decreases in the use of Evoked verbs and Situationally Evoked forms in Writing, whereas Participant C does not.

In the Contrast classification, both Participants each use approximately the same percentage of Contrast forms in the Conversation and Interview domains, but Participant G uses approximately 4 times less Contrast in the Written domain, whereas Participant C uses approximately 2 times less in the Written domain.

There is also a category that combines Contrast and Evoked for a total classification of use of Given information. Recall that Contrast is a specific type of Given information in that one of the two elements is related anaphorically to the other in terms of logical or pragmatic negativity. The total combined category is, for both Participants, the highest percentage of use in both the Conversation and Interview domains. In the Written domain, Participant G's use in the combined C + E category falls to one-half of what it was in the other two domains, whereas Participant C's use falls only to two-thirds of what it was in the other two domains.

In the Inferrable classification, Participant G shows a consistent increase of use from Conversation to Interview to Writing, whereas Participant C shows the highest use in the Interview domain. Notice also that of the four classifications, the Inferrable classification shows the least percentage of use by both participants. This is perhaps because many of the uses that might readily be classified as Inferrable in some other system of analysis (Prince's, for example) are actually classified as Contrasts in this system.

In the final classification, both participants use approximately the same percentage of Null forms in the Conversation and Interview domains, whereas Participant G shows more of a decrease of use in that classification in the Written domain than does Participant C. The specific categories coded under the Null classification are usually not considered to contain propositional information and as such are not commonly associated with given/new information studies. In this study, however, the Null category was developed to classify the use of categories 12–18 (Appendix C) specifically to examine differences in the use of such elements in the three domains of spoken and written language. In the specific categories of this classification, Participant C shows a consistent increase and differentiation of use in the Sentence Connector category between the three domains, whereas Participant G shows less marked differences in the use of this category. Both Participants use Intensifiers and Performatives markedly less in the Written domain than in the two spoken domains.

Tables 2.5 and 2.6, which use the extended categories developed in this study for the analysis of given and new information, clearly show that there are differences in how given and new information are distributed in spoken and written language, and therefore, how coherence is being established differently in the three domains. At the same time, it is also possible to look at individual differences between the two participants, to see how each, compared with the other, handled the distribution of given and new information in the three domains. According to the total percentages of use for the five classifications in the three domains, Participant C more consistently distinguishes between the three domains. Participant G, however, shows many similar percentages of uses for many of the categories in the Conversation and Interview domains. On the other hand, Participant G shows a greater overall distinction in the use of Given/New between spoken and written language than does Participant C. At least in the particular topic area examined in this study ("What Are the Problems and Pressures Faced by Graduate Students?") Participant C defines the three domains of use more clearly from each other, but Participant G observes a greater overall distinction (by mode) between written and spoken language.

2.4.4. Conclusion

As the first level (Section 2.3) of this study on linguistic structure differences was concluded with a caution against interpreting the results as evidence of universal differences between spoken and written language, a caution will be offered here also. It would be incautious, for example, to interpret the results of Section 2.4 as a universal indication that written language uses two to four times as much new information as given information compared with spoken language uses. What this section does offer is a new methodology within a discourse interactionist paradigm for investigating how coherence is established through manipulation of given and new information. Again, in order to establish a discourse continuum showing how coherence and given and new information differ in spoken and written language, other empirical studies would need to be done varying topic, audience, subject-participants, and domain. Context is constitutive of language use.

This study clearly indicates that when topic and participants were held constant and task-audience was structured to vary there were measurable differences between three spoken and written language domains at both the micro-structural level of analysis and at the macro-discourse level of analysis. On the one hand, although there are not simple, universal, exclusive differences between spoken and written language use, on the other hand, there are discernable differences between uses of spoken and written language ranging along a continuum based on genre and context considerations.

APPENDIX A: WERTH'S EMPHASIS SYSTEM

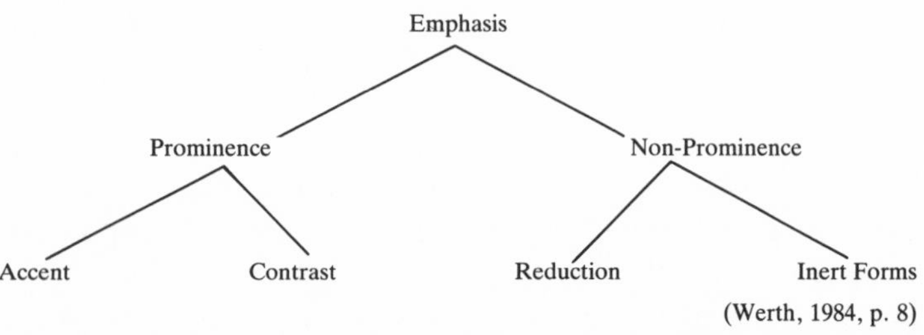

(Werth, 1984, p. 8)

Intonational *prominence* is reserved "for material which for some reason is made to stand out, and *non-prominence,* for recessive material" (Werth, 1984, p. 8). Prominence is bivalent, consisting of *accent* and *contrast;* non-prominence includes *inert forms,* which can never be made prominent, and *reduction.* The basic definitions of these terms are as follows:

- *Accent:* consists of two types, *information accent* and *attention accent.* (1) Information accent occurs on freshly introduced semantic material. (2) Attention accent occurs on previously occurring material that would normally be under the category of *reduction,* but for some reason has to be reaccented. The most common circumstance calling for reaccent is the need to renew the present relevance of some "decaying" information. Werth considers attention accent "simply a special form of information accent" (p. 9).
- *Reduction:* a form of non-prominence associated with semantic material that is being repeated merely "to keep the information in the 'current' file" (p. 9). Since in such cases there is a crucial link between a previous and a subsequent item, "reduction is an anaphoric operation" (p. 9). The information linked in this way need not be an example of strict identity.
- *Contrast:* an accented form related to a previous piece of information in a specific way. The previous piece of information must have a nega-

tive relationship with the contrasting item. Contrasting items may involve either basic negation or implicit or inferred relationships of negativity. The relationship between contrasted items is also fundamentally anaphoric.

- *Inert forms:* grammatical function words, such as particles, determiners, and complementisers, that carry little or no semantic information and are never accented. The category does not consist of *all* function words because some function words can accept contrast emphasis, for example quantifiers.

APPENDIX B: PRINCE'S CLASSIFICATION SYSTEM FOR ASSUMED FAMILIARITY

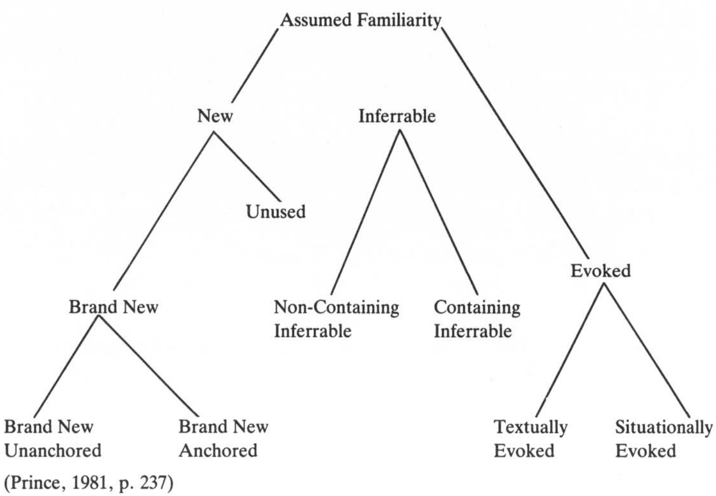

(Prince, 1981, p. 237)

1. *Brand New–Unanchored:* a semantically new entity introduced into the discourse.
2. *Brand New–Anchored:* a semantically new entity linked to another entity by being properly contained in it.
3. *Unused:* a new entity that has not yet been used in the discourse but which is assumed to be in the hearer's "model" and readily identifiable.
4. *Noncontaining Inferrable:* an entity that is Inferrable by logical or "plausible reasoning from discourse entities already evoked or from other Inferrables."
5. *Containing Inferrable:* an Inferrable in which what is referenced off of is properly contained in the Inferrable entity itself.
6. *Textually Evoked:* an entity that is already in the discourse model because it was once New or Inferrable.
7. *Situationally Evoked:* an entity that represents the discourse participants themselves or some salient feature of the extratextual context.

APPENDIX C: EXTENDED CATEGORIES FOR ANALYSIS OF GIVEN AND NEW INFORMATION DEVELOPED FOR THE CURRENT STUDY

1. *Brand New* (BN): the same category as that coded by Prince for a semantically new entity introduced into the discourse, with the difference that attributes and entities are coded separately.
   (a) I bought a *dress.*
   (b) It makes me feel *paranoid.*
2. *Brand New–Anchored* (BNA): the same category as Prince's but again used somewhat differently, both to code attached entities as in (a), but also to code a semantically new adjective attached to an entity as in (b).
   (a) He is a *friend of mine.*
   (b) I bought a *beautiful dress.*
3. *Brand New–Reintroduced* (BNR): this category follows Werth's system which distinguishes between Reintroduced and Reduced. A candidate for reintroduction is a concept or entity that has been previously mentioned but which has not been kept current in the discourse to the extent that it could undergo reduction at that certain point in the discourse. It is difficult to show examples of this category without looking at extended segments of discourse.
   (a) I have many problems . . . several intervening sentences. I would say that *problems* come under several different categories.
4. *Brand New Verb* (BNV): this category is not used by Prince. Here it is used to code verbs that carry new semantic information.
   (a) My parents *supported* me when I was an undergraduate.
5. *Unused* (U): this follows Prince's category for an entity that is assumed to be readily identifiable but unused previously in the discourse.
   (a) *Freud's* theories have had an enormous effect.
6. *Evoked* (E): this follows Prince's category for Textually Evoked, an entity or concept that was once New or Inferrable that is currently activated in the discourse model and, thus, highly available for pronoun reference, although not necessarily pronominalized.
   (a) Money is much more of an issue than *it* ever was.
7. *Situationally Evoked:* this follows Prince's category for references to the discourse participants themselves or to other salient features of the extratextual context.
   (a) *Let's* discuss the three things that *you've* set up as a kind of framework.
8. *Verb-Evoked:* This is a newly developed category that is intended to capture a distinction between verbs that are highly contextually expected as compared with verbs that are classified BNV. The BNV verbs contain more new information, are more vibrant and precise, whereas the EV verbs are more predictable and at times tend to be idiomatic. Examples of potential EV verbs (to be established by use in context) are "to be," "to have," "to do," "to make," "to get," "to go."

(a) He *gets* more financial support.
(b) It *makes* it a lot more difficult.

9. *Contrast* (C): this category follows Werth's system by coding an element (C) that is in negative anaphoric relationship with some other discourse (or possibly) common ground element.
(a) Well I *do* have some opinions about it.
(b) It's *not* just *money* . . . It's *not* just *time* . . . it's all these *other attitudes*.
10. *Inferrable* (I): following Prince's category, here the category refers to elements that are logically or pragmatically inferrable from the discourse or the common ground.
(a) I went to the post office and the *clerk* couldn't find a stamp.
(b) But when you pay the amount back and the *interest,* you pay the full amount.
11. *Containing Inferrable* (IC): following Prince, this category codes a set-member inference.
(a) *One* of the eggs is cracked.
12. *Performatives-Monitors* (P): this category codes performatives (such as "I think," "I know," "I doubt"), which are usually considered to be without their own propositional value but act as modifications (showing speaker/writer attitude) of propositions to which they are attached. The category also codes monitors (such as "well," "you know," "like"), which are used by the speaker/writer to acknowledge and monitor interaction.
(a) "I *feel* like I really don't want to pay for this experience twice.
(b) *You know,* what do you do?
13. *Intensifiers* (INT): this category codes such terms as "even," "just," "actually," "really," which also are nonpropositional but comment on propositions.
(a) . . . and the thing that *really* gets me is . . .
14. *Sentence Connectors* (SC): this category codes relative pronouns, complementizers, subordinating conjunctions and coordinating conjunctions when they are used within sentences.
(a) The other thing *that* I just wanted to say is . . .
15. *Discourse Connectors* (DC): this category codes metalinguistic terms (such as "first," "on the other hand," "to conclude"), which direct the hearer/reader to the structure of the text, as well as "and," "but," "however," when used at the beginning of sentences.
(a) *However,* it's not just money.
(b) The *first* idea is that . . .
16. *Question Words* (Q): this category codes question-formation words.
(a) *What's* going to happen to people?
17. *Quantifiers* (QU): this category codes quantifiers (such as "some," "any").
(a) He gets *some* grants.
18. *Feedback* (F): This category codes feedback (such as "umhumnh," "yes," "ok") in spoken language.

REFERENCES

Bakhtin, M. M. 1981. *The Dialogic Imagination: Four Essays.* Holquist, M. (Ed.). Emerson, C., and Holquist, M. (Trans.). Austin: University of Texas Press.

Bakhtin, M. M. 1986. *Speech Genres and Other Late Essays.* Emerson, C., and Holquist, M. (Eds.). McGee, V. W. (Trans.). Austin: University of Texas Press.

Basso, K. 1974. "The Ethnography of Writing." In Bauman, R., and Sherzer, J. (Eds.), *Explorations in the Ethnography of Speaking.* Cambridge: Cambridge University Press.

Biber, D. 1986. "Spoken and Written Textual Dimensions in English: Resolving the Contradictory Findings." *Language,* 62, 384–414.

Biber, D. 1988. *Variation Across Speech and Writing.* Cambridge: Cambridge University Press.

Brown, G. 1983. "Prosodic Structure and the Given/New Distinction." In Cutler, A., and Ladd, D. (Eds.), *Prosody: Models and Measurements.* Berlin: Springer-Verlag.

Chafe, W. 1979. "The Flow of Thought and the Flow of Language." In Givon, T. (Ed.), *Syntax and Semantics, 12: Discourse and Syntax.* New York: Academic Press.

Chafe, W. 1980. "The Development of Consciousness in the Production of a Narrative." In Chafe, W. (Ed.), *The Pear Stories: Cognitive, Cultural, and Linguistic Aspects of Narrative Structure.* Volume III of Advances in Discourse Process. Norwood, N.J.: Ablex.

Chafe, W. 1982. "Integration and Involvement in Speaking, Writing, and Oral Literature." In Tannen, D. (Ed.), *Spoken and Written Language: Exploring Orality and Literacy.* Norwood, N.J.: Ablex.

Chafe, W. 1985. "Linguistic Differences Produced by Differences Between Speaking and Writing." In Olson, D., Torrance, N., and Hildyard, A., (Eds.), *Literacy Language and Learning: The Nature and Consequences of Reading and Writing.* Cambridge: Cambridge University Press.

Chafe, W. 1986a. "Evidentiality in English Conversation and Academic Writing." In Chafe, W., and Nichols, J. (Eds.), *Evidentiality: The Linguistic Coding of Epistemology.* Volume XX of Advances in Discourse Processes. Norwood, N.J.: Ablex.

Chafe, W. 1986b. "Writing in the Perspective of Speaking." In Cooper, C., and Greenbaum, S. (Eds.), *Studying Writing: Linguistic Approaches.* Beverly Hills, Calif.: Sage Publications.

Chafe, W. 1987. "Cognitive Constraints on Information Flow." In Tomlin, R. (Ed.), *Coherence and Grounding in Discourse.* Amsterdam: John Benjamins.

Clark, H., and Clark, E. 1977. *Psychology and Language: An Introduction to Psycholinguistics.* New York: Harcourt, Brace, and Jovanovich.

de Beaugrande, R. 1979a. "Moving from Product Towards Process." *College Composition and Communication.* 30, 357–363.

de Beaugrande, R. 1979b. "Psychology and Composition." *College Composition and Communication,* 30, 50–57.

de Beaugrande, R. 1980. *Text, Discourse, and Process.* Norwood, N.J.: Ablex.

de Beaugrande, R. 1982. "Psychology and Composition: Past, Present, and Future." In Nystrand, M. (Ed.), *What Writers Know.* New York: Academic Press.

de Beaugrande, R. 1984. *Text Production: Toward a Science of Composition.* Norwood, N.J.: Ablex.

Flower, L., and Hayes, J. 1980a. "The Dynamics of Composing: Making Plans and Juggling Constraints." In Gregg, L., and Steinberg, E. (Eds.), *Cognitive Process in Writing.* Hillsdale, N.J.: Lawrence Erlbaum.

Flower, L., and Hayes, J. 1980b. "Identifying the Organization of Writing Processes." In Gregg, L., and Steinberg, E. (Eds.), *Cognitive Processes in Writing.* Hillsdale, N.J.: Lawrence Erlbaum.

Flower, L., and Hayes, J. 1981a. "A Cognitive Process Theory of Writing." *College Composition and Communication,* 32, 365–387.

Flower, L., and Hayes, J. 1981b. "Plans That Guide the Composing Process." In Frederiksen, C., and Dominic, J. (Eds.), *Writing: The Nature, Development and Teaching of Written Communication, Vol 2.* Hillsdale, N.J.: Lawrence Erlbaum.

Flower, L., and Hayes, J. 1981c. "The Pregnant Pause: An Inquiry into the Nature of Planning." *Research in the Teaching of English,* 15, 129–143.

Goody, J. 1977. *The Domestication of the Savage Mind.* Cambridge: Cambridge University Press.

Goody, J., and Watt, I. 1972. "The Consequences of Literacy." In Giglioli, P. (Ed.), *Language and Social Context: Selected Readings.* Harmondsworth, England: Penguin.

Gregory, M., and Carroll, S. 1978. *Language and Situation: Language Varieties and Their Social Contexts.* London: Routledge and Kegan Paul.

Halliday, M. 1967. "Notes on Transitivity and Theme in English (Part 2)." *Journal of Linguistics,* 3, 199–244.

Halliday, M. 1978. *Language as a Social Semiotic.* London: Edward Arnold.

Hasan, R. 1985. "Meaning, Context and Text – Fifty Years After Malinowski." In Benson, J., and Greaves, W. (Eds.), *Systemic Perspectives on Discourse, Vol 1.* Volume XVI of Advances in Discourse Processes. Norwood, N.J.: Ablex.

Heath, S. 1981. "Toward an Ethnography of Writing in American Education." In Whiteman, M. (Ed.), *Writing: The Nature, Development, and Teaching of Written Communication, Vol. 1.* Hillsdale, N.J.: Lawrence Erlbaum.

Householder, F. 1971. *Linguistic Speculations.* Cambridge: Cambridge University Press.

Hymes, D. 1972. "On Communicative Competence." In Pride, J., and Holmes, J. (Eds.), *Sociolinguistics: Selected Readings.* Harmondsworth, England: Penguin.

John-Steiner, V., and Tatter, P. 1983. "An Interactionist Model of Language Development." In Bain, B. (Ed.), *The Sociogenesis of Human Conduct.* New York: Plenum.

Lord, A. 1960. *The Singer of Tales*. Harvard Studies in Comparative Literature, 24. Cambridge, Mass.: Harvard University Press.

Matsuhashi, A. 1981. "Pausing and Planning. The Tempo of Written Discourse Production." *Research in the Teaching of English,* 15, 113–134.

Matsuhashi, A. 1982. "Explorations in the Real-Time Production of Written Discourse." In Nystrand, M. (Ed.), *What Writers Know.* New York: Academic Press.

McIntosh, A. 1966. "Graphology and Meaning." In McIntosh, A., and Halliday, M., *Patterns of Language: Papers in General, Descriptive, and Applied Linguistics*. London: Longman.

Nystrand, M. 1986. *The Structure of Written Communication: Studies in Reciprocity Between Writers and Readers*. Orlando, Fl.: Academic Press.

Ochs, E. 1984. "Clarification and Culture." In Schiffrin, D. (Ed.), *Meaning, Form and Use in Context.* Washington, D.C.: Georgetown University Press.

Olson, D. 1977. "From Utterance to Text." *Harvard Educational Review,* 47, 257–281.

Ong, W. 1977. *Interfaces of the Word.* Ithaca: Cornell University Press.

Prince, E. 1979. "On the Given/New Distinction." *Chicago Linguistic Society,* 15, 267–278.

Prince, E. 1981. "Toward a Taxonomy of Given-New Information." In Cole, P. (Ed.), *Radical Pragmatics.* New York: Academic Press.

Rubin, R. 1980. "A Theoretical Taxonomy of the Differences Between Oral and Written Language." In Spiro, R., Bruce, B., and Brewer, W. (Eds.), *Theoretical Issues in Reading Comprehension.* Hillsdale, N.J.: Lawrence Erlbaum.

Schafer, J. 1981. "The Linguistic Analysis of Spoken and Written Texts." In Kroll, B., and Vann, R. (Eds.), *Exploring Speaking-Writing Relationships.* Urbana, Ill.: National Council of Teachers of English.

Scinto, L. 1986. *Written Language and Psychological Development.* Orlando, Fl.: Academic Press.

Stubbs, M. 1980. *Language and Literacy: The Sociolinguistics of Reading and Writing.* London: Routledge and Kegan Paul.

Stubbs, M. 1983. *Discourse Analysis: The Sociolinguistic Analysis of Natural Language.* Oxford: Basil Blackwell.

Tannen, D. 1979. "What's in a Frame?" In Freedle, R. (Ed.), *New Directions in Discourse Processing, Vol. II.* Norwood, N.J.: Ablex.

Tannen, D. 1980. "A Comparative Analysis of Oral Narrative Strategies: Athenian Greek and American English." In Chafe, W. (Ed.), *The Pear Stories: Cognitive, Cultural, and Linguistic Aspects of Narrative Production.* Volume III of Advances in Discourse Processes. Norwood, N.J.: Ablex.

Tannen, D. 1982. "The Myth of Orality and Literacy." In Frawley, W. (Ed.), *Linguistics and Literacy.* New York: Plenum.

Vachek, J. 1973. *Written Language: General Problems and Problems in English.* The Hague: Mouton.

Vacheck, J. 1976. *Selected Writings in English and General Linguistics.* The Hague: Mouton.

Van Dijk, T., and Kintsh, W. 1983. *Strategies of Discourse Comprehension.* New York: Academic Press.

Vande Kopple, W. 1986. "Given and New Information and Some Aspects of the Structures, Semantics, and Pragmatics of Written Texts." In Cooper, C., and Greenbaum, R. (Eds.), *Studying Writing: Linguistic Approaches.* Beverly Hills, Calif.: Sage Publications.

Vygotsky, L. 1986. *Thought and Language.* Kozulin, A. (Ed., Trans.). Cambridge, Mass.: MIT Press.

Werth, P. 1984. *Focus, Coherence and Emphasis.* London: Croom Helm.

Wertsch, J. 1985a. (Ed.). *Culture, Communication and Cognition.* Cambridge: Cambridge University Press.

Wertsch, J. 1985b. *Vygotsky and the Social Formation of Mind.* Cambridge, Mass.: Harvard University Press.

3 *Repair in spontaneous speech: A window on second language development*

HENRY SHONERD

> The language learner must make his raincoat in the rain. (Klein 1986)
>
> Language use is the crucible of language development. (Langacker 1987)

3.1. INTRODUCTION

Consider the following sample of speech from a learner of English as a second language:

> He . . . receive . . . He received . . . his friend . . . from his friend . . . He received the letter from his friend.

The learner certainly gets his idea across, though, as we might expect from a learner, with hesitations, repetitions and adjustments, that is, repairs.

Or consider the following exchange during a lengthy conversation between another learner of English and a native speaker of English. The learner is describing his custom of watching the news on television, but is not sure of how to label a particular news segment:

Learner: (I watch) brief news. How say this . . . "brief news"?
Native speaker: Yeah, news in brief.
Learner: Ah . . . news in brief.

This conversational exchange involves collaborative repair, or other-repair, as contrasted with the previous example of self-repair.

In this chapter, I argue that both kinds of repair (self- and other-) are instrumental in the development of oral proficiency in the target language. These spontaneous repairs in the speech of second language learners do not present themselves simply as corrections. They represent an expansion of the language resources of the learner during the process of language use in social context. In this sense, repairs epitomize the interaction of language use and language development implicit in the raincoat and crucible metaphors quoted at the outset of this chapter.

A developmental interpretation of the repair process is in complete accord with the Vygotskian notion that human learning must be explained as an interaction of social and functional determinants on the one hand and biological determinants on the other. Repair is evidence for the functional and social side of the equation.

As an aspect of language, repair provides a window on what Vygotsky has called "higher mental functions." Such functions are marked by four essentials (Wertsch, 1985), all well demonstrated in the data in this chapter on repair. First, repair is social in origin. This is especially apparent in other-repair, but is equally present as approximation to conventional form and conventional semantic structure during self-repair. Second, such processes are self-controlled. This is evident not only in self-repair data but in other-repair as well. A large part of other-repair is elicited by the learner. Other-repair, in other words, is assisted production of speech where the locus of control is largely internal despite the external source of assistance. Third, repair is "intellectualized," that is, a metaprocess. It requires language awareness. Finally, repair involves mediation. This is doubly true: one, because as part of language learning repair requires the internalization of symbols (mediative devices, par excellence); two, because repair mediates the learning of new symbols by way of the symbols replaced by the repair.

Repair, then, provides a potentially rich vein of data for analysis of the development of language and thought. This chapter assays the utility of repair data in analyzing the course of development of English as a second language (ESL).

In the next section, I review briefly investigations of self-repair in second language speech by other researchers and then present in some detail findings of my own. I follow the same procedure in the following section on other-repair. Finally, I discuss the implications of research in second language repair for broader issues in the nature of language, language use, and language acquisition.

3.2. SELF-REPAIR IN SECOND LANGUAGE

3.2.1. Previous studies

Although self-repair has been the subject of a good deal of theorizing on the role of language awareness in second language acquisition (by Lado, 1964; Corder, 1967; and Krashen, 1981, among others), surprisingly little empirical research has been done. Three important published studies of research in self-repair in spontaneous second language speech are those of Seliger (1980), Fathman (1980), and Carroll, Dietrich, and Storch (1982). The first two studies are of learners of English as a second language, the last of learners of German as a second language.

Seliger argues (p. 88) that "correction reveals an awareness for the grammar of the language and the manner of planning and repair reveals the underlying processes or strategies utilized by the learner in the grammar construction process." He claims that repair is performance data that tells us how competence develops. Seliger's data include repetition in his repair data, arguing that the repetition reveals the tentative, hypothesis testing of much second language speech. This hypothesis testing is indicated also by rising intonation, indicating uncertainty by the learner, and repetitions without rising intonation, indicating the learner's conclusion that the repeated words are appropriate to the circumstances. Seliger posits two kinds of language learners: "the corrector [who] prefers to produce the utterance in whatever primitive form and work on perfecting the utterance after it has been produced" and "the planner [who] prefers to carefully plan his utterance internally . . . with a predominance of silent and filled pauses." (Note: This characterization of second language speech behavior parallels remarks by Maclay and Osgood [1959] in their study of repair in native speakers of English. These researchers characterized two styles of spontaneous speech – "slow and error free" and "fast and error full.")

As Seliger, Fathman included repetitions in her repair data. She notes the presence of discourse repairs, often in the form of topic abandonment, as opposed to corrections, which move form closer to intended meaning. The greatest number of corrections were lexical, constituting 40 percent of all corrections. Fathman noted among Korean students in her study (vis-à-vis the other subjects) a greater incidence of repetitions and corrections. Moreover, she found a greater proportion of corrections of bound morphemes among the Korean subjects. Thus, the selectivity of self-repair operated not only as a function of the type of unit repaired but also according to cultural and linguistic background.

Carroll et al. had the largest corpus of self-repair data. They collected 832 examples of self-repair from the spontaneous speech of four Americans and four Japanese learning German as a second language. However, their data were confined to the correction of bound morphemes. Therefore, their finding that the Japanese speakers had a higher incidence of self-repair is analogous to Fathman's finding of a greater incidence of corrections of bound morphemes among her Korean subjects.

The researchers found no correlation between the error rate of subjects and their rate of repair but did find a tendency for subjects to repair those morphemes with higher error rates more than those with lower error rates. Thus, articles had both a greater chance of error and of repair than personal pronouns. Here selectivity in self-repair seemed to be positively correlated with the relative difficulty of the unit repaired.

3.2.2. The present study

As part of a comprehensive study of second language learning strategies of literate adults (Shonerd, 1986), more than one thousand self-repairs from their spontaneous speech were recorded and transcribed. (Repetitions were not included in the repair data.) The learners were all enrolled in an intensive English program at a university in the United States. The twelve subjects of the study included six speakers of Japanese, three of Spanish, one of Chinese, one of Arabic, and one of Farsi. The recordings of their spontaneous speech were done during interviews (two-way dialogue), picture descriptions (monologue), and classroom interaction (one teacher and about ten students) over the course of three months.

Local repairs. Some of the repairs were clearly attempts to move what they were saying closer to the conventional form of expressing an intended meaning. This kind of self-repair I have labeled "local" according to the terminology of H. Clark and Clark (1977) in speech planning and execution and according to the terminology used by Dulay and Burt (1972) in second language error analysis. Here are examples[1] of spontaneous self-repairs of pronunciation, (bound) morphology, lexicon, and syntax, respectively, in the speech of the subjects of the study:

1. Three my friends *than . . . that* they are Iranian . . . and we don't speak.
2. *I like I liked* them talk about something.
3. I don't *love to like to* study . . . because I'm tired.
4. *I said him . . . I said to him* I began to interested in Indian culture.

These local self-repairs constituted 59 percent of the self-repairs during interviews, 53 percent of those during picture descriptions, and 63 percent of those during classroom interaction, or an average of 59 percent of the total of 1,016 self-repairs. On an individual basis, local self-repairs constituted between 46 and 66 percent of total self-repairs.

An analysis of the distribution of local self-repairs yielded the data shown in Table 3.1. In the conversation of the learners during interviews and classroom interaction, lexicon and syntax received the great-

Table 3.1. *Distribution (in percent) of local self-repair*

Context	Pronunciation	Morphology	Lexicon	Syntax
Interviews (N = 502)	11	24	37	28
Classroom (N = 36)	14	17	36	33
Picture task (N = 62)	13	34	32	21
Total (N = 600)	11	24	37	28

Table 3.2. *Distribution of repairs of Japanese and non-Japanese learners*

	Pronunciation	Morphology	Lexicon	Syntax
Japanese	6	30	29	35
Non-Japanese	11	18	43	27

est focus in the self-repair of these second language learners, followed by morphology in third place and pronunciation in last place. (Morphological repairs were most frequent during the monologues of picture descriptions.)

An analysis of individual behavior tended to confirm this ranking. The combined local repairs for the interviews, which comprised more than three-fourths of the corpus of all local self-repairs, revealed that syntactic repairs were the most prevalent for six of the twelve subjects, lexical repairs the most prevalent for five of the twelve and morphological repairs for one of the twelve. Pronunciation was the least prevalent for ten of the twelve.

Though the local self-repair of the entire group can be characterized by a focus on lexicon and syntax, there is relatively greater attention to morphological and syntactic repair by the Japanese and relatively greater attention to pronunciation and lexical repair by the non-Japanese. This is demonstrated in Table 3.2.

In judging the success of the local self-repair in moving an utterance closer to the conventions of the target language, there were four possible outcomes.

One outcome resulted when the repair was more native-like than the original utterance:

5. I see *much friends . . . a lot of friends.*

A second possible outcome was one in which the repair was *less* native-like than the original utterance:

Table 3.3. *Outcome of local self-repair (percentages)*

Context	More native	Less native	Equally native	Indeterminate
Classroom (N = 36)	78	11	3	8
Picture des. (N = 62)	82	8	5	5
Interviews (N = 502)	77	5	11	6
Combined (N = 600)	78	6	10	6

6\. . . . but *I under . . . I'm understand* the idea.

A third outcome occurred when self-repairs replaced equally native-like utterances. These repairs provide approximate synonyms for the original utterances rather than more correct forms:

7\. After that it's *speaking . . . talk.*

Finally, it was possible for the repair to be of indeterminate status, in terms of nativeness, when compared to the original utterance. In such cases, the repair does not move the form of the original utterance closer to a native-like target. The learner appears to recognize the need for a repair but is unsuccessful in replacing the original utterance with a native-like expression:

8\. *I can't . . . asked . . . I can't to ask . . . them.*

Consistently high success in achieving more native-like utterances is indicated by results from the analysis of the outcome of the repairs in the corpus of the study (Table 3.3).

Global repairs. Self-repairs like the following constituted a different category from the local repairs of the previous section:

9\. I take from the dictionary or *from the . . . if* the teacher explain something, I write it on the paper.
10\. *And I can't . . . then I can* understand English.
11\. *I need . . . I think* only with practice I have that.

Each of these repairs consists of a false start and a subsequent alteration that reflects a change in meaning of the utterance rather than a change in form that leaves meaning essentially unaffected. It appears that the meaning the learner is trying to put across is not simply being clarified by making the utterance more conventional – meaning is being altered. This kind of repair has been labeled "global" by H. Clark and Clark (1977) and Dulay and Burt (1972). When self-repairs were classified according to this local–global distinction, the behavior of second language learners was distinguished markedly from that of proficient speakers of English. As was pointed out in the previous section, local self-repairs constituted an average among the twelve subjects of 59 percent of the total self-repairs during interviews and 53 percent during the picture descriptions. Contrast this with self-repair rates of the interviewer (a native speaker of English) during interviews and of a control group of native speakers during picture descriptions. During two of the interviews taken at random, the interviewer made only two local self-repairs (or a total of less than three percent) from a total of seventy-five self-repairs. Of a total of twenty-five self-repairs performed by the five native-speaking controls during picture descriptions, none were local.

Thus, in comparing dialogue and monologue of second language learners and highly proficient speakers of English, there was a preference for local self-repairs by the learners and an overwhelming preponderance of global self-repairs by proficient speakers.

3.2.3. Interpretation of self-repair data

An analysis of the self-repairs of the ESL learners in the studies cited reveals several features that bear comment: (1) the selective nature of self-repair, (2) the success of second language learners in moving closer to conventional form during self-repair, (3) notable differences from the kinds of self-repairs made by native speakers of English, and (4) the elaborative character of many repairs.

Selectivity in self-repair. In general, the local self-repairs in these studies focus more on lexicon and syntax, less on morphology and even less on pronunciation. At the same time, the focus of self-repair is culture sensitive.

Of the corpus of local self-repairs in my own study, 37 percent were lexical. This is very close to the 40 percent figure in Fathman's research. This consistency suggests that self-repair as a strategy of second language learning stresses the importance of lexical development. Why this should be true may have to do with the intrinsic importance of lexicon to language development and language use, to the study habits of the learners, or other factors. Whatever the case, the consistency of findings opens the door to further research.

Another interesting finding in my study of second language learners is the relatively greater attention to morphological and syntactic repair and relatively less emphasis on pronunciation and lexical repair in the speech of Japanese compared with that of other cultural groups. The finding about morphological repairs is consistent with the studies of both

Fathman and Carroll et al. among their Asian subjects learning a second language. This consistency suggests strongly a sociocultural basis for self-repair beyond the psycholinguistic one of self-repair as a universal strategy of second language acquisition. At least two explanations seem plausible. These regularities of behavior may be imposed by differences between source and target language. On the other hand, pedagogic practices and socially prevalent learning "styles" may be influential. The issue is raised here, not to settle it, but to point out the potential of self-repair data in analyzing strategies of second language acquisition in social and historical contexts.

Success of self-repair. Many of the errors (i.e., nonconventional usage) of the subjects went uncorrected. There are several possible explanations for this. One is that the learner is simply unaware that an error has been made. This certainly must be the case some of the time. Another possibility is that the learner senses that an error has been made but is unsure that a repair will result in a more native utterance. In fact, 6 percent of local self-repairs by learners were indeterminate in their status. In those cases, the learners were aware that they had made errors but were unsuccessful in their attempts to produce more conventional forms. It is also likely that there are times when the learner judges before a repair is attempted that the repair will be unsuccessful and, on this basis, the learner decides against attempting the repair.

The third possibility, raised by Fathman (1980), is that learners must balance their efforts to match the conventions of the target language with the need for fluency in conversation. In some cases, learners may be aware that an error has been committed and be capable of correcting the error but sacrifice the correction to speed of output. Slobin (1979) has commented in general terms on the tension between two competing "charges" of language, clarity and quickness. For the sake of comprehensibility, second language learners must approximate the conventions of the target language. But, for the sake of keeping conversational turns and of coherence in discourse and cognitive processes, learners cannot afford to dwell too much on correctness in their speech.

The fact that the great majority of these local self-repairs (78 percent of the total) move production in the direction of a native target indicates that the learners are judicious in their use of repair. The learners evidently have good hunches as to what will work, making the repairs maximally communicative.

Differences in self-repair of learners and native speakers. The marked difference in the proportion of global to local self-repairs of learners and proficient language users is evidence that repairs are a window on language development.

The overwhelming preponderance of global repairs relative to local repairs in the speech of native speakers is consistent with research on false starts in the speech production of native speakers (Maclay and Osgood, 1959). Speakers must make decisions of a global nature in discourse planning (H. Clark and Clark, 1977). Global repairs are evidence for the efforts of the speaker in planning and maintaining discourse coherence. These repairs reflect the way in which thinking and speaking interact with one another in the development of discourse coherence (Vygotsky, 1962; Chafe, 1980). Self-repairs that operate at a more local level, such as the corrections of pronunciation, morphology, lexical choice, and word omission, are, evidently, at the service of some more firmly established local plan.

Second language learners risk more errors and have to focus greater attention locally in speech planning and execution than native speakers. Conventional linguistic units at all levels, from phonological to discourse levels, are less well entrenched for learners than for fluent speakers of a language. For fluent speakers, lower level units are so well entrenched that they can focus more of their attention on higher-level units in construction of coherent discourse than is true for learners. This would explain why a much higher percentage of the self-repairs of ESL learners than of native speakers of English should be local.

Elaborative nature of self-repair. Nooteboom (1980) characterizes self-repair as a process of "unspeaking." Although self-repair is, from one perspective, the replacement of one form by another, what underlies the self-repair may be a reanalysis of a linguistic unit previously used as an unanalyzed "chunk." Bowerman (1982) argues that such "reorganizational" processes are responsible for lexical and syntactic development in a first language. Hakuta (1974, 1976) and Wong-Fillmore (1979) make the same claim for grammatical development in second language: over time learners master the internal structure of "prefabricated patterns." The following self-repairs (from Shonerd, 1986) are plausibly the result of such a process of reanalysis:

12. I said, "*Dun . . . Don't* touch that thing."
13. I must do *anything everything* myself.
14. *I meet I met* her . . . Friday.
15. *I said him . . . I said to him* I began to interested.

In example 12, a Spanish speaker has gone from a partially conventional negative marking on the auxiliary (common among Spanish speakers learning English) to an even more conventional pronunciation profiling the presence of "not" within the contracted form. In example 13, the speaker is struggling with the differences between "any" and "every" within the compound form in which they appear. In example 14, the speaker's repair inflects a verb uttered originally in infinitival form. Uninflected verb forms are common and commonly repaired in this corpus (see example 2). The insertion in example 15 of "to" between the verb and its object marks a syntactic relationship between the two indicated in the original utterance only by the sequential order of the verb and object.

The point to be made here is that these self-repairs may represent the reanalysis of linguistic units unanalyzed at some earlier stage of second language learning. The self-repair itself represents, in microcosm, gradual refinement in the language abilities of the learner.

Repair, seen in this light, is more than a simple process of correction; it is an expansion of semiotic resources. The original utterance contains more than an error to be corrected; it provides a relatively simple structure on which a more complex and more native-like utterance can be based. Syntactic and morphological repairs are more apt than repairs of pronunciation and lexicon to have this quality of expansion. Consider the following self-repairs (also, from Shonerd, 1986), some of which attain a final outcome only after a series of approximations:

16. *He open . . . He keep op' . . . He keep book open.*
17. Maybe *don't . . . they don't leave.*
18. I don't know *he's . . . if he's* feeling . . . bad or if he's feeling good.
19. *It's the same love. It's the same kind of love.*
20. There is a man . . . *h' . . . he is . . . who . . .* who is exchange student . . . from . . . mm . . . from foreign country.
21. *Highway . . . they work . . . they work on the highway . . . they work on the highways.*
22. *He . . . receive . . . He received . . . his friend . . . from his friend . . . He received the letter from his friend.*

The clearly expansionary nature of these repairs is testimony to the "constructive effort" (Langacker, 1987) involved in the development of fluency in a second language.

3.3. OTHER-REPAIR IN SECOND LANGUAGE

3.3.1. Previous studies

Given the traditional role of the second language teacher as a model and enforcer of "good grammar," one might expect to find much relevant empirical research. This appears not to be the case. For example, in a review article on error correction in foreign language teaching, Hendrickson (1980) concluded that there was very little empirical basis to decide the answers to two basic and interrelated issues: how error correction should be done (when, how often, and by whom) and the value of other-repair for second language acquisition. However, Hendrickson's review disregarded important and relevant research in discourse analysis, in particular the work on other-repair. Error correction is only one kind of other-repair and cannot be understood in isolation from alternative forms of other-repair.

Probably the most rigorous and widely known research on the process of repair in conversational interaction has been done by Schegloff, Sacks, and Jefferson (1977). They have established a system for the analysis of repair in conversation based on the initiation of the repair (by self or by another) and the repair proper (also by self or by another). They found a strong preference for self-initiation and self-repair in regular conversation. There amounts to what is almost a taboo against other-repair in conversation between native speakers of English, at least among the subjects of the studies by Schegloff et al.

Several second language researchers, aware of these findings, have taken the broad view of "trouble spots" in native–nonnative conversation as captured in the analysis of other-repair, rather than reduce the research to a study of uninvited and potentially obtrusive error correction by teachers. Kasper (1985) has criticized the common tendency in classroom second language research to disregard all but teacher-initiated repair. Gaskill (1980) found that most repair in the classroom was self-repair and that other-correction was often "modulated." For example, an agreement with what a learner said effectively downplayed the fact that the native speaker was modeling a more conventional form for saying it. Unmodulated other-correction was often invited (i.e., initiated) by the learner with pauses and rising intonation. Chesterfield (1982) found that other-repair in native–nonnative discourse often occurred as a lexical "cloze" by the native during a word search by the nonnative. Phonological, morphological, and syntactic repair was, as a result, much less common.

Accompanying the narrow construal of other-repair as purely corrective taken by some second language researchers is the assumption that other-repair constitutes a conversational "incident" to be focused on by the interactants. This need not be the case. Jefferson (1972) has commented on the phenomenon in conversation between native speakers where repair sequences in conversation are sandwiched rather unobtrusively between turns devoted to some topic other than the repair itself. Day, Chenoweth, Chun, and Luppescu (1977) noted that corrective feedback in native–nonnative discourse generally occurred as the same sorts of unobtrusive "side-sequences." Conversational flow may be facilitated rather than disrupted by other-repair, since the repair is subordinated to the communicative intent of the interactants. When facilitative, the other-repair combines the discovery (or confirmation) of the correct form by the learner with the discovery (or confirmation) of the learner's intended meaning by the native listener.

Discourse analysis provides a perspective on other-repair unburdened by prescriptivist construals inherent in most current research. This is analogous to freeing research on self-repair from the shadow cast by looking simply for the correction of an error rather than the ongoing expansion of the language resources of the learner.

3.3.2. The present study

In the study of self-repair by adult second language learners of English (Shonerd, 1986), data on other-repair in native–nonnative interaction were also collected and analyzed. Generally, other-repair, like self-repair, was found sandwiched unobtrusively within the spontaneous flow of speech. As such, it was part and parcel of the communicative interchange, a convenient device for facilitating the interchange that did not divert attention to the topic at hand to explicit grammatical analysis. Moreover, much of the other-repair was either modulated by the native speaker or invited by the nonnative speaker. The new image we get of other-repair is that of a collaboration between more and less experienced users of English for the purpose of facilitating talk. In this vein, other-repair is appropriately thought of as assisted production.

Types of other-repair. Some of the repairs were paradigmatic in that they involved the replacement of one linguistic unit (originally uttered by the learner) by another, more conventional unit (offered by the native speaker). Some of the repairs were syntagmatic in nature involving the completion by a native speaker of an utterance begun by the learner. The latter was true of the following example of assisted production, which demonstrated the sort of lexical cloze procedure noted by Chesterfield (1982). In the following conversational exchange from an interview, a pause is taken as an indication to the native speaker (NS) of a word search on the part of the learner (nonnative speaker, NNS). (All of the following examples are taken from interviews.) The native speaker provides a lexical item, which the learner then repeats:

NNS: I want to buy a new tape recorder but I bought . . .
NS: speakers
NNS: speakers

Other-repair was sometimes elicited by the learner through paraphrase. This occurs in the following interchange in which the subject was describing his use of the language laboratory:

NNS: How do you say, "The one day I went . . . the next day no"? A day between?
NS: every other day
NNS: every other day

The following is an example of other-repair through hypothesis testing, analogous to the hypothesis testing during *self*-repair behavior noted by Seliger (1980). In this case, the more experienced language user is drawn into the repair process. In the first line of the interchange, the learner indicates his uncertainty about the correctness or appropriateness of a particular expression through rising intonation and a pause. The subject has just been asked if he uses audiotapes to study English:

NNS: Almost ever . . . ?
NS: Never?
NNS: No.
NS: Almost always?
NNS: Almost always . . . almost always it's only for listen.

This hypothesis testing can involve the learner giving more than one alternative, one of which is confirmed by the native-speaking interlocutor as in the following, where the learner is explaining how she encountered a native-speaking friend on the way to class:

NS: Where did you meet her?
NNS: In to the way on the way . . .
NS: On the way
NNS: On the way I met her.

Some other-repair occurs as a result of modeling rather than explicit correction, the sort of "modulated" other-repair noted by Gaskill (1980). This happens in the following exchange:

NNS: She's the sister of my grand-grandmother grandmother.
NS: Oh, she's the sister of your great-grandmother.
NNS: *great*-grandmother.

Assisted production was sometimes elicited through syllabic or root word cues, as when a learner talks about the value of travel abroad:

NNS: It's very profit . . . (with a pause and rising intonation)
NS: profitable
NNS: profit . . . profitable
NS: umhm
NNS: and very good experience

Another type of assisted production can take place through translation. Here the learner is describing his strategies of reading in English:

NNS: How do you say "subrayar"?
NS: underline
NNS: underline. Ah, it's easy. Underline the idea I don't understand.

Table 3.4 provides the distribution of other-repair according to categories exemplified previously. Repairs under "miscellaneous" consist of those elicited by the learner through translation, syllabic or word root cues, or unelicited other-repair "modulated" by the native speaker.

Response to assistance. Other-repair can appropriately be called assisted production if the assistance is somehow incorporated into the speech of the learner. The data from this study indicate that this can take place in a number of ways. One possibility is that the assistance is integrated into a larger constituent. This is exemplified in the following exchange from an interview in which the second language learner is talking about a movie (*Amadeus*) she has seen. The subject has trouble accessing a particular lexical item and is assisted by the interviewer:

NNS: I think . . . I thought he made opera . . . and ah . . . but . . . not king . . .
NS: prince?
NNS: Prince don't like his opera.

Another possible response to the assistance is simply to repeat the proffered linguistic element, as in the following example where the learner is describing his television watching habits:

NNS: Brief news. How say this . . . "brief news"?
NS: Yeah, news in brief.
NNS: Ah . . . news in brief.

Still another response to the assistance is a simple acknowledgment of the words offered by the interlocutor as appropriate to the meaning intended by the learner. This occurs in the following example where the learner is explaining his relationship to a person with whom he was staying:

NNS: How do you say, "distance relation, very distance"?
NS: Ah . . . yeah . . . "She's a distant relative."
NNS: Yeah.

A final possibility is for the learner to simply ignore the words offered by the interlocutor. This is apparently the fate of the following offer of lexical assistance during an interview involving an instructor (I) and a student (S):

Table 3.4. *Types of other-repair (percentages)*

	Correction	Cloze	Paraphrase	Hypothesis testing	Miscellaneous
Interviews (N = 154)	27	24	12	19	21
Classroom (N = 57)	43	33	3	0	21

Table 3.5. *Response (in percent) to other-repair*

	Integrated	Repeated	Acknowledged	Ignored
Interviews (N = 154)	37	57	5	1
Classroom (N = 57)	34	46	15	5

I: What is she studying?
S: Dentist . . . dentist . . . dentist
I: Dentistry?
S: Teeth.
I: Dentistry.
S: But my next door is Rita and Judy . . . She very good friend.

Responses by the subjects to the offers of assisted repair (i.e., other-repair) during interviews and classroom observation were distributed in the manner shown in Table 3.5.

Thus, a large percentage of the offers of assisted repair during interviews and in the classroom were utilized by the subjects to produce utterances, either through simple repetition or through the integration of the assistance into a larger constituent. Some kind of acknowledgment is apparent in most cases where the offered assistance is *not* utilized in producing an utterance.

Focus of other-repair. Table 3.6 presents the distribution of other-repair of the subjects according to the type of linguistic unit that is focused upon.

3.3.3. Interpretation of other-repair data

It is evident from these examples that other-repair cannot be characterized simply as correction. Vygotsky has provided a much more fruitful way of characterizing other-repair.

Self-repair is an intrapsychological process; other-repair is an in-

Table 3.6. *Distribution of other-repair (in percent) according to type of unit repaired*

	Pronunciation	Lexicon	Morphology	Syntax
Interviews (N = 154)	16	62	12	10
Classroom (N = 57)	12	68	3	17

terpsychological one. The former requires the private application of language awareness, the latter requires the application of language awareness collaboratively. When other-repair involves the scaffolding of language production of a less experienced language user by a more experienced one, we may speak appropriately of the "zone of proximal development" (Vygotsky, 1978). Vygotsky (p. 86) defines this zone as "the distance between the actual developmental level as determined by independent problem solving and the level of potential development as determined through problem solving under adult guidance or in collaboration with more capable peers."

Learner-centered nature of other-repair. As Klein (1986) has pointed out, the language learner can focus on only a limited number of aspects of the gap between current abilities and a more native-like target. This is true whether the gap is bridged by self-repair or by other-repair. There is an additional consideration with other-repair: whereas, in self-repair the delicate attentional processes of monitoring, matching (original utterance with its replacement), and repairing are completely in the control of the learner, in other-repair some of the process of speech production is external to the learner. Speaking a second language already involves a high load on the attentional capacities of the learner; integrating the repairs of others may result in an overload. Two conditions must hold for this not to occur. First, the learner must attend to the repair. Second, as with first language acquisition, other-repair in second language acquisition must be within the zone of proximal development of the learner. Other-repair has the advantage of providing the learner with additional semiotic resources for the production of the second language, but the disadvantage that the assistance may be either disregarded or unusable.

The data in Table 3.5 provide evidence that a large portion of other-repair is both attended to and usable by the learner in producing the second language. That this is the case is probably related to the findings in Table 3.4 that much of the assistance is, in fact, elicited. Rather than the image of passivity evoked by conceiving of other-repair purely as unelicited correction (cf. Hendrickson, 1980), we see language learners in charge of their own processes of speech production, even when, as in the case of other-repair, aspects of the process are external to the learner. This active involvement approach maximizes the extent to which these less experienced language users are able to make use of the semiotic means of more experienced language users.

Only about a quarter of the other-repair during interviews took place through overt correction. The percentage was closer to half in the classroom interaction. (There were seven cases of other-repair being offered by other learners in the classroom.) Further evidence of the important role of the teacher as an arbiter of form is the fact that a much higher percentage of all repair in the classroom was assisted than was the case outside of the classroom. The ratio of other-repairs to total self-repair during interviews was 154/844, or .18. The ratio within the classroom was 57/57, or 1.00. (The even number is pure chance.)

The preference for self-repair, or at least the self-initiation of repair (Schegloff et al., 1977), is therefore born out in the dialogue between native and nonnative speakers from which these repair data were obtained. Although the classroom interaction does not completely contradict this tendency, the preference is clearly attenuated in such a setting. This is probably related to teacher-centered patterns of turn-taking and topic initiation in the classroom.

Lexical focus of other-repair. During local self-repair (see Table 3.1) lexical and syntactic repair were nearly equal and accounted for approximately two-thirds of the total. During other-repair, lexicon alone is the focus of approximately two-thirds of the total, much greater than any of the other categories. This is a difference one might expect in comparing collaborative repair (other-repair) and noncollaborative repair (self-repair).

We have already seen that several of the mechanisms for assisted production favor a focus on lexical units. Among them is the cloze-like procedure where a second language learner elicits assistance through hesitation and rising intonation. Such a method of elicitation is more effective in focusing on a whole word to follow than on pronunciation, on a bound morpheme or on the arrangement of words in sequence. The same is true of translation as a means of effecting other-repair.

In English, single words are the prototypical units of meaning of the language. Dictionaries embody this prototypicality. The initial stages of acquisition of a first language testify to the fundamental importance of single words as indicators of meaning. A great deal of the private study reported by the subjects of this study was devoted to the study of single words. It is not surprising that, in seeking help from others in producing English, learners should find single lexical items easier to incorporate into their spontaneous speech than elements of pronunciation, morphology, or syntax.

There is yet another reason that one might expect other-repair to focus more on the lexicon than self-repair does. Lexicon is the component of grammar where the quantitative difference between the knowledge of a learner and an interlocutor (especially a native speaker) is likely to be the greatest. This is because the number of free morphemes in a language is much greater than the inventory of sound segments, intonational contours, bound morphemes, or syntactic structures. This quantitative difference between the semiotic resources of the native speaker and the learner may be responsible for the relatively greater focus on lexicon in other-repair.

3.4. REPAIR IN RELATION TO BROADER ISSUES OF LANGUAGE AND LANGUAGE DEVELOPMENT

This account of empirical work on repair in the spontaneous speech of second language learners makes a case for repairs as a strategy of second language learning and as a fruitful source of second language research data. Beyond this fairly narrow empirical focus, repair is an issue with broader methodological and theoretical implications. In the remainder of this chapter, I develop briefly the relation of repair to three such general areas: repair as a subset of a total repertoire of language learning (and teaching) strategies, repair in first language development, and the relation of repair to theories of language and language acquisition.

3.4.1. Repair as a strategy of analysis in language learning

The language learner has access to two general kinds of language learning strategies: use and analysis of the language (Shonerd, 1986). Strategies of *use* require a relatively fluent utilization of the symbolic units of the target language for production or comprehension. A prototypical use strategy is conversational practice. Strategies of *analysis* involve the segmentation of the flow of speech into its symbolic units (e.g., morphological and syntactic), the separation of these units into form and meaning, and the decontextualization of these units. Typically one thinks of the study of grammar and vocabulary as strategies of language analysis.

Strategies of use and analysis in second language learning can involve classroom study and interaction, a variety of technologies (film, audio and video recording equipment, and print), private study of the grammar of the target language and conversational interaction with friends who are native speakers of the second language. John-Steiner (1985a) and Shonerd (1986) have described in detail these "functional learning systems" (Vygotsky, 1978) of adult second language learning in which the most successful artfully interweave the use and analysis of the target language. A strategy prototypical of this interweaving of use and analysis is repair (self- and other-) during spontaneous speech. Such a strategy shows in microcosm the development in the learner of the resources of the second language.

To argue that repair may be instrumental in the process of second language learning does not mean it is necessarily a conscious and deliberate learning (or teaching) strategy. From one point of view, repair may simply be an incidental by-product of the effort to facilitate communication, but a product nonetheless. In the short-term context of face-to-face conversation, repair is primarily a communication strategy. However, this immediate communicative function in no way denies the possibility that repair is of developmental importance. Krashen (1981) and Tarone (1980), curiously enough, have argued that since repair is a communication strategy, it is of no importance in second language learning. The logical result of such reasoning would be the absurd conclusion that conversation is of no importance in language learning, since it is a communication strategy.

From a Vygotskian perspective, language has its sociogenetic basis not only in the conventions of its symbols but in the "scaffolding" (Bruner, 1966) available to language learners in the form of help from fluent users of a language. Social invention resides both in the conventions of language and in the conventional social structures for language learning. For the second language learner these include language classes and friendships with empathetic native speakers outside of class.

For the learner all of these possibilities constitute available resources. Other-repair during native–nonnative discourse can be seen in the same light. It provides the learner with access to the language abilities of more experienced language users when those abilities are of immediate utility – during the problem solving inherent in self-expression in a second language. Moreover, as with self-repair, other-repair is of immediate utility during communication, and has a dual long-range function in the development of second language ability.

3.4.2. Repair in first language development

Both self-repair and the ability to incorporate other-repair into one's own speech demonstrate metalinguistic awareness. Such awareness is present in first language learners. Vygotsky (1962) noted that a major aspect of this awareness (and one central to the repair process), knowledge of the separability of sign and referent, unfolded slowly in the child.

Early signs of this awareness have been discovered by more recent psycholinguistic research. Oller (1980) cites evidence that infants incorporate the sounds of the language around them into their babbling. Crib speech demonstrates (Weir, 1966; Bruner and Feldman, 1985) that children attend retrospectively to the form of the language around them and even practice intonational, phonological, and syntactic patterns of their interlocutors. Language play in the monologues and dialogues of children is a major indicator of the language awareness of children (Keenan, 1974; Cazden, 1975; Kucsaj, 1983). Children as young as four years of age are capable of adjusting their speech according to the age of their interlocutors (Shatz and Gelman, 1973). Children as young as three years of age are capable of revising (repairing) their speech in the face of misunderstanding by listeners (Gallagher, 1977; Garnica, 1977).

Some researchers have asserted that self-repair and, more generally, metalinguistic abilities are instrumental, even necessary, to first language development. E. Clark (1982) claims that self-repair shows in microcosm the process of language development in the child. Having internalized grammatical means in excess of production abilities, the child is capable of monitoring its own speech, matching it against a more adult form and repairing its speech accordingly. Differences in metalinguistic (Kahmi and Koenig, 1985) and metapragmatic (Savich, 1983) abilities have been shown to be associated with differences in the language abilities of normal and language-delayed children.

The elaborative nature of many self-repairs in the speech of second language learners cited in section 3.2.3 is similar to what has been found in L1 research. Weir (1966) has commented on the way in which her young first language subjects "built up" more complex syntactic units from more simple ones during their crib talk. Braine (1971) estimates that between 30 and 40 percent of the utterances of first language learners of his subjects from 24 to 30 months consist of such "replacement sequences." Miller (1979) has also commented on these expansionary repairs in young children. Though the self-repairs in the above adult L2 examples represent a much more advanced level of semantic development (hence, conceptual development), there is clearly a developmental connection between the self-repair strategies of the young first language learners and the older second language learners.

An information-processing model of human cognition has been used to explain self-repair in first language development. Vygotsky (1978) was familiar with the concepts of automatic and controlled processes (he used the terms "involuntary" and "voluntary"), which are an essential element of MacWhinney's (1978) analysis of children's self-repairs.

MacWhinney posits that the repair results from a mismatch between the form first uttered and the "weak form" (i.e., less automatic or more controlled linguistic unit) that replaces it. Since repair requires controlled processing, it requires scarce attentional resources, and must therefore be a "spotlight" in nature, rather than a "floodlight" (E. Clark, 1982). The characteristic of selectivity in self-repair (documented here in second language learners) is revealed over time as a shift from a preponderance of phonological repairs in younger children to more lexical and syntactic repairs in older children (E. Clark, 1982). Language itself reveals the spotlight nature of consciousness (Chafe, 1974). In this sense, the metalinguistic processes of self-repair are a window on language development, while language is an even larger window on the mind.

Although, as we have seen, the first language learner has a gradually evolving awareness of language itself, there is what amounts to a qualitative difference in this capacity in older, particularly highly literate, second language learners (the subjects of all major research on second language repairs). This rests on the second language learner possessing a more fully developed semantic system, more efficient memory heuristics, greater general problem-solving capacities, and basic principles of phonology and the pragmatics of language use (Ervin-Tripp, 1974). Since repair (both unassisted and assisted) relies on metalinguistic abilities, and since language awareness increases with age and literacy, we would expect repair to be at least as instrumental in literate adult second language learning as it is in first language learning.

3.4.3. Repair and theories of language and language acquisition

Some of the most well known second language theorists of the last three decades have discounted the role of self-repair in second language acquisition. Lado (1964) stated categorically that, "The person who has not yet fully learned a foreign language fails to notice his own mistakes." Corder (1967) paid enough attention to spontaneous second language speech to know that learners are capable of monitoring and correcting at least some departures from conventional form, but argued that the mistakes that these learners are capable of correcting are "no more important than slips of the tongue." Krashen (e.g., 1981) states that self-repair plays no role in second language acquisition, which, according to him, is determined entirely by the triggering of a language acquisition device by "comprehensible input." In fact, the sweeping claims of these theorists are based on skimpy (or nonexistent) second language repair data and disregard counterevidence from first language acquisition (ironic for Krashen's claim that first and second language acquisition operate identically). Lado is simply wrong factually; Corder's data are "clean" of "performance" data (Seliger, 1980), and Krashen's study of monitoring processes has been characterized as largely "subjective" and "anecdotal" (McClaughlin, 1978).

As pointed out earlier, other-repair has not fared any better as a focus of second language research (Hendrickson, 1980). Krashen (1981), for example, is as dismissive of the value of other-repair as he is of self-repair in second language acquisition.

The major reason for lack of interest in repair in language development is arguably the prevailing generative theory of language and language acquisition. Krashen is a self-avowed Chomskian and invokes the legendary language acquisition device in explaining the presumed "natural order" of morpheme acquisition. In fact, the generative paradigm militates against research in language repair on at least the following counts: (1) an almost total emphasis on comprehension, (2) the use of only "clean" language data due to the focus on ideal competence, (3) the dismissal of metalinguistic processes in language development, (4) assumed innateness of language faculty, and (5) language as a static and modular capacity (Chomsky, 1980).

On all five of these counts, the construal of repair as an important aspect of language development (first and second) departs from the generative paradigm: (1) during the repair process, production and comprehension interact; (2) repair is very much performance data, yet relies on emergent competence; (3) repair requires metalinguistic awareness, yet is embedded in fluent and relatively unmonitored speech; (4) repair exemplifies processes of language use in social context that are necessary for language development; and (5) repair is important for language development because language is a functional and dynamic semiotic system that cannot be explained in isolation from general cognitive processes. On every point, repair instantiates the interactive, nonmodular character of language.

3.5. SUMMARY AND CONCLUSION

This chapter began by pointing out that repair has received little attention in the study of language. Yet, a theoretical overview from a Vygotskian perspective and an empirical analysis of the speech repairs of second language learners indicates that repair provides an excellent window on language acquisition.

The empirical findings reported in this chapter support the idea that repair is instrumental to language acquisition: striking differences in the self-repair behavior of L2 learners and native speakers of the language, the spotlight nature of repair, and the success of learners during repair in moving utterances closer to target language conventions. Agreement among research findings of different investigators of repair indicate robustness of repair as a methodological tool: a preference for self-repair (or at least self-initiation of repair), culturally patterned differences in the focus of self-repair, and a marked deemphasis of pronunciation in adult (second language) repair in contrast to the findings of a focus on phonology in child (first language) repair.

This approach will appear peculiar to some. It considers speech production in all its messy glory as constitutive of acquisition, rather than degenerate performance data to be eschewed in favor of some sanitized picture of language competence. Repair instantiates the interaction between performance and competence in language use. It provides in microcosm a view of the reorganizational processes of language development, which, for the most part, remain covert.

This view may seem less peculiar if we consider repair as a general aspect of all creative endeavor: revision in writing and the composition of music, reformulation in scientific thinking, modification in the creation of visual art, and so on. In this, a developmental and interactionist language paradigm shares common ground with Chomsky's major insight that language use is a creative process. We may take a cue here from an interactionist study of creativity in "experienced thinkers" (including seminal figures in mathematics, literature, physics, and dance):

> I am interested in discovering the shared dynamics in the various processes of thought, while recognizing and exploring developmental, cultural and historical differences in the mastery of thinking. (John-Steiner, 1985b, p. 3)

An analysis of revision processes (including repair in speech) offers a way of exploring commonalities inherent in the shared dynamics of creative work while recognizing differences in developmental courses. For instance, we note the presence of repair in the speech of all language learners but differences in the nature of that repair due to culture and levels of language development. In the spirit of John-Steiner's study of the paths of development of experienced thinkers, repair in language development adds to understanding by focusing on processes rather than products.

Finally, as with all creative endeavor, speech repair instantiates the tension between the old and the new, between the social and the personal. Through repair, the creative effort inherent in language acquisition breaks free of the past not so much through the abandonment of old (and "bad") habits as through the elaboration and expansion of established knowledge. Self-repair is possible because of the internalization by the learner of the semiotic resources of more experienced language users, yet this internalization obeys individual developmental courses. Other-repair, involves on-line help from more experienced language users, yet the locus of control of the assisted production must be internal to the learner. Thus, the social scaffolding of language development, implicit in self-repair and explicit in other-repair, leads to greater individual freedom in the form of more proficient and creative use of a language. The power of an interactionist paradigm is that it recognizes the dialectic nature of all creative human endeavor.

NOTE

1. In all examples, the unit replaced and its replacement are italicized. Suspended dots (. . .) indicate hesitations.

REFERENCES

Baars, B. J. 1980. The competing plans hypothesis: An heuristic viewpoint on the causes of errors in speech. In H. W. Dechert and M. Raupach (Eds.), *Temporal variables in speech: Studies in honour of Frieda Goldman-Eisler.* The Hague: Mouton. 1982.

Baars, B. J., Motley, M. T., and MacKay, D. G. 1975. Output editing for lexical status in artificially elicited slips of the tongue. *Journal of Verbal Learning and Verbal Behavior,* 14, 382–391.

Bates, E., and MacWhinney, B. 1982. Functionalist approaches to grammar. In E. Wanner and L. R. Gleitman (Eds.), *Language acquisition: The state of the art.* Cambridge: Cambridge University Press.

Bowerman, M. 1982. Reorganizational processes in lexical and syntactic development. In E. Wanner and L. R. Gleitman (Eds.), *Language acquisition: The state of the art.* Cambridge: Cambridge University Press.

Braine, Martin D. S. 1971. The acquisition of language in infant and child. In Carroll E. Reed (Ed.), *The learning of language.* New York: National Council of Teachers of English.

Bruner, J. 1966. *Toward a theory of instruction.* Cambridge, MA: Harvard University Press.

Bruner, J., and Feldman, C. 1985. Lecture at the Psychology Department of the University of New Mexico, April 5.

Carroll, M., Dietrich, R., and Storch, G. 1982. *Learner language and control.* Frankfurt: Lang.

Cazden, C. B. 1975. Play with language and metalinguistic awareness: One dimension of language experience. In C. B. Winsor (Ed.), *Dimensions of language experience.* New York: Agathon Press.

Chafe, W. L. 1974. Language and consciousness. *Language,* 50, 1, 111–133.

Chafe, W. 1980. Some reasons for hesitating. In H. W. Dechert and M. Raupach (Eds.), *Temporal variables in speech: Studies in honour of Frieda Goldman-Eisler.* The Hague: Mouton.

Chesterfield, K. B. 1982. The role of children in adult second language learning. *Language Learning,* 32, 2, 305–329.

Chomsky, N. 1980. *Rules and representations.* New York: Columbia University Press.

Clark, E. V. 1982. Language change during language acquisition. In Michael E. Lamb and Ann L. Brown (Eds.), *Advances in developmental psychology,* Vol. 2. Hillsdale, NJ: Lawrence Erlbaum Associates.

Clark, H. H., and Clark, Eve. 1977. *Psychology and language.* New York: Harcourt Brace Jovanovich.

Corder, S. P. 1967. The significance of learners' errors. *IRAL,* 4, 161–169.

Day, R. R., Chenoweth, N. A., Chun, A. E., and Leppescu, S. 1977. Corrective feedback in native–nonnative discourse. *Language Learning,* 34, 2, 19–45.

Dulay, H. C., and Burt, M. K. 1972. Goofing: An indicator of children's second language learning strategies. *Language Learning,* 22, 235–252.

Ervin-Tripp, S. 1974. Is second language learning like the first? *TESOL Quarterly,* 8, 2, 111–127.

Fathman, A. 1980. Repetition and correction as an indication of speech planning and execution processes among second language learners. In H. W. Dechert and M. Raupach (Eds.), *Towards a cross-linguistic assessment of speech.* Frankfurt: Verlag Peter D. Lang.

Gallagher, T. M. 1977. Revision behaviors in the speech of normal children developing language. *Journal of Speech and Hearing Research,* 20, 303–318.

Garnica, O. K. 1977. Some prosodic and paralinguistic features of speech in young children. In C. E. Snow and C. A. Ferguson (Eds.), *Talking to children: Language input and acquisition.* Cambridge: Cambridge University Press.

Gaskill, W. H. 1980. Correction in native speaker–non-native speaker conversation. In D. Larsen-Freeman (Ed.), *Discourse analysis in second language research.* Rowley, MA: Newbury House.

Hakuta, K. 1974. Prefabricated patterns in the emergence of structure in second language acquisition. *Language Learning,* 24, 2, 287–297.

Hakuta, K. 1976. A case study of a Japanese child learning English as a second language. *Language Learning,* 26, 2, 321–351.

Hendrickson, J. M. 1980. Error correction in foreign language teaching: Recent theory, research and practice. In Kenneth Croft (Ed.), *Readings on English as a second language for teachers and teacher trainees.* Cambridge, MA: Winthrop.

Jefferson, Gail. 1972. Side sequences. In David N. Sudnow (Ed.), *Studies in social interaction.* New York: Free Press.

John-Steiner, V. P. 1985a. The road to competence in an alien land: A Vygotskian perspective on bilingualism. In James V. Wertsch (Ed.), *Culture, communication and cognition: Vygotskian perspectives.* Cambridge: Cambridge University Press.

John-Steiner, V. P. 1985b. *Notebooks of the mind: Explorations of thinking.* Albuquerque: University of New Mexico Press.

Kahmi, A. G., and Koenig, L. 1985. Metalinguistic awareness in normal and language-disordered children. *Language, Speech and Hearing Services in the Schools,* 16, 3, 199–210.

Kasper, Gabriele. 1985. Repair in foreign language teaching. *Studies in Second Language Acquisition,* June, 7, 2, 200–215.

Keenan, E. O. 1974. Conversational competence in children. *Journal of Child Language,* 1, 2, 163–183.

Klein, Wolfgang. 1986. *Second language acquisition.* Cambridge: Cambridge University Press.

Krashen, S. K. 1981. *Second language acquisition and second language learning.* Oxford: Pergamon Press.

Kucsaj, Stan A., II. 1983. *Crib speech and language play.* New York: Springer-Verlag.

Lado, R. 1964. *Language teaching.* New York: McGraw-Hill.

Langacker, R. W. 1987. *Foundations of cognitive grammar, Vol. 1.* Stanford: Stanford University Press.

Maclay, H., and Osgood, C. E. 1959. Hesitation phenomena in spontaneous English speech. *Word,* 15, 19–44.

MacWhinney, Brian. 1978. The acquisition of morphophonology. *Monographs of the Society of Research in Child Development,* no. 174, 43, 1–2.

McClaughlin, B. 1978. The monitor model: Some methodological considerations. *Language Learning,* 28, 2, 309–332.

Miller, Max. 1979. *The logic of language development in early childhood.* Berlin and New York: Springer-Verlag.

Nooteboom, S. G. 1980. Speaking and unspeaking: Detection and correction of phonological and lexical errors in spontaneous speech. In V. Fromkin (Ed.), *Errors in linguistic performance: Slips of the tongue, ear, pen and hand.* New York: Academic Press.

Oller, D. K. 1980. The emergence of the sound of speech in infancy. In G. H. Yeni-Komshian, J. F. Kavanagh, and C. A. Ferguson (Eds.), *Child phonology,* Vol. 1, *Production.* New York: Academic Press.

Savich, P. A. 1983. Improving communicative competence: the role of metapragmatic awareness. *Topics in Language Disorders,* December, 4, 1, 38–48.

Schegloff, E., Sacks, H., and Jefferson, G. 1977. The preference for self-correction in the organization of repair in conversation. *Language,* 53, 361–382.

Seliger, H. 1980. Utterance planning and correction behavior: Its function in the grammar construction process for second language learners. In H. W. Dechert and M. Raupach (Eds.), *Towards a cross-linguistic assessment of speech production.* Frankfurt: Verlag Peter D. Lang.

Shatz, M., and Gelman, R. 1973. The development of communication skills: Modifications in the speech of young children as a function of listener. *Monographs of the Society for Research in Child Development,* 38, 1–38.

Shonerd, Henry G. 1986. *Strategies of language use and language analysis in the development of oral fluency among literate adults learning ESL.* Ph.D. dissertation, University of New Mexico.

Slobin, D. I. 1979. *Psycholinguistics*. 2nd ed. Glenview, IL: Scott-Foresman.

Tarone, E. 1980. Communication strategies, foreigner talk and repair in interlanguage. *Language Learning,* 30, 2, 417–432.

Vygotsky, L. S. 1962. *Thought and language.* Cambridge, MA: MIT Press.

Vygotsky, L. S. 1978. *Mind in society.* Michael Cole, Vera John-Steiner, Sylvia Scribner, and Ellen Souberman (Eds.). Cambridge, MA: Harvard University Press.

Weir, R. H. 1966. Some questions on the child's learning of phonology. In F. Smith and G. A. Miller (Eds.), *The genesis of language: A psycholinguistic approach.* Cambridge, MA: MIT Press.

Wertsch, James V. 1985. *Vygotsky and the social formation of mind.* Cambridge, MA: Harvard University Press.

Wong-Fillmore, L. 1979. Individual differences in second language acquisition. In C. J. Fillmore, D. Kempler, and W. S.-Y. Wang (Eds.), *Individual differences in language ability and language behavior.* New York: Academic Press.

4 *Struggling for a voice: An interactionist view of language and literacy in Deaf education*

SHERMAN WILCOX

UNDERSTANDING DEAFNESS

We can understand deafness in two ways: as a disabling condition, or as a unique way of perceiving and understanding the world. According to the first view, the essential feature of deafness is the physical condition of not being able to hear. Deaf students are disabled compared to "normal" students – they are hearing-impaired. Under this pathological view, deafness is seen as a potential barrier to students' development into normal, hearing adults. The goal of education is to intervene as early as possible with effective techniques to remediate this condition. Parents, teachers, and other professionals must be prepared to identify social, cognitive, and language difficulties that might arise because of impaired hearing. Specialists are then brought in to treat these disorders.

According to the alternative, cultural view, deaf students are not impaired hearing students any more than Hispanics and blacks are "impaired" Anglos. They are instead people with a different but equally valid view of the world.[1] According to the cultural view, the goal of education is to facilitate deaf students' development into multilingual, multicultural, Deaf[2] adults. Teachers, parents, and others must be alert to situations in which obstacles, misunderstandings, and misinterpretations might arise because of differing views of the world. These become the topics for discussion and learning.

The cultural view does not deny that deaf students experience difficulties. The task is not merely, however, to identify and label these problems but to appropriately interpret their significance. In order to accomplish this, we must first understand the process by which knowledge is acquired.

On one hand, as John Dewey (1916:335) put it, knowledge seems to be

> the sum total of what is known, as that is handed down by books and learned men. It is something external, an accumulation of cognitions as

> one might store material commodities in a warehouse. Truth exists ready-made somewhere. Study is then the process by which an individual draws on what is in storage.

The acquisition of knowledge is understood as a passive, receptive affair. Dewey believed that this notion was mistaken and led to teaching that was lacking "in any fruitful connection with the ongoing experience of the students" (342).

Instead, Dewey (1916:344) believed that:

> Knowledge is not just something which we are now conscious of, but consists of the dispositions we consciously use in understanding what now happens. Knowledge as an act is bringing some of our dispositions to consciousness with a view to straightening out a perplexity, by conceiving the connection between ourselves and the world in which we live.

Knowledge is actively created by people in interaction with their world. "Education," Dewey wrote, "is not an affair of 'telling' and being told, but an active and constructive process" (38).

Toward a deaf epistemology

If we accept the pathological view of deafness and also believe that knowledge is external to a person, then it is natural to ascribe the source of deaf students' difficulties to their physical condition. Deafness clearly imposes a barrier between a mind waiting to be filled and the external source of knowledge. The result in education is domestication of the Deaf student. "Education for domestication is an act of transferring 'knowledge' " (Freire, 1985:102).

If we believe, however, that deafness can enable people to view the world differently and that knowledge is actively constructed, then we will expect that deaf people might arrive at a different understanding of the world than hearing people do. "If one changes the tools of thinking available to a child, his mind will have a radically different structure" (Vygotsky, 1978:126). The result in education is education for freedom. "Education for freedom is an act of knowledge and a process of transforming action. . . . Obviously learners are not seen as 'empty vessels,' mere recipients of an educator's words. Since they are not marginal beings who need to be 'restored to health' or 'saved,' learners are viewed as members of the large family of the oppressed. Answers for their situation do not reside in their learning to read alienating stories, but in their making history that will actualize their lives" (Freire, 1985:102–103).

The interaction of these two themes – the pathological versus the

Table 4.1. *Disabling and empowering pedagogies in Deaf education*

Issues	Disabling	Empowering
Where is the problem?	Inside the student Deafness	Interaction of dominant and dominated groups
View of Deafness	Pathological	Cultural
Educational practices	Effective methods Students as patients	Transformative action Students as agents
Student's relation to knowledge	Passive recipient Depositing	Active creator Creating and exploring
What should happen in the classroom?	"Fixing and filling"	"Dialoguing and exploring"
What is the role of the teacher?	Clinician/technician	Transformative intellectual
Effect on students	"The culture of silence," which leads from boredom through inaction to unconsciousness	"The struggle for voice," which leads from reflection through action to critical consciousness
What about reality?	Reality is given – student accommodates	Reality is opaque but can be illuminated – students transform reality

cultural view of deafness, and the conception of knowledge as actively created versus passively received – will form the basis for the exploration of language and literacy in the remainder of this chapter. As they impact on schooling, the two themes lead to two pedagogies of deaf education. The results of these two pedagogies – disabling and empowering – on the major issues in deaf education are shown in Table 4.1.

BREAKING THROUGH THE CULTURE OF SILENCE

In order to start our exploration we need a better understanding of the Deaf experience. One way to do this is to listen to the voices of Deaf writers. I start with an excerpt from a poem by the Deaf poet Ella Mae Lentz.

> We were simply talking
> in our language of signs
> When stormed by anthem driven soldiers
> Pitched a fever by the score of their regime.

They cuffed our hands, strangled us with iron reins.
"Follow me! Line up! Now sit!"
The captain, whip in hand,
Inflicts his sentence with this command:
Speak!
        "Sh–?"
Speak!
        "–i–?"
Speak!
        "–t?"

Damn your chains!
We'll pronounce our own deliverance
And articulate our message loud and clear.

And for the width of a breath
We grant each other asylum
Talking in our language of signs.

When they pound, pound, pound.
"Don't answer. Don't open. It's bad, don't."
The thunder rolls again.
"But I want to. I want to see.
Well maybe. I just want to see."
So step by step we succumb
Our silent agreement undone.
Come out of your dark and silent world
And join us in our bright and lovely world.

Look! Those whose ears work are signing!
Yes, but such queer speech they shape.
What waits out there?
To be fair we should see more.
Could it be they've rearranged the score?

And one by one
We go down the corridor of their sterile syntax,
Not knowing . . .[3]

Ella Lentz has clearly won the struggle to acquire a voice. Unfortunately, the majority of deaf students lose this battle. Deaf students are rarely in a position to write their own words, to construct their own sentences, or to author their own world. Deaf education most often inflicts sentences upon deaf students.

One form this infliction takes is defining Deaf students as those with an affliction. The Deaf world is not considered to be a separate but equal world. It is seen as a partial world, a "dark and silent world" of limited experience and false knowledge. Deaf education has made little effort to understand and incorporate the Deaf experience into the school curriculum. Instead, it has considered Deaf students as objects to be turned into images of the dominant, Hearing society. In such an atmosphere, the only reality for a Deaf student "is to be like, and to be like is to be like the oppressor" (Freire, 1970:33). The effect on students is what Freire has called the culture of silence, which leads from boredom to inaction to a state of unconsciousness. Bernard Bragg, one of the founders of the National Theater of the Deaf, has told of his experience in grade school.

> Spontaneous outbursts of laughter in the classroom were often stilled by scornful reprimands from our . . . teacher not so much because they were impolite or erupted at inappropriate times as because he said they sounded disgustedly unpleasant or irritating – even animalistic. Young and uncomprehending as we were, we were given long lectures on the importance of being consistently aware of what our laughter sounded like to those who could hear. . . . Compliments were often lavished upon those who came up with forced but perfectly controlled laughter – and glares were given to those who failed to laugh "properly" or didn't sound like a "normal" person. Some of us have since then forgotten how to laugh the way we had been taught. And there are two or three from our group who have chosen to laugh silently for the rest of their lives (reported in Gannon, 1981:355–356).

BITTER WORDS FROM THE SILENCED

Freire (1985:192) asks, "What happens when the dominated people finally realize their culture is not ugly as the dominators say? What happens when they see that their values are not so deplorable, that their presence in the world is not as despicable as the dominators say?"

For those willing to listen, another Deaf voice, Lex Lohman, has broken through the culture of silence in answer.

> Bitterweed[4]
> Beware the dark eyes on you in the street
> And the impersonal glances
> Of those who pass you by –
> They have no love for you, though you be their brother;
> Though you should cry for pity, there would be none.
>
> Growing in alien soil, the strange plant dies
> From rocks that press too hard, that block its root,
> Sent underground for nourishment in earth
> That holds no sustenance for such as come
> Unbidden through the tunnel of rain.
> Wherever you may go, the word shall pass

That you are stranger there, and you shall know
The unreceptive ground and fierce sunlight
In the press of hostile faces: they will shout
In a bitter voice the wisdom of the old,
Who have no will to live nor strength to die
And speak the blind prejudice of the stone,
And close the shadowy door.

Only the bitterweed can sink its root
Into the powerful rancor of the soil
And blossom forth in strong integrity,
Undaunted by a hatred. You must send
Your anger forth to rend the strangling rock
And with your strength build shelter from the sun;
And send them also
A word as bitter as theirs, as filled with hatred:
Then only will they let you pass in peace.

Deaf education is conceived as "education of the disabled" (see Cummins, 1986, for a similar account of minority education). The goal is to help the students overcome their pathology, their deafness – and join hearing people in our "bright and lovely world." Teachers are seen as clinicians who must cure their patients before they can fill their heads. What do Deaf people think of this approach? Guie C. Cooke provides a humorous but insightful glimpse in the poem, "Pests to Exterminate."

There is a pest we can't endure:
He is the one who has a cure,
And comes around with this or that.
Politely, we pass him his hat.
(If there's a cure we'd like to try
It's socking him upon the eye!)

There is a sense, though, in which Deaf education is truly education of the "disabled." The source of disablement is not within Deaf students. It is not the result of their deafness. Deaf students are rendered disabled by their interactions and struggles with the educational establishment. Myths – linguistic and cultural – are imposed on Deaf people's lives. Their struggle for consciousness is the struggle to illuminate these myths by questioning them, to shape their world by speaking their own words. The character Alice in Gilbert Eastman's play *Sign Me Alice II* says, "The hearing people do not treat me right. . . . Their ideas are false. They are hypocrites. They mold deaf people's lives. Not mine. Not my soul. I won't let them reshape me. . . . Deep in my body there is a flame."

Deaf education does not have to be disabling. There is an empowering alternative (Cummins, 1986). Bilingual, bicultural approaches to Deaf education can fan the flame by incorporating "knowledge and social relations that dignify one's own history, language, and cultural traditions" (Giroux & McLaren, 1986:221). Such an approach to Deaf education can empower students. It can enable them to question false ideas, to transform the world, and to mold their own reality.

In order to begin empowering Deaf students we must understand a simple fact: Deaf students do make sense of the world. If it looks like they do not, it is because our understanding has been mystified in two ways. Teachers often are not aware of what Deaf students are doing. Once we chose to ignore the Deaf experience, we lost our link to making sense of the sense the student makes. Teachers are also often unaware of what *they* are doing, especially in their language-mediated, finely tuned interactions (or, as is too often the case, out-of-tune interactions) with Deaf students.

MAKING SENSE OF THE WORLD

By listening to the voices of Deaf people we can also gain a glimpse of what the world looks like through their eyes. Ethnography is ideally suited to this task. The ethnographer assumes that the only way to discover how people understand the world is to accept the validity of their knowledge, "to grasp the native's point of view, his relation to life, to realize his vision of his world" (Malinowski, 1922:25). The point of this is not to "become Deaf" but to better understand what Deaf people are doing, how they make sense of their world. As Geertz (1983:58) explained:

> The trick is not to get yourself into some inner correspondence of spirit with your informants. Preferring, like the rest of us, to call their souls their own, they are not going to be altogether keen about such an effort anyway. The trick is to figure out what the devil they think they are up to.

In the sections that follow, I recount the experiences of a young Deaf child with the goal of discovering how she makes sense of her world (Wilcox & Corwin, 1990).

BoMee was born in Kang Won-do, Korea on March 26, 1984. She was born eight weeks prematurely, but apparently responded to sound as a neonate. Her lungs were not completely formed when she was born, and consequently BoMee developed chronic pneumonia. She was given streptomycin as an antibiotic during this time; the medication, as well as her premature birth and subsequent illness, are possible factors in the etiology of her deafness. BoMee is profoundly deaf with a 110 dB sensorineural loss in both ears.

BoMee was assigned to a foster family in Korea when her health returned at age 0;6. She stayed with this family until she was adopted. BoMee arrived in the United States on August 23, 1986, at age 2;5. She immediately started attending the local preschool for the deaf.

BoMee's adoptive mother, Joanne, teaches special education for the local school district, specializing in working with communicatively disordered, hearing children. Joanne has taken a few sign language classes and primarily signs English.

BoMee's adoptive father, Kim, is Korean and also was adopted by an American family. Kim holds a baccalaureate degree in sign language interpreting. He is a certified interpreter and employed as a classroom interpreter. Kim is fluent in American Sign Language (ASL) as well as signed English.[5] A hearing brother, Micah, was born when BoMee was 4;3.

BoMee's parents decided to provide as rich and healthy a learning environment for her as they could. They knew before she arrived that BoMee was deaf; because of their backgrounds – their knowledge of ASL and their acquaintance with deaf people and Deaf culture – they decided that they would make every effort to raise BoMee in a multilingual, multicultural environment. What does it mean to provide such an environment to a young deaf child? For Joanne and Kim, it meant the following.

BoMee is exposed to a wide variety of signing. Kim signs primarily ASL to her, and Joanne signs primarily English (typically using simultaneous communication, or speech and voice at the same time). When Micah was born, Joanne and Kim decided to sign to him also, not only so he would naturally acquire signed language but also so BoMee would see her parents signing to other children. Grandparents, aunts, uncles, nieces, and nephews all either took sign language classes or learned basic vocabulary from Kim and Joanne. One of BoMee's relatives was already a student in a local sign language interpreter program.

In addition, Kim and Joanne attempted to provide BoMee with a wide variety of models of Deaf adult signing. They routinely ask Deaf adults to visit and encourage them to talk with BoMee, tell her stories in ASL, and read to her by signing from children's storybooks. BoMee has many videotapes of Deaf adults telling stories in ASL.

BoMee is encouraged to recognize her multicultural background. She is exposed to Deaf culture and allowed to see this as a positive part of her cultural heritage. She also is exposed to and told about Hearing culture (the ways and values of hearing people).

BoMee's encounters with the Deaf community have been structured so that she can learn the ways and values of many different adults: educated, uneducated; professionals, workers; oral, signing; ASL users, signed English users, and so forth. Deaf adults are invited to take BoMee on short trips to parks or shopping, giving her the chance to talk with Deaf people and to see them interacting with hearing people.

Korean culture was an important part of BoMee's early life and remains so in her new home. Both parents are familiar with Korean culture and incorporate it into their home life (e.g., Korean holidays, food, customs, language, and stories).

Finding an identity

BoMee's multilingual, multicultural environment has had an influence on her social and cultural development in at least two ways. It has provided her with an environment in which clear and easy communication can take place with family, adults, and peers; and, it has provided her with a secure sense of who she is and where she fits into the world.

Young children clearly need free and easy communication to develop the finely tuned interactions so important to language development (Bruner, 1983). They also need it to resolve conflicts, to establish healthy relations with others, and to ease the ever-present fears of childhood (Meadow, 1968; Schlesinger & Meadow, 1972). This was especially true for BoMee.

Once, for example, BoMee was unable to go to sleep at her normal bedtime. She continued to jump out of bed, ask for water, horseplay, and do the various things a five-year-old does when avoiding sleep. Kim and Joanne were becoming rather irritated, so Joanne went into the bedroom to talk to BoMee. BoMee told her mother that at first she was postponing going to sleep because she had felt afraid of the dark. Later, she explained, as her parents became more and more irritated with her behavior, she found it even more difficult to relax and go to sleep because of the anxiety she felt trying to force herself to sleep quickly so that her parents would not become more upset.

Without the ability to communicate freely and easily with her parents, this situation would never have been discussed in such rich detail. Instead, BoMee's fear and anxiety would have gone unexpressed, and her parents would have had little or no insight into the cause of their daughter's behavior.

Deaf children often grow up not knowing what will become of them as adults. Since they rarely see deaf adults, they often assume that they will die or be killed before they become adults (Fletcher, 1987) or that they will suddenly become hearing since the world seems to be populated only by hearing adults.

BoMee had a similar misconception, related not to her deafness but to her adoption experience. One day, BoMee and Joanne were driving by the airport. BoMee asked, "That's the airport where I arrived, right?" Joanne said, "Yes, that's right." Then BoMee asked with a very gloomy expression, "Is it time yet?" Joanne, not understanding what BoMee was talking about, asked, "Is it time for what?" "To put Micah on a plane and send him away." BoMee remembered arriving at the airport on a plane when her Korean foster family sent her to the United States. She also knew, from stories that Kim had told her, that he too had arrived on a plane when he was adopted. BoMee was under the impression that parents must send their children away when they reach a certain age. This misconception was easy for Joanne to clear up. Clearly, though, the resolution of this misconception depended critically on fluent and easy communication between Joanne and BoMee.

Because of her exposure to a wide variety of Deaf adults, BoMee has a firm understanding of what it means to be a Deaf person; of the appropriate way to behave when associating with Deaf people; and of how she, as a Deaf person, can interact in a healthy and appropriate way with hearing people. An encounter with a hearing woman in a grocery store demonstrates her bicultural competence.

Hearing adults are easily attracted to BoMee; she is a cute, deaf girl who talks with her hands to her parents. Frequently, strangers want to pick her up, play with her, and give her candy or gum. Joanne has tried to teach BoMee that she doesn't have to let people touch her just because she is deaf, and that she should not accept candy or food from strangers. Once, in a grocery store, an older woman noticed BoMee and Joanne signing in the checkout line. "Oh, she's so cute," the woman bubbled. Then, she offered BoMee a stick of gum. Turning to Joanne, BoMee said, "Mom, tell her 'No thank you – I'm deaf, I'm not poor.' "

BoMee has a strong, positive sense of self-identity as a Deaf person. There is no indication that BoMee is confused or self-conscious about what it means to be deaf. On the contrary, she seems to think that being deaf is something that anyone could be proud of.

When he was 0;10, Micah had chronic ear infections and subsequently had to have grommets or "tubes" put in his ears. Before this surgery the mass of fluid in his ears had become adhesive, allowing little or no sound conduction to take place. Once, during this time, BoMee called to Micah, and he did not respond. Joanne explained to BoMee that because of the fluid in Micah's ears, he was temporarily "deaf." "Micah's deaf?" BoMee asked incredulously. She ran to Micah and signed, "Good boy, Micah!"

Watching others think

L. S. Vygotsky (1978:57) noted that thinking is a social activity. The roots of the higher cognitive functions begin in our interactions with others:

> All the higher functions originate as actual relations between human individuals. . . . Every function in the child's cultural development appears twice: first, on the social level, and later, on the individual level; first, between people (interpsychological), and then inside the child (intrapsychological).

In a natural language setting, children have access to all the language that is in their environment – not only talk that is directed to them, but also talk from adults to other children, from children to adults, from adults to adults, and the private or problem-solving speech of adults and children.

Educators often cite the need for access to this environmental talk as an advantage of total communication (Pahz & Pahz, 1978). In the experience of many Deaf people, however, total communication rarely lives up to its name (Bahan, 1989a). Parents and teachers frequently do not sign everything they say or sign it in such a way that it cannot be understood (Johnson, Liddell, & Erting, 1989; Marmor & Petitto, 1979). One type of speech that is especially likely not to be signed is speech that is clearly not intended for the deaf child: adult's problem-solving speech.

The Corwins sign all of their verbal interactions with BoMee. They also try, as much as possible, to sign their interactions with others when BoMee is present. About a month after BoMee arrived, they also decided to sign their private speech. Every time they were talking to themselves or verbally problem solving, they would sign "aloud." Some examples are: "Gee, what goes next in this recipe?" "I wonder where Kim is. Maybe he had a meeting." Every morning when they looked for their shoes they would sign to themselves, "Where are my shoes?" In about a week, they noticed BoMee in her bedroom signing to herself, "WHERE MY SHOES WHERE?" ("Where are my shoes?").[6]

This private speech continued to progress as BoMee's ASL developed. Soon, BoMee was signing her own private speech while she solved problems. Some examples are:

> (Trying a dress on a doll. The dress is just a little too small): HMMM. WRONG ME. THIS DRESS FIT HERE$_i$? THINK NOT. HMMM. FOR OTHER DOLL HERE$_j$. ("Hmmm. I'm wrong. Does this dress go on this doll? I don't think so. Hmmm. It goes on this other doll.")

> (Looking for her shoes): WHERE SHOES MINE WHERE? HMMM. THINK LEFT MY ROOM THERE MAYBE. NO, NO. KNOW, KNOW, KNOW. BEHIND CHAIR, KNOW. ("Where are my shoes? I think I might have left them in my room. No, no. I know, I know! They're behind the chair.")

The effects of her early exposure to interpersonal and problem-solving speech can be seen in BoMee's later problem solving. One day BoMee told a lie. Since she had started doing this fairly frequently, her parents decided this required a family meeting. They sat down with her and told her that they knew that she understood what she had done was inappropriate, and that they wanted to discuss with her what the consequences of this behavior should be. "Well," she signed in ASL, "in my opinion you have three choices. You can either take away my toys, give me a spanking (but I don't think that's a good idea), or give me time out. Of course, it's your decision." She was so sophisticated and serious in her manner that BoMee was given time out so that her parents could go into the other room and laugh.

Using the tools at hand

BoMee's early life was not conducive to language development. Her Korean foster family did not know any sign language, and BoMee received no special schooling or therapy. The extent of her language development during her first two and a half years was reflected in the "home signs" that her Korean foster family used with her. These were gestures that this particular family used to identify BoMee's basic needs (potty, food) and to name items (animal). She arrived in the United States with no more than five of these home signs.

Many professionals in deafness might assume that the use of home signs is a harmful practice since they are not part of a formal linguistic system. The Corwins feel, however, that this signed input served the useful function of making BoMee aware at an early age that motions of the hands can be meaningful. They allowed BoMee to learn that words (signs) can represent things in the environment. They served much the same function that phonetically consistent forms or protowords serve for young hearing children (see, e.g., Berko-Gleason, 1985:50, 72).

We have seen other deaf children who come to school without any idea of what words are for. This becomes an obstacle in their language and cognitive development. Perhaps because of the few home signs that BoMee had, she began to learn words for concrete objects fairly soon after she arrived in the United States. The first evening, for example, she learned DADDY, MILK, and KISS.

The family spends much time talking about language. They talk about ASL, English, signing, and speech; about why some deaf people speak and others don't; about when deaf people should use their voice and when they should not. At one point, BoMee was concerned with whether she would learn to speak like hearing people. At another, she wanted to know why all hearing people don't sign. All this talk has made BoMee quite aware of language in its signed, spoken, and written manifestations.

One indication of BoMee's metalinguistic awareness is her interactions with Micah. BoMee signs motherese to Micah. She works on expanding his language and its complexity in a natural way. One evening at the dinner table Micah signed "more." "You want more?" signed BoMee, emphasizing "more" to reinforce his attempt. "Here's some more. This is rice. You want more rice? That's right!"

BoMee's awareness of sociolinguistic variation extends to adults. She knows that some people talk and others sign; she also knows that some people sign and understand ASL while others only sign and understand English. As early as age 3;2 she recognized the variation in her home linguistic environment: she signed the game "This Little Piggy" in ASL to Kim and in English to Joanne.

BoMee seemed to develop an early affinity for ASL. We are not able to say why this occurred. Perhaps it is because ASL is a more "natural" language, one that is better suited to the visual modality (Supalla, 1986). It is also possible, however, that BoMee preferred ASL because of the early bond that developed between her and her father. Whatever the reason, BoMee went through a phase when, after her mother would sign something to her, she would turn to her father and say, "Say it the right way."

BoMee's awareness of sociolinguistic variation is now quite refined. Once, watching a videotape of the deaf actress and storyteller, Linda Bove, BoMee commented to Joanne, "That woman signs pretty good. I think she's deaf." The same tape featured a hearing woman who signed a story. "That other woman," BoMee continued, "doesn't sign that good. She's probably hearing."

BoMee is also quite adept at dealing with sociolinguistic variation at school. She knows that the teachers prefer English and speech to ASL.[7] She understands the idiosyncratic signs that deaf children with limited ASL or English vocabularies use, and she uses them with her deaf peers but not, for example, her parents. One day when Joanne was visiting the preschool, a young deaf boy ran up to BoMee and signed a word; it was clearly not an ASL or signed English word. Later, Joanne asked BoMee what the boy had said. "He said let's play the game where we chase each other around the playground," she explained. Puzzled, Joanne asked

BoMee how she knew that the boy had meant that. "Because that's what he said," was BoMee's matter-of-fact reply.

Deaf parents fingerspell to their deaf children. Hearing parents are often advised against this because it is assumed that deaf children who are unable to read and write lack the skills to make fingerspelling meaningful. ASL researchers have noted, however, that deaf children may make sense of fingerspelling not as a letter-handshape correspondence, but as a primary signed system (Akamatsu, 1985; Padden & LeMaster, 1985; Wilcox, 1992). In other words, deaf children may comprehend fingerspelling as a gestalt just as hearing children perceive speech as a Gestalt in the early stages of language development (Peters, 1983).

Joanne at first accepted the common wisdom that fingerspelling depends on spelling and was concerned when Kim began fingerspelling to BoMee. She had little formal language, much less any letter recognition. Within the first month, however, BoMee was fingerspelling her first word, B-U-S. It seems that BoMee understood this simply as a complex sign, because she could not read the word 'bus' or say which letters were in B-U-S. Later, though, when she started reading, these fingerspelled words quickly became sight vocabulary for BoMee.

BoMee has enjoyed stories and books since she was three years old, but the actual process of reading as it pertains to phonological symbols was often perplexing to her. Initially, she started reading words in context. "Don't Walk," "Open," "McDonald's," and "No Parking Any Time" were some of her favorites. Her family also helped her to read environmental print in the home such as "milk" and "cat food." Words for which she had some visual association seemed to come easily, but she still was not able to read even the shortest of stories.

One of the most remarkable events in BoMee's language development was her discovery of how to use the phonology of ASL to solve the problems she faced learning to read.

By about the age of five, BoMee was reading simple books. As Joanne would read to her and BoMee would pick out the words she knew, Joanne noticed that BoMee had difficulty remembering some words: 'that,' 'not,' and 'and' gave her particular problems.

Joanne tried using Dolch word cards with BoMee with minimal success. Just as Joanne began looking for other ideas, she noticed that BoMee was reading these words on her own.

In order to understand BoMee's solution, it is necessary to have a basic understanding of the phonology of ASL.[8] Signed words, like spoken words, are composed of minimal contrasting units – phonemes. As is true for spoken languages, ASL phonemes are composed of contrasting units called distinctive features.

Just as a hearing child first reads out loud, BoMee "signs out loud"

Figure 4.1.

when she reads. One day, Joanne was watching BoMee read and noticed that when she came to the word 'that' BoMee made the Y handshape (a phoneme of the ASL word THAT) with her right hand. With her left hand, BoMee moved the fingerspelled letter T from her thumb to her pinky finger. When Joanne asked what this meant, BoMee replied, "See, it looks like 'that.' T and T, see?" (see Figure 4.1).

The feature [+spread] is a feature of the Y handshape and other handshapes such as horn-Y (as in the sign MOCK). In the Y handshape, [+spread] is realized as the extension of the thumb and pinky finger. What BoMee had done was establish a relationship between this feature of the Y phoneme and the fact that in English orthography 'that' is spelled with a 't' at the beginning and the end. The two extended digits of the Y phoneme represented for BoMee the English grapheme 't' at the beginnning and end of 'that.' She had created a three-way link between the visual phonetics of signed language (the Y phoneme and its feature [+spread]), fingerspelling (the handshape T), and English orthography.

BoMee also showed Joanne the word NOT. NOT is produced with an open-A handshape. The open-A handshape shares the feature [+spread] with Y. It contrasts with the regular A handshape used in fingerspelling and in signs such as WITH.[9] BoMee demonstrated that the closed fingers of NOT can represent the English graphemes 'n' and 'o' and the thumb can represent 't.' Again, for BoMee the extended thumb represented the English grapheme 't.'

Finally, BoMee showed her mother how she remembered the English word 'and.' She explained, "Because it looks like 'and.' See the A, N, and D?" BoMee demonstrated how the shape of the hand in forming the

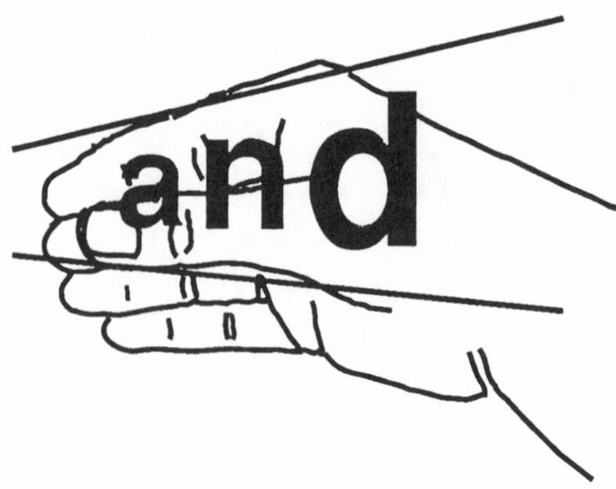

Figure 4.2.

word AND resembles the shape of the word 'and' in print by fingerspelling A, N, and D starting at the tips of the handshape and extending to the base of the palm (see Figure 4.2). Indeed, in print, the letters 'a,' 'n,' and 'd' increase from left to right, just as does the final handshape (flat-O) in the ASL word AND.

Eventually these words became sight words for BoMee and she discontinued using the phonological cues she had created for herself. She has not, however, discontinued using this strategy with new words. She had found a way to use her knowledge of the phonology of her preferred mode of communication, signing, to facilitate acquisition of her second language, written English.

Queer speech

The previous example showed how BoMee used the structure of signed language to facilitate her acquisition of English. Sometimes, however, what BoMee was taught about signed and spoken languages impeded her acquisition of English.

BoMee was introduced to the present progressive signed English suffix, -ING, in school. BoMee was already producing present progressive in ASL (verb plus head nod), as well as other verbal tense and aspect forms. She knew that in ASL, the tense marker is often placed at the beginning of a sentence: FINISH ME EAT ME, 'I ate.' It was no surprise to her parents when BoMee started producing sentences like -ING ME EAT ME, "I am eating."

It makes perfect sense. It follows the grammar of ASL. It expresses a concept that was obviously in BoMee's zone of proximal development. More important to her teachers, however, was the fact that BoMee used -ING as a free morpheme, a word. It was, in this sense, ungrammatical English, a language problem to be explained.

Teachers inflict the command to "Speak" but they also accept that students should sign. "Those whose ears work" are signing in Deaf education more and more. As Ella Lentz noticed, however, it is often "queer speech they shape."

This queer speech is called Manually Coded English (MCE). In an earlier section I suggested that teachers are often not aware of what they are doing. A critical gap in their awareness is their own language behavior, their signing. Teachers have very little idea about what these coded English systems that they rely on really are, how they are constructed, and what they accomplish.

These systems are inventions, engineered languages designed to represent natural language from one modality in another modality – spoken English becomes signed English (Wilcox & Wilcox, 1991). Thus, they are analogous to writing systems, which likewise represent spoken language in another modality. Like writing systems, MCE must answer two design questions: what will be represented (sounds, syllables, words, etc.), and where will the symbols (written marks, signed gestures) be obtained (by borrowing from existing systems or by invention).

For the example at hand, the solution to these two design questions is that words and affixes will be signed – as opposed, for example, to the two component sounds in -ING. The sign for EAT was borrowed (from ASL) and the sign for -ING was invented.

There is more to the story of -ING. The present progressive inflection in English is unstressed: '*eat*-ing' not 'eat-*ing*.' Notice that for the MCE solution the situation is reversed. The visual stress in the signed word EAT+ING does not correspond to the acoustic stress of the spoken word 'eat-ing.' When the -ING marker is added to a word in MCE, the stress shifts from the root word to the suffix: EAT-*ING*.

Hearing teachers are little aware of this subtle but critical difference. As hearing people, they rely more on the acoustic stress than the visual stress. We know that stress and intonation play an important role in young hearing children's language acquisition (Cruttendon, 1986; Peters, 1983). Should we expect otherwise for Deaf children? The only difference is that they are surely more attuned to the visual stress. From there, they take the ball and run, right into -ING ME EAT ME.

The teachers at BoMee's school took note of this language behavior. Their conclusion was that Deaf children always have difficulty with English present progressive. It is, they declared, a particular characteristic of the abnormal language development of deaf children.

Legitimizing the disability: Whose world is it?

Others also took note of the situation. About this time, Joanne took BoMee to be evaluated at the local school district. The diagnostician asked whether BoMee was using present progressive. Joanne replied "Yes." "You mean BoMee consistently signs -ING?" the diagnostician asked. Joanne told her that BoMee was not yet consistently using present progressive in English, but was using it quite regularly and properly in ASL. The diagnostician's assessment, duly entered into BoMee's permanent record: "Child has not acquired present progressive." Thus, BoMee was transformed from a creative language user to a disabled child with a developmental language disorder.

Deaf students do not come to school as passive, empty containers waiting to be fixed and filled. They are, like their hearing peers, active, critical learners. In spite of diagnostician's assessments to the contrary, lack of hearing leads to neither lack of knowledge nor inability to learn. It may, as we have seen, lead to different knowledge. This different knowledge may then lead the Deaf student, using her critical, constructive thinking, to arrive at a different understanding – of English grammar, for instance – from her hearing peers or from the hearing teacher. Finally, this different learning experience most certainly will be differently valued. But this is clearly a socially, culturally, and politically constructed accomplishment. It is, as Foucault (1980) understood, a matter of power, of determining who is charged with saying what counts as true knowledge.

It seems that BoMee has the world at her fingertips. But whose world is it (Bahan, 1989b)? From the hearing perspective – especially those such as teachers and diagnosticians who are in positions of authority to say what counts as right and wrong, normal and abnormal – there is but one reality. It is a hearing world, and deaf children must learn to live in it. In fact, the world is neither hearing nor deaf. It is as we create it, given our own unique perceptions, dispositions, and active, constructive minds. "The effective environment of any organism is never merely the objective situation in which he finds himself, but rather the product of an interaction between his unique organismic characteristics and whatever opportunities for experience his objective surroundings may provide" (John-Steiner & Souberman, 1978:125).

Straightening out perplexities

"Children solve practical tasks with the help of their speech, as well as their eyes and their hands" (Vygotsky, 1978:26). This is profoundly true for BoMee, especially when we consider that for her, speech is signed language. With regard to the practical task of reading, BoMee's solution is informative for at least three reasons.

First, it was BoMee's invention, not an outsider's intervention. Using the tools at hand, Deaf children can devise effective solutions to meaningful problems. For Deaf as well as hearing students, learning need not be an affair of being told but an active, constructive process.

Second, the strategy depended on BoMee's knowledge of ASL. The case is often made that ASL is detrimental, or at least of no help, to the acquisition of English by deaf children. This clearly was not true for BoMee. Her knowledge of ASL was critical to her literacy development.

Finally, it was a visual strategy. The relation between speech and writing, phoneme and grapheme, depends on sound. As hearing people, we may not think it is possible to use the structure of a language unrelated to English – a language in which phonemes are produced with the hands and perceived with the eyes – to establish a phoneme–grapheme connection. Indeed, there is no historical connection between ASL handshape phonemes such as Y, open-A, and flat-O and English graphemes. To BoMee, however, this was a natural way to bring her unique "dispositions to consciousness with a view to straightening out a perplexity" (Dewey, 1916:334). It was a stunning glimpse at a tiny spark of critical consciousness.[10]

Empowering teachers and students

The story of -ING suggests that teachers frequently are not critically aware of the impact of what they are doing, especially in their language-mediated interactions with Deaf students. For this, we must lay responsibility with teacher education and teacher accreditation. It is not only Deaf students who "go down the corridor . . . not knowing." Educators, whether they are hearing or deaf, must also struggle against the mystifications that are provided to them through the official curriculum, history, and their own unexamined beliefs. Just as education has disempowered Deaf students, teacher training programs continue to withhold knowledge from future teachers that would enable them to engage in active, critical dialogue with their Deaf students. Those few who are capable of doing this have become what Giroux and McLaren (1986:217; see also Giroux, 1988) call transformative intellectuals, "capable of articulating emancipatory possibilities and working towards their realization. [They] . . . treat students as critical agents, question how knowledge is produced and distributed, utilize dialogue, and make knowledge meaningful, critical, and ultimately emancipatory."

What can be done about this situation? How can Deaf education empower Deaf students? How can teacher training programs turn out Deaf educators who are capable of acting as transformative intellectuals?

First, we must reexamine the role of the Deaf community in Deaf education. As Elsasser and John-Steiner (1977:356) have remarked, "A student's sense of personal power and control emerges largely as a result of the increasing movement of his or her social group towards self-determination. In the absence of such movement educational intervention is most often futile." The Deaf community, the Deaf experience, Deaf culture, and Deaf history must become a part of the official school curriculum.

Second, we must examine and restructure teacher training programs and accreditation requirements. This movement is already underway in a limited way. Harlan Lane (1988) has pointed the way in his recommendations to the Commission on Education of the Deaf on restructuring Deaf education teacher preparation. Until the macrostructure of Deaf education requires it, though, we will continue to produce teachers of the Deaf who know more about vocal-fold physiology than they do about Deaf culture or ASL.

Third, we must all – Deaf and hearing, teacher and student – become critically aware of the language situation in Deaf education. Vygotsky (1978) tells us that language is a tool for thought. It is time to examine our tools – all of them: ASL, MCE, spoken English, written English, and whatever languages are being used in the Deaf student's home and community.

Bakhtin (1981:295–296) describes the importance to illiterate Russian peasants of becoming critically aware of their own complex language situation; the insight is equally applicable to Deaf students.

> Thus an illiterate peasant, miles away from any urban center, naively immersed in an unmoving and for him unshakable everyday world, nevertheless lived in several language systems: he prayed to God in one language (Church Slavonic), sang songs in another, spoke to his family in a third, and, when he began to dictate petitions to the local authorities through a scribe, he tried speaking yet a fourth language (the official-literate language, "paper" language). All these are different languages. . . . But these languages were not dialogically coordinated in the linguistic consciousness of the peasant; he passed from one to the other without thinking, automatically: each was indisputably in its own place, and the place of each was indisputable. He was not yet able to regard one language (and the verbal world corresponding to it) through the eyes of another language (that is, the language of everyday life and the everyday world with the language of prayer or song, or vice versa). As soon as a critical interanimation of languages began to occur in the consciousness of our peasant, as soon as it became clear that these were

> not only various different languages but even internally variegated languages, that the ideological systems and approaches to the world that were indissolubly connected with these languages contradicted each other and in no way could live in peace and quiet with one another – then the inviolability and predetermined quality of these languages came to an end, and the necessity of actively choosing one's orientation among them began.

Approaches to Deaf education which impose others' solutions, concepts, and truths on the student – not only old-fashioned, fix-and-fill, "banking concept" (Freire, 1970) approaches but also some bilingual/bicultural programs – are doomed to failure. The path to critical consciousness does not begin from without, but from within the Deaf student. The first step is true dialogue between teachers and students, which allows students to act not as patients but as agents in the discovery and transformation of their inner world of knowledge and outer world of sociocultural relations.

> The educator's role is to propose problems about the codified existential situations in order to help learners arrive at a more and more critical view of their reality. . . . He can never be a mere memorizer, but a person constantly readjusting his knowledge who calls forth knowledge from his students. For him, education is a pedagogy of knowing. The educator whose approach is mere memorization is antidialogical; his act of transmitting knowledge is inalterable. For the educator who experiences the act of knowing together with his students, in contrast, dialogue is the sign of the act of knowing. (Freire, 1985:55)

Discourses of power and truth

The interaction of language and culture in Deaf education is shown in Figure 4.3. The critical factors of language and culture are considered as they impact the Deaf student on a macro level (e.g., in pedagogy and ideology; teacher talk about Deaf students' language; culturally transmitted myths about deafness) and on a micro level (students' and teachers' bilingual/bimodal competence; the daily interactions between Deaf students, teachers, parents, and others and hearing teachers, administrators, diagnosticians, and others).

Interactions of language and culture on the macrolevel are called "discourses of power and truth." They include scenarios such as described here in which BoMee was labeled a language-disordered child by a diagnostician charged with "saying what counts as true knowledge." Interactions at the microlevel are called "interpersonal interactions." Many of them contribute not only to the moment-to-moment disablement of Deaf students but also to the creation of the "historical-cultural

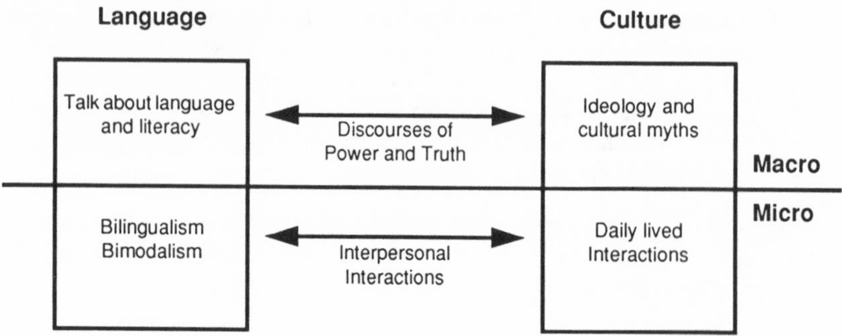

Figure 4.3.

configuration we have called the culture of silence" (Freire, 1985:72). Giroux (1981) elaborates:

> Culture . . . [is] defined not simply as experiences functioning within the context of historical structures and social formations, but as "lived antagonistic relations" situated within a complex of socio-political institutions and social forms that limit as well as enable human action. . . . It is a complex realm of antagonistic experiences mediated by power and struggle. . . . To rethink the concept of culture is thus to attempt to articulate not only the experiences and practices that are distinctive to a specific group or class, but also to link those experiences to the power exercised by the dominant class.

Clearly, ASL must play a much more active role in Deaf education. Students should be receiving formal classroom instruction not only *in* ASL but also *about* ASL. Students and teachers together must explore and discuss the languages of the community. This is occurring in only a limited way in very few experimental or proposed programs (Humphries, Coye, & Martin, 1989; Johnson et al., 1989; Strong, 1988).

That such an approach empowers disenfranchised communities is clear (Elsasser & Irvine, 1985; Freire, 1985; Shor & Freire, 1987). The reports of the people themselves are remarkably univocal. A Nicaraguan writer reports, "I realized that in order to study what I wanted I had to begin by studying my own language. I had to begin all over again. It was hard, but little by little I began with the Spanish and as I went along I discovered that it's a beautiful thing to study one's own language; I was beginning to understand so many things" (Randall, 1984:187). Mervin Garretson, a Deaf writer, expresses the same sentiment: "To know, once and for all, that our 'primitive' and 'ideographic' gestures are really a formal language on a par with all other languages of the world is a step towards pride and liberation" (in Gannon, 1984:367). Barbara Kannapell, a Deaf sociolinguist, says, "Once I learned that ASL is my native language, I developed a strong sense of identity as a Deaf person and a more positive self-image" (ibid.:372). A speaker of Virgin Island Creole pleads that, "as we strive to identify with the rich history of our enslaved foreparents, as we endeavor to become more patriotic, let us learn to cherish everything that belongs to us; this includes our Creoles. They are works of art created by our ancestors in bondage and, as such, are precious gifts to be treasured by all of us here in the English-speaking West Indies" (Richardson, 1985). In his 1913 film *Preservation of the Sign Language* George Veditz, a Deaf teacher and president of the National Association of the Deaf, offered the same plea.

> "A new race of Pharaohs that knew not Joseph" are taking over the land and many of our American schools. They do not understand signs, for they cannot sign. They proclaim that signs are worthless and of no help to the Deaf. Enemies of the sign language, they are enemies of the true welfare of the Deaf. . . . As long as we have Deaf people on earth, we will have signs. . . . It is my hope that we all will love and guard our beautiful sign language as the noblest gift God has given to Deaf people. (in Padden & Humphries, 1988:36)

Critical bilingual/bicultural education – in ASL and English, by Deaf and hearing teachers – must become the accepted method in Deaf education. Only in this way will educators cease to inflict sentences and instead enable Deaf students to discover and pronounce their own.

WRITING OUR OWN WORDS

Such an approach to education not only empowers language users, it also empowers and strengthens the suppressed language. Freire (1985:185) recognized this when he wrote, "A language can only develop when it is practiced in all domains and given opportunity to do so." In this regard, it is important to realize the effect that a writing system can have on a language. In the specific instance of Virgin Island Creole, Carrington (1981) has noted that "The . . . opportunity for the use of creole by the development of a writing system breaks the barrier that has shut out from information transfer, from 'language-hood' and from confidence, large numbers of people over several hundred years in this society, has shut them out from full communication within their society. . . . There is a need, a very deep need, for communication tools that allow people to share in the development of their society."

It is important not to underestimate the importance of writing to the integrity of languages and their users. Literacy is a double-edged sword (Coulmas, 1989:5):

> To those who cannot read and write, a book or any other written document manifestly demonstrates their own ignorance and powerlessness; of which fact the educated few can and, of course, do take advantage. One of the crucial consequences of the invention of writing becomes apparent here: it is a powerful instrument of social control.

Writing also "greatly enlarges the range of communication and, consequently, power" (ibid.:7). Some of the functions that writing affords in addition to those provided by spoken or signed language are (Coulmas, 1989):

1. *Mnemonic function:* writing can aid in preserving individuals' memory (e.g., lists) and a peoples' memory. "History becomes possible thanks to the mnemonic function of writing, as well as the accumulation of knowledge" (ibid.:12). Although they probably overstate the case when they claim that "prehistory is the study of peoples without writing, whereas history is the study of people who possess written texts" (Stuart & Houston, 1989:82), there is a sense in which literacy allows people to create their own histories, to "transform the world with their work and create their own world. This world, created by the transformation of another world they did not create and that now restrains them, is the cultured world that stretches out into the world of history" (Freire, 1985:14–15).
2. *Distancing function:* "writing is a distancing medium not only with respect to sender and receiver, but also as regards the sender and the message" (ibid.).
3. *Reifying function:* "The spoken word is ephemeral and spontaneous in its very essence. In writing, on the other hand, words become stable and tangible. As objects in their own right they become, moreover, depersonalized" (ibid.). In spoken and signed utterances the focus is on what the person means. In written works, the focus is more likely to be on what the words mean, independent of the author. This opens the avenue for users of the language to record and analyze it in ways otherwise quite difficult. "Writing provides the means of analyzing language because it turns language into an object" (ibid.:15).
4. *Social control function:* by committing words to writing we gain the potential for regulating social conduct by means of laws, policies, regulations, wills, and so forth. It is no accident that the words author and authority are etymologically related.
5. *Interactional function:* We usually think of speech or sign as the more interactional medium of communication. Writing, however, affords the possibility of a different type of interaction such as "instruction manuals, recipes, style sheets, etc., directed at an unspecified readership" (ibid.:14). In another sense writing is interactional because it allows the reader to review previous words and paragraphs. Videotapes of signed language and audiotapes of spoken language are only marginally interactive in this way.

6. *Aesthetic function:* While the notion of literature does not depend on writing (Frishberg, 1988), writing certainly makes possible new genres such as novels and certain types of poetry. It would be hard to imagine, for example, the poetry of E. E. Cummings without the written word and its layout on a page. An entire area of specialization, including typography and the graphic arts, has developed around the specialized aesthetic function that writing affords.

The question of writing signed languages, particularly ASL, has been a thorny one for many years. Many people, both advocates and opponents of the Deaf way, have noted the powerful potential of writing ASL. A. G. Bell (1883:217), for instance, believed that certain conditions were leading toward the production of a "defective race of human beings." One condition was the growth of a Deaf community. A second was the spread of American Sign Language, "a different language from that of the people at large . . . a language as different from English as French or German or Russian." Bell foresaw the power of writing ASL: "Another method of consolidating the deaf and dumb into a distinct class in the community would be to reduce the sign-language to writing, so that the deaf-mutes would have a common literature from the rest of the world" (Bell, 1883:219). Bell's evaluation of such a move was decidedly negative, even racist (Bahan, 1989c). My own belief is that Bell got his observation right but his conclusion wrong. Written ASL does hold the potential for empowering Deaf people, and this is precisely what we need. Why should the only avenue to literacy for Deaf people be through English?

The case is often made that for ASL, videotape is the equivalent of writing. Videotape certainly provides some of the functions of writing, such as the distancing and aesthetic functions. It allows people to preserve their words and to distribute some types of literature. Preserving spoken words on audiotape also serves many useful purposes, but it is not writing.

Those opposed to writing ASL counter that writing does not preserve the eloquence of ASL as it is signed by a Deaf person. This is true, but is hardly an indictment of writing ASL. Written English likewise does not preserve the eloquence of performance. Anyone who has ever heard Dylan Thomas perform his poem, "And Death Shall Have No Dominion," and compared that with the written words on the page of a book will attest to this fact. This is not a fault of writing, it is a potential that authors and performers of English literature utilize to their advantage. ASL authors and performers, it seems to me, should be afforded the same opportunities.

Consider a simple example. Literacy is not just something taught in classroom lessons. Children often incorporate written English into their games and personal lives. Why do we insist on denying Deaf children these experiences with their own language? Why must literacy for the Deaf students mean English literacy?

CHOOSING OUR OWN LANGUAGE

> The word in language is half someone else's. It becomes "one's own" only when the speaker populates it with his own intentions, his own accent, when he appropriates the word, adapting it to his own semantic and expression intention. Prior to this moment of appropriation, the word does not exist in a neutral and impersonal language (it is not, after all, out of a dictionary that the speaker gets his words!), but rather it exists in other people's mouths, in other people's contexts, serving other people's intentions: it is from there that one must take the word, and make it one's own. . . . Consciousness finds itself inevitably facing the necessity of having to choose a language. (Bakhtin, 1981:293–294, 295)

The choice is clear – for many Deaf people, the language of consciousness is ASL. But it is also impossible to overestimate the importance of writing our own words. Here too, the lesson is clear – literacy is not the problem, it is the solution. It is time for those concerned with Deaf students' struggles to find a voice to realize the importance of ASL literacy. ASL is a beautiful language. It captures and expresses the pride, the history, and the identity of Deaf people. But it is still an unwritten language. This does not diminish ASL as a language. It is an untapped potential. We need an accepted ASL writing system, and we need to explore its use in Deaf education.[11]

The movement to empower Deaf students to "pronounce their own deliverance and articulate their message loud and clear" is long overdue in Deaf education. We can only hope that one day, Deaf writers will also be able to spell out the terms of their liberation and write their stories in their own language. Maybe then the hearing, literate, educational establishment will begin to listen and see.

NOTES

1. See Baker & Cokely (1980), Padden & Humphries (1988), Woodward (1989), Wilcox (1989a, 1989b), and Wilcox & Wilcox (1991) for further discussion of the pathological and cultural views of deafness.
2. Following the commonly accepted convention proposed by Woodward (1972), I use the lowercase *deaf* to refer to the condition of not being able to hear and uppercase *Deaf* to refer to a group of people who share the same language, ASL, and culture.
3. This poem was originally conceived in American Sign Language; the text presented here is a transcription by the author of an English translation from

the videotape, "American Culture: The Deaf Perspective (Literature)," produced by Susan D. Rutherford for the San Francisco Public Library, 1984.

4. All poems with the exception of Lentz (see n. 3) appear in Gannon (1981).
5. See Baker & Cokely (1980) and Wilcox & Wilcox (1991) for further discussion of signed English and ASL.
6. ASL words are glossed as uppercase English words; fingerspelled letters are given in all uppercase with the letters in fingerspelled words separated by hyphens; English words and letters are given in single quotes; and English translations are given in double quotes.
7. The implications of BoMee's sociolinguistic competence are profound. Not only does BoMee recognize others' preferred language and level of competence; she also adjusts her language accordingly. Hearing teachers and diagnosticians frequently are not proficient signers. BoMee recognizes this and adapts. This presents a dilemma: how is it possible for these professionals to know whether they are observing BoMee's language proficiency or a reflection of their own?
8. See Liddell (1984), Liddell & Johnson (1989), Padden & Perlmutter (1987), and Wilbur (1987) for further discussion of ASL phonology.
9. As a matter of fact, substituting the A for the open-A handshape (e.g., in the ASL classifier for upright objects) is a mispronunciation common among adult, hearing signers.
10. This confirms the reports of Deaf persons that deafness has little to do with their sense of identity; a more appropriate description, according to Bahan (1989d), would be "seeing persons." See also Mather (1989) for an ethnographic description of how one teacher – a Deaf, native signer of ASL – used visually oriented strategies to help deaf children acquire communicative competence.
11. A proposal for such an ASL orthography is given in McIntire et al. (1987).

REFERENCES

Akamatsu, C. T. 1985. "Fingerspelling formulae: A word is more or less than the sum of its letters." In W. Stokoe & V. Volterra (eds.), *SLR '83: Sign Language Research*. Silver Spring, MD: Linstok Press.

Bahan, B. 1989a. "Total communication: A total farce." In S. Wilcox (ed.), *American Deaf culture*. Silver Spring, MD: Linstok Press.

Bahan, B. 1989b. "It's our world too!" In S. Wilcox (ed.), *American Deaf culture*. Silver Spring, MD: Linstok Press.

Bahan, B. 1989c. "What if . . . Alexander Graham Bell had gotten his way?" In S. Wilcox (ed.), *American Deaf culture*. Silver Spring, MD: Linstok Press.

Bahan, B. 1989d. "Notes from a 'seeing' person." In S. Wilcox (ed.), *American Deaf culture*. Silver Spring, MD: Linstok Press.

Baker, C., & D. Cokely. 1980. *American Sign Language: A teacher's resource text on grammar and culture*. Silver Spring, MD: T. J. Publishers.

Bakhtin, M. M. 1981. *The dialogic imagination*. (Edited by M. Holquist, translated by C. Emerson & M. Holquist.) Austin: University of Texas Press.

Bell, A. G. 1883. *Upon the formation of a deaf variety of the human race.* New Haven, CT: National Academy of Sciences.

Berko-Gleason, J. 1985. *The development of language.* Columbus, Ohio: Charles E. Merrill.

Bruner, J. 1983. *Child's talk: Learning to use language.* New York: W. W. Norton.

Carrington, L. D. 1981. A seminar on orthography for St. Lucian Creole, January 29–31. In *Language and development: The St. Lucian context.* Castries, St. Lucia: Folk Research Centre and Caribbean Research Centre.

Coulmas, F. 1989. *The writing systems of the world.* Oxford: Basil Blackwell.

Cruttendon, A. 1986. *Intonation.* Cambridge: Cambridge University Press.

Cummins, J. 1986. Empowering minority students: A framework for intervention. *Harvard Education Review, 56(1),* 18–36.

Dewey, J. 1916. *Democracy and education.* New York: Macmillan. (1966 Free Press paperback edition)

Eastman, G. 1983. *Sign me Alice II.* Washington, DC: Gallaudet College Press.

Elsasser, N., & P. Irvine. 1985. English and Creole: The dialectics of choice in a college writing program. *Harvard Educational Review, 55*(4), 399–415.

Elsasser, N., & V. John-Steiner. 1977. An interactionist approach to advancing literacy. *Harvard Educational Review, 47*(3), 355–369.

Fletcher, L. 1987. *Ben's story: A deaf child's right to sign.* Washington, DC: Gallaudet University Press.

Foucault, M. 1980. *Power/knowledge: Selected interviews and other writings, 1972–1977.* New York: Pantheon.

Freire, P. 1970. *Pedagogy of the oppressed.* New York: Seabury Press.

Freire, P. 1985. *The politics of education.* Granby, MA: Bergin & Garvey.

Frishberg, N. 1988. Signers of tales: The case for literary status of an unwritten language. *Sign Language Studies, 59,* 149–169.

Gannon, J. R. 1981. *Deaf heritage: A narrative history of Deaf America.* Silver Spring, MD: National Association of the Deaf.

Geertz, C. 1983. "From the native's point of view: On the nature of anthropological understanding." In C. Geertz, *Local knowledge.* New York: Basic Books.

Giroux, H. A. 1981. *Ideology, culture, and the process of schooling.* Philadelphia: Temple University Press.

Giroux, H. A. 1988. *Teachers as intellectuals: Towards a critical pedagogy of learning.* Granby, MA: Bergin & Garvey.

Giroux, H. A., & P. McLaren. 1986. Teacher education and the politics of engagement: The case for democratic schooling. *Harvard Educational Review, 56*(3), 213–238.

Humphries, T., T. Coye, & B. Martin. 1989. A bilingual, bicultural approach to teaching English, or How two hearies and a deafie got together to teach English. In S. Wilcox (ed.), *American Deaf culture.* Silver Spring, MD: Linstok Press.

John-Steiner, V., & E. Souberman. 1978. Afterward to L. S. Vygotsky, *Mind in society: The development of higher psychological processes.* Cambridge, MA: Harvard University Press.

Johnson, R. E., S. K. Liddell, & C. J. Erting. 1989. *Unlocking the curriculum: Principles for achieving access in deaf education.* Gallaudet Research Institute Working Paper 89-3. Washington, DC: Gallaudet University.

Lane, H. 1988. Educating the American Sign Language speaking minority in the United States. *Sign Language Studies, 59,* 221–230.

Liddell, S. K. 1984. THINK and BELIEVE: Sequentiality in American Sign Language signs. *Language, 60,* 372–399.

Liddell, S. K., & R. E. Johnson. 1989. American Sign Language: The phonological base. *Sign Language Studies, 64,* 195–277.

Malinowski, B. 1922. *Argonauts of the Western Pacific.* London: Routledge.

Marmor, G., & L. Petitto. 1979. Simultaneous communication in the classroom: How well is English grammar represented? *Sign Language Studies, 23,* 99–136.

Mather, S. A. 1989. "Visually oriented teaching strategies with deaf preschool children." In C. Lucas (ed.), *The sociolinguistics of the Deaf community.* San Diego, CA: Academic Press.

McIntire, M., D. Newkirk, S. Hutchins, & H. Poizner. 1987. Hands and faces: A preliminary inventory for written ASL. *Sign Language Studies, 56,* 197–241.

Meadow, K. 1968. Early manual communication in relation to the deaf child's intellectual, social, and communicative functioning. *American Annals of the Deaf, 113,* 29–41.

Padden, C., & T. Humphries. 1988. *Deaf in America: Voices from a culture.* Cambridge, MA: Harvard University Press.

Padden, C., & B. LeMaster. 1985. An alphabet on hand: Acquisition of fingerspelling in deaf children. *Sign Language Studies, 47,* 161–172.

Padden, C., & D. Perlmutter. 1987. American Sign Language and the architecture of grammatical theory. *Natural Language and Linguistic Theory, 5*(3), 335–375.

Pahz, J. A., & C. S. Pahz. 1978. *Total communication.* Springfield, IL: Charles C. Thomas.

Peters, A. 1983. *The units of language acquisition.* Cambridge: Cambridge University Press.

Randall, M. 1984. *Risking a somersault in the air: Conversations with Nicaraguan writers.* San Francisco: Solidarity Publications.

Richardson, S. 1985. *A gift to be treasured.* Manuscript submitted for publication.

Schlesinger, H. S., & K. P. Meadow. 1972. *Sound and sign.* Berkeley: University of California Press.

Shor, I., & P. Freire. 1987. *A pedagogy for liberation: Dialogues on transforming education.* Granby, MA: Bergin & Garvey.

Strong, M. 1988. A bilingual approach to the education of young deaf children. In M. Strong (ed.), *Language, learning and deafness.* Cambridge: Cambridge University Press.

Stuart, D., & S. D. Houston. 1989. Maya writing. *Scientific American, 261*(2), 82–89.

Supalla, S. 1986. *Manually Coded English: The modality question in signed language development.* Master's thesis, University of Illinois at Champaign-Urbana.

Vygotsky, L. S. 1978. *Mind in society: The development of higher psychological processes.* Cambridge, MA: Harvard University Press.

Wilbur, R. B. 1987. *American Sign Language: Linguistic and applied dimensions.* Boston: Little Brown.

Wilcox, S. (Ed.). 1989a. *American Deaf culture.* Silver Spring, MD: Linstok Press.

Wilcox, S. 1989b. "Breaking through the culture of silence." In S. Wilcox (ed.), *American Deaf culture.* Silver Spring, MD: Linstok Press.

Wilcox, S. 1992. *The phonetics of fingerspelling.* Amsterdam: John Benjamins.

Wilcox, S., & J. Corwin. 1990. The enculturation of BoMee: Looking at the world through Deaf eyes. *Journal of Childhood Communication Disorders, 13*(1), 63–71.

Wilcox, S., & P. Wilcox. 1991. *Learning to see: American Sign Language as a second language.* Englewood Cliffs, NJ: Prentice-Hall Regents (a publication of Center for Applied Linguistics).

Woodward, J. 1972. Implications for sociolinguistics research among the deaf. *Sign Language Studies, 1,* 1–17.

Woodward, J. 1989. "How you gonna get to heaven if you can't talk with Jesus? The educational establishment vs. the deaf community." In S. Wilcox (ed.), *American Deaf culture.* Silver Spring, MD: Linstok Press.

Part II

Mediational processes

A central concept in an interactional understanding of human thinking is "mediation." In his book-length treatment of Vygotsky's ideas, Wertsch (1985) argues that "Vygotsky made his most important and unique contribution with the concept of mediation" (p. 15). This was Vygotsky's view also; Wertsch quotes Vygotsky as stating "the central fact about our psychology is the fact of mediation" (ibid.). The six chapters in this section share a concern with mediation. Here we clarify the conceptual outlines of mediation that are assumed but not necessarily explicit in the chapters that follow.

"Mediation" refers to the tools, signs, and practices that contribute to qualitative changes in development. Jerome Bruner, in his introduction (1962) to the first translation of Vygotsky's work, points to the central quality of mastery in mediation: Vygotsky

> believed that in mastering nature we master ourselves. For it is the internalization of overt action that makes thought, and particularly the internalization of external dialogue that brings the powerful tool of language to bear on the stream of thought. Man, if you will, is shaped by the tools and instruments that he comes to use, and neither the mind nor the hand alone can amount to much. . . . And if neither hand nor intellect alone prevails, the tools and aids that do are the developing streams of internalized language and conceptual thought that sometimes run parallel and sometimes merge, each affecting the other. (Bruner, 1962, p. vii)

This is what Bruner calls Vygotsky's "mediational point of view. Concepts and the language that infuses and instruments them give power and strategy to cognitive activity" (Bruner, 1962, p. ix).

We find, however, that the term mediation is used in various ways – and sometimes in a way that dilutes the power of Vygotsky's conception. For example, a frequent use is that social interaction "mediates" the child's learning. While this is an important feature of an interactionist perspective and is related to the use we intend, it is not this use we wish to suggest here. Rather, "mediation" is used to refer to those means which become tools for thought, those means and practices which, through social interaction, become internalized and thus available for independent activity. The mediational means such as notched sticks and knots in the history of some groups, the use of language in written forms in other groups, and the varied oral discourse practices of all groups are examples of mediational means. The use of these means and their internalization is what distinguishes, in Vygotsky's view, elementary and higher psychological processes, as well as human behavior from that of other primates. Sign systems – the most important of which is speech – are a special type of stimuli that the individual comes to use as psychological tools that are "directed toward the mastery or control of behavioral processes – either someone else's or one's own – just as technical means are directed toward the control of nature. . . . the psychological tool alters the entire flow and structure of the mental functions . . . by determining the structure of the new instrumental act, just as a technical tool alters the process of natural adaptation by determining the form of labor operations" (Vygotsky, 1981a, p. 137).

The development of higher functions is characterized by "voluntariness" or conscious control: the internalization of signs, tools, and practices makes possible the control of one's own and other's activity – often referred to as self- and other-regulation. Although speech may be the most important of the sign systems, other forms of signs also play a significant role. Vygotsky's discussion of the development of higher forms of attention (1981b) suggests that the child's initial reaching or grasping behavior may be transformed, during the process of social interaction, so that the behavior of reaching for an object is transformed into the gesture of pointing to an object and the behavior becomes a *sign* by which the child can now signify "indication" combined with the preverbal intonation of desire to communicate "request" for a specific object to another.

According to Wertsch, mediation provided Vygotsky with an "overarching principle of development," which Wertsch labels the "decontextualization of mediational means" – "the process whereby the meaning of signs become[s] less and less dependent on the unique spatiotemporal context in which they are used" (1985, p. 33). Over time, mediational means transform psychological functioning. Vygotsky viewed "the introduction of a psychological tool (language, for example) into a mental function (such as memory) as causing a fundamental transformation of that function" (Wertsch, 1985, p. 79). Moreover, "psychological tools are not auxiliary means that simply facilitate an existing mental function while leaving it qualitatively unaltered. Rather, the emphasis is on their capacity to transform mental functioning" (ibid.). And further, "increasingly sophisticated forms of mediation (or more generally, representation) allow the developing human to perform more complex operations on objects from an increasing spatial and temporal distance" (p. 80).

These psychological tools and practices are social in two senses. Language, various systems for counting, mnemonic techniques, algebraic symbol systems, and other mediational means are *social* in the sense that they are products of sociocultural evolution. Psychological tools and practices are neither invented by the individual nor discovered in the individual's independent interactions with nature. Nor are they inherited in the form of instincts or unconditional reflexes. Instead, individuals have access to psychological tools and practices by virtue of being part of a sociohistorical milieu in which those tools and practices have been and continue to be culturally transmitted.

Second, psychological tools are social in the sense that they are acquired through the processes of social interaction. In the process of acquisition, not only the mediational means, but also the social organization of the activity is internalized. Contained then within this view of learning is the acquisition of volitional processes, the feelings and desires associated with the participants in the activity. It is not just behaviors, then, on which such a perspective focuses, but the fullness or wholeness of an activity as a cultural process, and development is seen as thoroughly situated in culture; the development of the individual is, as Vygotsky repeatedly noted, *cultural* development, "a process in which children grow into the intellectual life of those around them" (Vygotsky, 1978, p. 88).

Doubtless, all the chapters in this collection touch on mediation. The six in this section, however, focus our attention on the preschool and early childhood years when the development of mediational processes is most evident. Two of the articles explore the development of communication in the early preschool years by focusing on nonverbal processes; two articles examine the development of written language understanding in the preschool period; one article discusses an intervention project in which mothers learned to incorporate a new form of mediation into their interactions with their preschoolers; the last article focuses on visual representation patterns as mediation in the development of mathematical understanding in the elementary school period. Let us provide a brief introduction to each article.

In their article on "Nonverbal factors in the interpsychic to intrapsychic internalization of objects," David McNeill, Karl-Erik McCullough, and Martha Tyrone argue that "adults' gestures embody and thus display a host of assumptions about both the social and physical world – how complexity in objects 'naturally' breaks apart, what is a 'natural' chunk of information (such that it is believed to be processible by the child), what an 'action' is and what types there are, what counts as 'attention' and 'understanding', and what one's approach to objects ought to be, and thus what their meaning is." First, McNeill, McCullough, and Tyrone offer a fine-grained description of two styles that adults seem to adopt with children in their interactions with objects; next, they trace the internalization of gesture from 15 months to 26 months by a single child; in the third part of their paper, they present data comparing the interactional styles and nonverbal behavior of ten parent–child dyads, compared on the basis of gender and socioeconomic class. The controlled comparison uses a jigsaw puzzle task and coding scheme that orders the adult's actions "according to the degree of latitude left by the adult for the child's own action." They find differences between the inner city and suburban parents as well as between the parents of boys and girls. The inner city adults exert a higher degree of control over the child and constrain the child's actions to a greater degree, whereas the suburban adults seem to use a less constraining form of guidance and leave more of the action to the child. We would speculate that such differences are linked to the differential degrees of independence that these adults have experienced outside the home, both in their occupations and in their schooling (e.g., Oakes 1985; Willis 1979). However, the most striking finding in their comparisons was related to gender, not class, with adults treating girls "as actually unable to perform the task." This kind of negative assessment of female ability is not new, but the finding in this study is striking in its magnitude, especially given the age of the population and the potential influence of such nonverbal interactions.

Whereas McNeill, McCullough, and Tyrone examine nonverbal communication in relation to objects, Patricia Goldring Zukow and Kelly Duncan focus on the connection between nonverbal communication and the learning of language in "An ecological approach to the emergence of the lexicon: Socializing attention." They link Vygotsky's consideration of social interaction with J. J. Gibson's ecological approach to perception as a way to investigate the question of how infants are able to detect the conventional relations between words and world without which language acquisition is impossible. A key element in this process is the education or socialization of attention. They argue that "the mere co-occurrence of a perceptually sensitive infant and the availability of detectable information in the perceptual array does not guarantee that conventional relations will be detected." Rather, "to make the transition to linguistic representation, children must *perceive/notice* conventional lexical relations." They find that caregivers socialize the child's attention through the coordinated use of gesture and speech. While Goldring Zukow and her colleagues have found some instances of culture-specific differences in caregiving practices, the similarities in practices used to direct attention between cultures is very striking. In this study, the authors present findings from twelve Mexican families in which the mothers had very low levels of schooling and findings from six Anglo-American families in which all parents had at least some college education. They use videotapes of naturally occurring samples of activity in the homes of the participants and they provide fine-grained descriptions to show the social process in which the child's attention is directed to the "affordances" in the perceptual array.

In the first two chapters of this section we see the development of nonverbal and action- and object-oriented mediation processes. In the next two chapters we see the elaboration of verbal mediation in the development of children's understanding. Maria Silvia Barbieri and Liliana Landolfi develop an alternative to the Piagetian approach to the origins of explanatory processes. According to Piaget's view, "the origin of the explaining capacity is linked to children's increasing ability to formulate correct representations of causal sequences, and make appropriate use of the connectives expressing this relation between two or more events." Barbieri and Landolfi argue that Piaget's approach has led to a flawed understanding by failing to examine "the activity of explaining in an interactive context. . . . Things are explained to somebody, in the context of specific kinds of interaction and in relation to particular goals." In their study, Barbieri and Landolfi focus on the internalization of explanations of children aged 30 to 60 months during three phases of a standardized pictorial explanation task. By detailed coding of new and repeated mentions of specific information, they are able to trace the history of information through these exchanges over time. They identify an increasing internalization of content over the three weeks of the experiment and an increasing autonomy in the use of the strategies across the three ages. Their results suggest the internalization of naming, describing, and, to a lesser extent, interpreting during child–adult book reading and the value of such activity in the development of the ability to explain.

In the fourth chapter in this section, Carolyn Panofsky reports on the interactions of six children over a year's time during routine bedtime activity at home. This study views such bedtime story reading as a "leading activity" in the lives of these children, one that engages them in the development of a system of thought: "Cultural practices employed in socially assembled situations are learned systems of activity in which knowledge consists of standing rules for thought and action appropriate to a particular situation, embodied in the cooperation of individual members of a culture" (Rogoff, Gauvain, & Ellis, 1984).

Panofsky argues that the cultural practice of storybook reading must be understood within the context of the socially assembled situation of families in which the activity is constructed in a specific way, for it is not the same in all families, as the work of both Heath (1983) and Wells (1985) has shown. By examining transcripts of naturally occurring book-reading activity, Panofsky identifies seven functions of language in text-related discourse (i.e., discourse used to make sense of text, rather than used to regulate the social dimension of the activity). This categorization of functions shows the range of ways in which the children in the study were learning to mediate their understanding of text. After describing the various functions and providing examples of their use in context, Panofsky provides evidence of their internalization. From four episodes involving a single child during one year, she shows that the child's *initiation* of functions increased while the adult's initiation of the same functions decreased over the same period. Such data suggest the change from functioning that is dependent on another to independent functioning that Vygotsky theorized as occurring in the zone of proximal development.

In the fifth chapter in this section, Patricia A. Edwards and Georgia Earnest Garcia describe a year-long training program in which parents of at-risk youngsters learned new ways to read with their children. In this study, Vygotsky's concepts are applied to the learning of adults rather than children, with a university researcher/group leader functioning as the "more capable peer." In addition, the project used a kind of cooperative approach in which the participants modeled strategies and coached and provided feedback to each other. Over time, the group leader ceded control of the group to the parents as they took over increasing responsibility for the functioning of the group. Transcripts of group sessions and of videotapes of the parents' book-reading interactions with their children provide illustration of the workings of the program. This program is unusual in using a Vygotskian model for parent training.

In the final chapter in this section, Pat Cordeiro takes us into the classroom, in a study of sixth graders' "literate exploration of a broad mathematical concept, group theory." Vygotsky distinguished between scientific and spontaneous concepts to refer to the systematically elaborated knowledge transmitted in formal contexts in contrast to the knowledge that tends to be spontaneously generated in the informal contexts of everyday life. While teaching a sixth grade class, Cordeiro introduced a variety of mathematical ideas to get the students to "play" with the ideas in recognizable forms as well as to see the ideas in abstract structural ways. Along the way, each student keeps a journal of his or her own way of approaching the ideas both alone and with peers. As the teacher, Cordeiro also kept a journal, and through the article she uses entries from both student and teacher journals to illustrate their collective intellectual journey. Along the way, the children reflect on their own thinking processes, marvel at the insights and ideas of the "great" mathematical thinkers, and begin to combine their new mathematical concepts as tools for thinking, using these newly acquired ideas as tools for exploring new domains. Through this process – which engages the children through visual, spatial and kinesthetic means as well as verbal – the students' learning leads to the development of what Vygotsky referred to as a "mediated attitude" (1962, p. 108):

> The inception of a spontaneous concept can usually be traced to a face-to-face meeting with a concrete situation, while a scientific concept involves from the first a "mediated" attitude toward its object.

The mediated attitude is a way of understanding that is produced through a historically developed and socially transmitted system of concepts. Vygotsky argues that whereas "a child's everyday concept, such as 'brother,' is saturated with experience," her formally acquired scientific concepts tend to be "schematic and lack the rich content derived from personal experience" (1962, p. 108). Cordeiro's work suggests that by creating a rich environment for learning, the teacher can in some sense promote the cross-fertilization of the children's spontaneous and scientific concepts, providing the means for the learning of scientific concepts to be saturated with experience and to see everyday experiences in newly schematic ways.

As Vygotsky argued, children "grow into the intellectual life of those around them" (1978, p. 88). Another way of saying this is that through social interaction learners' consciousness is constituted by the mediational processes that have come, historically, to characterize the cultural activities, and hence the enculturated participants, of the world in which they live. The six chapters in this section provide various ways of viewing this development.

REFERENCES

Bruner, J. 1962. Introduction. In L. S. Vygotsky, *Thought and language.* Cambridge, MA: MIT Press.

Heath, S. B. 1983. *Ways with words.* Cambridge: Cambridge University Press.

Oakes, J. 1985. *Keeping track: How schools structure inequality.* New Haven, CT: Yale University Press.

Rogoff, B., M. Gauvain, & S. Ellis. 1984. Development viewed in its cultural context. In M. H. Bornstein & M. E. Lamb (Eds.), *Developmental psychology: An advanced textbook.* Hillsdale, NJ: Erlbaum.

Vygotsky, L. S. 1962. *Thought and language.* Cambridge, MA: MIT Press.
Vygotsky, L. S. 1978. *Mind in society: The development of higher psychological processes.* Cambridge, MA: Harvard University Press.
Vygotsky, L. S. 1981a. The instrumental method in psychology. In J. V. Wertsch (Ed.), *The concept of activity in Soviet psychology.* Armonk, NY: M. E. Sharpe.
Vygotsky, L. S. 1981b. The development of higher forms of attention in childhood. In J. V. Wertsch (Ed.), *The concept of activity in Soviet psychology.* Armonk, NY: M. E. Sharpe.
Wells, G. 1985. Preschool literacy-related activities and success in school. In D. Olson, N. Torrance, & A. Hildyard (Eds.), *Literacy, language and learning.* Cambridge: Cambridge University Press.
Wertsch, J. 1985. *Vygotsky and the social formation of mind.* Cambridge, MA: Harvard University Press.
Willis, P. 1979. *Learning to labour: How working class kids get working class jobs.* London: Saxon House.

5 *Nonverbal factors in the interpsychic to intrapsychic internalization of objects*

DAVID McNEILL, KARL-ERIK McCULLOUGH, AND MARTHA TYRONE

As is well known, Vygotsky (1962, 1978, 1981) argued that new achievements appear in children's mental (or cultural) development twice: first *inter*psychically, as part of the social interaction of the child with adults or older children, later *intra*psychically, as part of the child's own internal mental operations. In this way, the child is presented with and finally internalizes cultural knowledge, and this knowledge becomes part of the child's own way of thinking. It is the hypothesis of this paper that the adult's *gestures* during social interactions with children are an essential part of the communication and thus of the guidance that adults provide, and that the child's gestures are a crucial source of feedback for the adult. Depending on the gestural component, completely different communicative situations can develop, success or failure can occur, and the child's willingness to learn may be strengthened or weakened. All of these processes can be observed going on during adult–child interactions. Adult's gestures embody and thus display a host of assumptions about both the social and physical world – how complexity in objects "naturally" breaks apart, what is a "natural" chunk of information (such that it is believed to be processible by the child), what an "action" is and what types there are, what counts as "attention"; and "understanding," and what one's approach to objects ought to be, and thus what their meaning is. Adult's assumptions in these spheres are made manifest unwittingly in the gestures and other nonverbal behavior directed to children. The child's gestures also are crucial because these gestures trace for the adult the process of the child's internalization from the interpsychic to the intrapsychic and can reveal to the adult the child's current *zones of proximal development* – the areas of development that are just opening up to the child and are particularly ready to show learning. Mothers act very differently when they demonstrate to their children toys the operation of which they believe are within the child's capacity, and those that they think are beyond the child. Thus the object is presented, not just as an object, but as an object bearing assumptions about the child, the object, its cultural meaning, the nature of information and action, and many other factors. It is fair to say that in these interactions between children and adults, mundane though they are, lie some of the earliest significant segmentations of reality.

VYGOTSKY'S THEORY

Three aspects of Vygotsky's theory are relevant to this chapter and will be briefly discussed in turn: (1) the steps of development appear twice, first interpsychically, next intrapsychically; (2) development is characterized by successive zones of proximal development in which guidance by adults or more skilled children is crucial; (3) pointing is a gesture that reveals mental development in microcosm.

1. *Internalization: steps appear in mental development twice.* According to Vygotsky cognition necessarily has a social foundation. The mental processes of individuals are direct reflections of the social processes in which the individual participated during earlier stages of ontogenesis (Wertsch, 1979): "The essence of this law is that in the process of development, children begin to use the same forms of behavior in relation to themselves that others initially used in relation to them" (Vygotsky, 1981, p. 157). A corollary is that new mental developments appear first in a social context: "We could formulate the general genetic law of cultural development as follows: Any function in the child's cultural development appears twice, or on two planes. First it appears on the social plane, and then on the psychological plane. First it appears between people as an interpsychological category, and then within the child as an intrapsychological category. . . . The very mechanism underlying higher mental functions is a copy from social interaction; all higher mental functions are internalized social relationships. . . . In their own private sphere, human beings retain the functions of social interaction" (Vygotsky, 1981, pp. 163, 164). The adult's cultural knowledge (factual and presuppositional) is brought to bear in interactions with the child, and this sets up a structure "on the social plane." This eventually becomes, via internalization, the structure of the child's own knowledge on the "psychological plane." Thus the meanings of objects incorporate meanings that derive from the social interactions over these objects.

2. *Zones of proximal development.* Vygotsky wrote: "The zone of proximal development defines those functions that have not yet matured but are in the process of maturation, functions that will mature tomorrow but are currently in an embryonic state" (Vygotsky, 1978, p. 86). This concept of the zone of proximal development brings out the

crucial part played by interpsychic representations: "It is the distance between the actual developmental level as determined by independent problem solving and the level of potential development as determined through problem solving under adult guidance or in collaboration with more capable peers" (ibid.). Vygotsky's aphorism for describing mental growth was that development lags behind learning. This lag creates the zone of proximal development (Vygotsky, 1978, p. 90). A child acts differently with objects whose operation she has mastered compared to objects whose operation is far beyond her (whose zone of proximal development is yet to come), and still differently with those objects whose operation is just within reach (the zone of proximal development is now opening up). The child's own behavior with objects is a vital piece of feedback evidence that guides the adult, if the adult is ready to receive it.

3. *Pointing.* Vygotsky regarded the development of pointing as a microcosm of the child's entire cultural development (Vygotsky, 1981, p. 160). Specifically, he believed that all development passes through three stages, and that the successive transformations of pointing exemplify this sequence. Pointing starts out as unsuccessful grasping with movements added to indicate the desired object. Then it turns into movements indicating a desired object, aimed by the child not at the object but at an adult and to which the adult responds (Bates, 1976, p. 61). Finally the gesture is made for the child himself or herself, and an interlocutor is not necessary for it to occur. The form of the gesture thus changes during its journey inward and these changes objectively trace out the process of internalization.

In a similar way, adult gestures might trace out different packages of information at different stages of internalization as the adult responds to the child. Again, mothers may be more or less sensitive to the clues they are presented with. Bekken (1989) has documented an extremely heavy reliance on deixis in mothers' gestures to children, far higher than the same mothers' gestures to adults in the same context and with the same content of speech (talking about toys in the room). Thus gestures of mothers might also trace out the adult's estimation of the child's degree of internalization.

RECORDING AND CODING VERBAL AND NONVERBAL INTERACTIONS

To collect data on instructional interactions, we visited suburban middle-class or inner city working-class families with 2-year-old children either in their homes, at a Hyde Park (Illinois) school specializing in inner city African-American families, or at the University of

Chicago. The same families were videotaped at roughly 6-month intervals during a 2-year period. In each session a primary caretaker was present, and the procedures and instructions were the same: the caretaker was told to get the child to operate the toy, work the puzzle, or count the objects handed to her by an on-screen experimenter. The on-screen experimenter controlled the presentation of the objects but the caretaker was in charge of the child and the flow of the interaction. The on-screen experimenter would intervene if the interaction appeared to break down, and in these cases the experimenter also tended to become a participant; we have drawn examples from some of these experimenter–child interactions, below. The instructions to the caretaker rather vaguely stated that we were interested in what children "know" at different stages of their development, and asked the caretaker to induce the child to use the object; there was no suggestion that the caretaker was the primary object of our study. Most caretakers were mothers, one was a father, and two were adolescent sisters.

The interactions were transcribed and analyzed from videotape according to the coding scheme described in the appendix. Coding focused on instructional episodes of typically 2 to 5 minutes' duration involving single objects. A new episode was recognized only when the on-screen experimenter presented a new object; any redefinition of an already present object in terms of functional task by either the caretaker or the child was considered to occur within the same episode. Coders would record the following for each interaction episode: the object, a narrative account of the interaction, the exact speech of the adult and child, the zone of proximal development (i.e., the functional task addressed by the caretaker), any change of the zone of proximal development (e.g., when the child or adult redefined the task), the focus of attention of both the child and the adult, and the dynamics of the interaction, both verbal and nonverbal, in terms of interactional features along several dimensions. In all, the coding scheme drew on 32 categories and interactional features (not all of which would be important in any given interaction). The appendix gives two illustrative transcripts utilizing the coding scheme.

THE MEANINGS OF OBJECTS INSOFAR AS GESTURES ARE CONCERNED

We present two contrasting examples of nonverbal communication between young children and adults during naturalistic instruction. Our purpose is to demonstrate that nonverbal signals (signals both to and from the child) can be the primary channel of interpersonal cognition. This may be especially true at the early stages. We will also use these examples to illustrate the kinds of cultural knowledge about objects that nonverbal signals convey. Shatz (1982) found that adults simplify and set off as distinctive the gestures they address to 19- to 34-month-olds; thus they seem to make some conscious effort to adapt their gestures as a channel of communication.

1. Our first example illustrates that it is chiefly in the nonverbal actions of adults that they display assumptions about the nature of objects (how they are put together) and the nature of the child's information-processing chunks. The example is from a videotape made at the child's home. The child was a girl 18 months old and her mother was demonstrating a crank-operated toy (Mickey Mouse seems to be frantically eating spaghetti). The mother separates her own manipulations of the toy from manipulations that are part of her interaction with the child, and thus divides the demonstration into what she regards as "communicative" and "noncommunicative," and what this entails. She also presents the toy in two steps, the first a static display of the toy, then a demonstration of its action. Thus she divides the demonstration into "object" and "action." Finally, each of these divisions the mother estimates to be an appropriately sized information chunk. Thus she conveys information of a psychological sort as well, namely, what kinds and amounts of information the child's mind can actually take in.

The mother first examines the toy in a space close to her own body. Her gaze is on the object and withdrawn from the child (object-focused, not part of any communication). Then she moves the toy into the communicative space between herself and her child and holds up the toy in a static display (thus contriving that orienting precedes action, and taking care to present a static structure before a dynamic function); this is the kind of pointing at the second stage that Vygotsky outlined, but directed to the child as interlocutor. Then the mother removes the toy from the communication space (thus separating information-processing chunks) but immediately reintroduces to turn the crank (showing the function); this is also a kind of pointing, more like the first stage, in that action and pointing are not completely differentiated. When the mother stops cranking she moves the toy close to the child (another information-processing chunk) and for the first time actually says something: "mmm . . . like that spaGHEtti." This locus of a verbal comment might also be significant. Saying what she did, she provided an evaluation to go with the toy and indeed the child now pretends to remove some spaghetti and eat it (moreover, the stress on "spaghetti" seems to mark the utterance as evaluative and potentially referring to the child, rather than descriptive and referring to Mickey). The mother doesn't invite the child to work the crank at any point: apparently she thought cranking was not within a zone of proximal development (as indeed it was not, since this child never did succeed in turning the crank on this or any other toy). Eventually the child tires of the game and turns away. Not until then does the mother remove the toy from the communicative space and put it down (thus she regarded herself as an active but secondary participant in the child's play).

We see in this example a quite finely tuned interaction under the control of the mother but relying on feedback from the child. Nearly all of the messages are nonverbal. The one verbalization appears where an evaluative function seems useful. We also see how the mother's beliefs about the nature of the world and the child's information-processing capabilities are built into her nonverbal communications. For instance, the mother's actions exhibit her beliefs that:

- Form is separable from function (she separates the display of the form of the toy from the demonstration of its function).
- Orientation should occur before demonstration.
- "Natural" chunks of information are actions such as orientation, display without movement, display with movement, evaluation, and response by addressee. These are the chunks revealed in how the mother displayed the form and demonstrated the function of the toy, and in how she invited the child to play with it. Such chunks reflect hypotheses about information-processing units; to this mother, information is classifiable according to the type of action. Different adults may divide reality along other lines, but we should expect their movements to reveal how they divide and classify chunks of information as well.

If we were to characterize the world view embodied in this interaction, it would be the view that the world is analyzable and analysis is the mode of approach to it. The mother is the side of the interaction largely responsible for the analytic onslaught on the world in this case, and the child is receiving this understanding on the social plane – in Vygotskyian terms its understanding, insofar as it understands, is interpsychic.

2. Our next example is with a second little girl (19 months) and presents a contrasting world view, which we will characterize as the attitude that objects *are as they are;* they come to us, have canonical uses, and should be approached over obligatory routes that admit little deviation. (This is a caricature, but we are trying to be clear.) The adult presents the object as an unanalyzable whole and insists that it be received in this light by the child. As an approach to the object, the situation is less finely tuned than the preceding example. The situation in this example may have arisen because the mother doubts that the object is within the child's zone of proximal development, or may reflect a habitual pattern of approaching objects (future videotapes of the same mother and child will prize these interpretations apart). But this approach still provides instruction. The question is what message is being conveyed. Again,

knowledge is interpsychic, but the message now appears to be that the object is a given; it is sacrosanct and should be approached in a foreordained way.

A second feature of this example is that there was, in the same situation at the same time, a second adult – an on-screen experimenter – who also interacted with the child and with the same object. This experimenter's style was much closer to the style of the mother in the first example; that is, the experimenter was more analytic and expressed an approach to the object that presupposed it was something the child herself could construct. The emphasis was on building up the object rather than using it; thus the emphasis was less on following a "correct" path and more on construction. The goal of the experimenter's interaction was to get the child to create the object, in contrast to the mother's goal, which was to get the object to perform in a certain preestablished manner.

The object is a type of pop-up toy in which a Humpty Dumpty figure is perched on a platform. The Humpty Dumpty is made up of five separate layers. The intended use of the toy is to place Humpty Dumpty on the platform and then press a lever that causes the platform to tilt over and topple Humpty Dumpty down, who satisfyingly breaks into his five parts.

The child was relatively unresponsive to the toy. Her own acts with it were limited to knocking the Humpty Dumpty figure off with her hands. The mother's response to this absence of enthusiasm was as we described: she herself put Humpty Dumpty back together again and then directed the child to press the button: "push the button! push the button!" The child didn't respond, and finally the mother arranged herself behind the child, so that her arms were in the same position as the child's arms, and then took the child's right hand in her own right hand and mechanically pressed the child's hand down on the lever and said "push the button again!" Here the game is: operate the object just as you are supposed to (however determined).

The experimenter's interventions occurred when the mother was distracted from the immediate context by something else in the room. The experimenter's goal was to get the child to put the pieces back on the platform. She first invited the child to put Humpty Dumpty together. This overture received no reaction at all. The experimenter then picked up the pieces and offered them one at a time to the child. There was still no reaction and so the experimenter placed the bottom piece on the platform, and offered the next piece to the child and kept on offering pieces until the whole Humpty Dumpty figure was built up. In the end, the experimenter and mother had behaved in the same way, although the experimenter was less direct about it. But in the process she was conveying, in her actions, a quite different attitude toward the object and what to do with it. For the experimenter the game is: let's see what you can do with this.

In this example, the child's nonverbal feedback is: the toy is not part of a zone of proximal development; the mother's reaction was to provide guided compliance; the experimenter's reaction was to change the task to seek a new possible zone of proximal development.

We see in this example that adult actions exhibit beliefs such as:

- Form is not separable from function (the mother treats the object as an unanalyzable form that has just one function). This attitude is the reverse of the belief shown in the first example.
- Function is specific action (the mother seizes the child's hand to make it "work" in the proper way). This also contrasts with the first example.
- Objects are constructible by oneself (the experimenter's implicit message).

POINTING

Vygotsky, as mentioned earlier, analyzed a series of steps in which pointing is gradually internalized as a form of representation. At first, according to Vygotsky, pointing is unsuccessful grasping, aimed at the object; then it becomes symbolic, aimed at an adult; finally it is made for the child himself. This last step marks the internalization of pointing. This series of steps is separate from and predates the release of pointing from the concrete context of speech, the famous here and now. That is, representation by internalized means would appear to be a condition to be met before the child is able to refer to objects not here and times not now. Unless a child can represent objects to herself, she cannot invent means of referring to them when they are absent. In the following set of longitudinal observations, which span one child's development from 15 to 26 months, we see a child proceeding along the full Vygotskian series of steps. Pointing initially is linked with grasping, later is incorporated into social interactions with adults, and finally is part of the child's own efforts to represent the world. This development of internalized representations, however, occurs entirely with concrete pointing gestures, locked into the child's here and now.

At 15 months, the following were typical contexts in which our subject, J, pointed/grasped at objects:

(1) Reaches for toy chicks box in a pointlike movement.
(2) Reaches for a new toy.
(3) Points/reaches for toy being held by puppet.
(4) Gazes at own hands on toy and says "doll."

There is an almost total absence of pointing at this age other than deixis combined with reaching. The final example (4) is particularly important. The child examines her own hands and pronounces the name of an object that the hands might grasp. The connection between action and object, and the mediating role of the hands, are made visible in this example.

By 19 months, we find a different situation. J now includes the adult interlocutor in her acts of deictic indication, as in these examples:

(5) Watches adult and holds out hand, anticipating grabbing the toy; then reaches for it.
(6) Picks up puzzle piece and looks at it; looks at adult and responds to question; then points to piece and makes contact with board.

Deixis is still linked to acts of grasping, but added now is a further step: the child includes the adult in her loop. This is the interpsychic stage from which, according to Vygotsky, future developments must derive.

At 26 months, J's pointing has taken yet another step. She now points for herself, as shown by her linking pointing, not with acts of grasping or to the adult, but to her own attempts at representation.

(7) Names animal and points to its head.
(8) Asks where to put piece, then picks a space and points to it.
(9) Picks up a piece and looks for space; says "he goes here" (gaze is the deictic action here).
(10) Points to space (no contact), then looks at Mother and asks if the space is right.

The child's deictic indicators are organized as part of her attempts to achieve representations of where she should place the puzzle pieces. The example at (10), the one including the mother, is crucially different from the inclusion of the adult at 19 months, in (6), where the child responded to the adult's question; at (10), the questioner is the child. At 19 months, J held out her hand in anticipation of having the object given to her by the adult. At 26 months, the child looks at her mother and points to the space in order to validate her own representation that this is the right place for the piece to go. This is representation for oneself.

Although we find Vygotsky's account of how pointing develops applying insightfully to the three ages in J's development, this account also implies that J's development is not complete at 26 months. She performs overt deictic acts, not yet the invisible pointing that may be the final stage of development – only the directed gaze in the example at (9) suggests a completely internal representation.

Nonetheless, displaced verbal references appear at 26 months. The following interchange occurred at the beginning of our 26-month taping session; no equivalent references to events in the past appear at 15 or 19 months. J is recalling a trip to the zoo:

(11) Mother: Oh, and what did you see who had the diaper on?
(12) J: The little monkey.
(13) M: Yeah, the baby monkey had a diaper on, right . . .
(14) J: Baby monkey had a . . . [M laughs] he had a little diaper.
(15) J: He got lot toys in there.

The child displays the ability to represent past events, including a past event introduced on her own, in (15).

On the other hand, at 15 months, J displays only a partial displacement of reference. She uses her name for simulacra of herself. These are uses that dissociate her name from her actual person. However, they are still in the Now. They might be called references in the "not quite here and now." The example starts with J looking in a mirror and then shifts to a photograph:

(16) J points to mirror and says her own name.
(17) Adult: Is that J?
(18) M: J!
(19) J closes panel on which mirror is attached, looks to M and says her own name again.
(20) M: J? Yeah! (and nods).
(21) J turns head and looks at wall and points at picture, and says her own name with rising (questioning) intonation.
(22) M confirms: looks at picture and points, and says: J's up THERE in the pictures.

The child can use her own name to refer to images of herself. Nonetheless, at 15 months this is but partial displacement. There is no reference yet outside of the immediate physical situation. That kind of displaced reference is not evident before the 26 month example cited earlier.

Thus, at 26 months, J reveals an ability to represent the world to herself in two crucial areas, and they appear at the same stage: pointing for herself, and using language to refer to what is not here and now. Both steps imply the ability to represent the world internally, in a mental construction. Pointing, however, is still an overtly executed action, suggesting that the development of internal representation is not yet complete at this age.

INTERACTION STYLES

Earlier, we contrasted two styles that adults seem to adopt with children. In one, objects are sacrosanct, they are as they are given, and only one action with them is regarded as appropriate. In the other style, objects are tried out with a variety of actions, pragmatically seeking what might work. To examine these styles in more detail, especially to see how pervasively they appear in adult–child interactions, we selected one of the tasks, a jigsaw puzzle and board, to which all the children were exposed. We coded a variety of interactive features and compared, on these features, mothers and children from two socioeconomic groups, poor inner city families and middle-class suburban families. The following features of our interaction code can be ordered according to the degree of latitude left by the adult for the child's own action; they are listed from least latitude to most.

- Adult does task (adult places the puzzle piece into its slot for the child).
- Adult's hands on (the adult places her hands on the child's hands and moves them for the child to place the puzzle piece into its slot).
- Adult's reorientation (the adult changes the orientation of the puzzle piece in child's hand).
- Adult removes child's hand (the adult removes child's hand from a puzzle piece or from the board).
- Adult blocks child's wrong move (the adult stops the child before she places a piece into the wrong slot).
- Adult points with contact (the adult touches the puzzle piece or the slot).
- Adult points without contact (the adult points but does not contact the piece or slot).
- Adult displays for analysis (the adult holds up the piece and points at its distinctive identifying feature, such as long ears).
- Adult talks with analysis (the adult holds up or otherwise indicates the piece or slot and specifies in words the distinctive identifying feature).

We observed 10 adult–child dyads, 5 from each socioeconomic group. In most cases, the interacting adult was the child's mother, although in two cases other family members fulfilled this role (both in inner city families). The children ranged in age from 2 to nearly 4 years of age. On several coding features, the two socioeconomic groups did not differ appreciably. On five features, however, the groups had occurrence rates that differed by at least a 2:1 ratio; these differences are large and may be significant. They point to a consistent direction of *more control and less analysis* in the inner city group; they also point to a pattern (though less consistent) of *avoiding physical contact with the child* in the middle-class group. Table 5.1 presents the average number of interactive acts per minute in which the features appeared (highlighting indicates at least a 2:1 difference).[1]

Numerically, the rates per minute in Table 5.1 appear small, but if we extrapolate to the days, months, and years of a child's development, such different rates lead to quite large cumulative differences between

Table 5.1. *Comparison of the interactions with children in two groups*

	Suburban	Inner city
Does task	0.26	0.29
Hands on	*0.12*	*0.57*
Reorients	1.87	2.08
Removes hand	*0.06*	*0.35*
Blocks move	*0.06*	*0.40*
Points w/ contact	2.87	1.94
Points w/o contact	*0.68*	*1.44*
Displays analysis	*1.12*	*0.44*
Talks analysis	0.65	0.53

inner city and suburban children in experiences with objects. To run through the table, we see that the inner city caretakers, more than the suburban caretakers, took control of the children's hands and moved them for them (as illustrated earlier), removed the children's hands from the wrong pieces, blocked the children's wrong moves, and pointed at pieces or slots without contacting them. On the other hand, the suburban caretakers, more than inner city caretakers, pointed at pieces or slots by making physical contact with the target. The inner city caretakers thus present a consistent picture of exerting higher degrees of control over the child, tolerating less variation, and leaving less room for mistakes. At the same time, however, the inner city caretakers display more physical contact with their children. The suburban caretakers, in contrast, do fewer of all these things, including physical contact. The contrasting styles of pointing are particularly interesting. The suburban caretakers contact the object (although not quite twice as often as the inner city caretakers), and this may be to ensure that the referent of the pointing gesture is clear to the child; they then leave the action to the child. The inner city caretakers do not contact the referent in this explicit way, but rather point to its spatial locus and leave its identification to the child.

These inner city and middle-class differences, if generalizable, suggest a contrast along two dimensions of children's early experiences. In terms of interactions with objects the middle-class caretakers, more than the inner city ones, emphasize pragmatic adaptability and flexibility. Their method would appear to encourage an outgoing curiosity that might stand the child well in later schooling. On the other hand, in terms of interactions with the child herself as a child (as opposed to an object of instruction), inner city caretakers, more than middle-class ones, favor a hands-on style that certainly looks empathic, warm, and supportive. These dimensions may be causally related. When a child is draped over her mother while working on a puzzle (as we saw only with inner city mothers), there is built into the very geometry of the situation an invitation to the caretaker to intervene and help the child. Is there a trade-off between values in the care for children – is physical aloofness the price of flexibility and curiosity? Is close, possibly stultifying control the price of physical contact? Do parents understand the price they are asked to pay?

What could explain the inner city and suburban differences shown in Table 5.1 and the possible association just suggested with interaction values? We have thought of several possible explanations, but as yet have no basis for selecting among them; any one or all of the following could create the differences in Table 5.1: (1) Although the instructions to our inner city and suburban mothers were the same, the mothers may have had different understandings of what we, the experimenters, were after. Mothers strove to meet what they took to be our expectations but differed in what they took them to be. The middle-class mothers may have thought we wanted to see what the children were going to do on their own. They were content to let the situation unfold in its own way and felt no compulsion to regulate it. The inner city mothers in contrast may have regarded us as testing their children for what they knew. Not surprisingly, they would then have tried to demonstrate their child's capabilities. If this account is valid, neither the suburban nor inner city mothers can be said to have guessed our purposes, since we wanted to see how the caretakers attempted to teach the children and not to see what the children would do on their own. (2) The inner city and suburban mothers have different understandings of the nature of teaching itself. The suburban mothers, perhaps influenced by educational doctrines like the discovery method, may think of teaching as letting the child work at his or her own pace with just occasional interventions when failure looms. The inner city mothers, on the other hand, may understand teaching in the more active sense of getting the child to match how the mother herself is behaving or would behave in the same situation. If this explanation is valid, we should consider the costs and benefits of these contrasting educational philosophies and how they mesh with prevailing educational doctrines in schools and society in general. (3) The inner city and suburban mothers may have different teaching goals (as opposed to methods). It is said that the African-American community has a strong oral tradition for transmitting cultural knowledge. Such a tradition implies exact standards with an emphasis on verbatim correctness. Sperry (1991) indeed found in a rural Alabama black community that children were discouraged from making up fantasy stories because adults regarded such tall tales as "lies," distortions of reality demanding suppression. Honoring the verbatim would encourage high levels of intervention and this could extend to nonverbal performances of the kind investigated here. Factors (1), (2), and (3) help put the teaching styles of inner city mothers into interactional, pedagogical, and cultural perspective. The long-term consequences of this interventionist style, however, remain unclear.[2]

GIRLS AND BOYS

Our sample included five girls and five boys. A remarkable fact is that the interaction feature of Doing the Task occurred almost exclusively with the girls. This feature appeared at various points with all five of the girls, while only one of the boys had the task done for him, possibly because the caretaker in this case was his older sister. That is, caretakers treat girls – far from needing assistance – as actually being unable to perform the task. This tendency was the same in both socioeconomic groups, as the nearly identical rates of Doing the Task in Table 5.1 show. For boys, the average rate of the caretaker doing the task was .06 interactions per minute; for girls, it was 0.66 – an order of magnitude greater. (For most of the boys, the rate was 0; the sole boy for whom the caretaker did the task had a rate of 0.30, half the girl's average.) We cannot say what part of this 10:1 difference in the treatment of girls and boys reflects "reality," in which adults are responding to actual differences in ability, and what part is due to a social regime that assigns girls the role of being incompetent. The fact remains that boys and girls are treated very differently even at the age of two in respect to competence at putting together puzzles and presumably in other areas as well. Again, extrapolating across the years of development implies massively different experiences for the sexes on the dimension of their presumptive competence by caretakers.[3]

CONCLUSIONS

What do we learn from such interactions of grown-ups and children with toys? We will mention six points:

1. Even commonplace actions with objects are loaded with cultural messages and attitudes toward actions, objects, and the ways to approach them.

2. The same objects are viewed in quite different ways under different attitudes. It is not enough to specify the object, therefore, but one must also look at the manner of its presentation and, through this, at the

attitude and the cultural message. These kinds of differences, if systematic and cumulative, can have enormous effects on children when they are multiplied over the many interactions that children have with adults over objects. The child's eventual willingness to learn can be channeled by these kinds of experiences.

3. Vygotsky's theory gives us a perspective for understanding the effects of adult–child interactions. The play with the object becomes part of the interpsychic representation, the opening of a path to intrapsychic knowledge. Such differences could lead to important contrasts in a child's approach to objects in the world.

4. Vygotsky's theory also gives us insight into the changes in children's pointing when it makes the transition from action, to pointing for the child herself, by linking this to the growth of internalized representations. Displaced references to past events in the speech of children also do not appear until the child's pointing has shifted to become pointing for the child herself, suggesting that internalization of representations is the underlying process for both domains.

5. Socioeconomic groups differ in how they distribute their teaching efforts. Middle-class caretakers focus on making clear the referent, and leave the action to the child (with assistance if needed). Inner city caretakers focus on the child's action, and let the referent appear in this controlled movement. Accumulating over a child's developmental period, these differences can lead to massively different interaction regimes for children's instructional experiences.

6. Independently of socioeconomic group, caretakers treat boys and girls in contrasting ways in terms of being willing to take over the task and complete it for the child. This difference, summed over the development period, can also amount to massively different experiences.

In general, interactions with adults are important in children's mental and social development. This is the case for a systematic reason. Adult interactions are important because of the facts of internalization: knowledge must be interpsychic before it can become intrapsychic. This interpsychic to intrapsychic sequence settles on caretakers an enormous importance in shaping children's very picture of the world, their knowledge as well as their expectations of social interchange. Such is the implication of Vygotsky's theory, and such is the conclusion pointed to by our observations of adult–child interactions.

APPENDIX: INTERACTION CODING PROTOCOL AND ILLUSTRATIVE EXAMPLES

The typical videotaping session involves a parent/caretaker, a child, and an adult researcher on camera, with an additional researcher taking notes on the interactions. The taping sessions are no less than an hour in length each, and are subdivided into episodes involving different toys or "stimulus objects." The toys are introduced by the on-screen researcher to the caretaker and child, with the goal of inciting the caretaker to instruct the child as to its typical function.

After completion of the taping session, the videotape is marked with a frame-counter, which indexes the temporal location of each episode on the tape and the timing of the evolving dynamic within each episode. Each episode is then analyzed by a trained researcher into a coding scheme developed specifically for the research project. Generally speaking, episodes are coded from the point of introduction of a stimulus object to the caretaker–child duo, to the point of its removal.

The coding scheme

In this section, the coding scheme, which was inspired by the work of Barbara Rogoff (1986, 1990), is explained by describing each coded category in turn. The coding is illustrated in the appendix with examples drawn from the data base of already coded episodes.

The coding categories range from fairly objective characterizations of the participants' activity in the interaction to evaluative features of the interaction determined to be of relevance. The following subheadings constitute those features of the coding scheme recorded in separate columns in the spreadsheet within a single data block (a "subepisode"). Each is followed by a brief description of the sort of information contained within.

Object line: In order to group the coded data into manageable units, gross subdivisions within each episode are determined by shifts in the status of the "stimulus objects" with respect to the triad of on-camera participants. Each change of state, locus, function, or possessor of the object(s) marks the initiation of a new subepisode.

Speech: Parent/Adult:
Child:

Narrative: Parent/Adult:
Child:

Within each subepisode, task-related speech is transcribed for the on-camera triad. Then, a "narrative" of the task-related activities of the on-camera participants is developed by the coder. The speech and narrative of the caretaker/parent (M) and the on-screen researcher (A) are coded within the same columns (there is considerable overlap in their interactive status vis-à-vis the child).

ZPD (zone of proximal development): A characterization of the functional task being addressed by the caretaker is entered at the beginning of each episode, with an analysis of both the level of difficulty of the task for the child, and its degree of involvement in the task. Changes in these features are entered in the subepisode in which the change occurred.

Space main object is in (re: P/A & re: Ch): The position and any changes in the position of the main object with relation to the participants are indicated for each subepisode, if necessary.

PARENT/ADULT:

A characterization of the task-related activity of the caretaker (and the researcher, if necessary) follows for each subepisode.

Attention focus: This is tracked through the subepisodes for the caretaker (and the researcher, if necessary), with special attention to gaze, body orientation, and object manipulation.

The following six categories constitute a checklist of the caretaker's activity during each subepisode (and the researcher's, if necessary). Each category is further separated into both verbal and nonverbal actions.

Form: This specifies whether or not the caretaker engages in any verbal or nonverbal actions during the subepisode. Key words uttered by the caretaker are entered in the verbal column.

Initiates/responds: This specifies whether or not the caretaker tries to initiate or shift an instructional event, or responds to an attempt by the child to initiate or shift it. Attempts are further specified to indicate the new task.

Structures situation: This specifies whether the caretaker structures the situation to facilitate instruction. The method used may be further specified.

Handles hard part: This specifies whether the caretaker accomplishes a difficult part of the task or the entire task.

Transfers responsibility: This specifies whether the caretaker attempts to shift the responsibility for accomplishing a task to the child, as is often the case after the caretaker has "handled the hard part" of a task.

Bridges from familiar: This specifies whether the caretaker attempts to facilitate the child's involvement with a toy or task by associating it to something familiar to the child.

Then, ten types of interactive features are coded:

Does task: The caretaker or researcher accomplishes the task.

Hands on: The conditions for this feature require that the child's hand(s) be on the toy when the caretaker moves the child's hand, and that the caretaker's action be directed at forcing the accomplishment of the task.

Reorientation: The caretaker or researcher shifts the toy within the child's grasp in order to "correct" its orientation without restricting the child's movements.

Removes hand: The caretaker or researcher removes the child's hand from the toy.

Blocks wrong move: The caretaker or researcher prevents an action by the child by setting up a barrier.

Points with contact: The caretaker or researcher touches a relevant part of the toy.

Points without contact: The caretaker or researcher gesturally indicates a relevant part of the toy without touching it.

Displays for analysis: The caretaker or researcher holds up the toy to the child and gesturally indicates a feature relevant to the task.

Talks with analysis: The caretaker or researcher tells the child information about the toy relevant to the task.

Gestures for analysis: The caretaker or researcher "demonstrates" or mimics an action relevant to the task without touching the toy.

Finally, a couple of catchall features are coded for:

Marking by action: This specifies other actions taken by the caretaker which are not immediately relevant to the instructional episode but which seem to be significant.

Other: This is where any other information relevant to the activities of the adults in the subepisode may be entered.

CHILD:

A characterization of the child's activity is then developed, comparable to the Parent/Adult section.

Attention focus: This is tracked with special attention to gaze, body orientation, and object manipulation, just as for the caretaker.

A checklist different from that for the caretaker follows, which describes the child's activity during each episode, again with both verbal and nonverbal actions differentiated.

Form: This specifies whether or not the child engages in any verbal or nonverbal actions during the subepisode. Key words are entered in the verbal column.

Initiates/responds: This specifies whether or not the child attempts to initiate or shift to a new activity, or responds to an attempt to initiate or shift the instructional event made by the caretaker or adult.

Places self to observe: The child actively shifts gaze, position, or posture to observe objects in play or the task-related behavior of the adults.

Actively directs: The child actively determines the course of a subepisode. This will often co-occur with cases in which the child initiates a new activity, but will also include elaborations of activities by the child.

Feedback: This specifies whether or not the child is providing feedback, either positive or negative, intended or not, to the caretaker. This can include demonstrations of understanding (positive), or lack of interest (negative, either intended or not).

Other: This is where any other information relevant to the activity of the child in the subepisode may be entered.

Mismatches: Finally, mismatches between various aspects of the participants' activities are noted. These could include discordances within a single participants' actions (e.g., demonstrating something manually while verbally describing something else), or mismatches between the actions of different participants (see Church & Goldin-Meadow, 1986, for discussion of the issues of mismatching verbal and gestural symbols).

Examples of coded subepisodes:

Example 1: In this example the child tries to place animal figure puzzle pieces into a wooden board. The interactive style of the caretaker reflects a fairly high degree of control over the child. Notice that during the subepisode, the caretaker handles the hard part, but only after instancing the following interactive features: Hands on, Reorientation (twice), Blocks the Wrong Move, and Pointing with Contact. This episode also illustrates a type of Mismatch between caretaker and child.

Example 2: In this example the mother establishes a verbal Bridge from Familiar by making a ringing noise, which typically marks the initiation of a phone call. By taking up the previously introduced phone and pretending to be the caller, the mother is also Marking by Action. In the Notes section, the coder suggests a possible interpretation of the child's loss of interest in the role playing game.

	Subject 1: CT, 2;3 Animal Puzzle Episode	Subject 2: EA, 2;0 Telephones Episode
Frame #:	99800	5120
Object Line:	(puzzle in C's lap)	A places second phone next to first (first toy

		phone in front of C, receiver in C hand)
Speech: Parent/Adult:	Come on put him in there . . . push on it put him in . . . no don't take them out. Put that in . . . this way. Put him in.	Who you talking to? Ring, ring, telephone. Hello, how you doing? What's your name? Hm, what's your name?
Speech: Child:	Nope . . . no.	Ball
Narrative: Parent/ Adult:	M orients piece, hands to C, reorients piece in C hand, blocks C removing piece already placed, taps space, reorients piece in C hand, presses down on C hands, presses piece into slot.	A places new telephone in front of C. M takes receiver 1 and points to new telephone, attempts "phone" conversation.
Narrative: Child:	C tries to place piece, tries to remove other piece, continues attempt.	C passes receiver of phone 1 to M, pulls new phone to self and holds up receiver to ear, then picks up and examines phone itself, phone slips from grasp, points toward bag asking for ball.
Zone of Proximal Development:	(placing pieces in puzzle: difficult, interested)	imagining conversation – difficult, loses interest quickly
Object Relative to Parent/Adult:	(in C's lap, C sitting in M's lap)	(beside)
Object Relative to Child:	in lap	in front of, then in hand
PARENT/ADULT:		
Attention Focus:	C/toy	C/toy
Form: Verbal (V):	+	+
Form: Nonverbal (NV):	+	+
Initiates/Responds (V):	+R (no don't take them out.)	+I (phone conversation)
Initiates/Responds (NV):	+R (blocks move)	+I (A introduces 2nd phone and M takes up phone for "phone call.")
Structures Situation (V):	+	+ (ring ring, hello)

Structures Situation (NV):	+	+ (takes up phone 1)
Handles Hard Part (V):		
Handles Hard Part (NV):	+ (presses piece into slot, etc.)	
Transfers Responsibility (V):	+	+ ("telephone," intonation of notification)
Transfers Responsibility (NV):	+ (hands piece to C)	+ (points to telephone)
Bridge from Familiar (V):		+ (ring ring)
Bridge from Familiar (NV):		
Does Task:	+	
Hands on:	+ (presses down on C hands)	
Reorientation:	+ (2X)	
Removes Hand:		
Blocks Wrong Move:	+ (blocks C removing piece already placed)	
Points with Contact:	+ (taps space)	
Points without Contact:		+ (to 2nd phone)
Displays for Analysis:		
Talks with Analysis:		
Gestures for Analysis:		
Marked by Action:		M takes old receiver and begins role-playing conversation.
Other:		
CHILD:		
Attention Focus:	toy	toy, then bag of toys
Form (V):	+	+
Form (NV):	+	+
Initiates/Responds (V):	+R (complains at M's attempts to control action)	+I (attempts to terminate episode)
Initiates/Responds (NV):	+I? (C tries to remove piece)	+R (to phone call play)
Places Self to Observe:		
Actively Directs:		asks for new toy
Other:	C's attempt to remove piece was apparently in order to try to place new piece in same slot.	
Mismatches:	What M construes as attempts to assist C's	

completion of task C construes as interference, or shift in task.

Notes:

In order to carry on play phone conversation, C must pretend that (her) M is a different person, which may be too difficult, or just not interesting.

NOTES

An early version of this paper was presented by the first author at a conference at the University of Toronto, June 22–24, 1990. The research reported herein has been supported by a grant from the Spencer Foundation. For their help in this project, we wish to thank Kristin Avery, Desha Baker, Lori Bauer, Cynthia Butcher, Trung Dinh, and Rose Villacis.

1. In tapes shown by Colwyn Trevarthen, middle-class and working-class families in Edinburgh, Scotland, display similar interaction style differences to those we observe between inner city and suburban families in Chicago.
2. We are grateful to Sidney Hans and Rob Jagers for discussing these issues with us and for their insights into the possible factors influencing our inner city mothers. It is difficult not to regard the inner city interventionist style as frustrating children's exploratory spirit. We saw adults actively interfere while their children fiddled in a purposeless manner with toys, as if this kind of activity should be suppressed. We can't say, once again, exactly why this would happen, but it would seem to be a strong discouragement of exploratory activity.
3. We are planning a more extensive report of the phenomenon of sons and daughters being differentially treated by caretakers, chiefly by mothers.

REFERENCES

Bates, E. (1976). *Language and context: The acquisition of pragmatics.* New York: Academic Press.

Bekken, K. (1989). Is there "motherese" in gesture? Ph.D. dissertation, University of Chicago.

Church, R. B., & Goldin-Meadow, S. (1986). The mismatch between gesture and speech as an index of transitional knowledge. *Cognition, 23,* 43–71.

Rogoff, B. (1986). Adult assistance of children's learning. In T. E. Raphael (ed.), *The contexts of school-based literacy* (pp. 27–40). New York: Random House.

———. (1990). *Apprenticeships in thinking.* Oxford: Oxford University Press.

Shatz, M. (1982). On mechanisms of language acquisition: Can features of the communicative environment account for development? In E. Wanner & L.

Gleitman (eds.), *Language acquisition: The state of the art* (pp. 102–127). Cambridge: Cambridge University Press.

Sperry, L. L. (1991). The emergence and development of narrative competence in African-American toddlers from a rural Alabama Community. Ph.D. dissertation, University of Chicago.

Vygotsky, L. S. (1962). *Thought and language* (E. Hanfmann & G. Vakar, eds. & trans.). Cambridge, MA: MIT Press.

———. (1978). *Mind in society* (M. Cole, V. John-Steiner, S. Scribner, & E. Souberman, eds.). Cambridge, MA: Harvard University Press.

———. (1981). The genesis of higher mental functions. In J. V. Wertsch (ed.), *The concept of activity in Soviet psychology* (pp. 144–188). Armonk, NY: M. E. Sharpe.

Wertsch, J. V. (1979). From social interaction to higher psychological processes: A clarification and application of Vygotsky's theory. *Human Development, 22,* 1–22.

6 *An ecological approach to the emergence of the lexicon: Socializing attention*

PATRICIA ZUKOW-GOLDRING AND
KELLY R. FERKO

Infants who are learning to talk, toddlers engaging in book-looking interactions with caregivers, and preschoolers and kindergartners have something in common. At home and at school, all are novices immersed in new and unfamiliar cultures. All of these children must come to detect patterns in what, at first, is a seamless, continuous flow of perceptual information. Events in daily life are not media constructs edited to have sharply delimited beginnings or ends. Conversation is not composed of tightly organized and self-contained sound-bites whose meaning is unambiguous. Instead, life for a novice is much more like an unedited or candid home movie whose organization and structure is not immediately transparent. Cultural meaning will be emergent, gradually detected by guided participation in ordinary activities, not by passive viewing or solitary problem-solving.

How do these infant- and child-novices gradually come to recognize/identify, participate in, and communicate about events in either setting? We argue that novices are assisted in their development by caregivers, family members and teachers, in both settings. Caregivers talk about what is happening as events unfold. In the midst of engaging in almost any part of the daily routine, caregivers unwittingly and unceasingly transmit knowledge of cultural practices by directing young members' attention to the dynamic relations between themselves and what the environment might offer. To do anything and get it done (from eating to bathing to napping), infants must be continuously focused (and refocused) on the who, what, where, when, and why of daily doings.

In this chapter investigations of the emergence of the early lexicon will illustrate the theoretical underpinnings grounding this approach. Our thesis is that the matrix within which infants are guided to notice linguistic conventions is *social,* whereas the process by which this type of cultural information is detected is *perceptual.* A neo-Vygotskian perspective provides a means to examine the contribution of the interactional setting to children's emergent abilities, while an ecological approach (E. Gibson, 1969, 1984; J. J. Gibson, 1966, 1979) suggests a way to explain the child's detection of the information transmitted. Empirical evidence from research investigating the emergence of the lexicon will illustrate how caregivers direct infants' attention to important aspects of ongoing events. Caregivers use gestures to mark the relation between what is being said and what is happening. The focus of attention is gradually shifted from simply noticing animate beings and objects to the opportunities they may afford for action. This research suggests that there may be somewhat different preferences for directing attention related to cultural heritage (Zukow, 1987). If this finding is confirmed, then we might expect communicative mismatches when children from nondominant cultures enter school. In addition, studies of parent–child reading events underscore the importance of caregivers' guiding their children's attention during book-looking interactions (Ninio, 1980; Panofsky, 1986, 1989).

VYGOTSKIAN APPROACH

Few psychologists subscribe any longer to the notion that infants come into the world as "blank slates" with no natural abilities. However, infants *are* "cultural" blank slates. That is, cultural knowledge including linguistic knowledge is not somehow innate, but must be learned (Dent, 1990; Zukow, 1990b). Vygotsky (1978) argued that society and culture provide children with opportunities to develop (Wertsch, 1985). In this view, social interaction is considered to be the source from which all higher functions, such as voluntary attention, thinking, logical memory, and language, arise. According to Vygotsky, emerging abilities first appear during interaction with more competent members of the culture. Only later can the child perform without guidance. Mental functioning that is guided by a more competent person is termed the *level of potential development,* while the child's accomplishments achieved without such assistance are called the *level of actual development.* The area between fully guided and autonomous functioning is known as the *zone of proximal development.*

Many studies have shown that in these interactional settings caregivers carefully "scaffold" activities by building on what children already know (Bruner, 1977; Bruner & Sherwood, 1976; Gardner & Rogoff, 1982; Greenfield & Lave, 1982; Saxe, Gearhart, & Guberman, 1984; Snow, 1977; Wertsch et al., 1980; Wood & Middleton, 1975; Zukow, 1989, 1990a; Zukow, Reilly, & Greenfield, 1982). Initially, when caregivers begin to invite infants to become active participants in daily life, they carefully structure events so that the elements necessary to undertake the activity are in the appropriate configuration for action to take place. In this early phase the caregiver may act out both participants' turns in the activity (Snow, 1977). She or he will often demonstrate the action and may then do the infant's part as well (Zukow, 1989, 1990a) or put the passive child through the motions of the activity (Zukow, 1987). This complete "other-regulation" of the infant is gradually phased out as the infant begins to participate. Adjusting to the infant's growing contribution, caregivers modulate the information that they provide by setting up the preconditions for the child to act. For the most part when the infant falters and needs assistance, caregivers facilitate the infant's participation by making some missing information more prominent (Zukow, Reilly, & Greenfield, 1982). According to this view, when the infant eventually internalizes the structure of the activity, the infant can perform unassisted, "self-regulating" her or his own actions. As a part of his legacy, Vygotsky left us a means to characterize the interactive settings in which cultural knowledge is transmitted. According to Vygotsky's description of "the cultural development of attention," caregivers "who surround the child begin to use various stimuli and means to direct attention" (Vygotsky, 1981, p. 198). However, the means by which *infants detect* the information they are so carefully guided to notice has not been explicitly addressed.

The following account illustrates a caregiver's step-by-step guidance in the *zone of proximal development* without making explicit the information (in brackets) that the child may actually notice and use to guide her or his actions. When a child learns to roll a ball back and forth, the caregiver [will seat the infant a few feet away facing her or him. A seated position with legs apart keeps the infant sturdily seated. This seated configuration serendipitously provides a built-in guide for the trajectory of the ball while allowing freedom of movement in the infant's upper body. Attention will be monitored and may be directed to the ball by bouncing it in front of the infant or waggling it in her or his line of sight while saying *Look at the ball!*. At first the caregiver] will roll the ball [through the parted legs] to the child and then lean over and roll the ball back for the child as the caregiver says *Throw the ball.* The caregiver may also [place the infant's hands on the ball and] guide its return. Gradually the infant will be assisted to release and roll the ball with less direct physical contact. Eventually attempts will be made to control the ball's trajectory. [In this phase, the repeated retraction of the caregiver's outreaching arms accompanied by *Look, toss it here = toss it here!*[1] may be enough to visually guide the direction of the infant's action.] Examples such as these highlight the guidance that caregivers continuously and carefully provide. However, whether or how the infants might detect the information most relevant for achieving the task at hand (tossing the ball to the caregiver) from all the possibilities available has not been investigated until recently. To understand the potential importance of the perceptual information contained in the brackets, an ecological approach to perception will be explored.

ECOLOGICAL APPROACH

In this section, a means for investigating the emergence of the lexicon is developed from key ideas taken from the ecological perspective. Perceptual information that is made available during social interaction serves as a basis for applying ecological principles to the problem of lexical development. The point of the highlighted segments in the preceding example is to illustrate that infants are not faced with an infinite set of options when attempting to achieve whatever task is at hand. Instead, caregivers severely limit alternatives, so that infants can eventually detect the conventional relations between words and world. Kinesthetic, visual, tactile, and (possibly) auditory information specifies the trajectory of the ball as it travels from one person to another, making transparent the invariant[2] relation between *toss* and the directed action of the ball.

The ecological approach to perception was derived by James J. Gibson (1979) from the perspective of a creature in its environment. Gibson theorized that perceptual information specifies its source in the environment and is detectable. Reed (1988, in press), a student and biographer of Gibson, has asserted that organisms perceive, act on, and know their environment. The notion that perceiving guides action is one of the key principles informing the work of ecological psychologists. For instance, the powerful interplay between vision and action can be experienced by attempting (unsuccessfully) to engage in the most mundane activities, such as walking up or down stairs, getting on or off an escalator, or walking through a doorway while wearing inverting prisms or blindfolded.[3] Under the same difficult conditions a person might initiate a conversation with someone, conduct a meeting, or coordinate speaking parts in a play. The person would find out how much an individual depends on vision to tell her or him how to make finely graded adjustments in her or his movements. The flow of familiar visual information will elude the eyes' clumsy searching. A person may clutch for an unfindable banister. Unable to see where she or he is stepping, staggering alternating with paralysis may result when trying to find a first or last stair. When trying to talk, a person may find that there are awkward starts and stops if the eye gaze and postural cues of the conversational partner continuously slip from view. When seeing is disrupted, visually guided action is severely hampered. The information that we are temporarily unable to detect prevents us from continuously monitoring and ascertaining the opportunities for action afforded by the environment.

Affordances

Central to the ecological perspective is the notion of *affordance* for action. According to J. J. Gibson (1979), there is a complimentarity between an animal and its niche, such that the animate and inanimate elements in the environment afford or offer unique advantages and disadvantages to each creature. For example, a puddle of rain water on a slick surface offers splashing, jumping, slipping to a person and is a potential swim-in-able, land-on-able, or drown-in-able for a variety of insects. Dynamic creatures perceive what the physical world affords by detecting invariance in the perceptual (visual, auditory, tactile, kinesthetic) array. An ecological approach suggests that development at any level may rely on or be enhanced by directing a child to notice the affordances of socio-cultural relations, including language.

To explain the emergence of language, Dent (1990) has theorized that "language is connected to the world and is, thereby, learnable." Dent discusses how children might come to detect the relation between language devices, such as tonal inflections, words, surface syntactic forms, and events that occur during everyday life. Appealing to Millikan (1984), she has argued that language devices must correspond to stable patterns in the environment if they are to be adaptive and workable for language learners. Her position is solidly grounded in an ecological approach to perception (Dent & Rader, 1979; J. J. Gibson, 1966, 1979; Rader & Dent, 1979; Reed 1985, 1987). From this view, people directly perceive meaningful information, because the structure in the environment emerges and is detectable while interacting with it. People perceive what the physical world affords, whether object, organism, or event, by the detection of invariance in the perceptual (visual, auditory, tactile, kinesthetic) array. Therefore, language devices and their relation to the world are detectable.

The education of attention

How are affordances made prominent and available to infants? According to J. J. Gibson (1966, pp. 51–52) attention must be educated so that the development or differentiation of perceptual abilities can take place. Attention is educated by more competent members of society who promote the noticing of affordances (Reed, in press; Zukow, 1990b). As a result of these experiences, perceptual differentiation increases, resulting in the detection of new affordances. To understand language development, an ecological psychologist would examine what caregivers do to educate attention. Specifically, how do they make the affordances of linguistic devices detectable.

Affordances during interaction

The initial problem for the child is to relate what is being said to what is happening. For perceptual differentiation related to language development to take place, there must be a matching and linking between the infant's ability to detect stable patterns and the perceptual information specifying the relation between language and ongoing events. For example, where to throw a ball will *not* be specified by a mother's point accompanied by saying *throw it to Daddy!* unless the infant can complete the trajectory of a point. For the point to be effective, the infant must be able to trace the trajectory from the end of the index finger through space to the place where it intersects with the topic of the point (Zukow, 1983). In this example, the topic is a father who affords "catching" by having his arms and hands arranged to receive the ball (Zukow, 1983). Infants just learning to speak may orient in the direction of the gesture (Scaife & Bruner, 1975; Butterworth, 1989) but, in fact, may not be able to follow a trajectory to its end point (Zukow, 1990c). However, if father and infant are seated facing one another, the infant's outstretched legs along with those of the father will mark a visual and physically constraining avenue for the ball to travel. Then, if the father synchronizes repeatedly retracting his outstretched arms as he says *Throw the ball to Daddy!,* the message may be better suited to a child just beginning to talk. In this case, the entire pathway from the child to the father as well as the direction of the motion are made perceptually available. This perceptual information provides dynamic guidance for the infant's response by making prominent the next course of action while eliminating other alternatives. When engaging infants in new activities, caregiver messages may be ineffective or not immediately comprehended. In these situations, caregivers often reduce ambiguity by providing perceptual translations of their verbal messages (Zukow, 1983, 1990c; Zukow et al., 1982). In this case, the father may eventually reach out and roll the ball to himself.

SOCIALIZING ATTENTION

Ecological studies of the relation between the social environment embodied as caregivers, perception, and the development of language have been recently initiated. A key assumption guiding this approach is

Dent's hypothesis that language devices corresponding to recurring patterns in the environment are detectable. Work conducted to investigate the emergence of the early lexicon (Zukow, 1989, 1990a, 1990b) provides empirical support for Dent's suggestions. This research has documented how caregivers bring the relation between words and daily activities to their children's attention during social interaction.

To investigate the education of attention, interactions during which caregivers directed attention were analyzed. Selection of these interactions was informed by their hypothesized importance in ecological theory (Reed, 1988, in press). During these interactions caregivers make various aspects of ongoing events perceptually prominent. The infant's noticing of this information may promote perceptual differentiation and the detection of affordances. In addition, this decision was based on attention-directing's proposed contribution to successful interaction and communication, empirical findings confirming their relation to language development, and their common occurrence. Various scholars (Bates, 1976; Shweder, 1982) have asserted that (cultural) knowledge shared by all competent members is the foundation of successful communication. However, common understandings may provide a range of possible interpretations during interaction rather than consensus. How mutuality is achieved in any given situation has not been explained. In fact, the cultural knowledge and practices by which common understandings are attained among adults are usually taken for granted and only noticed when communication breaks down. In answer to this omission, we propose that during interaction the moment-by-moment basis for consensus is embodied as a shared focus of attention. In support for this proposal, several researchers have argued that the establishment and/or negotiation of joint attention by competent members provides the basis for exchanging information (Atkinson, 1982) or reaching a working consensus (Schegloff, 1972). Even less can be assumed when communicating with infants. Little regarding the infant's or novice member's knowledge can be assumed except that it is limited and the detecting of information is confined to the "here and now." Therefore, the practices used by the caregiver-expert to continuously establish a shared focus of interaction are especially important to the transmission and acquisition of cultural knowledge, including linguistic knowledge (Zukow, 1989; see Bruner, 1983; Wells, 1981 for related arguments). Recent investigations (Bruner, 1983; Adamson, Bakeman, & Smith, in press; Goldfield, 1987; Tamis-LeMonda & Bornstein, 1989; Tomasello & Farrar, 1986; Tomasello & Todd, 1983; Vibbert & Bornstein, 1989) undertaken for somewhat different ends have shown a relation between promoting shared attention and the emergence of the lexicon. However, the socio-perceptual processes underlying these findings have not been specified.

The development of the early lexicon also requires that the child detect the conventional relations that hold between the continuous streams of linguistic and perceptual information. Theoretical views that invoke innate biases appear to assume that simple spatio-temporal contiguity will serve as a satisfactory explanation of how children detect the relations between words and world. However, the mere co-occurrence of a perceptually sensitive infant and the availability of detectable information in the perceptual array does not guarantee that conventional relations will be detected. The conditions following from a spatio-temporal explanation would lead to the development of a very idiosyncratic lexicon. Specifically, the child might link the saying of a particular word with any aspect of the event that occurs simultaneously with the speech. The number of possibilities are open-ended. Given the spatio-temporal contiguity perspective, on being put to sleep for a nap, what prevents a child from relating a word such as *sing* to bird, sleeping, pillow, crib, window, clouds, tree, or any of the numerous other elements available during everyday events (Braunwald, 1978; Stemmer, 1983)? A child might relate a word, *bird,* to a property of it, *feathers,* a part, *wings,* or its location, *branch* (cf. Quine, 1960) rather than the whole animal. (For a discussion of these issues, see Zukow 1990b, p. 712.) No doubt this position can account for many of the nonconventional and/or idiosyncratic meanings that young children have been observed to express. Unguided or haphazard pairings very well may underlie under- and overextensions (Bowerman 1976; Braunwald, 1978), such as calling only canaries *birdie* or calling all men *daddy.*

To make the transition to linguistic representation, children must *perceive/notice* conventional lexical relations (Schmidt & Dent, 1985, 1986) before they can comprehend and produce them (Zukow, 1989). During attention-directing interactions caregivers often unite attention-directing gestures with speech. The caregiver is able to illustrate the conventional relation between speech and what it represents at the nonconventional level of perception and action (Schmidt & Dent, 1986; Zukow & Schmidt, 1987, 1988). We have called this process in which caregivers specify culturally relevant and socially shared topics perceptually for the child's benefit *socializing attention* (Zukow, 1989, 1990a). In socializing attention caregivers use both gesture and speech. In these situations the occurrence of a linguistic device, say a name, is actually coincident *both* with the presence of some stable pattern in the environment, the labeled topic of attention, and with the action directing attention to that object. For instance, the saying of "*Look at the bunny!*" co-occurs with the topic, a toy, being waggled in the child's line of sight, the gesture.

Method

We have drawn examples from a series of intra- and intercultural studies in the United States and Mexico (Zukow, 1989, 1990b; Zukow & Schmidt, 1987) to illustrate the generality of our findings. Although there appear to be culture-specific differences in caregiving practices related to folk theories of child rearing and child development among some of these families (Zukow, 1984), the similarities in practices used to direct attention between cultures is very striking (Zukow & Schmidt, 1987). Naturalistic videotapes of everyday interaction were collected in the home, because it is generally agreed that this is the context in which language development occurs. Great care was taken in preserving the ecological validity of these interactional settings. (For a more detailed description of the complete methodology, see Zukow, 1989, 1990b.)

Sample: caregivers. The Mexican caregivers came from the traditional rural culture of Central Mexico. Five families lived in Colonias Populares in Mexico City or on the outskirts in the Estado de Mexico; 7 families lived in a rural area (Ejido de Santa Ana y Lobos) in the state of Guanajuato some 175 miles northwest of the Federal District. Of the 12 families who participated in the study, only one mother had completed more than 4 years of primary schooling. Videotapings were made at 6-week intervals over a 9- to 12-month period. The 6 Anglo middle-class families resided in Santa Monica, California. All had attended at least a few years of junior college; some were professionals. Videotapings were made at one month intervals during a 2-year longitudinal study from 6 to 30 months of age.

Procedure. Each caregiver–child pair was videotaped for 30 minutes interacting in their home. Simultaneous audio-recordings were made of each videotaped session. These audio-recordings were transcribed by a native speaker according to the conventions established by Sachs, Schegloff, and Jefferson (1974) and Zukow (1982). In order to ensure that the researcher's interpretation of the activities was in agreement with that of the caregiver, the videotapes were reviewed with the caregiver immediately following each videotaped session. In cases of disagreement, precedence was given to the caregiver-expert's interpretation of events and utterances. The videotapes were then viewed and reviewed by independent coders to identify attention-directing interactions. The coders used protocols developed to differentiate various aspects of attention-directing in conjunction with the transcripts of the videotaped interactions. (See Zukow, 1989, 1990b.)

Attention-directing interactions. Attention-directing presentations have been defined here as a message directing the other interactant to coordinate her or his attention to that of the message-initiator for the duration of the specified activity (Zukow 1989, 1990b). To operationalize this definition, all instances of the perceptual imperatives, such as *Look!* or *Listen,* initiated by caregivers and directed to the target child were collected along with any accompanying attention-directing gestures. This collection provided an ethnographic basis for determining the range or scope of attention-directing gestures and topics. In addition to utterances such as *Look at the cat!, Look, get down!, Look, sweep over there!,* occurrences of attention-directing gestures in nonlinguistic and in other linguistic environments were collected as well, for example, pointing while saying *Over there!*

Attention-directing gestures. All actions associated with utterances accompanied by perceptual imperatives fell along a continuum of perceptual regulation that ranged from complete guidance or "other-regulation" by the caregiver to complete self-regulation by the child (extrapolated from analysis of problem solving) by Wertsch et al. [1980]. Secondarily, this dimension roughly describes a transition from nonconventional to conventional gestures. During attention-directing interactions the child's task is to determine which aspects of the ongoing interaction are being foregrounded.[4] The difficulty of the task depends on the perceptual support provided by the gesture used. In the first, SHOWING, the child's perception is controlled by the caregiver. For instance, some object of attention is rotated, loomed, waggled in(to) the child's line of sight. In the second, ACT-ON, the child is put through the motions of an activity or the child is positioned to experience the perceptual information, such as looming the child toward her or his own reflection in a mirror. In the third, DEMONSTRATING, an aspect of the ongoing activity is highlighted for an already attending child who is given an opportunity to participate. The fourth, POINTING, depends upon the child's ability to follow a trajectory of an object or the trajectory traced by a head nod or hand point to the place where it intersects with the object of attention. In the fifth, LOOK (i.e., uttering "look" without an accompanying gesture), words direct the child to coordinate her or his attention to that of the caregiver. (LOOKs are not considered in this chapter, because in these interactions it is the child's responsibility to detect the relation between words and world.)

Socializing attention is effective because of the perceptual salience of the gestures used to direct attention to topics of the interactional situation (Zukow & Schmidt, 1988). Take the following segment as an example.

Qualitative examples

Example 1: SHOWing an object (CBO8, 00:50)[5]

Cindy, aged 8 months, and her mother Yvette were seated on the bed in her parents' bedroom. Cindy was looking down at the various toys scattered around the bed, watching her mother manipulate them. Yvette picked up a rattle and moved it toward Cindy. Cindy lifted her head and focused her gaze on the rattle moving in front of her. Yvette rotated the rattle with her thumb and index finger, moving it back and forth around its vertical axis. As Yvette rotated the rattle, it produced noises. Carefully monitoring Cindy, Yvette ceased rattling as Cindy reached out and grasped the rattle with her right hand. Yvette released the rattle into Cindy's grasp. Cindy imitated her mother by rotating the rattle around the same vertical axis.

Many SHOW gestures appear to be optimal for displaying objects as an integrated whole. This SHOW involved a translational movement of the rattle, bringing it into the child's line of sight. According to J. J. Gibson (1979), *translation* produces the deletion of background surface texture in the optic array at the leading edge, with corresponding accretion at the trailing edge. Both the object and the trajectory or direction of the gesture are specified perceptually. The rattle is a relatively stable pattern in the visual array during this movement, presented against a background of shifting information. Further, the continuous deletion of surface texture in the background at the leading edge of the gesture along with a similar rate of accretion of surface texture at the trailing edge specifies the trajectory of the gesture. In SHOWs, attention is invited by the magnification or rotation of the topic. Further, the placement of the object usually intersects the line of sight of both caregiver and child, so that they are constrained to jointly attend to the same topic of attention and to monitor each other's gaze. In this case, the rattle is simultaneously being magnified and moved toward Cindy along this line. Visually, *magnification* involves an increase in the density of surface texture of the rattle and its enlargement in the visual field. As the rattle is brought toward Cindy there is a corresponding occlusion and diminishing of background information. Often the object is rotated about an axis at the apex of this movement. *Rotation* is a shift in the alignment of textural units across the topic surface. As the surface turns about an axis, information along one side is brought into view while information on the other is taken from view. In this example, the rattle is rotated around the vertical axis, 180 degrees one way and 180 the other, displaying the entire rattle. On many occasions this SHOW gesture would be accompanied by saying *Look at the ra::ttle!* or *Ra::tle!* The exaggerated vowel lengthening often co-occurs with the rotation of the rattle. The stilling of the rattle is delicately negotiated by caregiver and child as Cindy reaches toward it. From her ensuing action, Cindy displays that she has noticed both rattle and action.

Looming is another method caregivers use to make whole objects or persons prominent. When *looming* occurs, it is the symmetrical, accelerated magnification of a topic with a reciprocal decrease in the amount and access to information in the background.

Example 2: ACTing ON to loom a person (KJ12, 11:58)

At the end of a hallway in Lisa's house there was a full length mirror. As Lisa walked down the hallway holding Karen, aged 12 months, in her arms she said, *Who's that in the mirror? = who's that in the mirror?* When Lisa stopped directly in front of the mirror, Karen reached forward and pointed to the reflection of herself reflected in the mirror. Lisa acknowledged Karen's response by saying *Ka::re::n! That's right, Ka:re:n!*

In this case, as mother and child moved toward their images in the mirror, they slowly increased in size. As Karen leaned forward to touch her own reflection, it quickly grew larger in the mirror. Simultaneously, her expanding image blocked access to visual information behind her, including some of her mother's reflection. Lisa wittingly or unwittingly coordinated the saying of *Karen* with her daughter's reflection at its maximum, providing her with a sensitively timed co-occurrence of image and name.

Gestures are not limited to displaying the whole object, but have the potential to make tangible a broad range of semantic functions or linguistic devices. Different literal or singular gestures that are adjusted to the specifics of the situation may optimally display characteristics of particular topics. Preliminary evidence suggests that caregivers use rather distinctive gestures to display a variety of affordances.

In DEMOnstrations, caregivers facilitate the infant's engaging in an activity by modeling or by highlighting possibilities for action. Affordances are made tangible. The topography of a rough texture, such as corduroy, is traversed with a bouncing fingertip. The consistency of beaten egg white can be seen as it is rubbed across fingertips; balls are bounced; temperature extremes are mimed by elaborate avoidant responses.

Example 3: DEMOnstration of the texture of bristles (ZR12, 02:06)

Zeke, aged 12 months, and his mother were playing in the backyard. Zeke was crouching at the top of a few steps, while Ann was standing at the bottom. Ann held a broom directly in Zeke's line of sight and said, "Wanna play with the broom, Zeke?" Ann set the broom down in front of Zeke with the bristles of the broom positioned upward and within his reach. As Ann moved her fingertips across the bristles, she said,

"*Sti::::cky!*" describing the prickly sensation of the bristles on her fingertips. Zeke carefully watched his mother, reached out toward the broom, and stroked the bristles with his fingertips.

In this example, the translational movement of the hand over the bristles was quick, irregular, and bouncing. The disappearance of background surface texture as the fingertips covered the bristles along with its reciprocal reappearance at the trailing edge specified the trajectory of the gesture. The shallow, rapid, bumpy path of the fingers (superimposed on the complimentary swiftly changing background information) emerged as a repetitive, wavelike pattern that specified the uneven surface below.

POINT-traces follow the contours of animate beings and objects. For instance, contours are traced with the index finger while asking infants to look at handles of cups or body parts such as ears or eyes of toy animals.

Example 4: POINT-trace body part of a person (CB12, 03:50)
Yvette was seated on the living room floor, holding Cindy, aged 12 months, her daughter, with her right arm. They were looking at each other at eye level. Yvette used her left index finger to trace a line directly across her own closed eyelid, while she said, "*Eye.*" Cindy watched her mother and then pointed to her mother's eye. As Cindy pointed, Yvette repeated, "*Eye.*"

In this interaction, translation and rotation of the index finger reveal the extent and shape of the eye being traversed. The translational movement beginning at one corner of the eye and terminating at the other marked the horizontal boundaries of the eye. There is a graduated change in the acceleration of the alignment of textural units across the length of the finger as the tip moves over the eye. Along the vertical axis information is brought into view at the fingertip more rapidly than at the knuckle, specifying a convex surface. The beginning and ending of the point-trace and the saying of *eye* are coincident.

Example 5: POINT-trace to part of a toy (KJ12, 05:40)
Karen, aged 12 months, was seated on the living room floor somewhat in front of Lisa, her mother, playing with a puzzle. Karen was holding a puzzle piece shaped like a giraffe. Then Lisa pointed to the place where the giraffe fit into the puzzle. Karen looked at her mother pointing to the puzzle, but made no move to fit the piece into the puzzle. As Karen looked down at the puzzle piece she was holding, her mother leaned forward and used her index finger to trace the contour of the giraffe's long neck. While tracing back and forth over the gi-

raffe's neck, she said, "See the long neck?" After watching her mother trace the giraffe's neck on the puzzle piece, Karen attempted to fit the piece into the puzzle.

In this interaction, the length and contour of the giraffe's neck, a subsegment of the animal, is differentiated from the entire toy. Again, translation and rotation along a surface, this time an edge, displays just and only the part of the toy mentioned in the caregiver's utterance.

Using a *POINT,* an object or location can be made noticeable in an otherwise undifferentiated expanse of background. If the trajectory of a projectile, such as a rock or a point that traces the entire trajectory from eye to object, intersects with the background, the topic of attention will be unambiguously specified (Zukow, 1983; Zukow et al., 1982; Zukow & Schmidt, 1988).

Example 6: POINTing to a location (IGS, 6/4/82, 12:45:99)[6]

In this semi-rural suburb of Mexico City, Irene, aged 25 months, had been repeatedly sweeping with a branch on command. Her mother, Carlota urged her to *Barre!* (*Sweep!*). The sweeping caused huge billows of dust to drift down on everyone nearby. Finally, Carlota attempted to get Irene to move away by saying *Bién barrido, todo eso!* (*Well swept, all of that!*). She accompanied her speech with a point tracing the extent of ground to be swept. The point was not visible to Irene and specified a spot some 15 feet or more away. Carlota's next point accompanied by *Todo eso!* (*All of that!*) was visible. Irene, not comprehending replied *Eh?* (*Huh?*) to both points. Carlota's next point and speech *P'allá!* (*Over there!*) were not comprehended either. Finally, Carlota tossed a rock to the place to be swept as she said *P'allá! = Mira allí!* (*Over there! = look there!*). Irene rotated to follow the trajectory of the rock, watched it raise a puff of dust as it hit the ground, walked to the spot, and began to sweep.

While a competent member of the culture could infer the entire trajectory from the fragment traced by Carlota's index finger, apparently Irene could not. Infants just learning to speak may orient in the direction of a point (Scaife & Bruner, 1975; Butterworth, 1989) but in fact, may not be able to complete a trajectory to its end point (Zukow, 1990c). In the trajectories of the points and of the rock, translation produces an occlusion of background surface texture at the leading edge of the finger or rock with concomitant uncovering of that texture at the trailing edge. The rock or fingertip is a relatively stable pattern in the optic array, while the continuous covering and uncovering of background surface texture specifies the trajectory. The trajectory of the rock finally intersects with the ground, sending up a puff of dust. The momentary *deformation* of the surface sends up grains of dirt to occlude what is beyond it and mark the location for sweeping.

> *Example 7: POINTing to an object* (JLA, 8/19/82, 19:28:27)
> In San Juan Totoltepec in the Estado de Mexico outside Mexico City, the family of Julio Arizon, aged 30 months, gathered in their tiny kitchen to watch the preparation of a very festive and infrequent meal of chile relleno. Julio's aunt, Lola, was using an electric mixer to beat the egg whites. The children gathered in fascination to watch this unusual event. The frothing egg whites began to spatter to the delight of the children. Jorge, Julio's older brother, said *Mira ahi!* (*Look there!*) and pointed to and touched the egg white that had landed on his sister Vero's dress. He traced the entire trajectory of the point from the corner of Julio's eye until his finger touched the egg white. Julio stepped forward to touch the beaten egg white and rapidly wiped it on his shirt.

Again, the structure of the information available in the optic array revealed the trajectory of the point through translation. This particular interaction is important because it illustrates how ambiguity is avoided. While the referent *ahi* (*there*) in the utterance does not tell Julio whether to notice his sister, her dress, or the egg white on the dress, the end point of trajectory is clearly marked by Jorge's touching of the egg white. Differentiating an object from a larger whole or from the surface beneath it is not an unresolvable dilemma, as the literature might suggest (Baldwin & Markman, 1989; Golinkoff et al., 1989; Markman, 1989, in press; Woodward & Markman, in press; cf. Zukow, 1990c). Caregivers, including somewhat older siblings, can provide perceptual information that makes philosophically subtle distinctions a simple matter.

This is the first work that makes explicit the methods by which caregivers' actions are tailored to direct attention to the essential details of ongoing events. Problematic understandings are often resolved through guidance by the caregiver. Caregivers limit choices. They educate infants' attention by relating lexical items to ongoing activities as a matter of course. Educating the infant's attention to the relation between world and words occurs repeatedly as stable patterns are made noticeable across many dynamic experiences. These gestures uniquely display the affordances of the topic of attention expressed by the accompanying semantic functions or linguistic devices. If attention is guided, little ambiguity in interpretation need result.

Implications for schooling. An ecological approach to the emergence of the lexicon is promising. There may be enough information in interaction across contexts to specify language devices sufficiently for the early lexicon to develop. Once that has happened, a great deal of socio-perceptual boot-strapping might occur, so that more complex aspects of language development, such as reading events and classroom lessons, might proceed from this foundation.

In the home, socializing agents guide the emergence of the child's knowledge of her or his culture by educating the child's spontaneous attentional abilities to engender a shared perspective of the world. The relation between the nonverbal and verbal marking of these patterns and their recognition enables children to segment a seamless physical reality into everyday events shared by other members of the culture (Zukow et al., 1982; Zukow, 1989, 1990a, 1990b; see also Mehan & Wood, 1975; Mehan, 1982.) The emergence of the ability to identify and interpret events relevant to one's culture is a prerequisite to effectively participating in and communicating about those events.

We suggest that when a novice enters any "new" culture, socializing agents of the new culture will mark important aspects of the ongoing stream of information into events relevant to that culture. The problem is that different cultures and different cultural subgroups secure, convey, and direct attention to new information in different ways (Heath, 1983; Michaels, 1982; Philips 1972, 1983; Shultz, Florio, & Erickson, 1982; Zukow, 1987). The consequences of these differences have implications for transitions from one cultural milieu to another, for example, from home to school. The task of detecting culturally relevant information at school is facilitated by socializing practices congruent with the culture of the home, while miscomprehension appears to be rather general and not cultural, due to being a nonnative rather than a native speaker.

Another preliminary finding suggests that media (print or replicas of natural kinds) often affect the type of gesture used. That is, all the teachers point to print, while they demonstrate or act on a student to illustrate the affordances of objects (tracing the outer edge of an object to highlight shape versus moving the student's hand around the object's perimeter). In contrast, teachers of different cultural origins appear to display rather different gestural combinations and configurations to repair breakdowns in communication. Qualitative analyses are underway to determine how these variations in input may affect comprehension. Eventually stylistic differences in the classroom will be related to communicative patterns observed in the home.

In sum, we propose that (1) the process of socializing attention underlies the emergence of cultural knowledge; (2) the cultural practices that socialize attention can vary from culture to culture; (3) these practices are not necessarily interchangeable or mutually intelligible; and (4) the degree of congruence between home and school practices in socializing attention will affect the rate at which the child becomes a competent member in the culture of the school.

NOTES

Preparation of this chapter was partially funded by a grant awarded to the first author by the Michelle F. Elkind Foundation. Her research conducted in Mexico was supported by NIMH Postdoctoral Fellowship #5 F32 MH 07996-02 and by a Spencer Foundation Grant awarded to Patricia Greenfield. The U.S. data reported was funded by a grant to P. Goldring (Zukow) from the Spencer Foundation, the University of California Linguistics Minority Project, and the Social Sciences Research Council with the Foundation for Child Development.

1. Rapid offset/onset or latching is indicated by equal signs (=) (Sachs et al., 1974; Zukow, 1982). Colons (::) indicates syllable lengthening.
2. Invariance refers to patterns of organization (or relationships) in perceptual structure that is retained under transformation/remains stable despite superficial change (J. J. Gibson, 1966).
3. These descriptions are taken from informal experiments undertaken in courses on normal environments conducted by Harold Garfinkel in 1978–1979.
4. Because caregiver gaze is common to all attention-directing gestures, our analysis does not treat gaze separately.
5. (OBO8.00.50) identifies a particular infant, CB. The videotape was made within a few days of her 8th (08) "month"-date. The timecode was 0 minutes, 50 seconds when the tape segment described began.
6. (IGS, 6/4/82, 12:45:99) refers to infant IGS. The videotape was made on June 4, 1982. The timecode was 12 minutes, 45 seconds, and 99/100 as the interaction described began.

REFERENCES

Adamson, L., Bakeman, R., & Smith, C. B. (in press). Gestures, words, and early object sharing. In V. Volterra & C. Erting (Eds.), *From gesture to language in hearing and deaf children.* New York: Springer-Verlag.

Atkinson, M. (1982). *Explanations in the study of child language development.* Cambridge: Cambridge University Press.

Baldwin, D., & Markman, E. (1989). Establishing word-object relations: A first step. *Child Development, 60,* 381–398.

Bates, E. (1976). *Language and context: The acquisition of pragmatics.* New York: Academic Press.

Bowerman, M. (1976). Semantic factors in the acquisition of rules for word use and sentence construction. In D. M. Morehead & A. E. Morehead (Eds.), *Normal and deficient child language* (pp. 99–179). Baltimore: University Park Press.

Braunwald, S. R. (1978). Context, word and meaning: Toward a communicational analysis of lexical acquisition. In A. Lock (Ed.), *Action, gesture, and symbol: The emergence of language* (pp. 285–327). London: Academic Press.

Bruner, J. (1977). Early social interaction and language acquisition. In H. R. Schaffer (Ed.), *Studies in mother–infant interaction* (pp. 271–289). London: Academic Press.

Bruner, J. (1983). *Child's talk: Learning to use language.* New York: W. W. Norton.

Bruner, J., & Sherwood, V. (1976). Peekaboo and the learning of rule structures. In J. S. Bruner, A. Jolly, and K. Sylva (Eds.), *Play: Its role in development and evolution* (pp. 277–285). New York: Basic Books.

Butterworth, G. (1989, April). The current status of developmental theory and research. Paper presented at the Dynamical Psychology Workshop. Kansas City, MO.

Dent, C. (1990). An ecological approach to language development: An alternative functionalism. In C. Dent & P. G. Zukow, (Eds.), *The idea of innateness: Effects on language and communication research. Developmental Psychobiology, 23,* 679–703.

Dent, C., & Rader, N. (1979). Perception, meaning, and research in semantic development. In P. French (Ed.), *The development of meaning: Pedolinguistics series* (pp. 178–230). Japan: Bunka Hyoron Press.

Gardner, W., & Rogoff, B. (1982). The role of instruction in memory development: Some methodological choices. *Quarterly Newsletter of the Comparative Human Cognition, 4,* 6–12.

Gibson, E. J. (1969). *Principles of perceptual learning and development.* New York: Appleton-Century-Crofts.

Gibson, J. J. (1966). *The senses considered as perceptual systems.* Boston: Houghton Mifflin.

Gibson, J. J. (1979). *The ecological approach to visual perception.* Boston: Houghton Mifflin.

Goldfield, B. A. (1987). The contributions of child and caregiver to referential and expressive language. *Applied Psycholinguistics, 8,* 267–280.

Golinkoff, R., Bailey, L., Wenger, N., & Hirsh-Pasek, K. (1989, April). Conceptualizing constraints: Why and how many? In R. M. Golinkoff (Chair), *The case for "constraints" on lexical acquisition.* Symposium conducted at the Society for Research in Child Development. Kansas City, MO.

Greenfield, P. M., & Lave, J. (1982). Cognitive aspects of informal education. In D. A. Wagner & H. W. Stevenson (Eds.), *Cultural perspectives on child development* (pp. 181–207). San Francisco: Freeman.

Heath, S. B. (1983). *Way with words.* Cambridge: Cambridge University Press.

Markman, E. M. (1989). *Categorization and naming in children.* Cambridge, MA: MIT Press.

Markman, E. (in press). The whole object, taxonomic and mutual exclusivity assumptions as initial constraints on word meanings. In J. P. Byrnes & S. A. Gelman (Eds.), *Perspectives on language and cognition: Interrelations in development.* Cambridge: Cambridge University Press.

Mehan, H. (1982). The structure of classroom events and their consequences for student performance. In P. Gilmore & A. A. Glatthorn (Eds.), *Children in and out of school: Ethnography and education* (pp. 59–87). Washington, D.C.: Center for Applied Linguistics.

Mehan, H., & Wood, H. (1975). *The reality of ethnomethodology.* New York: Wiley.

Michaels, S. (1982). "Sharing time": Children's narrative styles and differential access to literacy. *Language in Society, 10,* 423–42.

Millikan, R. G. (1984). *Language, thought, and other biological categories: New Foundations for realism.* Cambridge, MA: MIT Press.

Ninio, A. (1980). Picture-book reading in mother–infant dyads belonging to two subgroups in Israel. *Child Development, 51,* 587–590.

Panofsky, C. (1986). Parent–child reading interactions: The importance of non-verbal behavior. In J. Niles & R. Lalik (Eds.), *Solving problems in literacy: Learners, teachers, researchers.* Rochester, NY: National Reading Conference.

Panofsky, C. (1989). The functions of language in parent–child book reading events. *Theory Into Practice, 28,* 120–125.

Philips, S. U. (1972). Participant structures and communicative competence: Warm Springs children in community and classroom. In C. B. Cazden, V. P. John, & D. Hymes (Eds.), *Functions of language in the classroom.* New York: Teachers College Press.

Philips, S. U. (1983). *The invisible culture: Communication in classroom and community on the Warm Springs Indian reservation.* New York: Longman.

Quine, W. V. O. (1960). *Word and object.* New York: Wiley.

Rader, N., & Dent, C. (1979). A theoretical approach to meaning based on a theory of direct perception. In P. French (Ed.), *The development of meaning: Pedolinguistics series* (pp. 146–177). Japan: Bunka Hyoron Press.

Reed, E. (1985). An ecological approach to the evolution of behavior. In T. D. Johnston & A. T. Pietrewicz (Eds.), *Issues in the ecological study of learning* (pp. 357–385). Hillsdale, NJ: Erlbaum.

Reed, E. (1987). James Gibson's ecological approach to cognition. In A. Costall & A. Still (Eds.), *Cognitive psychology in question* (pp. 142–175). New York: St. Martin's Press.

Reed, E. (1988). *James J. Gibson and the psychology of perception.* New Haven: Yale University Press.

Reed, E. (in press). The intention to use a specific affordance: A conceptual framework for psychology. In R. Wozniak & K. Fischer (Eds.), *Children's thinking: The effects of specific environments.* Hillsdale, NJ: Erlbaum.

Sachs, H., Schegloff, E. A., & Jefferson, G. (1974). A simplest systematic for the organization of turn-taking in a conversation. *Language, 50,* 696–735.

Saxe, G. B., Gearhart, M., & Guberman, S. R. (1984). Towards understanding social organization of early development. In B. Rogoff & J. V. Wertsch (Eds.), *Children's learning in the "zone of proximal development"* (pp. 19–30). San Francisco: Jossey-Bass.

Scaife, M., & Bruner, J. S. (1975). The capacity for joint visual attention in the infant. *Nature, 253,* 265–266.

Schegloff, M. (1972). Notes on a conversational practice: Formulating place. In D. Sudnow (Ed.), *Studies in social interaction* (pp. 75–119). New York: Free Press.

Schmidt, C., & Dent, C. H. (1985). The nature of lexical representation in natural language. Paper presented at the meeting of the International Linguistics Association, New York.

Schmidt, C., & Dent, C. H. (1986). Representation in the environment. Poster presented at the meeting of the International Society for Ecological Psychology, Philadelphia.

Shultz, J. J., Florio, S., & Erickson, F. (1982). Where's the floor: Aspects of the cultural organization of social relationships in communication at home and in school. In P. Gilmore & A. A. Glatthorn (Eds.), *Children in and out of school: Ethnography and education* (pp. 88–123). Washington, D.C.: Center for Applied Linguistics.

Shweder, R. (1982). Beyond self-constructed knowledge: The study of culture and morality. *Merrill-Palmer Quarterly, 28,* 41–69.

Snow, C. E. (1977). Mothers' speech research: From input to interaction. In C. E. Snow & C. A. Ferguson (Eds.), *Talking to children: Language input and acquisition* (pp. 31–50). Cambridge: Cambridge University Press.

Stemmer, N. (1983). *The roots of knowledge.* Oxford: Blackwell.

Tamis-LeMonda, C. S., & Bornstein, M. H. (1989). Habituation and maternal encouragement of attention in infancy as predictors of toddler language, play, and representational competence. *Child Development, 60,* 738–751.

Tomasello, M., & Farrar, M. J. (1986). Joint attention and early language. *Child Development, 57,* 1454–1463.

Tomasello, M., & Todd, J. (1983). Joint attention and lexical acquisition style. *First language, 4,* 197–212.

Vibbert, M., & Bornstein, M. H. (1989). Specific associations between domains of mother–child interaction and toddler referential language and pretense play. *Infant Behavior and Development, 12,* 163–184.

Vygotsky, L. S. (1978). *Mind in society: The development of higher psychological processes.* (Ed. M. Cole, V. John-Steiner, S. Scribner & E. Souberman.) Cambridge, MA: Harvard University Press.

Vygotsky, L. S. (1981). The development of higher forms of attention in childhood. In J. V. Wertsch (Tr. & Ed.), *The concept of activity in Soviet psychology* (pp. 189–240). Armonk, NY: M. E. Sharpe.

Wells, G. (1981). Becoming a communicator. In G. Wells (Ed.), *Learning through interaction: The study of language development* (pp. 73–115). Cambridge: Cambridge University Press.

Wertsch, J. V., (1985). *Vygotsky and the social formation of mind.* Cambridge, MA: Harvard University Press.

Wertsch, J. V., McNamee, G. D., McLane, J. G., & Budwig, N. A. (1980). The adult–child dyad as a problem solving system. *Child Development, 51,* 1215–1221.

Wood, D., & Middleton, D. (1975). A study of assisted problem-solving. *British Journal of Psychology, 66,* 181–191.

Woodward, A. L., & Markman, E. (in press). Constraints on learning as default assumptions: Comments on Merriman and Bowman's "The mutual exclusivity bias in children's word learning." *Developmental Review.*

Zukow, P. G. (1982). Transcription systems for videotaped interactions: Some advantages and limitations of manual and computer rendering techniques. *Applied Psycholinguistics, 3,* 61–79.

Zukow, P. G. (1983). An intra-ethnic comparison of the transition from nonverbal to verbal communication: Two case studies in Central Mexico. Unpublished manuscript.

Zukow, P. G. (1984). Folk theories of comprehension and caregiver style in a rural-born population in Central Mexico. *Quarterly Newsletter of the Laboratory of Comparative Human Cognition, 6,* 62–67.

Zukow, P. G. (1987, April). Socializing attention: Intracultural gestural variation and folk theories of child development in Central Mexico. Poster presented at the annual meeting of the Society for Research in Child Development, Baltimore.

Zukow, P. G. (1989). Siblings as effective socializing agents: Evidence from Mexico. In P. G. Zukow (Ed.), *Sibling interaction across cultures: Theoretical and methodological issues* (pp. 79–105). New York: Springer-Verlag.

Zukow, P. G. (1990a). Socializing attention and the emergence of linguistic representation: Intra-ethnic studies in Central Mexico. Unpublished manuscript, submitted for publication.

Zukow, P. G. (1990b). Socio-perceptual bases for the emergence of language: An alternative to innatist approaches. In C. Dent & P. G. Zukow (Eds.), *The idea of innateness: Effects on language and communication research. Developmental Psychobiology,* 705–726.

Zukow, P. G. (1990c). Verbal and gestural self-repair and elaborations of child-directed messages during attention-directing interactions. Unpublished manuscript.

Zukow, P. G., Reilly, J., & Greenfield, P. M. (1982). Making the absent present: Facilitating the transition from sensorimotor to linguistic communication. In K. E. Nelson (Ed.), *Children's language* (Vol. III, pp. 1–90). Hillsdale, NJ: Gardner.

Zukow, P. G., & Schmidt, C. (1987, April). Socializing attention in the U.S. and Mexico. Presented at the annual meetings of the Society for Research in Child Development, Baltimore.

Zukow, P. G., & Schmidt, C. (1988, April). Socializing attention: Perceptual bases for language socialization. Paper presented at the International Conference on Infant Studies, Washington, DC.

7 *Learning how to explain: The effects of mother's language on the child*

MARIA SILVIA BARBIERI AND
LILIANA LANDOLFI

Within the Vygotskian framework, explanations are a basic device for development and socialization. This chapter describes a study of mother–child interaction designed to analyze the contents and strategies of the mother's explanations, and their effects on the child. The aim was to test whether children incorporate maternal explanations and to explain how they do so.

However, before any study of the emergence of the explaining capacity in children can start, a definition of the object of inquiry is required.

An implicit assumption of our culture defines explanations as "the search for causes." In the psychological literature, Piaget is the most representative author of this approach. According to his view, the origin of the explaining capacity is linked to children's increasing ability to formulate correct representations of causal sequences, and make appropriate use of the connectives expressing this relation between two or more events. He discussed the issue of children's explanations in four books: *The Language and Thought of the Child* (first French edition 1923), *Judgement and Reasoning in the Child* (first French edition 1924), *The Child's Conception of the World* (first French edition 1926) and *The Child's Conception of Physical Causality* (first French edition 1927). At the time, he wanted to develop a treatise on children's logic aimed at describing the features of their reasoning. Egocentrism was a central concept for the author. He claimed that the lack of distinction between "subject" and "object" affected reasoning, understanding of reality, and use of language in children. As regards the social use of language, egocentrism leads children to collapse their own and other people's perspectives. Children talk as if the interlocutor should know and understand whatever they do; therefore, they produce confused and inefficient explanations that are lacking in the necessary explicitness. As regards the representation of reality, egocentrism leads children to superimpose their own experience onto physical and natural phenomena and to interpret them in "psychological" terms (i.e., animism, finalism, moral duty).

As regards the structure of reasoning, inability to create proper hierarchical relationships and insensitivity to contradictions lead them to create a generic link between two events in such a way that cause and effect are easily confused.

By studying causal questions (Piaget, 1923), causal sentence completion (Piaget, 1924), and explanations of natural phenomena or mechanical objects (Piaget, 1926, 1927) in children, Piaget came to the conclusion that before the age of 8, when egocentrism is overcome, children are not able to explain. To them, the word "because" is a vague and undifferentiated term having the meaning of "and." Moreover, the incorrect use of causal connectives reflects an incorrect causal reasoning "between the years of 6 and 9 when the relation indicated by because is incorrect; one can always assume that reasoning has been at fault . . ." (Piaget, 1924; Eng. trans. 1972, p. 9).

These conclusions deserve comment. In the Piagetian definition of explanation, two elements are central. The first is the privilege accorded to physical causality; only when children are able to master a correct explanation of a physical phenomenon can they be considered to have reached a correct understanding of causality. The second is the necessity of a correct and explicit use of causal connectives. Though Piaget defined the language as a "window on thought," he nevertheless attributed a primary role to most superficial devices of explanation, such as the correct use of "because." As a consequence, subsequent researchers following this line of work concentrated their efforts on analyzing, by means of different kinds of tasks, the use and comprehension of causal connectives. Their results supported Piagetian conclusions (for an extended review, see Donaldson, 1986), but are challenged on different grounds by the results of some recent research.

First, causal understanding and the mastery of causal language do not coincide. Piaget himself was aware of this issue, but, though he cautioned against a strict identification of language and thought in some points of his 1924 book, in fact the other view predominated in his theory. On the contrary, studies in cognitive development (Donaldson, 1986; Das Gupta & Bryant, 1989) show that when the events involved are familiar (i.e., the fall of an object for lack of support, the wetting of a cup by spilled water, etc.) even preschool children can properly master causality. The explanations requested by Piaget concerned complicated mechanisms (i.e., the functioning of a tap or a syringe) or natural phenomena and this may have rendered the explanation more difficult.

Moreover, studies on spontaneous production of causal language (Hood & Bloom, 1979; Bloom et al., 1980) in adult–child interaction show that children start in the third year of life to produce causal language and that this language is correct from the start. Children do not often produce causal connectives and mostly refer to psychological causality, but very few instances of cause–effect inversion can be found in their productions. In this direction, it is also worth remembering that the very few studies analyzing spontaneous production in adults showed that adults also very seldom refer to physical as compared with psychological causality, and do not often use causal connectives (McCabe & Peterson, 1988). In fact, when we read the two following examples we can easily agree on the fact that a type of sentence like (1) is acceptable and very common in everyday interactions:

(1) I had to take the car to the garage, the brakes were loose.
(2) I had to take the car to the garage because the brakes were loose.

Lastly, because Piaget emphasized the importance of an explicit and correct use of causal language as an indicator of correct causal reasoning, it took a long time before researchers realized that certain uses of the language can be more difficult to understand than others for very young children and that solving many of the tasks intended to tap causal knowledge requires sophisticated linguistic and metalinguistic knowledge.

For instance, a metalinguistic judgement is required when children are requested to detect anomalous ("silly" in the experimenter's words) sentences in which "because" in medial position is followed by an effect rather than by a cause (Corrigan, 1975; Emerson 1979) as it is shown in examples (3) and (4).

(3) The milk spilled because the glass fell off the table.
(4) The glass fell off the table because the milk spilled.

When children have to interpret "reversible" sentences (e.g., "X moved because Y moved"; French, 1988) in which the event following "because" is such that children cannot rely for comprehension on their knowledge of the world, the interpretation has to be based on a pure syntactic knowledge.

When children have to tell "what comes first" of two events mentioned in a causal sentence (e.g., the boy broke his leg because he fell off his bicycle) (Sullivan, 1972; Emerson, 1979), they have to draw a temporal inference from a causal statement. Although children might know that "because" introduces a cause, nevertheless they might not be good at extracting second-order information.

Therefore, the fact that children below the age of 8 are bad at solving these tasks does not mean that children do not understand causality but rather, according to Donaldson's hypothesis (Donaldson, 1986), that they lack the linguistic knowledge necessary to solve these tasks. Donaldson (1986) suggests that all these abilities may come later in development than the correct use of causal language.

A more radical criticism, however, can be addressed to the Piagetian approach. Our criticism stems from the idea that the presence of a causal predicate (either implicit or explicit, either referring to psychological, physical, or logical causality) is not sufficient to define an explanation. Causal explanations are only a subset of all the possible ways of explaining. Consider the following example:

(5) Two friends, A and B, are sitting at a beachside café. Suddenly, they hear a noise behind them like a roll of thunder.
A: What's that?
B: It's the barman taking out the garbage bins.

Despite the absence of any causal predicate, the reply is recognized intuitively as an explanation. In fact, in natural interactions there are many conversational moves that the interlocutors recognize as explanations without these having to contain any causal predicate, even in implicit form.

Some authors studying natural interactions or ordinary explanations do in fact acknowledge the existence of different forms of explanation, some of which do not contain causal predicates (Castelfranchi & Parisi, 1980; Antaki & Fielding, 1981; Barbieri, Colavita, & Scheuer, 1990; Landolfi, 1988). Relying heavily on Antaki and Fielding's (1981) work on ordinary explanations, Barbieri et al. (1990) have recently proposed a typology that they used to analyze child–child interaction, but which is intended to serve more general purposes. The following examples are drawn from the corpus that we are examining in this chapter. The typology considers three types of explanations:

1. Explanations of "what something is," which tell us how to "understand" a thing. They include definitions of objects or events, paraphrases, examples, and clarifications of meanings.

(6) The child (29 months) had erroneously identified a cash register with a telephone in the picture of the supermarket. In discussing this picture the mother says:
M: Here's the cash register, see?
C: What does the cash register do?
M: The cash register, which registers the money that the greengrocer receives.
C: That?
M: The greengrocer receives money (.2) from the sale of his fruit (.3) and he has to put all his money into this drawer (.1) and then to give a receipt he has to push the buttons on the cash register, OK, and after that (.2) he gives the receipt to the customer (.2) to daddy-cat who went to buy some fruit and vegetables.

M: C'è la ca:ssa, visto?
C: //E cosa fa la cass?
M: Il registratore di cassa eh segna i soldi che il fruttivendolo incassa.
C: Che?
M: Il fruttivendolo incassa dei soldi (.2) dalla vendita della frutta (.3) questi soldi: li de:ve mettere tutti dentro questo casse:tto (.1) e poi per fare lo scontrino: batte con- con le dita sui tasti di questo registratore di cassa, no, e dopo (.2) dà lo scontrino al compratore (.2) al al papà gatto che è andato a comperare la frutta e la verdu:ra

2. Explanations of "why something happens," which tell us about the physical events or teleological sequences that have brought about a given state of things.

(7) The mother of a 29-month-old child talks about the picture of the doctor.
C: Why are we going to the: where are we going here. To the: ?
M: Doctor's the physician.
C: Why?
M: Oh, well to have a check up, to see if we are all well. (.2) how we are growing (.2) how much we weigh (.2) if we have a cold (.2) if we are breathing well (.3) for all these reasons.

C: Perchè andiamo dal: qua dove andiamo. Dal?
M: Dottore no, dal medico=
C: =Perchè?
M: Eh, per farci visitare, per vedere se stiamo tutti quanti bene. (.2) come crescia:mo (.2) quanti chili abbia:mo (.2) se abbiamo il raffreddo:re (.2) se respiriamo be:ne (.2) per tutti questi motivi qua.

3. "Deductive" explanations, which clarify the basis for an inference, a judgement, or a conclusion.

(8) The mother of a 29-month-old child is discussing the picture of the doctor. She points to the picture of a piggy covered with many bandages.
M: See how many bandages this piggy has? He must have cut himself a lot (.2) just like you on your arm.

M: Hai visto quanti cerotti ha questo maialino? Deve essersi fatto tante ferite (.2) come la tua ferita sul braccio.

Only the last two types contain a causal predicate in an implicit or explicit form.

To understand what constitutes an explanation, consider again example (5). Removed from the context of the dialogue, B's utterance could be taken easily for a description. What makes it an explanation is A's question or, to be more precise, the fact that within the context, there is something obscure that needs "explaining," which is signaled in A's question. Our approach, in fact, is characterized by the idea that explanations are better defined by their context than by their content. In other words, it is difficult to understand the nature of explanations if we do not examine the *activity of explaining* into an interactive context (Barbieri, 1989; Landolfi, 1988). Things are explained *to* somebody, in the context of specific kinds of interaction and in relation to particular goals.

A conversational move becomes an explanation as a consequence of two facts. First, there is something in the context, either linguistic or extralinguistic, that is obscure – or is supposed to be such for the interlocutor – and needs clarifying (an explanandum). This need may be signaled by explicit questions, non-verbal cues, or it may be presupposed by the speaker when he or she is familiar with the partner and knows the scope of his or her knowledge, as it happens often in mother-child interactions. Second, in relation to this some more information is supplied (the explanans) with the aim of modifying the interlocutor's state of knowledge. For an explanation to be successful, at least to some extent, the relation between the explanandum and the explanans must be grasped by the interlocutor, and for this to happen the new piece of information supplied must be adapted to the interlocutor's state of knowledge in such a way as to – potentially – produce a change in it. In this approach, both partners contribute to the occurrence and success of the explanations, because it is the presence of an interlocutor with particular cognitive needs that guides the "explainer" in the selection of relevant content and choice of explanatory – rhetorical – strategies, in relation to a particular kind of interaction and the goals connected to it. Thus, explanations which are appropriate in certain circumstances can be quite inappropriate in others.

When the social dimension is forgotten, explanations are considered only as a mere cognitive problem, as a sort of problem solving. This is what happens in most of the approaches that define explanations on the basis of their content, such as the causality approach. In this case, "explaining," which is a social activity, is conflated with "understanding," which is instead an individual activity (Mosconi, 1989). Understanding is, hopefully, the effect of explaining, but not the core of it, as we can easily realize when we compare two sentences such as:

(9) Peter explained why the fridge broke.
(10) Peter understood why the fridge broke.

The emphasis on the interactional aspects of the explaining activity and its contextually bound nature make our approach closer to the Vygotskian perspective rather than the Piagetian.

Vygotskian approaches emphasize the importance of interaction and social experience for the development of language and cognition. In this perspective the role of structured information provided by adults and that of discourse practices in the formation of a shared representation of the world are very important. In our approach, learning to explain means that the child has to learn how to control those conventions (partly social and pragmatic, partly connected to selecting relevant contents) that govern the explaining activity according to the context in which it takes place. By "context," in this particular study, we mean two things: (1) a knowledge of the implications of the "frame" of the interaction; and (2) a knowledge of the events and scripts that, within specific discourses, lead to certain interpretations or reconstructions of facts being adopted.

It might be useful to give some examples concerning the frame examined, the interaction between mothers and preschool children engaged in "reading" books. Typically, the frame of reading books requires that a very young child knows that a book is an object used for doing very specific things. You read it by turning the pages, and you do not explore it in other ways such as chewing, throwing, or touching (Snow & Ninio, 1986). Furthermore, in the presence of a book, special kinds of language are produced that are related to its contents (labels or narratives), rather than others (action proposals, requests for actions, etc.). Children have to learn that, when faced with a book, they are supposed to "recount," that is, produce sequences of events connected by "and," "then," and "after," and expressed in a special narrative tone. Children have also to learn that when mother asks one kind of question, they are supposed to name certain objects and produce further related information, but when mother asks another kind – for example, "why" questions – they are supposed to reply with causes, reasons, or conditions. As regards the relation between what is done with the book and the actual contents of it, children have to learn that the pictures are connected to what is being said, and that they are "interpreted," that is, read for their conventional meaning (this is a doctor) rather than for their more immediate appearance (a man dressed in white), and, lastly, that certain final states of events depicted have one reconstruction that is more plausible than others, because of the context in which they occur (Nelson, 1986). For example, when there is a picture of carts colliding in a supermarket, it is more likely that a similar event has been caused by the hurrying or the carelessness of the main character than by a slippery floor.

We hypothesized that children develop the ability to explain through interaction with another, more expert, individual – in this case, the mother.

Young children of the age observed in this study (30, 45, and 60 months) seem to know the conventions connected to the fact that books are "read" and "narrated." Studies of even younger children frequently mention the progressive conventionalization of these activities. For example, Ninio

(Ninio & Bruner, 1978; Ninio, 1980a, 1980b; Snow & Ninio, 1986) has described the development of the book reading routine, and Nelson (1990) has described the first appearance of the "narrative" tone in a monologue produced by a little girl of 24 months before she fell asleep.

Therefore, our analysis will concentrate on the second aspect of contextual knowledge mentioned previously: the ability to use event knowledge and scripts to interpret pictures as representing sequences of events, that is the ability to "read/explain" a book by decoding its contents. All this involves a general, socially shared representation of the world being made explicit: Bruner (1986), for instance, points to narratives as one of the ways in which we give sense to the world.

The aim of this study is to investigate, in a Vygotskian approach, the origins of the child's ability to explain, and look for the origins of this skill in social interaction (Vygotsky, 1962; Hood, Fiess, & Aron 1982) and in the support provided by a more expert partner (in this case, the adult). Indeed, during the book-reading interactions with children of the age we examined, most of the maternal language can be considered as explicative in nature. Objects are named and defined according to their characteristics and functions, pictures are interpreted, contexts are created, and events are reconstructed. Reading books is an opportunity for considering and discussing about things that happen – or might happen – in the real world. In these interactions a zone of proximal development is created where children are introduced to the organization of knowledge and convention of their culture. How much do children internalize of the knowledge made explicit by their mothers? Our research strategy is based on an analysis of the child's production compared with the mother's during the ongoing session as well as after a given period of time (20 days), in order to see whether the child incorporates her explanations, and how she does so.

METHOD

The data we are presenting are part of a larger project. The project used an observational method that developed over four months. Twelve mother–child pairs were videotaped during four sessions, at 3-week intervals. Children were divided into three age groups (30, 45, and 60 months plus or minus 2 months).

Pairs interacted using a booklet especially prepared for the occasion by taking four separate pages out of a well-known book for children. This booklet depicted four situations (supermarket, doctor, playground, and animals) accompanied by a brief text. Each situation presented various activities that could be freely selected by mother and child for explanations or discussions. As a way of illustrating what has been discussed so far, consider the following Figure 7.1.

In Figure 7.1, at least four activities are taking place:

1. There are people buying and weighing some fruit (top left).
2. There are people buying and paying for vegetables (top right).
3. There are people buying meat and waiting while it is cut (bottom left).
4. There is Mr. Donato who has just been involved in an accident (bottom right).

Notice that at least three of these situations could be generalized as buying activities and all of them take place in a supermarket.

Every session was organized, as far as possible, into four phases as Figure 7.2 illustrates. As summarized in Figure 7.2, during the first phase, we intended to evaluate the child's baseline level of knowledge and understanding of the pictures/situations/events as well as his or her spontaneous report of what he or she was looking at. This is because we needed to know how much or how little children already knew before the input or second phase. During the second phase, the role of the mothers consisted in an explanation of the various events presented in the booklet. Children were allowed to interact but their contribution became mandatory during the third phase when they were asked specific questions as a way of checking the state of knowledge after the input phase. Finally, once again, children had to talk about the booklet without any specific prompt. The main goal, at this point, was to compare the child's production of the first phase with the fourth one, that is, after the input and input-check phases. In order to study the degree of generalization children could reach, different booklets were used in the fourth phase of session 2, 3, and 4. The generalization booklets presented identical contents (supermarket, doctor, playground, and animals) but the pictures, though in the same style, were different.

The sessions were videotaped and transcribed using the method proposed by Ochs (1979), which allows the insertion of both the linguistic and paralinguistic features.

In this paper we examine only the data concerning the first session and the first phase of the second where the subjects are examining the same booklet. Our analysis focuses on the language produced by the child at three times, subsequently referred to as phases 1, 2, and 3: the first and last phase of the first session, and the first phase of the second session 3 weeks later. Subjects who did not speak in any one of the three times were excluded. Thus the sample actually examined consisted of:

- 2 children (males), 30 months old.
- 3 children (2 males, 1 female), 43 months old.
- 4 children (2 males, 2 females), 61 months old.

Figure 7.1. The picture of the supermarket is reproduced from Richard Scarry, *Il secondo libro delle parole* (Serie: Leggere con Scarry). Milano: Mondadori Editore, 1986. Original edition: Richard Scarry, *Best First Book Ever!* (1979; the publisher is not reported).

	Phase 1	Phase 2	Phase 3	Phase 4
Function	Evaluation of child's baseline level of understanding or capacity of reporting the story without mother's prompts.	Presentation of the illustrated material integrated with explanations considered necessary by the mother.	Check of the comprehension level reached by the child after explanation.	Assessment of the child's learning and generalization.
Child's role	The child looks at the booklet and freely talks aloud about what s/he sees.	The child listens to the mother's explanations and s/he may intervene if desired.	The child answers to the mother's questions, s/he may ask questions too.	The child looks at the booklet and freely aloud about what s/he sees or remembers.
Mother's role	The mother is invited not to talk during this phase unless solicited by the child.	The mother explains the booklet following the illustrations and adding extra material when she believes it to be necessary for comprehension.	The mother checks the child's comprehension and encourages the child's production through prompts and solicitations.	The mother is invited not to talk during this phase unless solicited by the child.
Researcher's role	The researcher invites the child to look and talk about the booklet.	Silent.	Silent.	Silent.

Figure 7.2. Organization of the sessions.

DATA CODING

Data were coded jointly by the two authors. The language the children produced with reference to each picture was divided into units of information. We considered an information unit each segment, which could function in the context of conversation as a separable unit. Therefore a verb and its arguments, if expressed, were considered a unit. Smaller units were also possible, for example, single-word answers to a question, or single-word utterances intended to point out a relevant part of a picture. Each unit was coded on the basis of four categories: (1) the content of the information item; (2) its origin; (3) the interaction techniques by which it was produced; and (4) the linguistic devices used to express it. These categories make it possible to trace the content back to its origin and see how it is transmitted.

Content

Here we code whether the content mentioned by the child is new or has already appeared previously in the interaction and whether the child contributes something original. Included in this category are:

New mentions: the first mentioning of a person, object, event or situation.

Old mentions: the second or more mentioning of a person, object, event, or situation, using the same linguistic expression or a reduced version of it.

Paraphrases: use of the same content with different words.

(11) (Explaining the picture of the supermarket, the mother of a 29-month-old child said)
M: The cats are going to the supermarket to do the shopping.
M: La famiglia gatti va al supermercato a fare la spesa.
When mother is checking the child's understanding the child says:
C: The cats are going to PAM (the name of a local supermarket).
C: I gatti vanno al PAM

Expansions: a previously mentioned item is enriched with new material.

(12) (Playground picture, child alone at the beginning of second session; age 60 months)
C: The girl-kitten warns the boy-kitten that he's going to tear his trousers. He tears them . . . he wasn't careful.
C: La gattina avvisa il gattino che si sta per stappare i pantaloni. Se li strappa . . . non è stato attento
In her explanation, in the first session, the mother had said:

M: The girl-kitten warns the boy-kitten, "Watchout! You'll tear your trousers."
M: La gattina avverte il gattino "Attento! ti strapperai i pantaloni"

Origin

Some items of information appear many times in the course of the interaction. The history of an item is reconstructed by tracing it back to who first mentioned it.

The following example involves a little boy of 30 months, and what he says about the supermarket picture. His production in phases 3 (the first phase in second session) and 2 (the fourth phase in first session) is examined and then compared with the maternal production regarding the same topic in the previous phases. The example is given in chronological order to make it clearer for the reader (the informative items that reappear in the mother's discourse and in that of the child are italicized).

(13) **Session 1.1.** (Child 30 months, assessment of the child's baseline, picture supermarket)
C: Ah look a telephone, look here ((He takes a cash register for a telephone))

C: Ah guarda un telefono, guarda qua
((Scambia il registratore di cassa per un telefono))

Session 1.2 (First session, mother explains)
M: and here: but you know this gentleman. It's Mr. Donato this (.1) *this is Mr. Donato//*
C: // What's he doing
M: *He goes to the supermarket and tips* all the bottles of syrup, the packets of biscuits, the ice-cream, everything out of the cart, he's made a real mess. The tomato sauce, the jam, the fruit jelly, *the fruit juice,* the cheese.
C: Where's the fruit juice
M: Here ((reads)) fruit juice (.2) this one in this in this little bottle
C: Why does he tip it out?
M: *Oh: because this gentleman is a bit careless* (.1) look at this stuff (.2) *whack* (gesture) *he kicks the cart* (.3) *and tips everything out, all the things he's bought.*
C: That
M: He tips over all the things he bought (.3) the sugar the spaghetti (.5)
C: Why did he buy all those things
M: He'd done his shopping *and he kicked the cart accidentally* and tipped everything out (.2) let's turn over . . .

M: E qua: ma tu riconosci questo signo:re. è il signor donato questo (.1) questo è il signor donato//
C: // Che fa:

M: Va al supermercato e rovescia tu:tte le bottiglie di sciro:ppo le scatole di bisco:tti il gela:to TUtto quanto una: schifezza ha fatto. Il pomo:doro la marmella:ta la gelatina di frutta:il succo di frutta: il forma:ggio
C: Dov'è il succo di frutta
M: Eccolo qua (legge) succo di frutta (.2) questo in ques- in questa bottiglietta
C: Perchè lo rovescia
M: E: perchè questo signore é un po' sbadato (.1) guarda le cose (.2) pah: ((gesto)) dà un calcio al carrello (.3) e rovescia tutto: tutte le cose che aveva comprato
C: Che
M: Rovescia tutte le cose che aveva comprato (.3) lo zu:cchero gli spaghe:tti: (.5)
C: Perchè ( ) aveva comperato tutto
M: Aveva fatto la SPEsa e senza volere ha dato un colpo al carrello e ha rovesciato tutto (.2) giriamo la pagina . . .

Session 1.3 (First session, mother checks child's comprehension)
M: (.2) And what happens to this Mr. Donato?
C: He drops every- he kicks the cart and tips all the things he's bought (.1) Why does he tip?
M: *Because he's careless.*
C: Why?
M: He's careless and he's knocked the cart
C: Why does he knock the cart?
M: Why: because he wasn't looking where he was going and he knocked the cart (.4) and in here the cash register, what's that for . . .

M: (.2) E a questo signor donato cosa succede?
C: Rovescia tut- dà un calcio al carrello e rovescia tutte le cose che ha comprato (.1) perchè rovescia?
M: Perchè è sbadato?
C: Perchè?
M: È sbadato e ha dato un colpo al carrello.
C: Perchè ha dato u:n tolpo.
M: Eh perchè: non: non guardava bene dove metteva i piedi e ha dato un colpo al car- al carrello (.4) e in questo il registratore di cassa a cosa serve . . .

Session 1.4 (child alone at the end of the first session)
C: What's this?
M: What do you think?
C: *Mr. Donato has tipped out all the things he's bought,* he tips them out (.5) *by accident he kicked the cart* ((turns the page))

C: Questo cos'è?
M: Secondo te?
C: Il signor Donato ha rovesciato tutte le cose che ha Comprato le

rovescia (.5) per sbaglio ha dato un contr- un calcio contro al carrello ((gira la pagina))

Session 2.1 (child alone at the beginning of the second session, 3 weeks later)
C: *He kicks the cart and knocks all the things he's bought on the floor,* (.8) two tins, *the fruit juice:* two (.25)
M: (points) Here?
C: The fruit juice that – that's in the tin then (turns the page)

C: Dà un CAlcio al carrello e butta per terra tutte le cose che aveva COMPRA:to (.8) due balattoli il succo di frutta: du:e (.2.5)
M: ((indica)) Qua?
C: Il succo di frutta che – che è nel balattolo: poi ((gira pagina))

As this long example shows, certain items appearing in the first phase of the second session (such as the fruit juice) are taken directly from the mother's discourse. Others (such as the kick to the cart) are reproposed by the child himself in phases 3 and 4 of the first session before appearing again in the final discourse. Our coding method makes it possible to reconstruct this history by assigning codes to each repeated item of information. The codes refer to the phase of the session where the item was previously mentioned, up to its first mention.

Interaction techniques

Here, we code how the child produces the piece of information being examined, to see whether it is spontaneous or a result of prompting from the mother.

Spontaneous production: the child produces the item without any prompting.

Generic prompt: the child produces the item in response to maternal prompting of a generic nature (What can you see here? What's happening here?). For an example, see mother's conversational turns in session 1.4 and session 2.1 in example 13.

Specific prompt: the child produces the item in response to a specific prompt from the mother.

(14) ((Child 29 months, picture: animals. The mother is trying to make the child say "whale"))
M: Do you remember what the one in Pinocchio is called? Wha . . .
C: Whale.

M: Ti ricordi come si chiama quella di Pinocchio? Ba . . .
C: Balena.

Repetition: the child repeats the mother's words immediately after she has said them.

Linguistic devices used by the children

Here we analyze the complexity of the organization of meaning in the child's production and how this is reflected in the linguistic devices used to express it.

Naming: people, objects, events, and situations are labeled with a name.

Describing: the child describes what can be seen in the picture

(15) ((Child 29 months, picture: the doctor))
C: This is naked, this is naked too and here there are many bandages.
C: Quetto è nudo, pure quetto è nudo e qua ci sono ta:nti cero:tti.

Interpreting: the child gives meaning to the picture by relying on general knowledge and inferences.

(16) ((Child 61 months; picture: playground))
C: The two kittens are fighting.
C: Litigano due gattini.

Specifying: a previously mentioned item is identified by specifying it as in the following example.

(17) ((Child 61 months, picture: supermarket))
M: Look how many fruits are shown at the green-grocer's.
C: The lemons, the apples, the oranges (.2) the cherries =
M: Guarda quanta frutta è esposta dal fruttivendolo.
C: I limoni le mele le arance (.2) le ciliegie =

Making links: an item is given meaning through a connection being made with the child's previous experience or present life.

(18) ((Child 29 months; picture: playground))
C: This is July skating . . . ((seeing a picture of a fox cub on skates)) ((July is the child's sister)).
C: Questa è Giuli che pattina.

Because: the child refers, explicitly or implicitly, to a causal connection.

(19) C: He kicks the cart and knocks all the things he's bought on the floor (cause–effect).
((see session 2.1, example 11))
C: Dà un CAlcio al carrello e butta per terra tutte le cose che aveva COMPRA:to

Table 7.1. *Total number of pictures examined by each age group in the three phases (means in brackets)*

	30 months $n = 2$	43 months $n = 3$	61 months $n = 4$	Total
Phase 1	3	6	9	18
	(1.50)	(2.00)	(2.25)	
Phase 2	5	8	11	24
	(2.50)	(2.70)	(2.75)	
Phase 3	8	11	14	33
	(4.00)	(3.70)	(3.50)	
Total	16	25	34	75

Requests: these form a separate category. The child makes a verbal or non-verbal request for names, interpretations, explanations (And here? What's happening? Why? Many examples do appear in the child's production in example 13).

RESULTS

First, the number of pictures examined during each phase was tabulated. As it is shown in Table 7.1, there is an increase in the number of pictures examined, in all three age-groups, in the second and third phases compared with the first one (chi square $r = 6$; $p < 0.05$).

Differences due to age are not very marked when comparing the means; the increase in the number of pictures is mainly due to the fact that in the oldest group more children did talk during all three phases.

Then, all the items of information mentioned for each picture by the children were counted. Table 7.2 gives a general overview of the number of mentions for each phase in the three age-groups, but a clearer picture of the changes can be obtained by examining the median number of mentions per picture across the three phases. Table 7.3 shows the relevant data.

There is an increase in the number of mentions across the three phases. There is also an increase due to age in the comparison of 43- and 61-month-old children. The high figures observed for the 30-month-old group are due to one of the two subjects who is responsible for 90 out of 143 mentions. Actually this child did not talk very much unless prompted by the mother. When the mother did not intervene,

Table 7.2. *Total number of mentions in the three phases for each age group*

	Phase 1	Phase 2	Phase 3	Total
30 months	17	16	110	143
43 months	23	66	89	178
61 months	70	152	196	418
Total	110	234	395	739

Table 7.3. *Median number of mentions per picture in the three phases for the three age groups*

	Phase 1	Phase 2	Phase 3
30 months	5.0	1.0	11.0
43 months	2.5	5.0	7.0
61 months	5.0	9.0	12.5

his production was very low (see phase 2), but it increased greatly following the mother's prompting (see phase 3 and, to a lesser extent, phase 1). Although mothers were requested at the beginning of the session not to intervene during certain phases unless solicited by the child, some mothers felt that their intervention was necessary in order for the child to appear knowledgeable.

Lastly, each mention was coded according to whether it was an old mention or a new one, whether the information was mother- or child-originated, whether it was produced spontaneously or not, and according to the linguistic means with which it was expressed. This was the basis of all phase and age-group comparisons. The comparisons were made per picture, that is, considering the production relative to each picture. The choice had two reasons: first, we wanted to know what changes might occur after mother's input in the child's production regarding a certain picture; second, we wanted to obviate the fact that different children examined different numbers of pictures.

Given the fact that children's linguistic abilities were not the same and some of them were more likely to talk than others, only non-parametric statistics were used.

Two kinds of comparisons were made: (1) comparisons concerning the differences between the three phases, and (2) comparisons concerning the differences between the age groups.

Table 7.4. *Median number of mentions per picture in the three phases for the three age groups in the restricted sample (number of pictures examined in brackets)*

	Phase 1	Phase 2	Phase 3
30 months (pictures = 2)	4.5	4.5	15.5
43 months (pictures = 4)	2.5	5.0	7.0
61 months (pictures = 4)	4.0	7.0	8.0

COMPARISON OF PHASES

The comparisons between the three phases were made, independently of age, using Friedman analysis of variance by ranks and, when necessary, using the Wilcoxon test for two-by-two comparisons.

As it is shown in Table 7.1, there is an increase in the number of pictures examined across the three phases.

However, not all the pictures referred to in one phase are taken into consideration in the others. Therefore, in order to obtain a more cogent comparison between the different phases, this stage of our analysis was carried out only on those pictures which the subject referred to in all three phases of the study. In this analysis, the total number of pictures examined is 10 and the subjects are 6 (2 for each age group). The total number of mentions examined was 259. Table 7.4 shows the median number of mentions per picture in the three phases and for each age group in this restricted sample.

All the results show a difference between the first phase and the other two. There were no significant differences between the second and the third phase.

As far as the content is concerned, there was, in the three phases, a tendency for general linguistic production to increase, that is, the number of information items mentioned per picture was higher. The medians for the three phases were 3.5, 5.5, and 7.5 respectively (chi-square = 5.45, $df\,2$, $p < 0.06$).

As one might expect from a study of this kind, the number of New mentions decreased from the first phase to the other two, but the number of Old mentions increased. This means that in the second and third phases, the children produced items that had already been mentioned in the course of preceding phases of the first session. In order to do so,

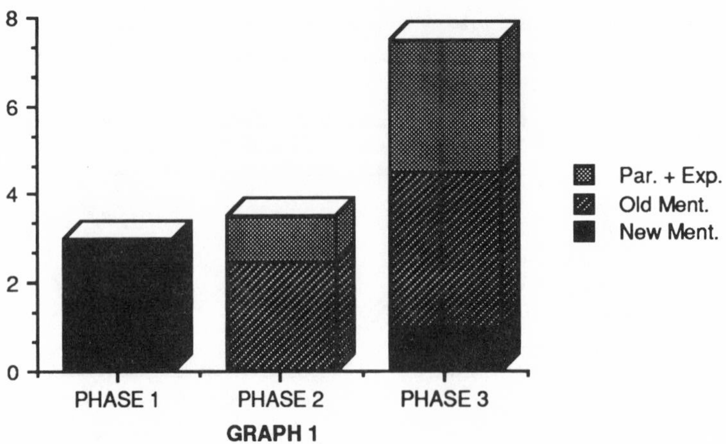

Figure 7.3. New and old mentions per picture in the three phases.

children either used the same words or reduced forms of things already said (Old mentions) or, more rarely, a more personalized form involving Paraphrases and Expansions. Medians of New mentions per picture for the three phases were 3, 0, and 1 respectively (chi-square = 6.95, *df* 2, $p < 0.05$). Medians of Old mentions per picture for the three phases were 0, 2.5, and 3.5 (chi-square = 7.55, *df* 2, $p < 0.05$). If to Old mentions we add also Paraphrases and Expansions, which all refer to items of information already mentioned, the effect is even stronger. Medians of Paraphrases plus Expansions per picture were 0, 1, and 3 (chi-square = 6.95, *df* 2, $p < 0.05$).

The analysis of the data concerning the origins of information shows that this increase in production is mainly due to the mention of mother-originated information. The production of information that originates from the child remains constant (medians per picture for the three phases = 3.5, 4, and 5 respectively, chi-square = 3.35, *df* 2, ns), and the production of information of maternal origin increases; medians per picture for the three phases were 0, 2, and 2.5 respectively (chi-square = 9.8, *df* 2, $p < 0.02$).

As regards the interactional aspects, we considered whether the child's production was spontaneous or dependent on some previous hint from the mother, that is, whether it followed a generic prompt, a specific prompt, or whether it was a repetition of the mother's words. The data show that children's production is sustained by maternal prompting.

Comparing the three phases, no differences were found as regards

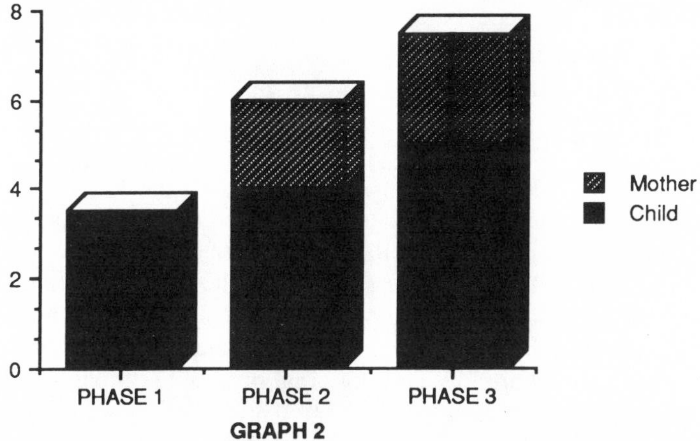

Figure 7.4. Origins of information per picture in the three phases.

spontaneous production that remains stable (medians per picture were 3, 4, and 2.5 respectively; chi-square = 0.35, *df* 2, ns). When children do not reproduce spontaneously the information supplied by the mother, mothers intervene with generic prompts, as can be seen in the following example.

(20) ((Child 43 months; picture: supermarket; mother explaining))
M: And this is instead the butcher's bench (.4) but in our supermarket you can't see it so well (.5) the steak, the minced meat (.3) the sausages (.4) and all these eno:rmous kni:ves (.5) here instead there is the paper (.3) for wrapping (1.5).

M: E questo è invece il banco della ca:rne (.4) ma lì al supermercato nostro non si vede così bè:ne (.5) la biste:cca, la carne trita:ta (.3) i wurstel (.4) e tutti questi colte:lli eno:rmi: (.5) qui invece c'è la carta (.3) per fare i pacchi (1.5).

(Child 43 months, phase 3)
C: ((looks at the booklet staying silent for a while)) The shop (1.5)
M: The:n,
C: The meat
M: Mh mh (2.5)
C: (she) Cuts (1.5)
M: Then, (1.2)
C: The knife
M: Mh mh (.3)
C: ((switches topic)) The carrots

C: Il negozio (1.5)
M: Poi,

C: La ca:rne
M: Mh mh (2.5)
C: Taglia (1.5)
M: Poi, (1.2)
C: Il coltello
M: Mh mh (.3)
C: Le carote

Comparing the child's production with the mother's explanation, we see that the child mentions the meat and the knives as the mother had previously done. The child's production, however, is sustained by a maternal request for more information. In short, the mother does not simply provide the child with information; she also makes sure that the child has remembered it. This maternal prompting, though of a generic nature, regards areas already covered previously, and stimulates the child to retrieve the information that has been provided. The number of items uttered in response to generic prompting increases in the three phases; medians per picture were 0, 1, and 2 respectively. Statistics on prompted production were not significant when comparing the three phases together, but the Wilcoxon test for two-by-two comparisons showed an increase between the first and the second phase ($T(10) = 6$; $p < 0.05$), between the first and the third ($T(10) = 4.5$; $p < 0.05$), and no differences between the second and the third phase ($T(10) = 18.5$; p ns).

The mentions following a specific prompt were only 8 out of 259 (3 percent). The use of specific prompts seemed to be related to the mother's interactional style because only 2 mothers out of 6 – 1 in the 30-month-old group and 1 in the 61-month-old group – used it, whereas generic prompting was used by all mothers. Repetitions amounted to 19 (7 percent). Due to the small numbers occurring in the two categories, no statistics were computed on repetitions and the production following specific prompts.

In general, children's favorite devices were naming, describing, and interpreting. These groups represented 42, 16, and 24 percent respectively of the initial production. The Friedman analysis of variance by ranks used to compare the three phases did not provide significant results in any of these categories or in the others examined, indicating that children continued to make use of their favorite linguistic devices in their production. However, the Wilcoxon tests for individual comparison showed an increase in descriptions between phases 1 and 2 ($T = 7.5$, $n = 10$, $p < 0.05$; medians per picture, 0.05 and 1), and between phases 1 and 3 ($T = 8$, $n = 10$, $p < 0.05$; medians per picture, 0.05 and 1). The difference between phases 2 and 3 was not significant. Interpretation provided similar results: for phases 1 and 2, medians per picture were 0 and 2 ($T = 4.5$, $n = 10$, $p < 0.05$); for phases 1 and 3 medians per picture were 0 and 1.5 ($T =$

$9, n = 10, p = 0.05$). No significant difference was found between phases 2 and 3. The latter results indicate that children incorporate the maternal information, but often reproduce it through their own linguistic devices.

A marginal but interesting observation concerns the tendency for the number of interpretations (mostly of maternal origin) to decrease between phase 2 and phase 3. In fact, phase 2 takes place at the end of the first session, only a few minutes after the information has been supplied, whereas phase 3 occurs 3 weeks later. The following example illustrates the point.

(21) ((Child 43 months; picture: supermarket; end of first session – phase 2))
M: You have to explain, you know (long pause)
C: That he has knocked down everything while he was running.

M: Devi spiegarmi tu sai.
C: Che ha buttato giù tutte le cose mentre stava correndo.

(phase 3)
C: The piggy (1.5) here tips over (everything)
C: Il maialino (1.5) qui rovescia.

During the explaining phase the mother had said
M: Look what this gentleman has done. He was running and he knocked down the carts full of stuff (.3) see? everything has fallen on the ground (.2) the fruit pie, the syrups//
C: //This?
M: This also fell on the ground.
C: Poor guy.
M: Poor guy (4) now he will have to pick up everything again (.3) here you shouldn't run.

M: Vedi cosa ha combinato questo signore correndo ha rovescia:to i carrelli pieni di roba (.3) hai visto? tutto è caduto per terra (.2) la crosta:ta gli sciro:ppi//
C: //Que:sto:
M: Anche questo è caduto per te:rra =
C: Pove:ro!
M: Poveri:no (4) adesso dovrà raccogliere tutto di nuo:vo (.3) qui non biso:gna correre.

Comparing the mother's explanation and the child's production in phases 2 and 3, it appears that the child remembers that the topic has been discussed with the mother, but not all the information supplied can be retrieved; therefore it is reported in a simplified form.

COMPARISON OF AGE GROUPS

The main concern of this study was to investigate the changes across phases. However, age comparisons were also carried out. These analyses concerned the coded measures for the overall number of pictures examined by children of each age group during all three phases. They were performed by means of the Kruskal-Wallis analysis of variance by ranks for groups of independent data. There were 16 pictures for the group aged 30 months (2 subjects), 25 pictures for the group aged 43 months (3 subjects), and 34 pictures for the group aged 61 months (4 subjects); the total amount of mentions examined was 739 (see Tables 7.1 and 7.2). As previously mentioned, in the first age group, one of the two subjects had a very high production; he is responsible for 63 percent of the production of this age group. Most of this production was prompted by the mother and, of course, maternal prompting pushes the child to exploit all of his or her knowledge. Despite this fact that flattens the effect of age, some differences did appear between the 30- and the 61-month-old groups. The significant comparisons, however, concerned mainly the differences between the 43- and the 61-month-old groups. To illustrate the differences between the three groups some qualitative examples will be given.

The main change as a function of age is an increase in the child's autonomous production.

First, there is a rise in general production. The medians per picture for the three groups were 7.5, 6, and 9 respectively ($H(2,75) = 6.8$, $p < 0.05$). The Mann-Whitney test for individual comparisons showed a significant difference between the group aged 43 months and the one aged 61 ($U\,(25, 34) = 259$, $p < 0.02$). No differences were found between 30 and 43 months ($U\,(16,25) = 168$; $p = 0.40$). The difference between 30 and 61 months, though not significant, is anyway larger ($U(16,34) = 204$; $p = 0.15$). Though not at a large extent, 5-year-olds (group 3) produced more information items.

It is worth noting that, for a large part, the source of the items produced by the older children lay in knowledge that they already possessed. While the quantity of information items originating from the mothers remained constant in all three age groups, indicating that the child turns to the adult for information at all ages, the quantity of items originating from the child increased with age. Medians per picture for the three groups were 4.5, 3, and 6.5 respectively ($H(2,75) = 10.14$, $p < 0.01$), and the Mann-Whitney tests showed a significant difference between the third group compared with the other two – group 1 versus group 3, $U(16,34) = 159$, $p < 0.05$; group 2 versus group 3, $U(25,34) = 240$, $p < 0.01$ – but no differences between group 1 versus group 2 ($U(16,25) = 199$; ns). So the children aged 61 months differed from the others with respect to the quantity of information about the world that they possess, and which they obviously brought with them to the session.

As regards the linguistic devices adopted, there was no difference in the age groups in the quantity of Describing ($H(2,75) = 3.1$; ns) and Naming ($H(2,75) = 3.0$; ns), but there is an interesting increase in the children's ability to "read" the pictures by interpreting them ($H(2,75) = 12.7, p < 0.01$). Once again, the third group was distinct from the other two. Medians per picture for the three groups were 0.5, 0, and 2 – group 1 versus group 3, $U(16,34) = 178.5, p = 0.05$; group 2 versus group 3, $U(25,34) = 217, p < 0.01$; but no differences for group 1 versus group 2, $U(16,25) = 157.5$; ns). Despite its high production, group 1 nevertheless gave fewer interpretations. Since the ability to interpret pictures is closely linked to the ability to recognize conventional indicators, it may be supposed that the improvement in this ability is linked to the children's increasing internalization of interpreting strategies previously learned from the adults.

An additional sign of growing autonomy is the decrease in questions: the youngest children asked more questions than those in the older groups. Medians per picture for all three groups were 1, 0, and 0 respectively ($H(2,75) = 5.6, p < 0.05$).

Some qualitative examples will illustrate our points more clearly. The following are examples of production in the second phase (end of first session). The first example concerns the 30-month-old child who did not produce unless prompted, and in this phase the mother did not intervene. The second concerns a 43-month-old child and the third a 60-month-old child.

(22) ((Child 29 months; picture: supermarket; end of first session – phase 2))
C: Look (.5) how nice! they are buying ((turns the page))
C: Guarda (.5) che bello! comprano ((gira la pagina))

(23) ((Child 43 months; picture: supermarket; end of first session – phase 2))
C: What is this? (.5)
M: What do you think it is, tell me where we are (.5) what do you see (.5)
C: Where there are the fruits.
M: Eh! and then? (1.5)
C: Where they sell.
M: Uh uh (2.5) what do they sell, you have to explain, you know (long pause)
C: That he has knocked down everything while he was running.
M: And then? (turns the page)

C: Cos'è Questo? (.5)
M: Secondo te cos'è, raccontami dove sia:mo (.5) cosa ve:di (.5)
C: Dove ci sono le frutta.
M: Eh! e poi? (1.5)
C: Dove si vende.
M: Uh uh (2.5) cosa si vende, devi spiegarmi tu sai (lunga pausa)

C: Che ha buttato giù tutte le cose mentre stava correndo
M: E poi? (gira pagina)

(24) ((Child 61 months; picture: supermarket; end of first session – phase 2))
C: Daddy-cat has gone shopping with the kid-cat (1.2) to the market (1.3) the lemons (.5) the a- the apples (.3) the oranges (.3) cherries, the tangerines (.3) and the grapes (1.5)
M: It doesn't matter if you don't remember what that is. Go on. Then?
C: The corn.
M: Mh
C: The pears (1.5) the strawberries
M: Mh and what happens in this market?
C: The pineapples (1.) xxxx ((unclear))
M: I can't hear you.
C: Here there is mummy-cat (1.8) she has gone shopping.
M: Talk clearly I can't understand anything.
C: She has gone to buy sausages (3.2) the ham ((whispers)) (.6) sausages (.4) the piggy (.3)
M: Shall we turn?

C: Il papà ga:tto è andato a fa:re col gattino la spesa (1.2) al merCAto (1.3) i limoni (.5) le me- le mele (.3) gli aranci (.3) ciliegie i mandaranci (.3) e: l'Uva (1.5)
M: Non fa niente se non ti ricordi cosa è quello. andiamo avanti Allora?
C: Granturco.
M: Mh
C: Le pe:re (1.5) le fragole.
M: Mh (1.5) e cosa succede in questo mercato?
C: L'ananas (1.) xxx ((non chiaro))
M: Non ti sento.
C: Qua c'è la mamma GA:tta (1.8) è an:daTA a compra:re:
M: Parla bene che non si capisce niente.
C: È andata a comprare le salsiccie, (3.2) il prosciutto ((sottovoce)) (.6) salsiccie (.4) la maialina (.3)
M: Giriamo?

As can be seen in the examples, the initial production of the oldest child is longer than that of the other two children. Moreover, some items (corn, pears, strawberries, pineapples, and sausages) are mentioned by the child for the first time in this phase. Lastly, the interpretation concerning mummy-cat going to buy sausages is also a child's production, paralleling a previous interpretation of the mother, who had mentioned daddy-cat going to shop with his child. Let us compare what the child said with mother's explanation. Mother mentions general categories, that is, fruit and vegetables, but the child specifies them. In his production the child adds new items and uses mother's interpretations to create new ones.

(25) ((Mother of 61-month-old child explaining supermarket))

M: There are many families of tiny animals going to the market and buying many things. There is daddy-cat with his child-cat and they go and buy fruit at the greengrocer. Look how many fruits are shown at the greengrocer's.
C: The lemons, the apples, the oranges (.2) the cherries =
M: = the grapefruits grape. Later on you will tell me, now I am telling you OK?
C: (nods)
M: And here who is this guy, the hippopotamus who goes to buy the vegetables and there is the cat looking and this is the doggy at the cash register who pushes on the keys to cash the money. Here they sell the fruit and on the other side they sell the vegetables (.4) here instead there is the butcher's department where miss piggy sells the meat (.2) hanging there is the ham, the pork cutlet and the steak (.2) the machine to mince the meat to make minced meat (.5) and here look what has happened, a disaster . . . ((goes on talking about the disaster))

M: Ci sono tante famiglie di animaletti che va:no al merca:to a compra:re ta:nte co:se c'è il papaà col gattino e vanno a comprare la frutta dal fruttivendolo. vedi quanta frutta è esposta dal fruttivendolo.
C: I limo:ni le mele gli aranci (.2) ciliegie =
M: = i pompe:lmi u:va: poi racconti tu adesso ti racconto io va bene?
C: ((annuisce))
M: E qui, chi è questo qui, l'ippopotamo che va a comprare la verdu:ra e c'è il gattino che gua:rda e QUESTO QUI è il cagnolino che batte i tasti per incassare i soldi:ni. di QUA vendono la frutta e da quest'altra parte vendono la verdura (.4) qui invece c'è il reparto del macella:io dove la signorina maialina vende la ca:rne. C'è appeso il prosciu:tto la braciola di maia:le e la biste:cca (.2) la macchina per macinare la carne e fare la carne macinata (.5) e più in qua guarda cosa è successo un disastro! ((va avanti a parlare del disastro))

DISCUSSION

The results of this study show a considerable transfer of information from mother to child in the course of the learning session (see comparisons between phases 1 and 2). There is also evidence that these items are still in the child's memory three weeks later; though the difference between phases 2 and 3 is not significant, the median of Old mentions in phase 3 is larger than that in phase 2. This transfer of information is directly visible in the distribution of the origins of items in the three phases. While the number of items having their origin in the child did not change, the number of items that originated from the mother increased between the first phase and the others.

There are also indirect signs of this transfer. In particular, there is an increase in Interpretations between the first phase and the other two. Interpretations are an indicator of the ability to recognize the conventions of certain types of representation of characters and events. In our data they are mostly of maternal origin. The children in the sample we examined seemed to adopt the strategy described by Snow and Goldfield (1983) in an analogous context of book reading: "In the context X, say what other people have already said." A similar strategy seems to be adopted by little ones, not only in the context of book reading, but also in their acquisition of new words (Harris et al., 1988). It would seem appropriate, therefore, to consider the role of this strategy of appropriation in the development of children.

This claim does not imply that no element of personal elaboration comes into play in the process. As far as our data are concerned, there is a clear indication that what is incorporated is the content, but this is reproduced in a reduced or simplified form. Whereas maternal discourses are fairly elaborate (as shown in example 13, where "tipping over everything" is illustrated by a long list of the things tipped over, and then defined concisely as "a real mess"), children's reproductions make use of the linguistic devices they happen to prefer and to master depending on their age – describing, naming, and, to a lesser extent, interpreting.

As we have already said, the autonomy of children increases with age: they ask fewer questions, bring a greater amount of preestablished knowledge of the world into the session, and elaborate the material to be absorbed in a more personal way. In short, smaller children depend heavily on their mothers as a source of information and they tend to repeat, though in a simplified form, what the adult said. Older children instead show a more considerable degree of personal elaboration. We believe, however, that this happens because maternal information has been internalized. In the first place, none of the children, not even the oldest, in phases 2 and 3 gave a reading of the pictures that differed substantially from that presented by his or her mother, for example, by proposing an alternative explanation for the events depicted. In the second place, the increased amount of interpreting in the older children shows a greater ability to read the pictures according to established, shared conventions.

CONCLUSIONS

In the psycholinguistic literature, book reading has been mainly studied as an activity especially relevant to the acquisition of language (Snow & Goldfield, 1983; Ninio & Bruner, 1978; Ninio, 1980b) and to the development of literacy (Snow & Ninio, 1986). Here we would like to suggest that this activity also has a role in the development of the explaining capacity in children.

In discussing the Vygotskian approach to the children's learning of explanations, Hood et al. (1982) presented a set of questions concerning this issue. The most relevant of them were: (1) how does the child come to understand how the world is? (2) how does he come to understand how to understand? (3) what is acceptable as an explanation in our society and culture? (4) what role do communicative exchanges play in learning how to explain? Hood et al. (1982) considered only causal language. Although we are proposing a different definition of explanation, based on pragmatic features and on context, we nevertheless consider our study a contribution to an answer to these questions.

In book reading, the world is "object-of-contemplation" rather than "things-for-action," and in a book many different objects, situations, and events can be represented in a single page where they are organized and grouped according to a preestablished logic. The discussion of this topic between mother and child offers a great opportunity for a shared representation of the world. It is one of the contracts of book reading that pictures represent what happens – or might happen – in the real world (Snow & Ninio, 1986). Mothers often make this link explicit (see examples 8, 20) but children are also aware of this (see example 18). Under this contract a large amount of knowledge is supplied about what you do – or what you should not do – in such a context (see examples 11, 21), and about the objects involved and their functions (see example 6). Our results give evidence of a considerable transmission of contents from mothers to children (learning how the world is).

However, the language of the mother can also offer the child a subtler kind of knowledge, that is, the knowledge concerning the way you know what things are and the discursive strategies that are appropriate when you have to show and transmit your knowledge through language (learning how to learn). A butcher's bench can be recognized because it has meat, knives, and a machine to mince meat; a cart collision is linked to its antecedents and consequents; a general category is given significance by specifying the items belonging to it. All these explaining strategies do appear in the discourses of the mothers. The fact that all this information is made explicit helps the child to learn what are the relevant features to be selected and mentioned in reporting this knowledge and what is the way of doing it. Though in a simpler form, the productions of the children show an impressive similarity of contents – and for cause–effect sequences also of linguistic forms – if compared with explanations received. In the follow-up of the analysis, when children's production concerning the generalization booklets will be studied, it will be possible to check how much children have learned about distinguishing relevant and marginal features and selecting the right ones in contexts that are similar but not identical to the learning context.

The data analyzed until now are not sufficient to give evidence of the process of children's learning of discursive strategies. In the production of the oldest group, however, it is possible to notice the presence of discursive strategies, such as specifying (see example 24), that very frequently appear in the explanations addressed to younger children. This might indicate some evidence that internalization of maternal discursive strategies has occurred.

One of the main functions of explanations in adults' and children's interaction (Orsolini & Pontecorvo, 1989) is the "argumentative" function, that is, the use of explanations to keep a point or to support a position against the arguments of the partner. In such a context, it does certainly matter whether a child is able to reason not in order to act, but in order to select relevant features, create temporal and causal links, and form categories and produce the right examples. All of these intellectual activities are practiced in mother–child interaction during book reading; this is one of the very first contexts where language is used to show and exploit knowledge.

Previous research (Snow, 1981; Wells, 1985) demonstrated that there is a correlation existing between narrative language skills and later school achievement and literacy development in children. The study of the relationship between some cognitive activities carried on during early child–adult book reading and later children's argumentative capacity may be a task for future research.

TRANSCRIPTION NOTATION

(( ))	Paralinguistic information and/or transcriber comments
(1.4)	Pause length expressed in tenth of a second
:	The sound is lengthened
=	Latched turns, no time space between turns
–	False start
//	Simultaneous start up between two speakers
CAPITALS	Stress
Comma	Low rise intonation
Period	Falling intonation
Question mark	Rising intonation
Exclamation mark	Exclamatory utterance

REFERENCES

Antaki, C., & Fielding, G. (1981). Research on ordinary explanations. In C. Antaki (ed.), *The psychology of ordinary explanations of social behaviour.* London: Academic Press.

Barbieri, M. S. (ed.). (1989). *La spiegazione nell'interazione sociale* (Explanations in social interaction). Torino: Loescher.

Barbieri, M. S., Colavita, F., & Scheuer, N. (1990). The beginning of the explaining capacity. In G. Conti-Ramsden & C. Snow (eds.), *Children's Language,* vol. 7. Hillsdale, NJ: Erlbaum.

Bloom, L., Lahey, M., Hood, L., Lifter, K., & Fiess, K. (1980). Complex sentences: Acquisition of syntactic connectives and the semantic relations they encode. *Journal of Child Language, 7,* 235–261.

Bruner, J. S. (1986). *Actual minds, possible worlds.* Cambridge MA: Harvard University Press.

Castelfranchi, C., & Parisi, D. (1980). *Linguaggio conoscenza e scopi (Language, knowledge and goals*). Bologna: Il Mulino.

Corrigan, R. (1975). A scalogram analysis of the development of the use and comprehension of "because" in children. *Child Development, 46,* 195–201.

Das Gupta, P., & Bryant, P. E., (1989). Young children's causal inferences. *Child Development, 60,* 1138–1146.

Donaldson, M. (1986). *Children's explanations.* Cambridge: Cambridge University Press.

Emerson, H. F. (1979). Children's comprehension of "because" in reversible and non-reversible sentences. *Journal of Child Language, 6,* 279–300.

French, A. L. (1988). The development of children's understanding of "because" and "so." *Journal of Experimental Child Psychology, 45,* 262–279.

Harris, M., Barrett, M., Jones, D., & Brookes, S. (1988). Linguistic input and early word meaning. *Journal of Child Language, 15,* 77–94.

Hood, L., & Bloom, L. (1979). What, when and how about why: A longitudinal study of early expressions of causality. *Monographs of the Society for Research in Child Development,* vol. 44, no. 6.

Hood, L., Fiess, K., & Aron, J. (1982). Growing up explained: Vygotskians look at the language of causality. In C. Brainerd & M. Pressley (eds.), *Verbal processes in children.* New York: Springer Verlag.

Landolfi, L. (1988). Explanations as a joint activity: Co-construction of knowledge in second language classroom. Unpublished Ph.D. thesis, University of Southern California.

McCabe, A., & Peterson, C. (1988). A comparison of adult's versus children's spontaneous use of "because" and "so." *Journal of Genetic Psychology, 149* (2), 257–268.

Mosconi, G. (1989). Un'analisi psico-retorica della spiegazione (A psychorhetorical approach to explanations). In M.S. Barbieri (ed.), *La spiegazione nell'interazione sociale (Explanations in social interaction).* Torino: Loescher.

Nelson, K. (ed.). (1986). *Event knowledge.* Hillsdale, NJ: Erlbaum.

Nelson, K. (1990). The beginning of narrative competence in speech for self. Paper Presented at the Fifth International Congress for the Study of Child Language, Budapest, 15–20 July.

Ninio, A. (1980a). Picture book reading in mother–infant dyads belonging to two subgroups in Israel. *Child Development, 51,* 587–590.

Ninio, A. (1980b). The ostensive definition in vocabulary teaching. *Journal of Child Language, 7,* 565–573.

Ninio, A., & Bruner, J. S. (1978). The achievement and antecedents of labelling. *Journal of Child Language, 5,* 1–15.

Ochs, E. (1979). Transcription as theory. In E. Ochs & B. Schiefflin (eds.), *Developmental Pragmatics.* New York: Academic Press.

Orsolini, M., & Pontecorvo C. (1989). La discussione in classe come contesto per imparare a spiegare. (Classroom discussion as a context for learning how to explain). In M. S. Barbieri (ed.), *La spiegazione nell'interazione sociale* (Explanations in social interaction). Torino: Loescher.

Piaget, J. (1923). *La langage et la pensée chez l'enfant.* Neuchâtel: Delachaux et Niestlé. English translation. *The language and thought of the child.* New York: Meridian, 1955.

Piaget, J. (1924). *Le jugement et le raisonnement chez l'enfant.* Neuchâtel: Delachaux et Niestlé. English translation. *Judgment and reasoning in the child.* Totowa, NJ: Littlefield, Adams, 1972.

Piaget, J. (1926). *La répresentation du monde chez l'enfant.* Paris: Alcan. English translation. *The child's conception of the world.* London: Routledge & Kegan, 1965.

Piaget, J. (1927). *La causalité physique chez l'enfant.* Paris: Alcan. English translation. *The child's conception of physical causality.* Totowa, NJ: Littlefield, Adams, 1972.

Snow, C. E. (1981). Literacy and language: Relationships during the preschool years. *Harvard Educational Review, 53,* 165–189.

Snow, C. E., & Goldfield, B. A. (1983). Turn the page please: Situation specific language acquisition. *Journal of Child Language, 10,* 551–569.

Snow, C. E., & Ninio, A. (1986). The contracts of literacy: What children learn from learning to read books. In W. Teale & E. Sulzby (eds.), *Emergent literacy: Writing and reading,* Norwood, NJ: Ablex.

Sullivan, L. (1972). Development of causal connectives by children. *Perceptual and Motor Skills, 35,* 1003–1010.

Vygotsky, L. S. (1962). *Thought and language.* Cambridge, MA: MIT Press.

Wells, G. (1985). Preschool literacy-related activity and success in school. In D. R. Olson, N. Torrance, & A. Hildyard (Eds.), *Literacy language and learning.* Cambridge: Cambridge University Press.

8 *Developing the representational functions of language: The role of parent–child book-reading activity*

CAROLYN P. PANOFSKY

It is a commonplace of our educational wisdom that young children should be read to. Not only is this belief widely held in popular thought but within the professional educational community as well (Teale, 1984). Yet it is not sufficient to say that reading to children is a key to literacy. As research (e.g., Heath, 1982, 1983; Wells, 1982, 1985) has shown, not all children who are "read to" at home do well in early literacy instruction.

Critical to the experience of adult–child book reading is the nature of that activity. In her ethnographic study of children from three communities, Heath (1982) found, for example, that when adults looked at books with very young children, all engaged in the kind of pointing-and-naming games, which Ninio and Bruner (1978) referred to as "ritual naming." However, once children's vocabulary needs diminished, some parents demanded an end to verbal interaction during book reading – children were expected to "be quiet and listen" – while other parents allowed the verbal interaction to remain a part of the activity. In a similar kind of contrastive finding in his longitudinal study, Wells (1985) found no correlation between looking at picture books with later literacy development but did find a significant correlation with the reading of stories and later success. Wells proposes that both the rich language of stories and the sort of talk that arises from stories "prepares the child to cope with the style of teaching and assessing that is so frequently observed in schools":

> As a result of the stories that are read to him, [the child's] world stretches beyond the present actuality into the world of imaginary characters whose actions and feelings he is invited to try to understand in terms of his own experience. Equally importantly, stories read are drawn upon as a means of making sense of the objects, people, and events in his day-to-day environment. (1985, p. 245)

The comparative research by both Heath and Wells suggests that the quality of the language used by parents and children during book reading is important in the child's development: certain kinds of verbal interactions are correlated with success in literacy in the context of schooling. Not surprisingly, parent–child book reading has been the focus of much research activity in the past decade and several comprehensive reviews explore the breadth of this work (Teale 1984, 1986).

The present study seeks to extend our understanding of parent–child book reading by focusing on the language of parent–child book reading activity, to describe the uses of language that the child develops. These uses of language comprise an accumulated knowledge, built up over several years of joint book-reading experiences, which the young learner brings to her or his school reading instruction. In order to address the issue of knowledge accumulated over the preschool period, the research examined the activity of a small number of children of several ages over a relatively long period of time[1] and observed their activity in its "naturally occurring context" of homes.

THEORETICAL FRAMEWORK

Notions of context specificity inform contemporary views of human action. Where once researchers held notions about generalized competencies and cognitive skills, newer conceptions refer to specific contexts of activity based on research findings that have displaced the notion of generalized cognitive competencies (e.g., Newman, Griffin, & Cole, 1989; Scribner & Cole, 1981). In investigations across a varied range of disciplines – cognitive and developmental psychology and psycholinguistics to ethnography of communication, linguistics and sociolinguistics – there is an emerging consensus about the centrality of context in the processes of human action. For example, Rogoff and her colleagues have argued that from the perspective of functional theories, "ways of thinking and behaving are not characteristics of the person separate from the context in which the person functions" (Rogoff, Gauvain, & Ellis, 1984, p. 556). No longer can cognition and context be considered separately but instead they must be studied as an integrated system, "to consider the systemic relation between all aspects of context and the action of the person in the integrated cognitive event" (Rogoff, 1982, p. 126).

An important task, then, for understanding human action and human development is the description of significant contexts in which development takes place. Following the work of L. S. Vygotsky (1978, 1987) theorists (e.g., Laboratory of Comparative Human Cognition [LCHC], 1983; Rogoff, 1982; Rogoff, et al. 1984; Wertsch, 1985) have argued that context – conceived in the comprehensive sense as both the immediate context of social interaction and the larger sociohistorical context in which that interaction is generated – is the significant unit in the analysis of mind (LCHC, 1983; Wertsch, 1985). Rogoff et al. (1984, p. 557) have summarized the approach this way:

> Rather than focusing on individual responses to environmental stimuli as the unit of analysis, the Vygotskian approach focuses on the concept of *activity*. . . . The cultural practice theory of the [Laboratory of Comparative Human Cognition] . . . focuses on activity by identifying "socially assembled situations" as the unit of analysis rather than working from characteristics of individual persons or cultures. "Socially assembled situations" are cultural contexts for action and problem solving that are constructed by people as they interact with one another. Cultural practices employed in socially assembled situations are learned systems of activity in which knowledge consists of standing rules for thought and action appropriate to a particular situation, embodied in the cooperation of individual members of a culture.

Such a theory emphasizes "the *practice* of socially constructed modes of thinking, where cognition involves *doing* goal-directed action" (Rogoff et al., 1984). In related work, Scribner and Cole (1981) defined "practice" as "a recurrent, goal-directed sequence of activities using a particular technology and particular systems of knowledge" (p. 236).

As contexts in which children learn, a "socially assembled situation" at home is likely to differ significantly from the socially assembled situations typical in other settings such as schools. The purposes and goals of apparently similar activities – such as reading – may differ and the relationships and roles of participants will differ as well. At home, the purposes and goals of an activity are usually continuous with the child's ongoing experiences and valued by others in her intimate social network. The child's active participation will be a pivotal factor in the home situation, where the choice to withold participation or to participate on one's own terms or in one's own way exerts a definitive role. By contrast, at school the purposes and goals of an activity may be difficult for a child to understand and a child's lack of participation can go unnoticed and unnoted. At home, the child's participation is the sine qua non: if the parent, for example, wants book reading with the child to occur, a way must be found to engage the child's active involvement. "Apprenticeship" has recently been used to refer to such teaching/learning relationships in which teacher and learner collaborate on the activity and where the learner's participation is under his or her control (John-Steiner, 1985; Rogoff, 1990). Unlike activity in formal and group learning environments, the one-to-one relationship of apprenticeship cannot proceed in a one-sided manner. As Rogoff (1986) explains,

> adults do not work alone. If children give no feedback or guidance as to their needs or understanding, adults can do little. . . . Children play an active role in their own learning. Not only do they assist the adult in setting the level of the lesson; through their motivation and self-directed attempts to learn, they require the adult to provide information or help. . . . together the adult and child manage teaching and learning in a process of *guided participation.* (emphasis in original)

The adult's guidance consists of the way he or she structures the situation on several levels, such as the assignment of roles in the activity as well as the verbal guidance along the way. In studying parent–child book reading, I found parents' structuring to be of central importance (Panofsky, 1987). In all of the families, children were given the role of selecting which books to read and in every case this was a role assignment which carried more than a negligible amount of power: parents sometimes expressed a dislike for one of the choices or a preference for a book to which the child objected, and occasionally went to great lengths to try to coax or cajole a change, but it was always the parent who gave in. It is interesting that even when parents claimed to "hate" a particular book, they would not overrule the child's choice. Yet these were not notably "permissive" parents, nor were such incidents limited to the observation periods. The explanation is that overruling the child's authority in this way would threaten to undermine the child's desire to participate; the boundaries of the activity were under the child's control. Indeed, there were many ways in which book reading seemed to be a kind of privileged and protected activity. Not only were children given the role of choosing books, but also they tended to control both the initiation and conclusion of book-reading activity. Parents almost never refused a child's request to read and they routinely gave in to requests to "read one more," even when they wanted the session to end. Parents also structured the interaction during book reading in a reciprocal way: if children pointed to a picture or asked a question when the adult was reading, these actions were never treated as interruptions as they would have been during other activities but were welcomed as opportunities for dialogue. Indeed, these multiple levels of structuring could not have been better designed to provide for lengthy sessions of talking about books.

For the participants in this study, the socially assembled situation of book-reading activity was structured to maximize the active participation of the children and to support their progressive "appropriation" of various parts of the activity. "Appropriation" refers to the developmental process in which as novices children first learn to *respond* to a given action or use of language by another and, with time and experience, begin to "take over" in Bruner's words (1983) the function as shown by their ability to now *initiate* an action or use of language that earlier they could, at most, respond to. This shift, revealing the takeover of strategies and processes of the expert by the novice, has been documented in many studies of book-reading activity by Snow and her colleagues (e.g., Snow & Goldfield, 1982; Snow, Nathan, & Perlmann, 1986). What has been examined in much less detail has been the varied functions of language during book-reading activity.

THE STUDY OF LANGUAGE FUNCTIONS

In several approaches to the study of language, a concern with the functions of language in social context has occupied a central place. In both the functional-systemic tradition identified with Halliday (1978, 1985) and the ethnography of speaking approach articulated by Hymes (1972, 1974), prominence is given to the "context of situation" in the examination of language. In both perspectives, language is seen as variable depending on a set of social factors, including domain, activity, participants, and community. Hymes argues that

> since every community has a variety of linguistic means, speaking always entails a choice (deliberate, spontaneous, automatic) among them. From the standpoint of communication in general, this extends to the choice of speech itself, as opposed to other means (vocal, gestural – a whistle, a scream, a note, a turning away), and as opposed to silence. . . . Whether one speaks, and, if one speaks, the way in which one speaks, are elements of choice and hence of the meaningfulness of language.
>
> To deal with language from this standpoint, we may make use of a concept that has come to prominence . . . the concept of *verbal repertoire*. . . . The term properly implies that people have available a variety of ways of speaking. We may understand *verbal repertoire* more precisely in terms of two interrelated aspects of speech. There are the *means of speech* that people have available, including the meanings associated with the use of one or another of these; and there are the *contexts of situation* in which speech is used, including meanings associated with these. . . . The set of patterns relating means of speech and contexts of situation may be said to constitute the ways of *speaking* of a person, a group, or a community. (1972, pp. xxiii–xxiv, emphasis in original)

Halliday has commented extensively on the patterning of speech in various contexts, elaborating on the constraining dimension of context (1973, 1978, 1985). In an early proposal for a contextual view of language use, Halliday argued that much of our speech in daily life takes place in

> fairly restricted contexts where the options are limited and the meaning potential is, in fact, rather closely specifiable. Buying and selling in a shop, going to the doctor, and many of the routines of the working day all represent situation types in which language is by no means restricted as a whole, the transactional meanings are not closed, but nevertheless there are certain definable patterns, certain options which typically come into play. . . . When we talk of "social functions of language," we mean those contexts which are significant in that we are able to specify some of the meaning potential that is characteristically, and explainably, associated with them. (1973, p. 347)

This notion of the contextual constraints on language brings us full circle to our original notion of situated activity. Context refers both to the immediate and ongoing social interaction of the assembled participants, as well as the sociohistorical dimension of the socially assembled situation and the cultural practices of those participants. The sociohistorical context both constructs or provides for the socially assembled situations in which participants operate and constrains the interaction of which their practical activities are comprised. To understand what is going on during any specific book-reading event, one must know the recurrent properties of the activity (which can be taken as indicating, if not fully revealing, its sociohistorical embodiment). Such an investigation is a hermeneutical process, rather than a linear one, with recursive steps back and forth between the two levels of analysis. Understanding the patterns of decision making and reciprocal interaction discussed earlier were central in conducting the analysis of language functions.

In order to analyze the functions, then, it is necessary to incorporate the sociohistorical elements of parent–child book-reading activity in the families who were studied. From Heath's (1983) study in three communities, one would not necessarily expect to find the same set of elements, the same "context" of activity, in all families. However, because the families participating in my study shared a common set of beliefs and practices regarding literacy (while differing in economic status and ethnicity), it was not surprising that they "organized" the activity in the same way as well. The most important aspect of this organization was the child-centered focus of the pattern, as manifested in the two elements referred to earlier: (1) the adult's authority as decision maker was subordinated to the child in that the child had a significant or controlling role in all decisions that were related to his or her interests (e.g., which books to read, the sequence of choices, the repetition of choices, the concluding of the activity); (2) the speaking roles were "egalitarian" in that any interruptions by the children were accepted. These elements are deeply consistent with what LeVine (1980) calls "the egalitarian ideology of middle-class America as applied to the relations between generations" (where "middle class" is taken as designating a cultural orientation rather than simply economic status). Cross-cultural studies of child rearing and child development have helped to illuminate this ideology, which LeVine (1980, p. 78) captures in a useful way:

> Middle-class Americans place a great deal of emphasis on self-confidence and self-reliance in individual development. They see their young children as needing a great deal of enthusiastic encouragement to acquire the confidence in themselves that will enable them to become self-reliant, equipped to meet the challenges of life without undue dependence on others. Hence the interest in and emphasis on talking to babies, responding to their slightest attainments with applause, and continuing to use praise as a reinforcer as the child gets older. The model implicit here is one of pumping encouragement in during the early years to obtain the child's autonomy later on. *At first you try to make a child feel good about any initiative he or she takes, and later you selectively but enthusiastically give verbal approval to displays of self-reliant behavior.* (emphasis added)

Such *displays* of behavior to the parent, which rely on reciprocal roles in dialogue, are central to what the child is learning. Given the value placed on those displays, it is not surprising, then, that parents expend considerable creativity in promoting the child's active participation through language – generating in language the varied possibilities for display. In this way, parents "managed" the cognitive and affective quality of the activity, providing ways "to relate" to the text both with thoughts and feelings, and serving the dual purpose of engendering enthusiasm for reading and skills for school success. After four years of this nightly apprenticeship, children can easily reverse roles to play the teacherly questioner with younger siblings or provide elaborate explanations of character and plot.

In the study of language functions, there has been a long-standing distinction between two major functions or uses of language (Brown & Yule, 1983). One function "serves in the expression of content . . . and [the other is] involved in expressing social relations and personal attitudes" (Brown & Yule, 1983, p. 1). The expression of content can be called a representational or ideational function, while the expression and regulation of social relations can be called an interactional or relational function. Not surprisingly, this same global distinction was found in the discourse of book-reading activity. However, what may seem surprising given other research is that the representational function predominated. I refer to this as potentially surprising because although there has been extensive research on children's use of interactional language functions (e.g., Ervin-Tripp & Mitchell-Kernan, 1977), comparatively little work has addressed the use of language for the ideational or representational "axis" of language function. Such language, however, is likely to be needed for successful participation in classrooms. An important point is that bedtime storybook reading comprises an intensely focused activity in which the representational functions of language are given primary attention.

In fact, for much-read-to children, book reading interactions may be seen as a "leading activity" (Meacham, 1977, p. 227) in the development of language for representation:

> At each stage in development, a particular activity can be characterized as a "leading" activity, not because it is most frequent, but rather because it is within the context of this activity that mental processes are reorganized and new activities are differentiated. The sequence of leading activities depends on the specific social and historical conditions of the developing child.

The use of representational language certainly occurs in domains other than book-reading activity. Yet the intensity, focus, and recurrence of these dyadic sessions lasting at least a half hour and occurring every night seem to set this activity apart from other speech situations.

THE TAXONOMY OF LANGUAGE FUNCTIONS

With this fuller understanding of the context of book reading, we turn to the detailed discussion of the functions of language during the activity. As mentioned earlier, there were the two global functions, interactional and representational. The interactional functions related to the activity itself – talk that negotiated what would be read and when; the interactional functions initiated and ended the activity and the sequence of different books which were read during the activity. Thus, the actual reading was bounded by the interactional language function. Even the youngest participants in the study seemed fully able to control the interactional functions of language: from the beginning of the study even the 2-year-olds were able to initiate, as well as respond to, all of the subfunctions of interaction. These included regulating self, other, and objects to accomplish control at the activity level:

"Read this now." (Child directs sequence of stories)
"You sit there." (Child directs seating arrangement)
"Me hold it." (Child physically controls the book)
"I turn." (Child controls page turning)
"Not yet." (Parent controls appropriate time for page turning)

Between beginning to read and ending each text, the use of interactionals occurred very rarely, only to signal who or when to turn pages or to "repair" the text-based conversation when one participant didn't understand the other (typically when the parent wasn't sure what the child had said). Most interactionals occurred during negotiation of activity beginnings and endings and for book choice, much like negotiating the agenda and the adjournment of a meeting. Overall, the interactional function accounted for 5 to 15 percent of the utterances during any 30- to 50-minute session. Since "off-task" talk rarely accounted for even 1 percent of the utterances during any total book-reading session, the amount of representational talk was 85 to 95 percent of all the talk that occurred during book reading activity. Where interactional talk was activity-related, representational talk was text-related. Interactional language was used to negotiate the activity, while representational talk was used to negotiate the meanings of text. In this talk, as we will see, children were developing a variety of ways for *representing* text and self in relation to text – an early and important subset of representational functions of language that are valued in school activities.

THE REPRESENTATIONAL FUNCTIONS

This text-related or representational discourse comprised a seemingly large and varied set divisible into seven subfunctions. Despite this variety, however, the discourse should be seen as constrained – the set of "allowable options" that bounded the discourse. The seven functions were identified as follows: attentionals, pictorials, connectives, inferentials, emotives, imaginatives, and recitations.[2]

Pictorials, connectives, and inferentials were the most frequently used, but all participants utilized all of these functions, and the use of the functions varied developmentally both for individuals and across ages.

The discussion that follows gives a definition and several examples of each function, followed by a discussion of several passages from the transcripts.

Attentionals are utterances in which one of the participants seeks to orient the attention of the other participant through verbal and nonverbal means such as "Look" accompanied by pointing. Attentionals were typically followed by a pictorial or a connective.

Pictorials are utterances in which joint attention of parent and child was focused on a picture and verbal information was added to make sense of the picture. This verbal information was of two kinds: informational or indicative utterances such as labeling ("That's a butterfly") or specifying of attributes ("It's upside down!"); and interpretive or inferential utterances (in the sense of interpreting or inferring *conventions*) about pictures. The following set of utterances illustrates these possibilities: "See the tear? He's crying." Here the first utterance is indicative and the second is interpretive.

Connectives are utterances in which a connection was made as a kind of strategy for making sense of text. Connections were made within and between text (intra- and inter-textual), and between text and self or text and world (extra-textual). Connectives may be used to connect any of the following combinations: picture-text ("Where's the little house?"); text-text within the same story ("Remember it said – "); text-text between two stories ("That's like in the other story when – "); text-self or picture-self in terms of past experiences ("That's what you look like when you jump off high places"); text-self or picture-self in terms of acting out ("I can make a face like that"); text-world knowledge or picture-world knowledge ("They make suitcases out of alligator skins").

Inferentials are utterances in which comments or questions go beyond the text (or beyond the conventional inferences referred to under pictorials). These include predictions or evaluations about the why or how of events or things, such as "Do you think the fish will like the cake?"; predictions or evaluations about the why or how of character's actions, or talk of feelings, such as "He should try to get it by climbing up the tree, then . . ."; personal extrapolations ("If I were there, I would . . .") and extrapolations that refer to another participant ("If you were there, you would . . ."); and metacommunication about words and stories, including explanations of word meanings and discussions of "what's real" (such as "That shows he's just dreaming").

Emotives are utterances that express or identify feelings. Several subfunctions were identified: explicit or expressive utterances of own feelings or opinions ("Oh, no!" or "This is scary!"); explicit or expressive utterances about another's feelings or opinions ("I bet he's scared"); and laughter and other paralinguistic responses to text.

Imaginatives are utterances in which the child acts out the role of a reader or of a participant in the text. Three subfunctions were identified: word play, such as spontaneously making up rhymes or elaborating on text; mock reading that is nonsensical but readerly (it "sounds like" the intonation of oral reading); and answering text-embedded questions (when this is contrary to the parent's expectation, rather than following a preestablished parent–child routine).

Recitations were utterances in which the child recited actual or textlike utterances, and which were either elicited by the parent, initiated by the child, or were a kind of spontaneous shadowing or anticipation. Four subfunctions were identified: initiations by the child which were memory-based; elicitations, prompts, or corrections by the parent; text-echoing; and content anticipation by the child (such as at the point of page turning when a phrase is divided between two pages).

In global terms, the emphasis on various functions, as reflected by their differential usage, was found to shift as follows:

1. interactions with the youngest children tended to focus on conventions of labeling and pictorial interpretation and thus relied extensively on the attentional and pictorial functions;
2. interactions then shifted focus to the creation of extra-textual connections between the text and the child's knowledge and experience of self and world outside the text and thus came to rely more extensively on the connective function;
3. interactions next led to discussions and interpretations of physical and psychological aspects of actions and events in the text and thus relied increasingly on the inferential function.

Although the use of the functions has been presented in a numerical sequence, this should not be taken as suggesting a stagelike model. For one thing, stage models imply "moving beyond" some earlier stage and "not going back," yet even the oldest children sometimes used functions and strategies that typified the activity of the least experienced children, and even the youngest children were able to participate in the use of all functions to some degree.

A selection of data focusing primarily on the three dominant functions – pictorials, connectives, and inferentials – will illustrate their use in context. One of the children in the middle age-group, a boy of 4;1 at the time of a midyear session, provides evidence of impressive development, especially in the use of the connective and the inferential functions. The session began with a first-time reading of *Curious George flies a kite* by H. A. Rey (1958). Although this book was unfamiliar to both parent and child, they had read several other Curious George books many times before; just as the mother began reading, the child announced "I'm going to be Curious George when I grow up," as he sat with a monkey-doll beside him which he called Curious George. Early into the story, the child reiterated this claim, demonstrating a use of connection between self and text. (Utterances illustrating functions to be discussed will be in boldface and referenced by numbers in the margin; italicized portions are written text):

Example 1

M: *George could do a lot of tricks with his ball too. This was one of the tricks. He could get up on the ball like this or he could do it this way with his head down. This was another trick George could do, he could hold the ball on his head like this.*

1 C: **I can do that. I'm going to be Curious George when I grow up.**

M: You're going to be Curious George when you grow up? I think you already are. *Look, no hands. What a good trick. But where did the ball go?*

C: [unintelligible]

M: You aren't Curious George yet? *George ran after it. The ball had gone into another room. There was a big window in the room but George liked to look out of that window. He could see a lot from there. He let the ball go and looked out.*

2 **Do you see the window?** [looks to C]

C: [nods]

3 M: **Where's the window in the book?**

C: [points]

M: There it is. *George could see Bill on his bike and a lake with a boat on it. George could see a big house with a little garden and a little house with a big garden. The big house was the house where Bill lived. But who lived in the little house. George was curious. Who could live in a house so little?*

C: I don't know.

4 M: **Where's the little house?**

C: [points]

5 M: **That's the big house.** Look, look. [pointing]

C: Oh, look at that.

6 M: **Yeah, that's a little teeny weeny house.** Who could live there?

C: I don't know.

M: *George had to find out so he went to the big garden. The garden had a high wall, but not too high for a monkey. George got up on the wall. All he had to do now was jump down so George jumped down into the big garden.*

7 **You jump off of things like that, don't you? That's how you look [pointing] when you come jumping down.**

8 C: **Yeah, out of the window.**

Throughout this sequence, we see the participants jointly constructing a variety of connectives. In the exchange about the big house and the little house, the message is that one expects a correspondence between the words in the text and the pictorial representation on the page. Although parents never directly and explicitly state such an expectation, there is considerable evidence suggesting that children in the study all came to internalize such an expectation. The initiation of connective questions by parents were routinely answered by children with increasing success. Additional evidence is that the children asked text-picture questions when they could not find the picture corresponding to something mentioned in the text, sometimes even saying, "I can't find the [thing mentioned in the text]."

In the sequence referring to "jumping off things" the mother does not say, didactically, that one should look for connections with one's own experience. But by indexing experiences from other domains known to the child, adults enact such connections, and in the later data there are numerous instances of children enacting such personal connections independently.

The connective function also involves intra-textual and inter-textual connections. In the former, the procedure is to look for a connection with another point, earlier or later, in the text; in the latter, the procedure is to identify a connection with another text. In the following example, the parent responds to the child's puzzlement by indexing the notion that upcoming text is likely to answer current uncertainty:

Example 2

M: *The bunny was off like a shot. George did not look; now he had to wait a little. One, two, three, four, he waited.*
C: Then when, how he got him?
9 M: **How did he find him?**
C: [Nods]
10 M: **Let's find out [turning page].**

In the next episode, after the baby bunny has been safely returned to its house, there is a picture both mother and child are unsure about. The mother plays out the "mystery," which is also in the text, by using picture interpretations:

Example 3

M: *When he came to the wall, he could see something funny in back of it. George got up on the wall to find out what it was.*
11 **What do you think that is?**
12 C: **Um, a hitter.**
M: A hammer?
C: No, a hitter, like when you hit something.
M: Oh, a hitter, like a stick or something.
C: [nods]
M: *He saw a long string and a long stick. A fat man had the long stick in his hand. What could the man do with the stick that long? George was curious. The fat man was on his way to the lake and George was on his way to the lake too.*
13 **What does the man have?**
14 C: **A fishing pole.**

At the end of the story, we find an example of the child initiating an inter-textual connection.

Example 4

15 C: . . . **Remember that one that has the elephant when he blows up the balloon?**
16 M: Oh, yeah, **when he got a hold of balloons –**
17 **C: Yeah, den he tried to get down, den he landed on a tree, den he gave all of the balloons to da circus, huh?**
M: Uhuh.
C: Dat was neat, huh?

This is a rather surprising example of inter-textual understanding. Yet, it is important to recall that this child was extremely fond of Curious George stories and the Curious George character, and the story with which he connects had been read many times and recently. At the same time, his ability to make this connection suggests a significant involvement with these materials and helps to account for the inferential understandings to be explored next, which are surprising for a child of his age and for a first time reading.

Inferentials

Early in the story, Curious George lets a baby bunny out of its cage to play with it in a walled-in garden, and the bunny disappears; after the disappearance, George goes to search for a piece of string:

Example 5

M: . . . *George took the string and went back to the bunny house.* See that little bird? Do you know what he's saying to George?
C: What?
M: He's saying "bad monkey." *Mother bunny was at the door. George let her out and put the string on her and Mother Bunny knew what to do and away she went with her head down and her ears up. All George could do was hold the string and run after her.*
18 **What do you think Mother Bunny is going to do?**
19 C: **Find.**
M: Find the baby bunny?
C: [nods agreement]

The exchange of interest begins at the end of the mother's second turn: "What do you think Mother Bunny is going to do?" The child is asked to predict what will happen next. The answer is implied but not directly stated in the foregoing text. The mother initiates this inferential question, and the child knows how to respond appropriately.

In the next example, the child's question indicates that he is able to initiate appropriate predictive questions as well. Here, Curious George is fishing from the end of a dock:

Example 6

M: *George looked into the water; that big red one there with a long tail. He was so near, maybe he could get it with his hands. George got down as low as he could, and put out his hand.*
20 C: **Will he fall in dere?**
M: What?
C: Will he fall in dere?
M: Will he fall in there? I don't know, let's see. [turns page] Oh, you were

right! *Splash, into the lake he went. The water was cold and George was cold and wet too. This was no fun at all.*

21 C: **He shoulda just got his two hands down dere, den put his feet on dere [pointing].**
M: Yeah, he could have hung on to the dock with his feet, 'cause his feet are like hands, aren't they?

First, the child asks, "Will he fall in dere?" accurately predicting what will happen, and later speculates on what the character "should have" done. Later, the child initiates another speculative sequence, excitedly breaking in while his mother is still reading. This time he speculates about how George could "rescue" a kite from a tree:

Example 7

M: . . . *They let the kite fly for a long time till Bill said "I will get the kite down now. I must go home and you should too." But when Bill pulled the string in the kite got into the top of a high tree. Bill could not get it down. "Oh my –*

22 C: **You know how – he can climb and get in dere and den he can, den he will find it, and den he will get dat part dat he will put down.**
M: That might be a good idea. *"Oh my fine new kite. I cannot let go of it. I must have it back," said Bill, "but the tree is too high for me." But no tree is too high for George. He went up to the top in no time. Then, little by little, he got the string out of the tree.* You were right, John. *George is a monkey, and monkeys can climb. Down he came with the kite. . . .*

A little later in the story George is left alone with the kite. He tries to fly it and is carried into the air by the kite. In this example, the mother initiates an inferential comment about the monkey's internal state to which the child replies with another rescue plan. However, the mother responds by citing previous textual material that invalidates his plan. Finally, when George is rescued, the child infers his emotional response:

Example 8

M: *George did not like it one bit. He wanted to get down, but how? Not even a monkey can jump in the sky. George was scared. What if he never got back, maybe he would fly on and on and on. Oh, he would never, never be so curious again, if just this one time he could find a way to get home.* Poor George. He's scared up there.

23 C: Yeah. **How 'bout, how 'bout he let the kite go away up in the sky and then he can jump in the pool.**
M: He can jump in the water? It said that he couldn't jump in the sky that high, not even a monkey can. *Hummhumm. What was that? George could hear something and then he saw something fly in the sky just like a kite. It was a helicopter and in the helicopter, hooray, was the man with the yellow hat.* Look.

24 C: **He's happy, huh?**

Table 8.1. *Percentage of each utterance function initiated by the parent (P) and child (C) during selected sessions throughout the year*

	1st quarter		2nd quarter		3rd quarter		4th quarter	
	P	C	P	C	P	C	P	C
Connectives	37	5	45	25	28	12	14	23
Inferentials	21	4	31	6	29	21	25	42

At the end of this episode of the monkey's rescue, the child recalls a strikingly similar episode in another Curious George story, which was discussed earlier as an example of inter-textual connection.

During the reading of *Curious George flies a kite* there were various connective and inferential questions and comments initiated by both the parent and child, along with other functions. Table 8.1, which includes both connective and inferentials from sessions throughout the year, presents a picture of change in the percentage of initiations by this parent and child of each function.

The increasing use of various functions emerged first in the questions and comments of the parents and were gradually appropriated by the children. At the beginning of the year, we see that almost all initiations of both connectives and inferentials are made by the parent. The fact that less than half of all connectives and only a quarter of all inferentials are initiations means that the rest are responses or follow-up discussion and suggests that considerable follow-up is required to enable the child to understand and participate in the use of the functions. At the second quarter, the child has begun to initiate a substantial percentage of connectives but still initiates only a few inferentials. In addition, connectives require substantially less follow-up discussion, as 70 percent are initiations; at this point, then, we see the child shift from participation in the use of connectives that is dependent on the adult to the child's independent control (in the form of initiations) of this representational function. In the third quarter, the child also exhibits significant control of the inferential function, and by the end of the year his use of both the connective and the inferential functions shows clear independence by outnumbering the adult's use of either function by nearly two to one. In the last two quarters the number of connectives that are initiations has declined to less than half of all utterances coded as the connective function, which seems anomolous in view of the earlier interpretation of low percentages reflecting the need for follow-up discussion; however, now the responses appear to reflect parents' tendency to restate or extend the child's initiations, rather than to make sure the child understands. An example of parental restatement and extension occurs at the end of example 5 when the mother agrees, "Yeah, he could have hung on to the dock with his feet, 'cause his feet are like hands, aren't they?"

CONCLUSION

The shift in the use of functions from a predominance of parent initiations to a predominance of child initiations shows the development of cognitive processes modeled by Vygotsky (1978, p. 57):

> Every function in the child's cultural development appears twice: first, on the social level, and later, on the individual level; first, *between* people (*interpsychological*), and then *inside* the child (*intrapsychological*). This applies equally to voluntary attention, to logical memory, and to the formation of concepts. All the higher functions originate as actual relations between human individuals. . . . *The transformation of an interpersonal process into an intrapersonal one is the result of a long series of developmental events.* (emphasis in original)

It is important to see the development of cognitive processes as social in origin, rather than individual, in the way that Vygotsky does. Cognitive processes, such as those reflected in the language of the preschool child highlighted in this discussion, develop in recurrent and intensely focused social interactions like those which occur during book reading. Access to opportunities for participation in such valued social practices is crucial. It is important to note that Vygotsky refers to the child's "cultural development" because he is concerned with the development that takes place in the sociohistorically constituted, or cultural, practices of the child's world. Increasing numbers of scholars are coming to speak of culturally valued practices, genres of power (Lemke, 1988) or simply a "culture of power" (Delpit, 1989) that operates in our schools. Lemke (1988) argues that "education does not do enough to empower people, to place in their hands tools they can use for their own purposes and the skills to use them."

By identifying the specific and varied representational functions of parent–child discourse during book reading, as well as the interactional processes of such exchange, this research offers a way to model instruction for children who have not had the advantage of such apprenticeship before formal schooling. Research by McCartney (1984) suggests that schools can impact development in the way I am suggesting. She found that, regardless of family background factors, the ways that language was used in teacher–child interactions in preschools had a significant impact on the development of cognitive-language processes in children.

As educators, our task is to foster children's interaction with the language of valued social practices.

NOTES

An earlier version of this paper was presented at the Fifth International Congress for the Study of Child Language, Budapest, Hungary, July 15–20, 1990.

1. The language of parent–child book reading was investigated during a longitudinal ethnographic study of family book-reading events in the homes of six preschool children. Families selected were ones in which shared book reading was considered to be an essential element of children's early experiences. The children were selected to cover the range of ages from 2 to 6, and were observed periodically for a year. At the beginning of the year, two of the children were approximately aged 2;0, two were 3;6 and two were 5;0. At each age there was a child of each sex and one whose family background was identified as Hispanic and one as Anglo. Naturally occurring book-reading events were observed in each of the homes every 6 to 8 weeks, to provide data from 36 sessions. Each session, lasting 30 to 50 minutes, was audiotaped and a third of the sessions were also videotaped; field notes were kept on all sessions and all audiotapes were transcribed.
2. The designation of the functions has been modified from earlier versions (Panofsky, 1987, 1989) in which pictorials were labeled as referentials, connectives were labeled procedurals, and attentionals were one of the subdivisions of procedurals.

REFERENCES

Brown, G., & G. Yule. 1983. *Discourse analysis.* Cambridge: Cambridge University Press.

Bruner, J. 1983. *Child's talk.* New York: Norton.

Delpit, L. 1989. The silenced dialogue: Power and pedagogy in educating other people's children. *Harvard Educational Review* 58: 280–298.

Ervin-Tripp, S., & C. Mitchell-Kernan. 1977. *Child discourse.* New York: Academic Press.

Halliday, M. A. K. 1973. The functional basis of language. In B. Bernstein, Ed., *Class, codes and control.* Vol. 2. London: Routledge & Kegan Paul.

Halliday, M. A. K. 1978. *Language as social semiotic.* London: Edward Arnold.

Halliday, M. A. K. 1985. Systemic background. In J. Benson & W. Greaves, Eds., *Systemic perspectives on discourse.* Vol. 1. Norwood, NJ: Ablex.

Heath, S. B. 1982. What no bedtime story means: Narrative skills at home and school. *Language in Society* 11: 49–76.

Heath, S. B. 1983. *Ways with words.* Cambridge: Cambridge University Press.

Hymes, D. 1972. Introduction. In C. Cazden, V. John, & D. Hymes, Eds., *Functions of language in the classroom.* New York: Teachers College Press.

Hymes, D. 1974. *Foundations in sociolinguistics.* Philadelphia: University of Pennsylvania Press.

John-Steiner, V. 1985. *Notebooks of the mind.* Albuquerque: University of New Mexico Press.

Laboratory of Comparative Human Cognition. 1983. Culture and cognitive development. In W. Kessen, Ed., *Handbook of child psychology.* Vol. 1. New York: Wiley.

Lemke, J. 1988. Genres, semantics, and classroom education. *Linguistics and Education* 1: 81–99.

LeVine, R. 1980. Anthropology and child development. In C. Super & S. Harkness, Eds., *New directions for child development: Anthropological perspectives on child development.* San Francisco: Jossey-Bass.

Meacham, J. 1977. Soviet investigations of memory development. In R. Kail & J. Hagen, Eds., *Perspectives on the development of memory and cognition.* Hillsdale, NJ: Erlbaum.

McCartney, K. 1984. Effect of quality of day care environment on children's language development. *Developmental Psychology* 20(2): 244–260.

Newman, D., P. Griffin, & M. Cole. 1989. *The construction zone.* Cambridge: Cambridge University Press.

Ninio, A., & J. Bruner. 1978. The achievement and antecedents of labeling. *Journal of Child Language* 5: 1–15.

Panofsky, C. P. 1987. The interactionist roots of literacy: Parent–child book reading and the processes of cognitive socialization. Unpublished doctoral dissertation, University of New Mexico.

Panofsky, C. P. 1989. The functions of language in parent–child book reading events. *Theory into Practice* 28: 120–125.

Rey, H. A. 1958. *Curious George flies a kite.* Boston: Houghton Mifflin.

Rogoff, B. 1982. Integrating context and cognitive development. In M. E. Lamb & A. L. Brown, Eds., *Advances in developmental psychology.* Vol. 2. Hillsdale, NJ: Erlbaum.

Rogoff, B. 1986. Adult assistance of children's learning. In T. E. Raphael, Ed., *The contexts of school-based literacy.* New York: Random House.

Rogoff, B. 1990. *Apprenticeships in learning.* New York: Oxford University Press.

Rogoff, B., M. Gauvain, & S. Ellis. 1984. Development viewed in its cultural context. In M. H. Bornstein & M. E. Lamb, Eds., *Developmental psychology: An advanced textbook.* Hillsdale, NJ: Erlbaum.

Scribner, S., & M. Cole. 1981. *The psychology of literacy.* Cambridge, MA: Harvard University Press.

Snow, C., & B. Goldfield. 1982. Building stories: The emergence of information structures from conversation. In D. Tannen, Ed., *Georgetown University Roundtable on Language and Linguistics 1981.* Washington, DC: Georgetown University Press.

Snow, C., D. Nathan, & R. Perlmann. 1986. Assessing children's knowledge about book-reading. In L. Galda & A. Pelligrini, Eds., *Language, play and story.* Norwood, NJ: Ablex.

Teale, W. 1984. Reading to young children: Its significance for literacy development. In H. Goelman, A. Oberg, & F. Smith, Eds., *Awakening to literacy.* Exeter, NH: Heinemann.

Teale, W. 1986. The beginnings of reading and writing: Written language development during the preschool and kindergarten years. In M. R. Sampson, Ed., *The pursuit of literacy.* Dubuque, IA: Kendall/Hunt.

Vygotsky, L. S. 1978. *Mind in society.* Cambridge, MA: Harvard University Press.

Vygotsky, L. S. 1987. *Collected works.* Vol. 1. New York: Plenum.

Wells, G. 1982. Story reading and the development of symbolic skills. *Australian Journal of Reading* 5: 142–152.

Wells, G. 1985. Preschool literacy-related activities and success in school. In D. Olson, N. Torrance, & A. Hilyard, Eds., *Literacy, language and learning.* Cambridge: Cambridge University Press.

Wertsch, J. 1985. *Vygotsky and the social formation.* Cambridge, MA: Harvard University Press.

9 *The implications of Vygotskian theory for the development of home-school programs: A focus on storybook reading*

PATRICIA A. EDWARDS AND
GEORGIA EARNEST GARCIA

How are programs organized to assist low-income parents to prepare their children for school? Surprisingly, we know little about this question, particularly as it applies to the theoretical principles researchers and educators have used to develop home-school programs. This question becomes increasingly important as more attention is directed toward the education of children who traditionally do not fare well in school (see Garcia, Pearson, & Jimenez, 1990). Yet book-reading programs continue to be developed for low-income parents and children with scant descriptions of the theoretical principles employed.

One aspect of Vygotsky's work (1962, 1978; Wertsch, 1984), the zone of proximal development, focuses on what adults – parents or teachers – do to stretch children's learning. Another aspect suggests that learning must be socially situated, and that for learners to move through the zone of proximal development they must internalize what they have learned through social interaction. In order to do this, learners need to be given the opportunity actively to construct and interpret academic tasks. While Vygotsky did not detail how more capable peers or adults were supposed to help stretch children's learning in this fashion, other researchers influenced by Vygotsky have used his theory to experiment with scaffolding, guided participation, and reciprocal teaching (Collins, Brown, & Newman, 1989; Palinscar & Brown, 1984; Rogoff, 1984). Yet, to our knowledge, few researchers, if any, have used the different aspects of Vygotsky's theoretical model, and the practical suggestions of other researchers influenced by Vygotsky, to stretch parents' learning and, especially, parents' learning of book-reading strategies (Edwards, 1991). This chapter reports on a program (Parents as Partners in Reading) designed and developed by the first author to assist nonmainstream parents develop the type of strategies needed to successfully read with their children.[1] In the chapter, we also describe how Vygotskian theory and derivatives of the theory were used to structure the book-reading program. Lastly, we discuss the implications of the program for increased parental and child participation in schools and note the implications of using a Vygotskian framework to develop other home-school programs.

BACKGROUND OF STUDY

A variety of programs have been developed to help low-income parents improve their children's performance in school (see Garcia et al., 1990; Henderson, 1987; Wilson, 1983). Several of the more recent programs have focused on parent–child storybook reading (Arrastia, 1989; Edwards, 1990a; Gaj, 1989; Goldsmith 1989). This activity is viewed positively by the schools (Teale, 1981) and thought to help increase children's print and phonological awareness (see Edwards & Garcia, 1991; Garcia et al., 1990). Through storybook reading, children hear written language, begin to relate written language to spoken language, and become aware of the features of print. As Gaj (1989) points out, storybook reading also is a way to create connections between parents and children, capitalizing on the shared history, intimacy, and motivation that makes the parent a unique teacher. Children who are successfully engaged in storybook reading at home are thought to be more likely to be interested in storybook reading in school. Observations of mainstream parents reading books to their children have revealed that these parents frequently use a variety of successful book-reading strategies that allow the parent and child to engage in school-like interactions (see Baghban, 1984; Heath, 1982; Hoffman, 1982; Kasler, Roser, & Hoffman, 1987; Taylor, 1983). Similar observations of nonmainstream parents reveal that storybook reading is not as common an event in their homes and that many nonmainstream parents are not familiar with the types of book-reading interactions common in school (Anderson & Stokes, 1984; Edwards, 1989; Heath, 1982; Teale, 1986).

One of the overriding criticisms of the research on nonmainstream parents has been that few suggestions are offered for improving parental participation in book reading (Ninio, 1980; Farron, 1982; Heath, 1982; Heath with Thomas, 1984; McCormick & Mason, 1986). While researchers have supported the notion that nonmainstream parents could profit from receiving assistance in how to share books with their children (Spewock, 1988; Sledge, 1987; Pflaum, 1986; Swift, 1970), only a few programs have actually been developed (Arrastia, 1989; Edwards, 1990a, 1990b; Gaj, 1989; Goldsmith 1989).

Efforts to assist nonmainstream parents with their children's literacy development have not always been effective. First of all, parents who were not successful participants in the school system are not always eager to participate in home-school literacy programs (see Edwards & Garcia, 1991). Second, some of these parents may not be fluent readers or those who are fluent may not be confident in their literacy abilities. Third, program developers not only have to specify and demonstrate successful book-reading strategies, they also need to facilitate parents' ownership of these strategies so that they will feel comfortable with storybook reading and continue to engage in it once the program has ended. Fourth, for a home-school program to influence nonmainstream children's performance in school, teachers and administrators need to be willing to accept the participation and knowledge of these parents and children. Last, a major drawback to the development of storybook programs has been that this line of work frequently has been seen as an attempt to acculturate instead of empower nonmainstream parents and their children (see Auerbach, 1989; Edwards & Garcia, 1991).

Description of the parents as partners in reading program

Theoretical overview. Vygotsky's concept (1962, 1978) of the zone of proximal development stresses that cognitive functioning occurs first on the social level, between people, and that the child then internalizes this functioning in individual development. The concept of the zone of proximal development focuses on the developmental phase where the child has only partially mastered a task but can participate in its execution with the assistance and supervision of an adult or more capable peer. Even though the interaction may be verbal, nonverbal, or a combination, Rogoff and Wertsch (1984, p. 1) state that "the zone of proximal development is this dynamic region of sensitivity in which cognitive development advances."

Current research has extended Vygotsky's ideas to a wider range of mental functions (see Rogoff & Wertsch, 1984). The research has also included work with infants, preschoolers, school-age children, and adolescents at home, at school, at work, and in the laboratory (Saxe, Gearhart, & Guberman, 1984; Rogoff, Malkin, & Gilbride, 1984). More recently, Vygotsky's theory has been used to interpret the Reading Recovery Model (Clay & Cazden, 1990) and for instructing Reading Recovery teachers and children (Gaffney & Anderson, 1991). The success of this theoretical model with other learners led the first author to propose that this model could be used to assist nonmainstream parents in learning to share books with their children. The author was particularly interested in employing scaffolding, guided participation, cooperative small groups, and social interaction principles.

Organization of the book-reading program

Twenty-five low-income mothers (18 African-American and 7 white) from a small, rural community located in the southeastern United

States participated in the program. None of the mothers had received prior training in book-reading, although they had completed an average of 9.5 years of schooling. Prior to soliciting the parents' participation, the university leader met with the school's administrators and kindergarten and first-grade teachers. She asked them to recommend all those children who they thought were not going to succeed because she wanted to show them that these children and their parents were capable of succeeding despite their low socioeconomic status (for discussion of the teacher and administrative components, see Edwards, 1991). Along with the teachers and school administrators, "natural" community leaders (among others, a popular bar owner and a priest of the predominately African-American parish) helped to solicit the participation of the mothers by encouraging them to attend and providing them with necessary transportation and daycare.

Of the 25 children who participated, 1 was enrolled in a high-risk program for four-year-olds, 9 were enrolled in developmental kindergarten, 7 were enrolled in a regular kindergarten, 5 were enrolled in a transitional first grade, and 3 were enrolled in a regular first grade. There were 14 girls (10 African-American and 4 white) and 11 boys (8 African-American and 3 white).

The book-reading program operated from October 1987 to May 1988 and consisted of 23 two-hour sessions divided into three phases: coaching, peer modeling, and parent–child interactions. Each phase lasted for approximately six to seven weeks. Not all of the mothers attended every session, and the children only attended the last phase of the program. It should also be noted that even though the parents shared with the university leader that they were engaged in book-reading interactions at home, this information cannot be verified because observations of parents and children reading together at home were not conducted.

The program was held in the school library, and parents were given access to the teacher resource room throughout the week to view videotapes or to discuss strategies with each other or with the university leader. The school librarian also encouraged the parents to check library books out under their children's names.

Prior to the implementation of the program, the university leader had asked the teachers to help define and model book-reading strategies that would be videotaped for the parents' viewing. In the process of defining the strategies to be implemented, the teachers revealed that they could not always delineate what they did, or wanted to do, when they read to children. Through the development of the videotapes they became more aware of the types of strategies that seemed to promote children's print and phonological awareness. The teachers and university leader derived the book-reading strategies from two sources. One set was derived from

Resnick et al.'s (1987) mother–child observational checklist, where attention is drawn to four dimensions of the parent–child interaction: body management (e.g., sitting opposite child, partially encircling the child), book management (e.g., parent permits child to explore book, links items in text to child's life), language interaction (e.g., labeling and describing pictures, giving words to child's vocalization), and affect (e.g., praising child, pausing for child's response). The second set of strategies, derived from the work of Ninio and Bruner (1978), provided the parents with a general progression of steps to follow in reading a story (e.g., attention-getting, questioning, labeling, and providing feedback). Teachers became familiar with both sets of strategies and selected particular dimensions to model for parents. A fuller description of the topics covered in the book-reading sessions and sample lessons in each of the three phases (coaching, peer modeling, parent–child interaction) are available elsewhere (Edwards, 1990a).

Implementation of the book-reading program

Phase one: Coaching. During the first phase, the university leader met with the parents as a group. In these coaching sessions, the university leader helped the mothers understand the importance of supporting their children's literacy development. Additionally, throughout the coaching sessions the university leader modeled book-reading behaviors and introduced teacher videotapes. A "scaffolded dialogue" was employed throughout these sessions and in the teacher–child interaction sessions. For example, when parents did not fully understand a strategy or how to use it, the university leader would prompt and support them (or referred them to an appropriate teacher tape explaining a particular strategy), enabling them to use strategies that would have been unattainable otherwise.

The mothers were encouraged to take on the roles of conversational informants and partners during the coaching phase. In the first session the mothers rarely responded to questions from the university leader or made comments to her, but were encouraged to respond and/or make comments in later sessions. A transcript of the first book-reading interactions during the coaching phase on October 12, 1987, demonstrates how the university leader encouraged the mothers to react and/or respond as conversational informants or partners (see Table 9.1).

As time passed, the dialogue between the mothers and the university leader increased in complexity. The university leader was able to conclude from the mothers' comments that they had begun to view book reading as a routinized and formatted language event between mother and child. They had also learned the importance of adjusting their lan-

Table 9.1. *Transcript of the first group taped book-reading session, recorded October 12, 1987*

Speaker	Utterance	Nonverbal	Text
Leader	{Reads the text.}		"a little ghost a happy ghost a sad ghost a friendly ghost Boo"
Leader	How would you explain to a child the difference between *big* and *small?*	Showed to parents the pages that read "a big ghost" and "little ghost"	
Parent	I'm big. You are small.	Other parents nodded in agreement.	
Leader	Yes, that's a good example. Can anyone else think of other examples.	Parents were silent.	
Leader	How would you explain the concept *happy?*	Showed the parents the page that read "a happy ghost"	
Parent	A giggly noise.	Some parents did not seem to agree with this parent's concept of happy.	
Leader	You mean you laugh when you are happy.		
Parent	Yes.	Other parents nodded in agreement.	
Leader	Can someone else give me another definition of happy?		
Parent	When you feel good about something.	Other parents nodded in agreement.	
Leader	I like the way you are responding.	Parents smiled.	
Leader	How do you feel when you are sad?		
Parent	You feel down and out.	Parents smiled.	

Table 9.1 (*cont.*)

Parent	You feel like you want to be by yourself.	Parents nodded in agreement.
Leader	How would you explain "sad" to your child?	
Parent	You do not feel like laughing.	Parents nodded in agreement.
Leader	That's a good way to put it.	
Leader	How would you explain the concept of "scary"?	
Parent	A dog.	
Leader	You mean a dog makes you feel scary?	
Parent	Yes.	Parents smiled.
Leader	But for each kind of dog you could get a different meaning of "dog." Are all dogs scary?	
Parent	No.	
Leader	It might be important to make that point clear to your child. Can anyone else tell me what "scary" means?	Parents listened.
Parent	Ghost makes me think of "scary." You know, Halloween time.	
Leader	Yes.	Parents smiled.
Leader	What does "boo" mean?	
All parents	Scary!	Parents laughed.
Leader	When someone says "boo," it makes you feel scary.	
All parents	Yes.	

Table 9.1 (*cont.*)

Leader	Did you enjoy this book?	
All parents	Yes.	
Leader	Just as I have encouraged you to explain these concepts to me, you have to explain them to your children.	Parents nodded in agreement.

guage to their child's level of understanding. Further, the mothers began to assume a number of roles during book reading (e.g., monitor, director, cooperative negotiator, informer, interpreter, and co-responder). They were also able to more easily label and describe pictures, link text to life and life to text, ask and answer questions about words and pictures, and vary their voices. Of utmost importance, the university leader observed that each mother in her own individual way seemed to be acquiring an understanding of which book-reading skills to use when reading certain books as well as what it meant to share books with her children.

The mothers frequently stayed after the scheduled sessions to review tapes and interact with the leader. In these sessions, the parents would ask the university leader to explain further the strategy the teacher modeled on the tape as well as to discuss ways they could implement the strategy at home with their children. For example, after viewing a tape of labeling and describing pictures, one parent asked "When reading books to your child is it important to point to pictures?" The following dialogued occurred between the mother and university leader:

Leader: Yes, it is important to label and describe pictures. It helps children to know exactly what you are talking about when you are reading to them and it also broadens their vocabulary. It is also a way for you to involve your children in the story. In other words, you are drawing their attention to the print in the book.

Parent: I never realized that I should pay such careful attention to pictures and objects in the book until I watched this tape. I just quickly read the book. I did notice that my child would want to stop and look at pictures, but I would get angry when he wanted to stop. I just wanted to finish the book.

The mothers were also invited to come back to the school during the week and view teacher tapes at their leisure. If parents had questions about the teacher tapes, they could either write their questions down on paper or tape them on a tape recorder. At the beginning of the next parent session, the university leader would address the parents' questions. Lastly, parents were encouraged to become part of their children's classrooms, and many of them accepted the invitation. For example, Jeanette, mother of Erica, a child in the four-year-old at-risk program, agreed to read to her child's class once a month.

Phase two: Peer modeling. The objective of this phase was to help the mothers manage the book-reading sessions and strategies. This phase was specifically based on Vygotsky's (1978, p. 86) work: "The zone of proximal development defines those functions that have not yet matured but are in the process of maturation." His work also suggests that the acquisition of skills progresses from a stage in which the teacher and learner jointly collaborate to perform a cognitive task (interpsychological plane), to a stage in which the learner has internalized and can regulate the process himself or herself (intrapsychological plane). The university leader's role in this stage was supportive, and served to (1) guide mothers' participation in bookreading interactions with each other, (2) find connections between what the mothers already knew and what they needed to know, (3) model effective book-reading behaviors for the mothers when such assistance was needed (encourage them to review teacher tapes), and (4) provide praise and support for their attempts.

In the initial peer group session, the university leader informed the mothers that the peer group sessions were organized to prepare them to read with their children on a one-to-one basis. She also informed them that the peer group sessions would allow them to practice with each other what they learned in the coaching sessions with her. The process of internalization for the mothers was gradual, but slowly they began to control and guide the book-reading sessions themselves. The fact that the mothers were gradually taking control of the book-reading sessions reflects Vygotsky's notion that learning can be transferred from the inter- to the intrapsychological plane. Even though the mothers assumed primary control of the book-reading activity, the university leader continued to support their efforts.

Rogoff's (1984) concept of guided participation extends Vygotsky's concept of the zone of proximal development and describes the university leader's participation and interaction with the mothers during the peer group phase. According to Rogoff,

> adults do not work alone. If children give no feedback or guidance as to their needs or understanding, adults can do little to structure the zone

> of proximal development. Children play an active role in their own learning. Not only do they assist the adult in setting the level of the lesson; through their motivation and self-directed attempts to learn, they require the adult to provide information or help. (1984, p. 27)

Based on Rogoff's concept of guided participation the university leader finely tuned her interactions with the mothers, thus ensuring proximity between what "[the mothers] already [knew] and what [they needed to know]" (p. 32). Consider the following example in Table 9.2 of one mother's *initial* attempt to model for her peers what she would do in a book-reading interaction with her daughter. The mother, Jeanette, volunteered to discuss the book *Stop and go, fast and slow* by McLenighan (1982). She began by asking questions about the picture on the cover of the book and elaborating on the concepts that she could discuss with her child, Erica.

When Jeanette finished sharing with the other participants how she would share this book with her young daughter, the university leader asked the mothers for suggestions. Jeanette, the only one to offer verbal comments, said: "I should have talked more about the pictures and the colors in the book." While the other mothers did not make any verbal comments to Jeanette, they did show in their body language that they agreed that she should have talked more about the pictures and colors in the book.

As the mothers became more comfortable with the peer modeling, they began to voice their opinions and offer suggestions to their peers about how to improve their reading interactions with their children. In addition, the mothers provided their peers with specific examples and strategies they used when they shared books with their own children at home. The mothers' story talk increased in complexity, and they seemed to enjoy having the opportunity to share their ideas with their peers. In fact, several of the mothers mentioned that they particularly liked the social interactions and the cooperative atmosphere within the group. One mother stated that "She liked all the support and encouragement she received from the other mothers." Another mother said "I especially like it when the mothers share with me how their children are behaving during book reading because I can compare my child's behavior to other children."

Phase three: Parent–child interaction. During this phase, the university leader ceded control of the sessions to the mothers and functioned primarily as a supportive and sympathetic audience. Specifically, the university leader offered suggestions to the mothers as to what book(s) to use in reading interactions with their children and provided feedback or

Table 9.2. *Jeannette's initial attempt to model for her peers, recorded December 7, 1987*

Jeanette:	What are some of the things in the picture?
Jeanette:	Does a bird fly fast or slow? [Jeanette says that most of the time her child would answer "fast" because she knows that birds fly fast and not slow.]
Jeanette:	What about the turtle?
Jeanette:	What about the snail? [Jeanette explains that a turtle is slow, but a snail is slower.] Jeanette opens the book and discusses the following concepts as she reads:
	Go and stop. [Jeanette states that she would ask her child to walk. Then she would say, "Are you going or stopping?"]
	Bottom and top. Jeanette uses a table as an example to teach this concept. She says that she would show her child the top of the table and explain that the bottom is underneath.]
	Left and right. [Jeanette would have her daughter hold up her right hand and then her left.]
	Day and night. [Jeanette explains that "when the day is over, then come the night." "What is over? When there is no more daylight outside, that is night."]
	Hide and seek. [Jeanette says that Erica knows about this game, but she would explain that seek means that she is "seeking her out."]
	Yes and no. ["Erica knows the difference between yes and no," Jeanette exclaims!]
	Summer and snow. [Jeanette simply says, "Summer is hot, and snow is cold."]
	Do and say. ["I would explain to Erica that when she is playing outside, she is doing something; but when she is sitting beside me, she usually say something."]
	Go and Out. [Jeanette says that go means to "go in a door," and out means "coming out."]
	Smile and pout. [Another mother says that you could explain that a person sometimes pouts when they're told no.]
	Boy and girl. [Jeanette says that her little girl knows the difference between a boy and a girl.]
	Straight and curly. [Jeanette says that this one is easy because her hair is curly, and Erica's is straight.]
	Peace and war. ["Peace mean helping each other," explains Jeanette, "and war is fighting with someone."]
	Win and lose. ["Win means you come in first," says Jeanette, "and lose mean you come in last."]
	End and beginning. [Jeanette says that the beginning would be where the book started, and the end is where it stops.]

modeled book-reading strategies when necessary. In this final phase, the mothers shared books with their own children and implemented book-reading strategies they learned in the previous two phases (coaching and peer modeling). Through these interactions, the mothers learned the importance of involving their children in a bookreading interaction. They seemed to recognize that children

> need to interact with the reader – their parents – to extend ideas, to question their own understanding, and to relate their ideas to experience. (Flood, 1977, p. 867)

Table 9.3 is a transcript of another mother: Charlene's initial attempt at sharing with her son, Kyle, a first-grader, the book *Chatty chipmunk's nutty day* shows a very lively and relaxed interaction between Charlene and Kyle.

During this interaction, Charlene and Kyle engaged in three participatory strategies observed by Doake (1985) – mumble reading, cooperative reading, and completion reading. Echo reading, the fourth participatory strategy Doake observed, seemed to emerge as children became familiar with certain stories. For example, Kyle mumbles along as Charlene reads to him. His "mumble reading" then merges into "cooperative reading." For instance, after Charlene announced "our book is called *Chatty chipmunk's nutty day,*" Kyle immediately said, "by . . ." This indicated that he was mumbling along as she was reading to him. Throughout the story Charlene creates many opportunities for Kyle to engage in the dialogue. She verifies his knowledge about the text. She labels pictures, expands the story events, provides additional context, emphasizes print, and encourages him to make predictions about the text. She corrects his responses in a positive manner and encourages him to evaluate his own explanations. Further, she praises him for his participation in the reading interaction by saying, "Very good, thanks," and Kyle jokingly asks "For what?" Over the seven-week period, Charlene and Kyle continued to enjoy their reading interactions. Kyle began to probe Charlene's knowledge of text and requested explanations that enabled Charlene to relate the events in the text to his life.

Videotaping the sessions. All three phases of the book-reading sessions were also videotaped. Videotaping the first phase of the program (coaching) gave parents and the university leader the opportunity to review specific sessions. It also gave parents who were unable to attend a particular session the chance to view the session that they had missed.

By videotaping sessions during the second phase (peer modeling) parents were better able to evaluate their own behavior abilities because

Table 9.3. *Transcript of Charlene and Kyle, recorded February 22, 1988*

Speaker	Utterance	Nonverbal behavior
Charlene	I'm Charlene Alexander and this is Kyle and this is our second session. Our book is called, *Chatty chipmunk's nutty day,* um, Susan Gruber.	Kyle squirms and moves rapidly from one side of the mother's lap to the other.
Kyle	By	
Charlene	Excuse me, by Susan Gruber. "Here is Chatty Chipmunk." Where is she? In the tree. Chatty likes to dig. He lives in his home in the ground. Where does he live? In the ground.	
Charlene	How did he make his home in the ground?	
Kyle	He dug a hole.	
Charlene	"He lives near a pine tree. He likes to run and play." You've seen pine trees before.	
Kyle	Yeah.	
Charlene	Where?	
Kyle	At my grandma's house.	
Charlene	Right, she's got a pine tree. "He likes to look for nuts to eat. 'Chitter-chitter-chatter,' he says. I like to eat nuts. Chatty looks for nuts. He looks under the pine tree – no nuts here. He looks under the cherry tree – no nuts here. He looks under the oak tree – 'Chitter, chitter, chatter here are the nuts, here are nuts to eat.' " Where did he look for nuts?	
Kyle	Under the cherry tree.	
Charlene	Where else?	Kyle turns back the pages in the storybook to find the answer.
Kyle	Under the pine tree.	

Table 9.3 (*cont.*)

Charlene	"He eats some of them." What's he going to do with the rest?	Kyle scratches his face.
Kyle	Eat them.	
Charlene	No, the ones that he's not going to eat.	
Kyle	Save em?	
Charlene	Let's find out. "Now where should he hide the nuts? Should he hide them in the oak tree?"	
Kyle	Yes!	
Charlene	Let's see – "no, a squirrel will find them. Should he hide them in the garden?"	
Kyle	No.	
Charlene	Why not?	Makes puzzled faces.
Charlene	You don't know?	
Kyle	Yea, I know.	
Charlene	Why?	
Kyle	Cause they take 'em.	
Charlene	Who will take them?	
Kyle	The man that lives in the forest.	
Charlene	The man that lives in the forest? "No, the rabbits will find them. Should he hide them in the grass?"	
Kyle	No.	
Charlene	Why? Who's going to find them in the grass?	
Kyle	The weasel.	
Charlene	The weasel, let's see. "No, the birds will find them. Should he hide them near the house?"	
Kyle	No.	
Charlene	Who do you think's going to find them near the house?	
Kyle	The cat.	
Charlene	Ah-hah, you saw him, huh?	Kyle giggles.

they could actually see some possibilities for improvement. Having the opportunity to watch their videotaped interactions with other parents encouraged the parents to try harder and to learn from their peers. It also allowed the university leader to monitor the parents' progress toward learning how to share books with their children.

Videotaping during phase three (parent–child interaction) was essential. Without it, both parents and the university leader would not have been able to monitor the parents' progress properly or see where they needed to improve. And without the benefit of the instant video replay, the university leader would not have been able to point out specific parent problems or stages of progress.

The use of videotaped sessions was a wonderful teaching and learning device. But it should be noted that the university leader prepared the parents for it. Her eagerness to tape the sessions did not take precedence over parents needs' and preferences. In every case, however, parents agreed to the taping.

Collaborative evaluation of the book-reading sessions

Evaluation of the book-reading sessions occurred throughout all three phases of the book-reading program. Both the university leader and the parents continuously observed and made notes about the effectiveness of the sessions. Throughout all three phases, the parents demonstrated their ability to understand, interpret, relate, discuss, and implement what they were learning. While the university leader was teaching, she observed the parents' behavior and mentally made notes of their progress. At the end of each book-reading session, the university leader asked the parents to evaluate the effectiveness of the session by using two evaluation instruments – the parent's response sheet and the parent's learning log.

The parent's response sheet. The parent's response sheet was a vehicle through which each parent could reflect on the session as it came to a close, focus on its key points, and select one point to work on during the week. Because some of the parents were unable to write their comments, the university leader asked other parents to assist them or she offered her assistance. She also suggested that parents work in groups of twos and threes or asked parents to record their comments on a tape recorder. These comments were transcribed later. Additionally, the parent's response sheet was valuable because it summarized what each parent remembered and considered important to implement or retain. It provided the university leader with another means of monitoring parents' progress.

The parent's learning log. The university leader felt that it was important for parents to reflect on what they were learning and how it applied to their experiences in trying to read to their children. The university leader further believed that it was important for parents to record their progress on daily or weekly log sheets and to keep them in a binder. If some parents could not write at all, she asked them to record their comments on a tape recorder or solicited the help of someone with whom they felt comfortable to write their comments for them.

The leader asked parents to bring their logs to each session and put their handouts in the binder. She read the parents' logs before she met with them to discuss their progress. The log sheets listed six possible response stems to complete: In this week's session I learned . . . ; At home I will work on . . . ; I am reading better because . . . ; I need to improve on . . . ; My child listens to the story better because . . . ; I still don't understand . . .

Researcher's evaluation of the program

The most important result of the book-reading program was that the mothers came to understand the teacher directive to them to "read to their children." Not only did they understand what it meant, they were able to articulate their knowledge of book reading to the university leader and their peers. Further, they were able to guide their children's participation in bookreading interactions. They came to understand the importance of supporting their children in their move toward becoming confident and competent readers.

DISCUSSION AND CONCLUSIONS

Although one way to evaluate this program is on the basis of the parents' and children's increased ability to engage in the storybook reading interactions, it is important to note that the program demonstrated a number of other benefits and strengths. For example, one reason that the program was successful was that the researcher was able to elicit the support of the parents in this endeavor. For this to occur, the social climate of the program had to be positive. Parents had to feel that they not only were going to learn something that would be valuable to them and their children, but that they also were true partners. As demonstrated in the transcripts in Tables 9.1, 9.2, and 9.3, the structure of the program encouraged the parents' active participation throughout all three phases. The parents were encouraged to ask questions, to use their own experiences to guide their participation, and to use their own dialect to communicate with their children, the other parents, and the researcher.

Although not all of the parents were confident in their initial book-reading capabilities, they demonstrated that, with guidance, they were able to read the types of books shared with their kindergarten and first-grade children, and that they also were able to help their children increase their phonological and print awareness. One reason that they were able to do this is that the first phase of the program allowed them to view book-reading strategies in a nonthreatening manner. During this phase, they also became acquainted with the types of predictable and repetitive books that are appropriate for beginning readers. Additionally, the program delineated the types of strategies that would help promote their children's phonological and print awareness and motivate them to become involved in storybook reading.

Interestingly, as the parents learned about the value of reading predictable and repetitive books, they also increased their own awareness about reading, eventually learning to use the structure of the stories to help their own oral reading and to engage their children in dialogue through the use of comprehension strategies (e.g., predictions, confirmations, inferencing). This development reflects the type of ownership that is necessary for a home-school program to help parents and children participate more fully in school-based literacy events.

One of the strengths of this program was that the participants did not have to perform perfectly. Consistent with Vygotsky's concept of proximal development, they were free to try out strategies in a nonthreatening environment. By modeling this type of framework for the parents, the researcher demonstrated the advantage of using scaffolding to stretch their children's learning. Jeanette's discussion of how she would share a book with her daughter, Erica, demonstrates that she was aware of the need to build on what Erica already knew.

The second and third phases of the program, the peer modeling and parent–child interaction, seemed to demonstrate the value of allowing participants to construct meaning together. This is an aspect of Vygotskian theory that was not mentioned earlier but which seemed to be a key element in the success of the program.

An issue not explicitly discussed in this description of the book-reading program was the negative attitudes held by the teachers and school administrators toward the children and their parents. In order to address some of the negative attitudes and misconceptions teachers and administrators had concerning nonmainstream parents and children, the university leader developed a course on family literacy and invited both teachers and administrators to attend.

Too often teachers and administrators erroneously assume that nonmainstream parents do not participate in their children's schooling because they are not interested in their children's education (Hughes, 1979; Mack, 1987; White, 1975). This assumption ignores current research that has shown that nonmainstream parents have a high regard for education (Goldenberg, 1987; Viadero, 1989). It also fails to take into account that storybook reading and storybook interactions are literacy and language events that are culturally bound (Au, 1983; Garcia & Pearson, 1991; Heath, 1982a, 1982b; Philips, 1983). If parents and children from cultures that have no tradition of bedtime storybook reading events are to engage in them, then they must be shown how to do so. Although teachers may tell parents to read to their children, they do not always tell parents what they mean by this directive. Goldenberg's (1987) study of Hispanic parents reveals that these parents were willing to help their children with literacy tasks but were frustrated when their efforts were rejected by their children's teachers. One of the problems suggested by this study, and implied in reviews related to the at-risk situation (Garcia et al., 1990), is that teachers may not know what to do when children come to school without the requisite print and phonological awareness needed to benefit from literacy instruction as it currently is implemented in schools.

Although we do not know to what extent the program changed the teachers' and administrators' attitudes about the participation and capabilities of other nonmainstream parents and children, we would suggest that the program encouraged them to acknowledge that nonmainstream children are capable of participating in school-based literacy activities with the appropriate types of instruction, whether this be from the parent or the teacher. We also look forward to the day when teachers truly build their instruction on the strengths that children bring with them to school. For this to happen, however, we need more research on language and literacy in nonmainstream settings, and more teacher training (both pre- and in-service) to help teachers not only acknowledge their own cultural biases regarding language and literacy, but also learn how to incorporate into their literacy instruction language and literacy activities common to nonmainstream children (see Edwards & Garcia, 1991; Garcia et al., 1990).

Finally, we think that the Vygotskian framework underlying the program allowed it to become a program of empowerment rather than acculturation. Through the program, nonmainstream parents learned what was expected of their children in school. They also became aware of what their children were capable of doing with the appropriate guidance. Their own confidence in their reading ability and ability to help their children with school activities increased. Through their children's participation in the program, they helped to ensure that their children would have the print and phonological awareness necessary to benefit from the traditional school-based literacy activities. Lastly, they gained confidence interacting with school personnel. Toward the end of the program, two of the parents became parent trainers in an extension of the program. More recently, one of the parent trainers was hired as a tutor at the school. The parents' increased knowledge about their capabilities and that of their children should help to provide them with the type of knowledge needed by parents if they are to hold schools accountable.

NOTE

1. By nonmainstream, we mean low-income parents who traditionally have not actively participated in the American educational system.

REFERENCES

Anderson, A. B., & Stokes, S. J. (1984). Social and institutional influences on the development and practice of literacy. In H. Goelman, A. Oberg, & F. Smith (Eds.), *Awakening to literacy* (pp. 24–27). Exeter, NH: Heinemann.

Arrastia, M. (1989). Mother's reading program. In *First teachers: A family literacy handbook for parents, policy-makers and literacy providers* (pp. 34–34). Washington DC: Barbara Bush Foundation for Family Literacy.

Au, K. H. (1983). Participation structures in a reading lesson with Hawaiian children: Analysis of a culturally appropriate instructional event. *Anthropology and Education Quarterly, 11*(2): 91–115.

Auerbach, E. R. (1989). Toward a social-contextual approach to family literacy. *Harvard Education Review, 59*(2), 165–181.

Baghban, M. J. M. (1984). *Our daughter learns to read and write: A case study from birth to three.* Newark, DE: International Reading Association.

Clay, M. M., & Cazden, C. B. (1990). A Vygotskian interpretation of Reading Recovery. In L. C. Moll (Ed.), *Vygotsky and education: Instructional implications and applications of sociohistorical psychology* (pp. 206–222). Cambridge: Cambridge University Press.

Collins, A., Brown, J. S., & Newman, S. E. (1989). Cognitive apprenticeship: Teaching the craft of reading, writing, and mathematics. In L. B. Resnick (Ed.), *Knowing, learning, and instruction: Essays in honor of Robert Glasser.* Hillsdale, NJ: Erlbaum.

Doake, D. B. (1986). Learning to read: It starts in the home. In D. R. Tovey & J. E. Kerber (Eds.), *Roles in literacy learning* (pp. 2–9). Newark, DE: International Reading Association.

Edwards, P. A. (1989). Supporting lower SES mothers' attempts to provide scaffolding for bookreading. In J. Allen & J. Mason (Eds.), *Risk makers, risk takers, risk breakers: Reducing the risks for young literacy learners* (pp. 222–250). Portsmouth, NH: Heinemann.

Edwards, P. A. (1990a). *Parents as partners in reading: A family literacy training program.* Chicago: Childrens Press.

Edwards, P. A. (1990b). *Talking your way to literacy. A program to help nonreading parents prepare their children for reading.* Chicago: Childrens Press.

Edwards, P. A. (1991). Fostering early literacy through parent coaching. In E. Hiebert (Ed.), *Literacy for a diverse society: Perspectives, programs, and policies* (pp. 199–213). New York: Teachers College Press.

Edwards, P. A., & Garcia, G. E. (1991). Parental involvement in mainstream schools: An issue of equity. In M. Foster (Ed.), *Readings on equal education, II: Qualitative investigations into schools and schooling* (pp. 167–187). New York: AMS Press.

Farron, D. C. (1982). Mother–child interaction, language development, and the school performance of poverty children. In L. Feagans & D. C. Farron (Eds.), *The language of children reared in poverty* (pp. 19–52). New York: Academic Press.

Flood, J. (1977). Parental styles in reading episodes with young children. *The Reading Teacher, 30,* 864–867.

Gaffney, J., & Anderson, R. C. (1991). Two-tiered scaffolding: Congruent processes of teaching and learning. In E. Hiebert (Ed.), *Literacy for a diverse society: Perspectives, programs, and policies* (pp. 184–198). New York: Teachers College Press.

Gaj, N. (1989). MOTHERREAD, Inc. In *First teachers: A family literacy handbook for parents, policy-makers and literacy providers* (pp. 27–30). Washington, DC: Barbara Bush Foundation for Family Literacy.

Garcia, G. E., & Pearson, P. D. (1991). The role of assessment in a diverse society. In E. Hiebert (Ed.), *Literacy for a diverse society: Perspectives, programs, and policies* (pp. 253–278). New York: Teachers College Press.

Garcia, G. E., Pearson, P. D., & Jimenez, R. T. (1990). *The at-risk dilemma: A synthesis of reading research.* (Study 2.2.3.3 b). Champaign: Reading Research and Education Center, University of Illinois.

Goldenberg, C. N. (1987). Low-income Hispanic parents' contribution to their first-grade children's word recognition skills. *Anthropology and Education Quarterly, 18,* 149–179.

Goldsmith, E. (1989). Parent readers program. In *First teachers: A family literacy handbook program for parents, policy-makers and literacy providers* (pp. 19–26). Washington, DC: Barbara Bush Foundation for Family Literacy.

Gruber, S. (1985). *Chatty chipmunk's nutty day.* Mahwah, NJ: Troll.

Heath, S. B. (1982a). Questioning at home and at school: A comparative study. In G. Spindler (Ed.), *Doing the ethnography of schooling: Educational anthropology in action* (pp. 96–131). New York: Holt, Rinehart, & Winston.

Heath, S. B. (1982b). What no bedtime story means: Narrative skills at home and school. *Language in Society, 11,* 49–76.

Heath, S. B., with Thomas, C. (1984). The achievement of preschool literacy for mother and child. In H. Goelman, A. Oberg, & F. Smith (Eds.), *Awakening to literacy* (pp. 51–72). London: Heinemann.

Henderson, A. T. (1987). *The evidence continues to grow: Parent involvement improves student achievement.* Columbia, MD: National Committee for Citizens in Education.

Hoffman, S. J. (1982, March). *Preschool reading related behaviors: A parent diary.* Paper presented at the Third Ethnography in Education forum, Philadelphia.

Hughes, J. M. (1979). A commitment to parent education. In W. G. Hill, P. Fox, & C. D. Jones (Eds.), *Families and schools: Implementing parent education* (Report No. 121) (pp. 6–9). Denver: Education Commission of the States.

Kasler, L. A., Roser, N. L., & Hoffman, J. V. (1987). Understanding of the forms and functions of written language: Insights from children and parents. In J. E. Readence & R. S. Baldwin (Eds.), *Research in literacy: Merging perspectives.* Rochester, NY: Thirty-sixth yearbook of the National Reading Conference.

Mack, P. (Chair). (1987). *Report of the Black Concerns Study Committee.* Washington, DC: National Education Association.

McCormick, C., & Mason, J. M. (1986). Intervention procedures for increasing preschool children's interest in and knowledge about reading. In W. Teale & E. Sulzby (Eds.), *Emergent literacy: Writing and reading* (pp. 90–115). Norwood, NJ: Ablex.

McLeninghan, V. (1982). *Stop and go, fast and slow.* Chicago: Childrens Press.

Ninio, A. (1980). Picturebook reading in mother–infant dyads belonging to two subgroups in Israel. *Child Development, 51,* 587–590.

Ninio, A., & Bruner, J. (1978). The achievement and antecedents of labeling. *Journal of Child Language, 5,* 1–15.

Palinscar, A. M., & Brown, A. L. (1984). Reciprocal teaching of comprehension-fostering and comprehension-monitoring activities. *Cognition and Instruction, 1,* 117–175.

Pflaum, S. W. (1986). *The development of language and literacy in young children* (3rd ed.). Columbus, OH: Charles E. Merrill Publishing.

Philips, S. U. (1983). *The invisible culture: Communication in the classroom and community on the Warm Springs Indian Reservation.* New York: Longman.

Resnick, M. B., Roth, J., Aaron, P. M., Scott, J., Woling, W. D., Laren, J. J., & Packer, A. B. (1987). Mothers reading to infants: A new observational tool. *Reading Teacher, 40,* 888–895.

Rogoff, B. (1984). Adult assistance of children's learning. In T. E. Raphael (Ed.), *The contexts of school-based literacy* (pp. 27–40). New York: Random House.

Rogoff, B., Malkin, C., Gilbride, K. (1984). Interaction with babies as guidance in development. In B. Rogoff & J. V. Wertsch (Eds.), *Children's learning in the "zone of proximal development"* (pp. 31–44). San Francisco: Jossey-Bass.

Rogoff, B., & Wertsch J. V. (1984). Editors' notes. In B. Rogoff & J. V. Wertsch (Eds.), *Children's learning in the "zone of proximal development"* (pp. 1–6). San Francisco: Jossey-Bass.

Saxe, G. B., Gearhart, M., & Guberman, S. R. (1984). The social organization of early number development. In B. Rogoff & J. V. Wertsch (Eds.), *Children's learning in the "zone of proximal development"* (pp. 19–30). San Francisco: Jossey-Bass.

Sledge, A. C. (1987, April). Mother–infant literacy knowledge. Paper presented at the annual meeting of the American Education Research Association, Washington, DC.

Spewock, T. S. (1988). Training parents to teach their preschoolers through literature. *Reading Teacher, 41,* 648–652.

Swift, M. S. (1970). Training poverty mothers in communication skills. *Reading Teacher, 23,* 360–367.

Taylor, D. (1983). *Family literacy: Young children learning to read and write.* Exeter, NH: Heinemann.

Teale, W. H. (1981). Parents reading to their children: What we know and need to know. *Language Arts, 58,* 902–911.

Teale, W. H. (1986). Home background and young children's literacy development. In W. H. Teale & E. Sulzby (Eds.), *Emergent literacy: Writing and reading* (pp. 173–206). Norwood NJ: Ablex.

Viadero, D. (1989, March) Minorities aspirations found high in early grades. *Education Week, 8* (23), 5.

Vygotsky, L. S. (1962). *Thought and language* (E. Hanfmann & G. Vaker, Eds. & Trans.). Cambridge, MA: Harvard University Press.

Vygotsky, L. S. (1978). *Mind in society: The development of higher psychological processes.* Cambridge, MA: Harvard University Press.

Wertsch, J. V., (1984). The zone of proximal development: Some conceptual issues. In B. Rogoff & J. V. Wertsch (Eds.), *Children's learning in the "zone of proximal development"* (pp. 7–18). San Francisco: Jossey-Bass.

White, B. L. (1975). *The first three years of life.* Englewood Cliffs, NJ: Prentice-Hall.

Wilson, S. H. (1983). Strengthening connections between schools and communities: A method of improving urban schools. *Urban Education, 18*(2), 153–177.

10 *Vygotsky in the classroom: An interactionist literacy framework in mathematics*

PAT CORDEIRO

This is an account of what happened in one elementary school classroom when teacher and students dwelt for a while in what Newman, Griffin, and Cole (1989) call the "construction zone," a realm of socially mediated interactions and Vygotsky's zone of proximal development. The domain was literate exploration of a broad mathematical concept, group theory, a view and a topic usually unavailable to American sixth graders.

My goals (I was at that time the classroom teacher) were to give young students an opportunity "to do what mathematicians do," to explore and make connections between seemingly disparate realms, to construct mutually a literate understanding of a mathematical principle, to participate in a process of concept formation, and to have time to experience cognitive change. I hoped to develop a mathematically rich context, broad enough to encourage

> the "construction zone," a magic place where minds meet, where things are not the same to all who see them, where meanings are fluid, and where one person's construal may preempt another's. (White, 1989, p. ix)

The instructional methodology was an interactionist literacy framework. I was concerned with maintaining a rich classroom climate that would facilitate three of Vygotsky's findings: first, cognitive change proceeds from interpsychological to intrapsychological; second, school learning introduces the zone of proximal development, which "characterizes mental development prospectively" (Vygotsky, 1978, p. 78); and third, "the development of the child's spontaneous concepts proceeds upward, and the development of his scientific concepts downward" (Vygotsky, 1962, p. 108).

Central to the theme was the notion that abstract conceptual development arises from concrete, contextualized experience provided to the learner at an early age in a supportive, interactive manner. Thus Vygotsky's finding that interpsychological development proceeds to intrapsychological cognitive change was actualized. Here, formal systems are learned first in an informal way in a familiar context. Abstract, conceptual learning can occur and be internalized when the tasks are contextually appropriate: "A formal system can be manipulated in a formal way. It is an easy but dangerous move from this to the conclusion that it is also learned in a formal way" (Donaldson, 1963, p. 33).

In an effort to promote concept development in pre-adolescents, to develop powers of thinking, to sow seeds of curiosity, to "get behind" the computational surface of traditional instruction, I have engaged students in thinking about some "big ideas" in mathematics. We have considered the nature of infinity (Cordeiro, 1988), the implications of Riemannian non-Euclidean geometry ("What if those tracks did meet?"), and, as discussed here, aspects of group theory. I have tried to enable young students to become mutually and socially invested in new ideas.

> Whether or not any child in the class becomes a world-class mathematician, we have nonetheless fulfilled the first requirement: we have made the introduction to the concept . . . a playful and exploratory experience, which has optimized the chance for independent thinking. Further, each child in that class comes away feeling that what they thought . . . was important, not wrong, and a new direction. (Cordeiro, 1988, p. 564)

Big ideas in rich contexts have three requisites. First, they are concepts that can be explored and extended into a variety of contexts. Big ideas encompass more than one case, are generalizable, and often have implications across disciplines. In philosophy, for instance, the concept of justice is a big idea. We can consider justice from many perspectives and in many contexts. We can discuss its implications in social sciences and literature, as well as in philosophy.

Second, the evolution of a big idea in the classroom begins with the teacher's instructional intention to develop a concept. This evolution may begin with a consideration of the concept itself, as when a teacher introduces the word "justice" and begins discussion to develop a definition, or understanding may grow slowly through involvement with specific cases that involve the concept. Mathematical big ideas may involve traditional computation and application to a degree, but in a broad, conceptual context. A teacher setting out to work with infinity, for example, would explore this concept both algorithmically and metaphorically.

> What my students and I have tried to do in these infinity studies was to "play" with the ideas, to carry them as far as they would go in the realm of fantasy and imagination, to be a little silly with them, to try to allow the terminology and ideas to sink into common currency, so that they became the stuff of daily experience. (Cordeiro, 1988, p. 557)

Finally, big ideas are concepts that continue to intrigue the experts (Davidson, 1990). From Plato on down to modern philosophers, "justice" as a big idea continues to be a concept which is debated, dependent on context.

In a study of big ideas in a rich context, learning is interactive, child to child and child to adult. The role of the adult will be to provide optimal conditions for learning (Cambourne, 1988) and to "provide guidance in creating links between the context of a novel problem and more familiar problem contexts, allowing the application of available skills and information" (Rogoff & Gardner, 1984, p. 96).

> The teacher offers the learner a kind of loan of himself or herself, some kind of auxiliary equipment which will enable the learner to make transitions and consolidations he could not otherwise have made. (Hawkins, 1973, p. 9)

This is Vygotsky's zone of proximal development:

> the distance between the actual development level as determined by independent problem-solving and the level of potential development as determined through problem-solving under adult guidance or in collaboration with more capable peers. (1978, p. 86)

The child performs a higher cognitive skill first in a social setting with an adult and then, with assistance and support, internalizes the function. "Human learning presupposes a specific social nature and a process by which children grow into the intellectual life of those around them" (Vygotsky, 1978, p. 88).

> The cognitive ability that occurs in the interaction is apparent in the adaptations made by the participants as the novice gains greater understanding of the problem and as the expert evaluates the novice's readiness to take greater responsibility for the cognitive work. (Rogoff & Gardner, 1984, p. 95)

Donaldson (1978, p. 109) notes that "children, even quite young ones, will not let themselves be passively led. They will actively invent and discover, using what we tell them as a starting point." Resnick (1976) observes that the adult task is to find teaching rules that will enhance the possibility of discovery, rather than choosing between rules *or* discovery.

In a classroom that is exploring a big idea, there is opportunity for students to diverge, to pursue aspects of the idea that appeal just to them. Students can assume "complementary problem-solving roles" (Forman & Cazden, 1985, p. 343). In this rich environment, the classroom becomes a laboratory; the students and teacher, researchers.

The concepts that are these mathematical big ideas are explored in a concrete, interactive way in Vygotsky's development of "spontaneous" concepts as opposed to the acquisition of "scientific" concepts: "The interrelation of scientific and spontaneous concepts is a special case within a much broader subject: the relation of school instruction to the mental development of the child" (1978, p. 93).

Vygotsky (1962, p. 108) further points out that these two start far apart, and "move to meet each other":

> One might say that *the development of the child's spontaneous concepts proceeds upward, and the development of his scientific concepts downward,* to a more elementary and concrete level. This is the consequence of the different ways in which the two kinds of concepts emerge. The inception of a spontaneous concept can usually be traced to a face-to-face meeting with a concrete situation, while a scientific concept involved from the first a "mediated" attitude toward its object.

In the exploration of big ideas, the "face-to-face" meetings are the daily classroom activities out of which grows the child's understanding of the concept. The "mediated attitude" then follows with guided discussion between child and adult, developing observations into ideas. The adult further mediates by generating the next activity in the curriculum, based on conclusions drawn from the previous one.

Vygotsky stresses the function of reciprocal structures in this evolution of concept. He points out that

> in working its slow way upward, an everyday concept clears a path for a scientific concept and its downward development. It creates a series of structures necessary for the evolution of the concept's more primitive, elementary aspects. . . . Scientific concepts in turn supply structures for the upward development of the child's spontaneous concepts toward consciousness and deliberate use. (1962, p. 109)

EXPLORING GROUP THEORY WITH PENTOMINOES

Group theory, "the supreme art of mathematical abstraction" (Bergamini & Editors, 1963, p. 173), is a theory of a particular kind of set – a set being any collection of entities: "Group and set theory are both used to compare the tools of different branches of mathematics and to make them as freely interchangeable as possible." Group theory is an abstract theory covering cases in three separate realms: algebra, the arithmetic of arrangements, and geometry.

When sets function within the postulates of group theory, they obey a particular set of rules, or postulates, in regard to an operation such as multiplication or a transformation such as rotation. Four postulates govern group theory: Closure, Identity Element, Inverse, and Associative (Boyer, 1968).

An understanding of group theory enables learners to begin to form mental linkages between areas of mathematical thinking. Further, it enables them to explore the relationship between "pure" mathematics and the concrete world of applications. Because group theory "lays bare the structural patterns in mathematics" and allows one to "cross over into other branches of mathematics and borrow tools, methods, or simply precedents" (Bergamini & Editors, 1963, p. 173), it is particularly valuable as a concept.

Kamii (1985, p. xii) points out that "young children literally *reinvent* arithmetic." If children are not allowed to "reinvent mathematics," if the learning environment is not rich enough to allow data to be collected by the learner and hypotheses to be formed as a result, then concept development will be stunted. In Vygotskian terms, scientific concept development will take place without the requisite spontaneous concept development.

Here, group theory is explored in a methodology, utilizing Vygotskian theories of concept development. Mathematical studies of a concept like group theory are explored through concrete, interactive elements that fall within the axioms of the theory. This allows teacher and students, learners together, to consider how "situationally dependent" figures "enter into a symbol system," differentiating "fixed properties from situational function" (Bamberger & Schon, 1978, p. 40).

This sixth-grade class was comprised of students of mixed abilities. The classroom was self-contained: all students stayed in the class together all day with minor exceptions and functioned as a learning unit. We all used student desks, arranged in a circle. This was a class that had a high interest in theory and performed well in a variety of learning areas. They very much enjoyed new ideas and "learning hard things." This class had routinely worked with concrete objects in learning mathematical concepts. These "math manipulatives," however, usually led to computational outcomes.

This study came late in the year, well after we had established positive conditions for learning (Cambourne, 1988) as a supportive setting for our learning. My role as teacher involved, in part, the training and "scaffolding" (cf. Cazden, 1979; Wood, Bruner, & Ross, 1978) of response mechanisms that are eventually to become internalized as the learners' self-monitoring mechanism. "Scaffolding" is the term for external supports given to learners in interactional settings to assist them in the learning process: "the teacher's selective intervention provides the supportive tool for the learner . . . thereby allowing the learner to accomplish a task not otherwise possible" (Greenfield, 1984, p. 118). This is the application of Vygotsky's zone of proximal development combined with the notion of interpsychological learning leading to intrapsychological growth.

Learners learn from the scaffolds provided. "Scaffolding holds the task constant, while simplifying the learner's role through the graduated intervention of the teacher" (Greenfield, 1984, p. 119). Eventually, the learner's greatest, most omnipresent respondent is the self. Scaffolding as a response mechanism allows the internalization of the scaffold as a self-monitoring device.

We began our study of group theory by exploring the world of pentominoes, those five-square geometric shapes that lend themselves to so much exploration (see Figure 10.1).

We used Marion Walter's (1971) *Teacher's guide for a unit in informal geometry.* Walter outlines quite clearly how to lead children through developing an understanding of concepts and relates her lessons to their origins in group theory. Pentominoes are a geometric set that falls within the postulates of group theory when subjected to the transformation operation. Walter says:

> The integers under addition, the rationals under addition, and the rationals *without zero* under multiplication form groups. . . . Many sets of motions in geometry form groups. This unit gives the children an easy introduction to groups on an informal level. They do not need to learn any definitions yet, but they can gain some firsthand experience with them. (1971, p. 77)

Students developed idiosyncratic methods for determining and charting all twelve shapes on graph paper and expressing their understanding of their process and approximations. At this stage, they recorded their process in learning logs, or dialogue journals (cf. Graves, 1989; Staton, 1988; Shuy, 1988; Staton, Shuy, Peyton, & Reed, 1988):

> First I made a straight line. Then I took a square off and put it on the bottom. Then I took the square that I moved to the bottom and moved it to the side of the square. After that I made a square out of four squares and added a square on the side. Then I kept moving them around and I finished.

Interpsychological processing may show itself through classroom talk and group work. Or it may occur as the students "talk" to an imaginary audience in a dialogue journal. In dialogue journaling the interactions are slowed down and made visible as students write out the learning processes becoming internalized. Newman et al., (1989, p. 73) point to the possibility for such "external devices" as writing to be "windows into the evolution and appearance of cognitive constructs."

Other students drew on prior knowledge for strategies, activating spontaneous concept formation. One student made mental use of a

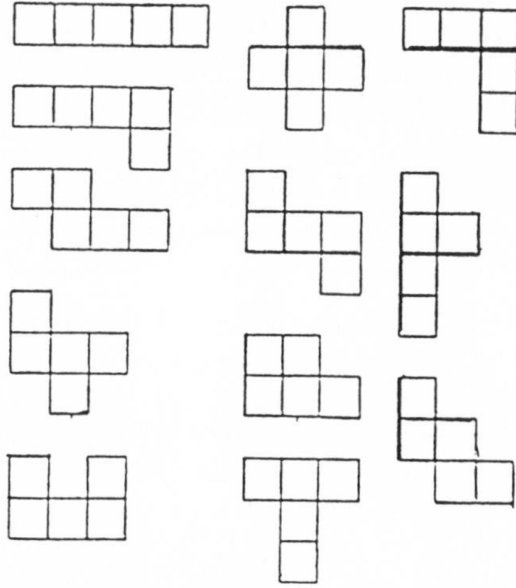

Figure 10.1. The twelve basic pentomino shapes.

video game that involves constructing and manipulating some of the basic twelve pentomino shapes. He then discovered the rest. Some students reported that they "just thought about five squares, moved it around a little until I couldn't find any more." For these students the visualization of the shapes was sufficient.

The problem became being sure that one shape was not simply one already discovered in a different position. The basic twelve shapes are all different, none are simple transformations of another. Students developed a variety of strategies for checking up on themselves and their work. "I just guessed then I checked them to be sure they weren't flipped"; "I basically moved the blocks around and checked if they were the same but just switched. I checked by seeing if they were upside down or sideways."

Some students recorded a planned strategy for determining the twelve shapes; "First I started with this [shows a shape], then I began moving one block at a time, so I would have something like this. I kept on doing this until I could think of no more."

Some students reported that comparing with friends was essential to their process, they sought response, a direct sign of the powerful interpsychological processing going on throughout this study. One reported in working with a friend that "another thing that helped was using the board – I would erase without messing the paper up."

One student wrote:

> What I did is looked at five squares. I brainstormed about how many ways I could make a shape without duplicating the other ones I had. Then I would sit and just look at the graph paper and move around. I would also try taking one shape that I had and take another and put the boxes in different places.

Students planned ahead to how they would solve a problem like this the next time: "I will draw it again. I will just draw, not think about it – I will just draw it."

> I found the shapes by first just drawing all I could think of. After that I checked them to see if I had them but changed around. I then thought some more, found a few. Then I traded a few with my friends, I mean, I saw what they had and they saw what I had. I then had all my shapes.
>
> I think if I did this project again I would definitely want a full working strategy to make it easier and much quicker.

Flower and Hayes (1981, p. 39) say that such planning "can reduce a vast problem to manageable size." And, while writing itself is "a complex problem-solving process" (p. 55), writing as we have seen becomes a tool in other problem-solving expeditions. In a foreword to Staton et al.'s, (1988) book on dialogue journal communication, Bruner (1988) points out that such journaling directly supports and activates the theories of Vygotsky.

> It takes as its fundamental assumption the one posited by the great Russian genius, Lev Vygotsky, that thought is internalized dialogue, that thoughts and ideas are first acquired by someone through dialogue, become internalized, and then elaborated into differentiated thought. Here, the idea of dialogue is used to encourage learning, used as a means of aiding students to more effectively digest the materials and knowledge that they are becoming acquainted with. (p. vii)

As we explored finding the various shapes – for I worked at this, too, demonstrating the learning, using large, inch-square graph paper on the classroom easel – we talked incessantly and moved around a lot. We resorted from time to time to pretending to move the shapes in the air, kinesthetically. The visual-spatial among us, me included, spent a lot of time looking. The linguistically oriented made lists and more charts. Some students sang and chanted as they worked. We worked for a long time, taking two long sessions before everyone was satisfied.

I remember the first time I ever had to do an assignment like this. It was in the spring of my high school junior year and I was taking the College Board examinations. Part of the text involved choosing between five shapes that had been rotated and flipped, transformations of the model on the left of the little line. Unable to get up and move around, which was what I felt like doing, I resorted to rotating a lot in my chair, trying desperately not to disturb the other test-takers. It was then I learned the meaning of kinesthetic intelligence, as I found out that the only way I had a prayer of getting those questions right was through the native intelligence involved in my whole body.

Restrained as I was, I did not think very well. I had no experience in this kind of mathematical learning and I had to "invent" prior knowledge on the spot. The prior knowledge I drew on was the world at large and my bodily experience in it. Teachers helping students to build a progressive pyramid of experience in this area need to expect and encourage a lot of physical movement. It is the translation of prior knowledge to paper.

I wrote in my journal at this point: "I haven't yet used the term 'group theory.' No one yet has asked why we are doing this."

Once when I stopped them to say that we were doing group theory, two boys on my team said, "Mmmmmm . . ." The others went back to what they were doing. While they were very interested during the discovery period of this, they were not particularly concerned with "the big picture." The task for them (Newman et al., 1989) was playing around with the patterns and similarities, not the same task as the one I envisioned.

The process I observed was purely trial and error. I got curious about whether computation would help anyone to work with pentominoes, which are multiples of five. I devised a game in which we had to cover a four-by-five grid paper mat with pentominoes. The object was to place a pentomino on the mat so that your partner could not place another. As we played this game, I asked how many of "the straight" shape, the one with five squares in a row, would it take to cover the mat. Everyone counted. No one multiplied or divided to find the answer. They did not automatically make use of the tools at hand, multiplication tables, to solve this problem.

I asked, "If two pentominoes are placed on this mat, how many spaces will be uncovered?" Students began again to count. Someone asked which two shapes I would be using, not realizing that any two pentominoes would yield the same result. No one automatically said "Ten." I concluded that it is a leap to transfer computation to a real-life situation. When I have to determine how many days are left in a month, I usually count on a calendar. Only rarely do I subtract, and then I don't always trust the result. Computation is most often learned algorithmically and, in Vygotskian terms, that is scientifically, top-down.

Following the exploration of the pentominoes, we focused on the variety of "moves," or transformations that could be made with the straight shape, such as rotating or flipping it over in various ways. We made drawings and charts of the transformations we had used. (See Figure 10.2.)

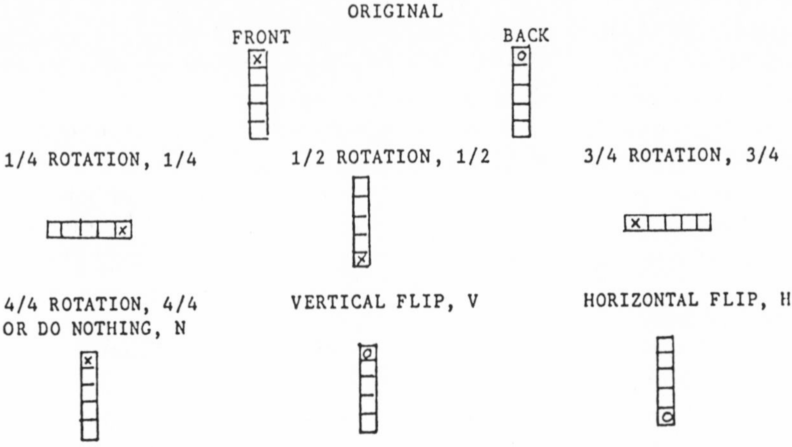

Figure 10.2. Some possible transformations with the straight pentomino shape.

As students worked, they moved around a lot and talked. Groups were formed according to their own variety of social and intellectual understandings. Two particular students worked together, as they often did, because they both understood first visually. Having been together before, they know this of each other and made use of it. Two others often worked together because they both liked to get into really "big projects" with keys and legends and large size or length. Two others worked together because they always talked and thought a lot first before doing any work on paper. Having been brought up in a Vygotskian fashion, having grown accustomed to processing interactively first, they naturally relied on moving from inter- to intrapsychological learning.

We moved on to the pentomino cross-shape. In working with the straight shape, we had realized that an infinity of transformations was possible so had limited them to the cardinal orientations. In working with the cross-shape, we worked within a template, a cutout of the cross, thus severely limiting the moves possible. Once transformed, the cross-shaped pentomino had to fit back inside the template and we again drew and charted the results. (See Figure 10.3.)

Following Walter, we developed a chart that showed the equivalence between a single transformation and two consecutive transformations with the pentomino. On this chart (see Figure 10.4) the two consecutive transformations are charted on the axes as "move listed on vertical axis *followed by* move listed on the horizontal axis." Inside the chart are the equivalent single-move transformations. Thus, a one-quarter motion

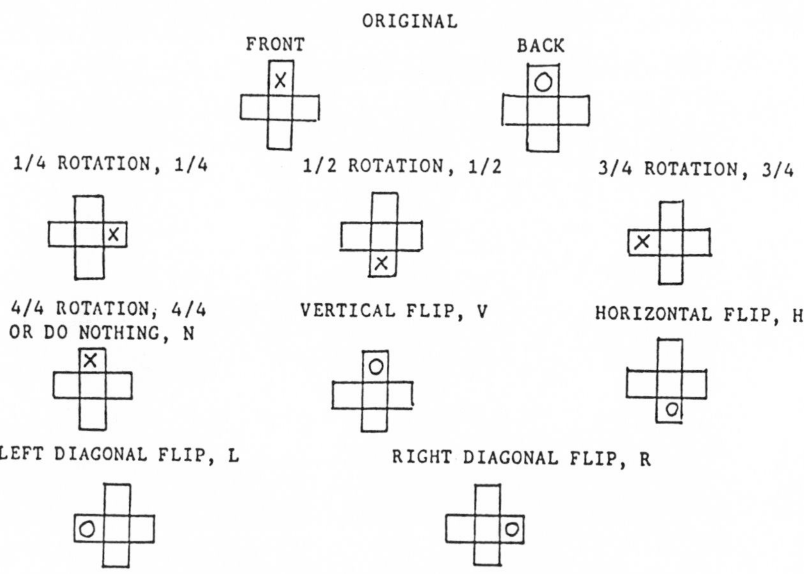

Figure 10.3. Some possible final positions after making one transformation with the cross-shaped pentomino.

Second Motion

First Motion / Followed by *	N	½	H	V	¼	¾	R	L
N	N	½	H	V	¼	¾	R	L
½	½	N	V	H	¾	¼	L	R
H	H	V	N	½	L	R	¾	¼
V	V	H	½	N	R	L	¼	¾
¼	¼	¾	R	L	½	N	V	H
¾	¾	¼	L	R	N	½	H	V
R	R	L	¼	¾	H	V	N	½
L	L	R	¾	¼	V	H	½	N

Figure 10.4. Chart of two-transformations and the equivalent single transformation (from Walter, 1971, p. 38).

		Second Motion							
	Followed by *	N	½	H	V	¼	¾	R	L
First Motion	N	N	½	H	V	[illegible]	[illegible]	[illegible]	[illegible]
	½	½	N	V	H	[illegible]	[illegible]	[illegible]	R
	H	H	V	N	½	L	[illegible]	[illegible]	[illegible]
	V	V	H	½	N	R	[illegible]	[illegible]	[illegible]
	¼	¼	¾	R	L	½	N	[illegible]	[illegible]
	¾	¾	¼	L	R	N	½	[illegible]	V
	R	R	L	¼	¾	H	V	N	[illegible]
	L	L	R	¾	¼	V	H	½	N

Figure 10.5. Chart of two-transformations and the equivalent single transformation, showing partial symmetry shading (from Walter, 1971, p. 37).

(¼) followed by a horizontal flip (H) has as its equivalent the single motion, right diagonal flip (R).

This chart is similar in structure to a computational chart, such as one used to tally multiplication facts. Students soon noticed the similarity, having much experience with such computational charts. They pointed out the developing diagonal symmetry in both. But they also soon noticed that the symmetry in a motion chart is not complete. (See Figure 10.5.)

Some students also worked with other pentomino shapes, having wondered if this similarity to computational charts only occurred with the cross-shaped pentomino. They proved that it did not.

Some of them wrote:

> We basically did what we did on the last chart but it was easier (at least for me). I guess it would have been quicker though if we did it with a symmetrical line down the center.

> [We] worked together and we pulled it off and we each did about the same. We both figured it out with the cross and we picked colors for each different sign.

> The first thing I did was to make the shape. Then I put the number 1 on the front and 2 on the other. Then I made a chart. It's like a times chart. So I took a problem, say ¼ + *DR* [diagonal right flip] which

> would end up like this [shows cross shape] and the only way you can get there in one move is a horizontal.

> Making the chart was confusing for me. I kept on getting DR and DL [diagonal right and diagonal left flips] mixed up, and I couldn't remember if a diagonal went horizontal or vertical.
> I didn't notice that the chart was symmetrical until now.
> The 1/4, 2/4, 3/4, and 4/4 were the easiest ones to do, because no flipping was involved.
> The N move was the easiest because the answer was always the same as the second move.

> I was in a group of three. . . . One of the problems we had, well, I had, was when you had N [no move] 4/4 [rotated fully]. Because they're both the same but you have to check which one fits the puzzler right. It is pretty easy. I enjoy doing things like this. Here is my math graph [graph is taped to the journal page]. I had no strategies. I learned a lot with the moves we did with the shapes.

> We didn't really have any problems. Although a few times we didn't understand what to write. The DR and DL were a little confusing. I basically had a chart set up and template so I could do the charted moves, then try it in one move. That's what [we] did to complete [our] chart. If you have any questions, just ask because I can't think of anything else to tell you.

As students continued to work with the pentomino shapes, all the groups used paper cutouts. Not all members of each group handled them; some were recorders. Once symmetry was discovered in the charts, the cutouts were used as a check. But students did continue to use the paper cutouts. Walter suggests that once students are working with the eight transformations possible with the pentomino "cross" shape,

> Now many students may need a paper cutout to convince themselves that the two motions suggested are correct. Again, each answer can be checked by the students at the board who can use the paper cutout. (Walter, 1971, p. 36)

Walter would have gone crazy with my class. They *all* used paper cutouts. And what is more, they used them throughout this unit, even with the straight shapes that came before, a study she feels they will do in their heads. I guess she envisions me at the board with the one shape and selected students. Not in my class. We had cut paper all over the place, everyone had individual little pentomino shapes, boxes, "straights," crosses – some students were working in colored chalk on giant charts on the board, others worked with me on inch-square graph paper on the large, class easel. The artifacts of this "big idea" were a part of our daily

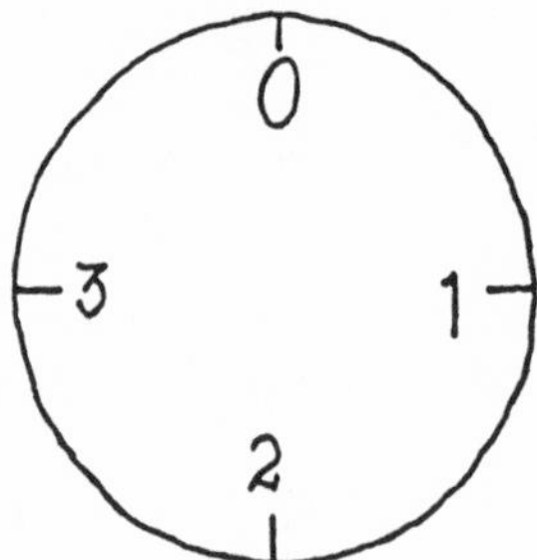

Figure 10.6. Modulo 4 "clockface."

living. We were immersed in our shapes and charts. There was a great deal of spontaneous concept formation going on.

MOVING ON TO MODULAR MATHEMATICS AND BEYOND

At this point we took leave of Marion Walter and began a study of "Mod Math." One student said, "Did you make this name up just for us?" It has such a nice, modern ring to it. But, "No," I said, "It's short for modular mathematics, which means it's like a clockface." No one said "That doesn't make sense." And so we moved right into it.

It was our Magnum Opus of Big Ideas. Mod Math in June – it was just the thing. By the end of the year, our room fairly sang with Mod Math.

In mod math, the clockface mathematics, we deal with a finite set of numbers, which are arranged around a circle like a clockface (see Figure 10.6) and which conform to the postulates of group theory. Each set begins with 0, so, for example "mod 4," or more properly, modulo 4, would contain the numbers 0, 1, 2, and 3, equally spaced around a clockface. To count, we begin at 0 and count around, and when we pass 3, in modulo 4, we arrive again at 0. So if we count to five in modulo 4, we arrive at 0. If we count to seven, we arrive at 2. If we wanted to add two and three, we would start at 0, count two, taking us to 2, and then count three more, taking us to 1: therefore, $2 + 3 = 1$ in modulo 4.

We thought that we would make a chart like we had made for the pentomino transformations. There the set was under the operation "followed by." Here the set of finite numbers, 0 to 3, would operate under the operation of addition and so the chart would seem familiar, looking like the computational addition and multiplication facts charts we were so used to. We began. Students went into their self-selected groups and worked on developing a chart for modulo 4 (see Figure 10.7).

Most students opted to color in their charts to show the reflection that

+	0	1	2	3
0	0	1	2	3
1	1	2	3	0
2	2	3	0	1
3	3	0	1	2

Figure 10.7. Addition chart, modulo 4.

0	1	2	3	3	2	1	0
1	2	3	0	0	3	2	1
2	3	0	1	1	0	3	2
3	0	1	2	2	1	0	3
3	0	1	2	2	1	0	3
2	3	0	1	1	0	3	2
1	2	3	0	0	3	2	1
0	1	2	3	3	2	1	0

Figure 10.8. Four-section chart, modulo 4 with transformations.

occurs over the diagonal. We *knew* that these would reflect symmetrically over the diagonal because we had explored similar addition and multiplication charts so often. Students began in groups to experiment with other modulos. Everyone also tried coloring in four-section modulo 4 charts that were reflections and flips of each other, extending the color patterns across other small sections (see Figure 10.8).

The afternoon came to an end and we went home. The next day we came in and, scrapping all other plans, went right to work on our mod math. As we began work on modulo 5, students talked about their extracurricular thinking about this big idea. One of the most telling aspects was that many had found modular mathematics aspects outside the classroom.

One related his transfer of knowledge as he talked about how a baseball diamond was a modular system. After you run the bases and come home, you run around the bases again. It is a finite, closed set. Other students related their newborn understanding of mod math as they recognized that their parents' car odometers were modular systems, that trains ran on modular systems, and that any kind of route was a system of modular mathematics. We looked again at the clock face and the calendar year, and speculated about time and the future. Were any of these *really* modular, finite, or were they all moving into the future, different, and infinite? Is everything ever the same, even when you go around it again and again?

We talked briefly, too, of the similarity between all the charts we had explored, the "facts" charts, the pentominoes transformational charts, and now, the modular charts. We were not too specific as to the group theory postulates that governed these similarities. I often made mention of them and once even wrote them out on the board: Closure, Identity, Inverse, Associative. But even with explanations, they lacked appeal at this stage of playful learning. We continued to talk about why these similarities occurred. It was sufficient, it seemed, for most of the students that I simply said that all of these sets fell under the postulates of group theory. They said they could see that this was true, even if they did not understand it in all its mathematical grandeur. What they really liked was doing the math, counting around the clockface, looking for patterns. It was looking for patterns and finding them that really got them going.

Here, working in the zone of proximal development, learners went beyond the normal realm of sixth-grade understanding. They began to make connections new even to me. I wrote in my journal, "It was good to see a link between the pentomino 'cross' chart and 'mod math.' " They wrote:

> I learned that mod math is related to what we did yesterday. I also learned about all the different patterns.
>
> One thing I thought that was interesting was the mod math. I really liked how it came together.

We began on this day to chart other "mods." Some students worked out their own modular patterns. Some got interested on whether there was an upper limit on modular mathematics, would there ever be numbers that were too big for "wrapping the can," a metaphoric way of describing counting around a modular number system resembling a clockface. One student, entranced with color, worked in modulo 64, the number of crayons in those wonderful big boxes of Crayola crayons, creating a large, bright chart that took a very long time to make.

I introduced them to the "stretched" modular patterns found in

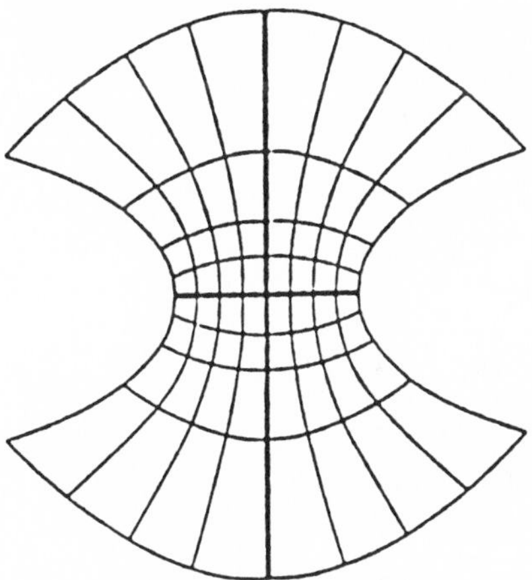

Figure 10.9. Deformed modulo 4 chart, transformed (from Bezuszka, Kenny, & Silvey, 1978, p. 33).

Bezuszka, Kenney, and Silvey's (1978) *Designs from Mathematical Patterns*. Here, modular mathematics square designs are deformed into diamonds and warped shapes. Each basic pattern is reflected vertically and horizontally across a four-section, deformed design. Figure 10.9 shows a deforming of Figure 10.8.

This was the part of the study that really took off. These sixth-graders had been waiting all year to color – just to color. It was the time of year and the end of childhood when they asked "Do you have any coloring books or any pictures that we could, you know, just color?" They wanted to play with color and contrast.

But now they could make their own coloring patterns. And they were able to use their well-honed skills of prediction and patterning to decide in advance what colors to assign to the various answers that would come up in different mods. That was the substance of the classroom talk.

They spent hours on these designs. Using the four-section design, deformed or plain, students followed a four-step procedure. First, they chose a modulo and created a single chart for it. Next, they assigned a different color to each number. Third, using the chart as a reference, they colored in a four-section design, coloring the first section, the "anchor" section according to the number chart they had made. Then, they used translations, reflections, or rotations to color sections two, three, and four.

The game for the rest of us at this point was to look at the colored design without any numbers and to determine what modulo had been

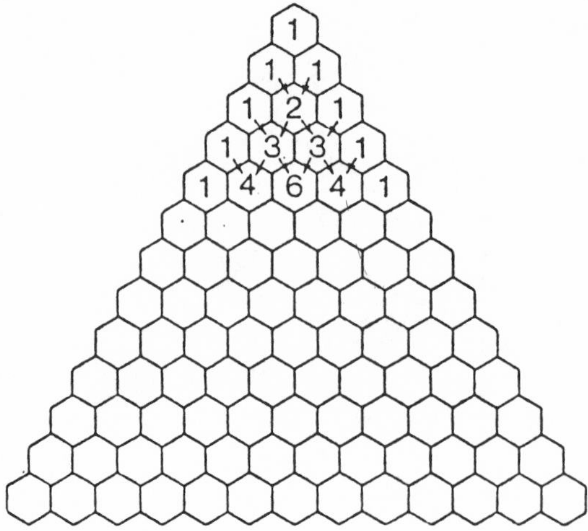

Figure 10.10. Traditional Pascal's triangle (from Bezuszka, Kenney, & Silvey, 1978, p. 66).

chosen and what transformations had been performed on the original design. We did a lot of thinking and talking to figure out some of them.

We talked a lot about how we thought of these things. Vygotsky's beliefs about the change from inter- into intrapsychological growth were most evident as students shared thoughts on thinking. In fact, one of the most interesting subjects under discussion during this period was "how I think of things," with different students describing how she or he went about thinking a problem through. The comparison of thinking strategies made for most interesting conversation for these sixth-graders. Much inter- and intrapersonal intelligence (Gardner, 1983) was tapped. When a big idea is explored in a rich context, thinking is the substance of discussion.

I introduced one student to Pascal's triangle (see Figure 10.10), showing him this special array that Pascal discovered. As with so many aspects of this study, we marveled together on the mind that had envisioned such possibilities. Exploring other's minds was the real substance of our talk and discovery as we colored and composed, created and colored, talking and moving all the while.

As we discussed Pascal's triangle, other students got interested. We were working on the big paper on the easel and talked about how the triangle actually originated many centuries ago in China and Persia but was popularized in the Western world by Blaise Pascal (1623–1662). In Pascal's triangle, a geometric, triangular arrangement, the number 1 is

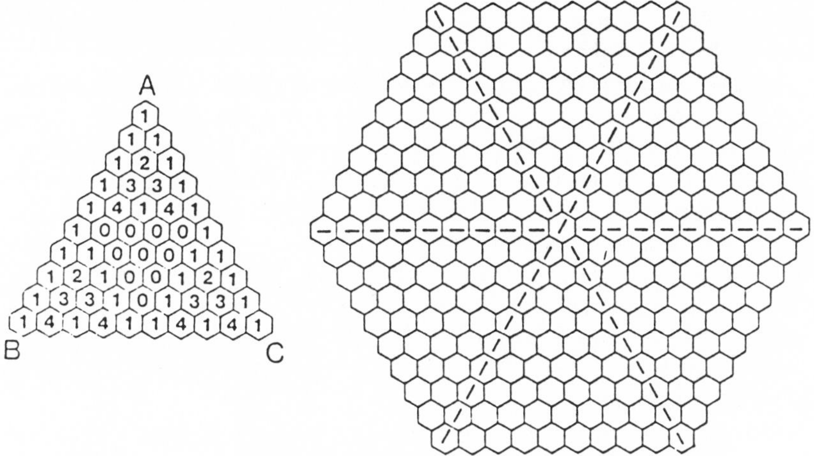

Figure 10.11. Tessellated Pascal's triangle, modulo 5 (from Bezuszka, Kenney, & Silvey, 1978, p. 78).

repeated along two sides; "every other number within the triangle equals the sum of the two numbers diagonally above it" (Bezuszka et al., p. 66).

Most students began to work with Pascal's triangle. The infiniteness of possibility fascinated them. And because of the work in modular mathematics, it was moments before someone saw the possibility of creating Pascal's triangles in different mods. Because they had been working in color, they automatically began color coding this work and found, to their utter delight, incredible patterns appearing, "chaos"-style (cf. Gleick, 1987) within the triangles.

And because they had so recently worked in pattern transformation, they transferred this learning to Pascal's triangle and we began to work with circular designs that repeated the patterns discovered by color. These were tessellated Pascal's triangles arranged around a center point in a hexagon. Varieties of these circular, tessellated patterns are available in Bezuszka et al. (1978). (See Figure 10.11.)

Some of these were very hard to do. Most students did the number work in pencil on the triangle and then went back to do the color coding. Some still "wrapped the can" to do the modular mathematics. Some made mathematical mistakes, which were not evident until the designs were color coded. We used some "white out," that liquid paint that covers typing mistakes, and went on with the design. I mostly served as troubleshooter during this period, working in the students' zone of proximal development, although I did find time to develop my own modulo 5

Pascal's triangle in color on the big easel. I had some help – once in a while students worked with me in my zone of proximal development – and we had a lot of fun.

I also bought crayons, markers, and colored pencils. Parents helped out, too, and old crayon boxes and marker sets, long forgotten, were enlisted in the effort. The coloring instruments of choice were colored pencils, although markers covered any penciled-in numbers better. We talked coloring all day long. And we worked with construction paper to mount the designs on contrasting colors. Sometimes we despaired at the colors in the school supply closet but generally they were good and true.

We talked about a poster of Fibonacci numbers and we came across the Sieve of Erasthones. We liked Wahl's (1988, p. 71) words, "a gadget invented by Erasthones." One of the most powerful aspects of doing big ideas in a rich context is the possibility to thus explore living history by working with people's mathematical ideas in concrete form. In a classroom set up for thinking, exploration, play, and immersion, students talk the history of thinking as they discover mathematical concepts.

Not all students took this side trip with me. Many were much too busy working on their modular math, tessellated Pascal's triangles. Three students made a huge chart on the wall out of four pieces of 12-by-18-inch oaktag and thought they would try to create the world's biggest Pascal's triangle "in the round, modulo 60." They created a "legend," a crayoned and color-coded chart, carefully squared in raw umber. In each square is a number, the name of the color that will match it, and a "swatch" of that color. Exploring the names of colors was one of the great satisfactions for these students in this project.

We see here an example of what Newman et al. (1989, p. 16) described as "appropriation," a feature of learning taking place in the zone of proximal development in which both teacher and student make use of each other's work by appropriating it and turning it to extended use:

> The crucial step . . . was neither taught directly nor invented spontaneously by the children. Rather it emerged in the interaction as the teacher appropriated the trial and error attempts of the children and used them to instantiate the expert strategy.

In this case, as occurred throughout the study, the task itself, as I had defined it, was continually appropriated and redefined by the students as they made the study their own. And I, in turn, appropriated their appropriation, as one learning piggybacked on the other.

> The appropriation process is reciprocal, and cognitive change occurs within this mutually constructive process. While instructional interactions favor the role associated with the teacher, we cannot lose sight of the continually active role of the child. (Newman et al., 1989, p. 58)

We made a bulletin board by classifying the tessellated mods into factor groups, predicting that similar patterns might appear. A student who enjoyed this sort of thing designed it. After some discussion, we arranged it in thirds, labeled 2, 3, and 5 for the prime factors. And there was a special section for prime-number modulos. We called the bulletin board "Charts of the System of Cardinal Numbers Modulo n Under Addition." A great title. No one ever asked what it meant.

Students wrote about their experiences with modular math:

> I haven't had any problems with Mod Math. I think it's fun making designs and coloring them in. I just finished a Mod 5 design. It looks very pretty. I am now working on a Mod 10 chart with [another student].

> I think doing the mods are pretty fun. I have just finished coloring mod 2. It came out pretty. I think. I learned that you can't go any higher than 118 in mod math (60) 59 + 59 = 118. [My friends] are doing mod 60 so I think it's going to take a while to color it.
>
> Right now I am doing mod 3. It's pretty interesting. I also learned that you can find a mod in so many different shapes.

> In mod math I am doing pretty well. It is so similar to what we have been doing before. Right now I am thinking of a rule for mod math 4. I have to finish coloring it, too.
>
> I discovered so many patterns and shapes in mod math. It's a pretty neat method.
>
> Next I will be working on Mod 5. It is just like 4. They are similar, except they add on another number.

> M.o.d. [*sic*] math is easy. The clock face* [student includes a diagram of one showing modulo 3, marked with an asterisk, at the bottom of the page] is easy to catch on to. I'm good at m.o.d. math.

I wrote in my journal on May 18:

> Things are getting very exciting with this group theory work. We talk about so many ideas. We talk about what it means to take number systems apart the way we feel we are doing with mod math.

> We spend a lot of time predicting what might happen to snarls (what we called certain, "chaos"-style sections of the colored modular Pascal's triangles; also nicknamed "diblets") when the modular numbers are higher multiples. We compare predictions of what bigger Pascal's triangles might look like. We say, "I predict . . ." and someone immediately says, "Yes, but . . ."

We began to talk about the notion of *congruence* as it is used mathematically. We knew congruence in geometry, but we had never thought about how it might apply to numbers. Now that we had been exploring group theory, here in "the construction zone," we saw that there are underlying similarities across several fields that previously seemed unrelated: number systems, arithmetic, algebra, and geometric systems. This knowledge has opened up our minds a little to other possibilities of connections.

In order to discuss this concept, I had to do some reading (Willerding & Hayward, 1968; Stein, 1963) and I said so. The students were with me; we had all been learners together right along.

No one seemed to worry that these things are hard to understand. Everyone seemed to know that we were about trying to find connections in the mathematical world and that perhaps when all of us were older we might want to know more about the connections. For now, it was sufficient to know that congruence had a broader meaning than one shape covering another on a desktop.

We continued to pattern, predict, and color. The factor spaces on the bulletin board were beginning to fill up. We began to talk about how what we had been doing was "tiling the plane." We talked about floor tiles, and wall tiles, and what kind of shapes might lend themselves to tiling themselves. Could any shape be used to tile? Probably not, because some shapes do not fit together well. We deceided with Rucker (1987) that, of regular polygons, three shapes tile the plane – triangles, squares, and hexagons. Irregular polygons can be made to tile the plane.

What Rucker taught us that we had not known was that the three-dimensional world also can be "tiled." Here, we were all in the zone of proximal development, with Rucker leading me and me leading the students. Consider soap bubbles, says Rucker; they are hexagons and that is why they fit together so nicely into piles of soap bubbles. They "tile" the three-dimensional plane, or, if you like, they fill the three-dimensional space completely because they tile.

This discussion led us into talking about the world of crystals. We knew that crystallography was related to group theory:

> The theory also helps scientists when they glimpse patterns darkly in nature. It has been used, for instance, to analyze configurations of molecules and crystals – arrangements important in the chemistry of human genes or in the "solid circuits" of sophisticated electronics. (Bergamini & Editors, 1963, p. 173)

We did not have much time left in the year but we began to tile the two-dimensional plane to see what might happen. Some students fell in love with periodic tiling as if they had never seen or done it before, even though they had. Others wanted to explore the possibilities in non-periodic tiling, so I read a little further. We tried Rucker's (1987) idea of working with irregular pentagons, which fit together but do not create a repeating design. We tried to do enough different designs, both periodic and non-periodic to be able to compare and contrast them and draw some generalizations. For without being able to generalize, we could not do our favorite thing, predicting.

Clearly, the symmetry of a shape or pattern affects its ability to tile periodically. We tried to tile with Penrose (1989) tiles, with their fivefold symmetry, just to see what would happen. (See Figure 10.12.)

We talked as we worked about the ideas that mathematicians thought were behind some of these concepts. Rucker points out that Penrose tiles may serve as a model for how the universe might be built up.

> It is conceivable that our universe is, at some deep level, made up of many, many copies of a few very simple components that can only be linked together in certain definite ways. The surprising lesson of the Penrose tiles is that one can have simple rules and components that necessarily combine to make a vast complicated whole! (Rucker, 1987, p. 110)

We went back to our interest in soap bubbles and crystals when we read in Peterson (1988) that Penrose had "tiled his plane" three-dimensionally by working with pairs of rhombohedra. Reading this out loud and trying to understand it got us to thinking out loud about how one goes about filling a space with three-dimensional shapes. Penrose had worked on these problems for the mathematical love of it, but he did think of the implications for crystallography. We read in Peterson (1988, p. 207) that in 1984, the world of crystallography discovered tiny metallic crystals made of aluminum and magnesium. These crystals showed a fivefold symmetry and according to the laws of crystallography that was not possible.

As we read all of this and tried to grasp its significances, traveling well on the edges of all of our zones of proximal development, we were struck by the following passage: "According to the well-established suppositions of crystallography, formalized in the branch of mathematics known as group theory, only a small list of rotational symmetries is possible for crystals" (Peterson, 1988, p. 207). Imagine that, we said, crystallography in group theory. There it is again, we said.

We read that Branko Grunbaum, an expert on the mathematics of tilings, has proposed a theory of adjacencies to describe tilings and crystal forms, "specifying how one piece is connected to its neighbors . . . an alternative to the group-theory approach traditionally used by crystallographers and other researchers" (Peterson, 1988, p. 211).

That's what it said, we said, group theory again. We read on:

> Whereas group theory emphasizes the importance of a pattern's overall rotational-symmetry properties, the adjacencies model takes a local

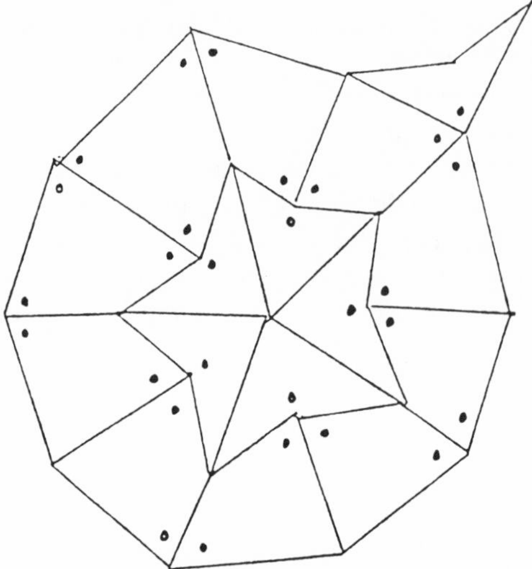

Figure 10.12. Penrose non-periodic tiling, student version.

> approach, specifying how one piece is connected to its neighbors. In fact adjacency rules generate many interesting patterns that can't be described by symmetries and group theory. (p. 211)

We sat back, amazed at the minds that think of all these things. That was the main subject of our talk at this point in the study. No one was really concerned with the postulates that governed the theory or how they played themselves out in the charts. We were much more involved with the "really big idea," the idea that a field that had been governed so long by one theory was now looking at a completely different theory, one that looked at things from a completely different point of view, one that found its history in the work of artists and craftsmen, who "relied on their own empirical rules and schemes" (p. 212).

> In a sense, the adjacencies way of looking at tilings isn't particularly new. For millennia, artists and craftsmen have created intricate, pleasing designs and repeating patterns on walls, on woven fabrics, on pottery without relying on the tenets of group theory to guide their work. They relied on their own empirical rules and schemes, which more often than not simply stated how one tile or shape fits with another. Once the rules and tile shapes are selected, the type of patterns that emerge is set. (p. 212)

That just about did it for us – weavers and potters and group theory. The whole study had come full circle. I knew that Vygotsky was smiling, that the spontaneous concept formation had just had its face-to-face inception with the scientific concept formation. But it would take a long time for it all to be sorted out. As Newman et al. (1989) point out:

> Internalization, by definition, is an individual process. It is also a constructive process rather than an automatic reflection of the external events. But the child does not have to leave the zone and then work on internalizing in splendid isolation. The internal and external constructive processes are occurring simultaneously. (p. 68)

And what was the main subject of interactive classroom talk at this point? Penrose, of course. What impressed us most was that the problem of tiling the plane in fivefold symmetry could not be solved within the bounds of the thinking at that time. It took a mind like Penrose's to "break set," to come up with a totally new way of looking at things before the problem could be solved. This really impressed us. We spent a lot of time talking about how people think and how some people go about doing something like "breaking set," solving a problem by looking at things in a completely new way. We said, think of Branko Grunbaum, coming up with a new theory that looked at a problem in a new way, by looking at the edges instead of at the middle.

We tried to consider objects in the room by looking at the edges instead of at the middle, to activate Grunbaum's adjacencies theory in our own classroom. It made us talk about the connections between things instead of the things themselves.

We talked about how mathematics goes back and forth from the real world of work and objects to the theoretical world of objects and ideas. Penrose says he thought what he thought out of pure enjoyment, for the love of math. And then, there was an application, just looking for some thinking to go behind it.

But mostly we talked about how great minds think. This was modeling in a grand style. We had all explored the world of thinking and mathematics. We had reached some pretty good conclusions on our own. We had grabbed the tail of group theory. It amazed us to see how far it could be taken.

CONCLUSION

An extended course of exploration, "a profoundly social process" (John-Steiner & Souberman, 1978, p. 131), such as the one described permits a clear vision of how classroom instruction can be when what Holdaway (1989) describes as a "generative curriculum" is in place. As students and teacher work together in the zone of proximal development, the task shifts, "subject to the social processes in which temporary alliances are created" (Newman et al., 1989, p. 73). With its shift, changes occur in the resultant interpsychological learnings. The task as I saw it did not always conform to the task as the students constructed it.

While the resultant learnings supported my early goals, they also fulfilled generated goals, goals that appeared during the course of study as we learned together in "the construction zone." I had narrowly seen the study as an opportunity to explore the world of mathematics. I had not been prepared to see in children's minds the "revelation of this internal, subterranean developmental network of school subjects" (Vygotsky, 1978, p. 91). I had not, for instance, expected us to focus finally on the power of the human mind and its manifestation in mathematics. Nor had I seen an exploration of group theory as an opportunity to expand our notion of patterning in the world around us. I had underestimated the minds of children.

Exploring big ideas in a rich context is a way of glimpsing people's minds. Dowdy (1971, p. 57) looks to group theory as a way of showing students something about "the way a mathematician works." For as children's understanding of a concept grows, they are able to follow the inception of a new idea. They can appreciate an Erasthones, a Fibonacci, a Pascal, or a Penrose. For they are stretching their minds too – they are trying for themselves to "break set," to make new connections and draw new conclusions, to look at things in a new way.

> Any investigation explores some sphere of reality. An aim of the psychological analysis of development is to describe the internal relations of the intellectual processes awakened by school learning. . . . If successful, it should reveal to the teacher how developmental processes stimulated by the course of school learning are carried through inside the head of each individual child. (Vygotsky, 1978, p. 91)

Also, like Newman et al. (1987), I had not expected my own understandings to be changed by dwelling so long in "the construction zone," but they were "as a result of carrying out a joint activity with others who had a different analysis of our shared situation" (p. 31). Further, I find as time goes by that my cognitive growth continues; my own "developmental process lags behind the learning process" (Vygotsky, 1978, p. 90).

These changes in learnings, goals, and cognitive directions, springing from variant and evolving definitions of task, are accountable through Leont'ev's (1981) idea of appropriation in which a child acquires the use of culturally elaborated tools by appropriating them in a socially mediated activity and, in the process, may create or attribute new interpretation. Appropriation in a classroom encounter occurs when both teacher and students make use of and interpret each other's socially mediated responses as the learning event proceeds.

> The children may take the [zone of proximal development] in unanticipated directions based on their own appropriation of what the teacher makes available. In this respect, the functional system of the zone of proximal development may not be characterized by an invariant task – the task as negotiated by the child and teacher may in fact change. While the dominant task definition is that of the teacher and the dominant movement is toward the adult system, each step is an interactive construction with a variety of possible outcomes. (Newman et al., 1989, pp. 74–5)

We particularly saw this happening as the study moved from pentominoes into modular math and beyond. As the students began to grasp underlying implications, as patterning as a guiding factor rose to the surface of attention, task definitions diverged, student from student, and student from me. This occurs because the instructional model is what Monson and Pahl (1991, p. 51) call "transactional," with "students engaging in a transaction between what is known and what is unknown."

Wertsch (1985) points to the need to specify how the child performs under adult guidance since Vygotsky made only "few comments" on this point. Descriptive studies such as this one support Vygotsky's observations that "direct teaching of concepts is impossible and fruitless" (1962, p. 83) and that "verbal intercourse with adults thus becomes a powerful factor in the development of the child's concepts" (1962, p. 69). But the necessary reciprocal nature of appropriation of task definition, idea generation, and conceptual development is a key element in promoting mutually profitable relationships between teacher and students. All must be active participants in a curriculum that has a generative, and not a pre-ordained nature.

Vygotsky has said of children, "learning awakens a variety of internal development processes that are able to operate only when the child is interacting with people in his environment and in cooperation with his peers" (1978, p. 90). The same is here held true for teachers.

> The teacher reciprocally applies the process of appropriation in the instructional interactions. In constructing a zone of proximal development for a particular task, the teacher incorporates children's actions into her own system of activity. (Newman et al., 1989, p. 63)

Cazden (1992) reflects that "Teaching is value-laden, interventionist work." But as this study illustrates, students actively involved in a rich context do some intervening, too. They affect the growth of both the study and the teacher's understanding. Then, teachers "learn to reflect on their own everyday knowledge, especially to discover and to trust their informal ways of knowing" (Bamberger, 1979, p. 2).

Schon (1983, pp. viii–xi) calls this teachers' "knowing-in-practice, most of which is tacit":

> Indeed, practitioners themselves often reveal a capacity for reflection on their intuitive knowing in the midst of action and sometimes use this capacity to cope with the unique, uncertain, and conflicted situations of practice.

Teachers are often not comfortable with their own mathematical understanding (Hyde, 1989; Thompson, 1985) but must remember that they are good learners themselves. Mathematics is a topic in which it has always been assumed that "explicit adult instruction . . . could be the only source of growth" (Cazden, Cordeiro, & Giacobbe, 1985). However, Vygotsky's description of the role of practical, spontaneous concept development relative to mediated, instructional, scientific development gives new insight into children's mathematical growth. As Vygotsky writes, "We have given him a pennyworth of instruction, and he has gained a small fortune in development" (1962, p. 96).

Translating interpsychological learnings into intrapsychological learning in everyday lives is possible in classrooms that have an everyday life, those classrooms which permit learners to live coherently in optimal surroundings. In this setting, a rich context can flourish.

The appearance of extraschool applications of modular mathematics supports the assumption of the shift to intrapsychological learning in this opaque process. This artifact of cognitive change, these "new system functions" are what Newman et al. (1987, p. 74) call

> the "next step" of intrapsychological system, attributable now to the child and available for the child as he coordinates in new interpsychological situations with teachers or peers or in the relative isolation that we would call "independent."

There are many implications that can be drawn from this work. We can see that it is possible for students to sustain interest over a lengthy period of time when they engage in conceptual thinking. In fact, in order to work on conceptual studies of this type, it is essential that much time be provided. Since we are, in fact, attempting to follow fully Vygotsky's (1962) suggestion that we strive for the "face-to-face inception" of spontaneous, bottom-up, concretely acquired concepts with scientific, top-down, abstractly acquired concepts, we must give recognition to the immensity of the learning tasks at hand.

In such a full presentation of Vygotsky's beliefs about concept development, students experience that "natural" order of scientific process, characterized by Armstrong (1980, p. 122) as "fundamental to scientific and mathematical awareness." One student described this study of group theory as "dismantling numbers" as we searched for patterns in Pascal's triangles, as good a definition as could be given.

We know from Vygotsky's work that "the development of scientific concepts runs ahead of the development of spontaneous concepts" (1962, p. 106). So we are secure in presenting abstract conceptual thinking during student "play" with a concept. But we remember that Vygotsky goes on to point out that "the development of a spontaneous concept must have reached a certain level for the child to be able to absorb a related scientific concept" (p. 108). So we allow plenty of time for spontaneous concept formation, the "face-to-face meeting with a concrete situation," before attempting to pursue the related scientific concept in depth, for it takes "a mediated" attitude toward its object (p. 108).

This all takes time – lots of time. Part of the time is used up in the students' mental effort to work things out in their own way, according to their particular combination of intelligences (Gardner, 1983). As the foundation of spontaneous experience is laid, the theoretical scientific concept can be integrated into the experiential. But, as Cazden (1992) points out, "once that foundation is in place, scientific concepts can stimulate further development." The effect is a dialectic (Vygotsky, 1978), spiraling between intra- and interpsychological growth.

We can also draw the implication that for students at this age, at this stage of thinking development, the study of mathematics should be about more than numbers; it should be about the concepts which underlie the numbers and their interrelatedness. Mathematics at this stage should not be discipline-bound, teaching geometry separately from algebra and arithmetic, or from literacy and social interaction.

> We found that intellectual development . . . is not compartmentalized according to topics of instruction. Its course is much more unitary, and the different school subjects interact in contributing to it. While the processes of instruction follow their own logical order, they awaken and direct a system of processes in the child's mind which is hidden from direct observation and subject to its own developmental laws. (Vygotsky, 1962, p. 102)

This view of intellectual development in an exploratory atmosphere is predicated upon the teacher's intention to trust students to learn and student's belief in that intention. Hawkins (1972, p. 110) warns us about "our failure to assign dignity to children's exploration of the world."

> Teachers have a moral duty not to abandon hope – to be constantly in search of changes in procedures which will have the effect that they can

> teach those children they now find unteachable, can initiate them into worthwhile activities into which they cannot yet see ways of initiating them. (Passmore, 1980, p. 29)

Duckworth (1986, p. 42) believes that the role of the teacher is to give validity to a view of the importance of one's own knowledge, "to make it absolutely clear that what they think is O.K. with you."

Where will students go with this new knowledge? As one student said to me, "Will we have more of this in high school?" I had to answer candidly that he might and he might not. As a student, I had not been exposed to these concepts. But I shared my hope that knowing that these ideas are out there will drive some students to seek out teachers who can teach them more than I know.

I had hoped to lay "the basis for the subsequent development of a variety of highly complex internal processes in children's thinking" (Vygotsky, 1978, p. 90). In attempting to do so, I enjoyed the "exaltation of the power inherent in all children's minds" (Cazden, 1992). I found that in "the construction zone," many can build together what one cannot imagine alone.

REFERENCES

Armstrong, M. 1980. *Closely observed children: The diary of a primary classroom.* London: Writers and Readers.

Bamberger, J. 1979. "Music and cognitive research: Where do our questions come from, where do our answers go?" Paper presented at the American Educational Research Association, Annual Meeting, April 8–12, San Francisco, CA.

Bamberger, J., & D. Schon. 1978. "The figural-formal transaction." D.S.R.E. Working Paper supported by a grant from the Ford Foundation, June.

Bergamini, D., & the Editors of Time-Life Books. 1963. *Mathematics.* New York: Time-Life Books.

Bezuszka, S., M. Kenney, & L. Silvey. 1978. *Designs from mathematical patterns.* Palo Alto, CA: Creative Publications.

Boyer, C. 1968. *A history of mathematics.* New York: John Wiley & Sons.

Bruner, J. 1988. "Foreword." In J. Staton, R. Shuy, J. Peyton, & L. Reed, Eds., *Dialogue journal communication: Classroom, linguistic, social and cognitive views.* Norwood, NJ: Ablex.

Cambourne, B. 1988. *The whole story.* New York: Scholastic.

Cazden, C. 1979. "Peekaboo as an instructional model: Discourse development at home and at school." In *Papers and reports of child language development, #17.* Stanford, CA: Stanford University, Department of Linguistics.

Cazden, C. 1992. "Active learners and active teachers." In *Whole language plus: Essays on literacy in the United States and New Zealand.* New York: Teachers College Press.

Cazden, C., P. Cordeiro, & M. E. Giacobbe. 1985. "Spontaneous and scientific concepts: Young children's learning of punctuation." In G. Wells & J. Nicholls, Eds., *Language and learning: An interactional perspective.* London: Falmer Press.

Cordeiro, P. 1988. "Playing with infinity in the sixth grade." *Language Arts, 65, 6,* pp. 557–566.

Davidson, P. 1990. Personal communication. Boston: University of Massachusetts.

Donaldson, M. 1963. *A study of children's thinking.* London: Tavistock.

Donaldson, M. 1978. *Children's minds.* New York: W. W. Norton.

Duckworth, E. 1986. *Inventing density.* Monograph published by Center for Teaching and Learning, University of North Dakota, Grand Forks.

Flower, L., & J. Hayes. 1981. "Plans that guide the composing process." In C. Fredrickson & J. Dominic, Eds., *Writing: The nature, development, and teaching of written communication; Volume 2, Writing: Process, development and communication.* Hillsdale. NJ: Lawrence Erlbaum.

Forman, E., & C. Cazden. 1985. "Exploring Vygotskian perspectives in education: The cognitive value of peer intraction." In J. Wertsch, Ed., *Culture, communication and cognition: Vygotskian perspectives.* Cambridge: Cambridge University Press.

Gardner, H. 1983. *Frames of mind: The theory of multiple intelligences.* New York: Basic Books.

Gleick, J. 1987. *Chaos: Making a new science.* New York: Viking.

Graves, D. 1989. *Investigate nonfiction.* Portsmouth, NH: Heinemann.

Greenfield, P. 1984. "A theory of the teacher in the learning activities of everyday life." In B. Rogoff & J. Lave, Eds., *Everyday cognition: Its development in social context.* Cambridge, MA: Harvard University Press.

Hawkins, D. 1972. "Nature, man and math." In *The informed vision: An essay on science education.* Reprint. New York: Agathon Press, 1974.

———. 1973. "What it means to teach." *Teachers College Record, 75, 1,* pp. 7–16.

Holdaway, D. 1989, Personal communication. Denver: Third Annual Regis College Whole Language Institute.

Hyde, A. 1989. "Staff development: Directions and realities." In P. Trafton & A. Schulte, Eds., *New directions for elementary school mathematics: 1989 Yearbook of National Council of Teachers of Mathematics.* Reston VA: National Council of Teachers of Mathematics.

John-Steiner, V., & E. Souberman. 1978. "Afterword." In L. Vygotsky, *Mind in society: The development of higher psychological processes.* M. Cole, V. John-Steiner, S. Scribner, & E. Souberman, Eds. Cambridge, MA: Harvard University Press.

Kamii, C. 1985. *Young children reinvent mathematics: Implications of Piaget's theory.* New York: Teachers College Press.

Leont'ev, A. 1981. *Problems of the mind.* Moscow: Progress Publishers.

Monson, R., & M. Pahl. 1991. "Charting a new course with whole language." *Educational Leadership,* March, pp. 51–53.

Newman, D., P. Griffin, & M. Cole. 1989. *The construction zone: Working for cognitive change in school.* Cambridge: Cambridge University Press.

Passmore, J. 1980. *The philosophy of teaching.* Cambridge, MA: Harvard University Press.

Penrose, R. 1989. *The emperor's new mind: Concerning computers, minds, and the laws of physics.* New York: Oxford University Press.

Peterson, I. 1988. *The mathematical tourist: Snapshots of modern mathematics.* New York: W. H. Freeman.

Resnick, L. 1976. "Task analysis in instructional design: Some cases from mathematics." In D. Khlar, Ed., *Cognition and instruction.* Hillsdale, NJ: Lawrence Erlbaum.

Rogoff, B. & W. Gardner. 1984. "Adult guidance of cognitive development." In B. Rogoff & J. Lave, Eds., *Everyday cognition: Its development in social context.* Cambridge, MA: Harvard University Press.

Rucker, R. 1987. *Mindtools: The five levels of mathematical reality.* Boston: Houghton Mifflin.

Schon, D. 1983. *The reflective practitioner: How professionals think in action.* New York: Basic Books.

Shuy, R. 1988. "Discourse level language functions: Complaining." In J. Staton, R. Shuy, J. Peyton, & L. Reed, Eds., *Dialogue journal communication: Classroom, linguistic, social and cognitive views.* Norwood, NJ: Ablex.

Staton, J. 1988. "Dialogue journals in the classroom context." In J. Staton, R. Shuy, J. Peyton, & L. Reed, Eds., *Dialogue journal communication: Classroom, linguistic, social and cognitive views.* Norwood, NJ: Ablex.

Staton, J., R. Shuy, J. Peyton, & L. Reed, Eds. 1988. *Dialogue journal communication: Classroom, linguistic, social and cognitive views.* Norwood, NJ: Ablex.

Stein, S. 1963. *Mathematics, the man-made universe: An introduction to the spirit of mathematics.* San Francisco: W. H. Freeman.

Thompson, A. 1985. "Teachers' conceptions of mathematics and the teaching of problem solving." In E. Silver, Ed., *Teaching and learning mathematical problem solving: Multiple research perspectives.* Hillsdale, NJ: Lawrence Erlbaum.

Vygotsky, L. 1978. *Mind in society: The development of higher psychological processes.* Cambridge, MA: Harvard University Press.

———. 1962. *Thought and language.* E. Hanfmann & G. Vakar, Eds. Cambridge, MA: MIT Press, 1962.

Wahl, M. 1988. *A mathematical mystery tour: Higher thinking math tasks.* Tucson: Zephyr Press, 1988.

Walter, M. 1971. *Boxes, squares and other things: A teacher's guide for a unit in informal geometry.* Washington, DC: National Council of Teachers of Mathematics.

Wertsch, J. 1985. "Introduction." In J. Wertsch, Ed., *Culture, communication and cognition: Vygotskian perspectives.* Cambridge: Cambridge University Press.

Wood, D., J. Bruner, & G. Ross. 1978. "The role of tutoring in problem solving." *International Journal of Behavioral Development,* 2, pp. 131–147.

White, S. 1989. "Foreword." In D. Newman, P. Griffin, & Michael Cole. *The construction zone: Working for cognitive change in school.* Cambridge: Cambridge University Press.

Part III

Functional systems

The challenge of adult literacy acquisition and the mastery of specialized forms of writing have become of special interest to educators and psychologists within the past three decades. A variety of approaches govern their efforts. Some educators emphasize traditional methods, including drills (see Kazamek's discussion, 1988), paying little attention to the specific cognitive and emotional needs of adult students. A more powerful approach was developed by Moffett (1981), who emphasizes the expressive aspects of writing, and considers formal features, such as spelling and punctuation of secondary importance. The approaches of particular relevance to the chapters presented in this volume are those in which functions of literacy are examined as practiced and taught in different societies. As Heath (1980, p. 126) writes: "Literacy acquisition is often a function of society-specific tasks, which are sometimes far removed from those of formal schooling, and are not conceived of as resulting from effort expended by 'teachers' and 'learners.' "

Scholars who approach literacy as a societal process of which the individual learner is a part rather than its sole focus bring an interdisciplinary point of view to its analysis. The functions, contexts of use, as well as the historical conditions in which writing has developed in a particular community, provide researchers such as Scribner and Cole (1981) part of the framework for the study of literacy in nonschool settings. The social view of literacy put forth by Paolo Freire (1970) has had a substantial impact upon the teaching of literacy. His influence is due, in part, to his philosophy in which he stresses the necessity of students and learners to constitute a community, and then to examine together the functions of literacy within their own, historically shaped circumstances. Juan Daniel Ramirez's paper in this section presents such an approach: he emphasizes the daily life of his adult students, addresses issues and problems where writing is relevant to their actual concerns, and views the uses of literacy in a sociocultural context. In comparing Ramirez's paper on adult learners in Spain to that of Francine Filipek

Collignon with Hmong immigrants (both in this section), an interesting difference in gender attitudes toward learning surfaces. Whereas the men of southern Spain are absent from beginning literacy classes, due, Ramirez speculates, to a possible fear of being seen as limited by the women and the community, Hmong students include both men and women in classes at all levels of proficiency. The Hmong women's attitude toward themselves as learners is quite striking; studying alongside men intimidates them. Uprooted from their agricultural communities, both men and women recognize the critical importance of literacy in their new, industrialized countries. But the women see themselves as limited in their skills to working solely with their hands whereas they see men as learning "with their heads."

Examining the cultural sources of language use and knowledge acquisition in the lives of adult learners is seen as a necessity by the three contributors to this section. In Michele Minnis's analysis of legal writing, she focuses on the role of class and ethnicity as powerful influences in the ways in which students approach the task of acquiring the highly specialized forms of legal literacy. Minnis suggests that for many law students and professors, childhood experiences, such as heated debates at the family table, are part of their early socialization leading to success. These students, drawn from the majority culture, are prepared for the argumentative forms of legal reasoning. They and their professors have a difficult time recognizing that different styles of interaction and values govern the childhood experiences of their peers drawn from minority communities. To the latter, deference and cooperativeness across generations are a primary mode of interaction with which they approach their law school experiences. The acquisition of new, domain-specific values and skills – whether in law school or in urban factory settings – confronts the subjects of the chapters to follow. The writers rely upon interactionist theory to clarify some of the issues raised by their work as literacy teachers and they suggest new pedagogical approaches in the joint construction of their students' emerging spoken and written discourses.

A central notion in their use of a sociocultural theoretical framework is that of "functional systems." The value of this concept is particularly noticeable in the analysis of cognitive stability and change: in the realization that for adults who are entering unknown cultural settings, not all of their approaches to learning will be new. Some aspects of their perceptual, cognitive, and interpersonal processes remain stable, while others are undergoing, in the course of cultural and intellectual adaptation, important shifts, additions, and transformations. Thus, adult learners, while engaged in new and demanding tasks, combine rapid change with familiar approaches, constructing new functional systems. Newman, Griffin, and Cole (1989) have suggested that adapting Luria's use of functional systems – which were of particular use to him in his analyses of brain injury – provides an excellent framework for the study of cognitive change and representation. Their use of this notion includes *cognitive* and *interpersonal* variables, both of which are central to the study of literacy development. In the following quotation they describe their view of some aspects of the "interpersonally constituted functional systems" with a particular relevance to the representation of cognitive mastery:

> The theoretical position we are proposing focuses on the changes within the functional system and the variable cognitive and interpersonal mechanisms that play a part in the system. . . .
>
> In the standard framework [of cognitive science] external devices, like talk and charts and writing, bear an opaque and perhaps uninteresting relationship to internal structures. In our mediational framework they are windows in the evolution and appearance of cognitive constructs. They are an essential part of the functional system that gives the actors as well as the analysts access to changes that are occurring. . . .
>
> In the standard framework representations are static; communicative comprehension requires an equivalence of representations. In our historical framework, representations are dynamic and communication proceeds with a series of "as if" relations where partial constructs are appropriated and revised. (1989, pp. 72–73)

In discussing the early stages of reading acquisition, Ramirez gives many examples of the appropriation of partial constructs as learners struggle with the phonetic and semantic aspects of texts. Collignon suggests that writing tools are appropriated by Hmong learners as connected to their sewing implements – in both instances their use of tools is linked to their needs to give shape to their experiences.

In our own research with Pueblo children (John-Steiner & Osterreich, 1975), we found the concept of functional systems very valuable. Researchers usually describe Native-American children as shaped by their visually potent environment: Alfonso Ortiz (1969) gives many examples of a "people's picture of the way things are." Evidence that Indian children excel in imaginal and spatial skills has been collected for over 50 years (Bland, 1970, 1974; Dennis, 1942). Children score high on certain visual tests and are less proficient on tasks measuring verbal proficiency. In light of these findings, a visual–verbal polarity is frequently used in describing how Native-American children learn. But such a simplification leads to poor research and poor theory. As our study evolved, so did our thinking about Pueblo children. Rather than using a simple polarity in learning styles, we explored the way in which children integrated various styles and strategies of learning. In relying upon the notion of functional systems, as discussed by Cole and Scribner (1974) in their cross-cultural research, we were able to document how children linked newly acquired symbol systems with previously developed, culturally patterned cognitive processes. We confirmed some of Luria's (1979) observations, namely, that

> complex, conscious activities are initially carried out in an expanded way. In its early stages, complex thinking requires a number of external aids for its performance. Not until later in the life of the child or in the course of mastering a particular form of activity does thinking become condensed and converted into an automatic skill. (p. 126)

The process of condensation described by Luria is not limited to children. The beginning literacy efforts of adults, as described by Ramirez, show many repetitions and a pulling apart of words. Slowly, novice readers start hearing their own words and, with the help of their teachers, link form and meaning.

One of the most interesting features of "functional systems" is the notion of "variable mechanisms," namely, that a particular task can be performed by variable means. Newman et al. (1989, p. 72) suggest: "In our functional systems, there may be variable representations corresponding to the variable mechanisms that can still get the task done." In the mastery of literacy and of specialized forms of writing, this feature – a reliance upon variable means – provides a significant tool for analyzing the role of culture in acquisition. As Collignon explains, Hmong women prefer those methods of literacy acquisition that are based on their earlier learning of sewing. There are hundreds of patterns in the Hmong "paj ntaub"; these are acquired slowly during childhood while the novice is observing, copying, correcting. Adult Hmong women like to use copying and dictation as part of their literacy learning, incorporating into their functional systems new content and symbols, but also maintaining some continuity in their approaches to challenging tasks.

In Ramirez's and Minnis's work, similar notions are apparent. These authors rely upon sociocultural theory to assist them in examining the particular challenges faced by adult learners. They recognize that culturally embedded forms of learning require a lengthy process of mastery as well as reorganization of existing functional systems. In helping students interpret texts, teachers in Ramirez's literacy programs rely upon colloquial expressions as well as terms derived from the instructional material expressed in more formal language. He writes of their reliance on various genres and discourses, which are first separate in the students' repertoires, but which become, with the teacher's help, linked into new functional systems of comprehension and representation. There is also an interesting parallel between Ramirez's work on literacy and Wilcox's study (in this volume) of signed language. Both authors show how novice learners use private speech in guiding their activities when faced with new problems or challenges. The adult speaker acquiring literacy needs to process written speech at several levels of organization. Luria (1982, p. 166) describes this process as follows: "Written speech involves several processes at the phonemic level, such as the search for individual sounds and their contrasts, the coding of individual sounds into letters, and the combination of individual sounds and letters into complete words." When words are read slowly, the linking of the externally produced forms are matched with difficulty to their internal representation. In the course of the matching process, the novice asks herself questions, guiding her process with the aid of private speech.

Teachers of adult learners are faced with a difficult task; their assistance, while greatly needed, cannot be based on interactional patterns and learning materials used with children. Instead, literacy workers have to understand the culture, the motivation, and the interests of adult learners. Ramirez and Collignon have developed methods, based in part on Paolo Freire's contributions, which take these concerns into consideration.

The challenge of acquiring legal discourse is a difficult one for all students. It is particularly demanding for minority law students, who are expected to fit into a traditional, competitive, and highly structured educational environment. Failing to adopt these values, and the legal discourses that govern classroom interactions, minority students are frequently seen as incapable of acquiring "lawyerly thinking." Minnis analyzes the cognitive and linguistic skills needed, *but not taught,* for the successful completion of law assignments. By showing what these skills consist of, she provides a model for an alternative approach to current legal education, one in which students are consciously and supportively socialized into their future profession. Such a model contrasts with the present situation, where students experience their classes "as contest(s) between opponents."

The students who are successful in combining their traditional socialization with the strategies needed for survival in law school develop new functional systems. These functional systems are constructed with the aid of individuals who are aware of the students' need to build cultural, cognitive, and attitudinal bridges between the students and their new environment. They rely upon the learner's zone of proximal development. While the first use of the concept of "functional systems" by Anokhin and Luria (see Luria, 1979, p. 124) emphasized new, physiological connections in the brain, in more recent uses of this notion, the interpersonal and cognitive aspects of human dynamic systems have been stressed. This current usage is well documented in the chapters that follow.

REFERENCES

Bland, L. 1970. *Perception and visual memory of school age Eskimos and Athabascan Indians in Alaskan villages.* Monograph No. 1, Human Environmental Resources Systems, Anchorage, AK.

Bland, L. 1974. Visual perception and recall of school age Navajo, Hopi, Jicarilla Apache and Caucasian children of the Southwest. Unpublished doctoral dissertation, University of New Mexico, Albuquerque.

Cole, M., & S. Scribner 1974. *Culture and thought: A psychological introduction.* New York: Wiley.

Dennis, W. 1942. The performance of Hopi children on the Goodenough Draw-a-man test. *Journal of Comparative Psychology* 34(3).

Freire, P. 1970. *Pedagogy of the oppressed.* New York; Continuum.

Heath, S. B. 1980. The functions and uses of literacy. *Journal of Communication* 29(2): 123–133.

John-Steiner, V., & H. Osterreich. 1975. Learning styles in Pueblo Children. Final report, National Institute of Education, Albuquerque, NM.

Kazamek, F. 1988. Necessary changes: Professional involvement in adult literacy programs. *Harvard Educational Review* 58(4): 464–487.

Luria, A. 1979. *The making of mind.* Cambridge, MA: Harvard University Press.

Luria, A. 1982. *Language and cognition.* New York: Wiley.

Moffett, J. 1981. *Active voice: A writing program across the curriculum.* Montclair, NJ: Boynton/Cook.

Newman, D., P. Griffin, & M. Cole. 1989. *The construction zone: Working for cognitive change in schools.* Cambridge: Cambridge University Press.

Ortiz, A. 1969. The study of the education of Indian children. *Senate Hearings before the Special Subcommittee on Labor and Public Welfare,* Part I. Washington, DC: U.S. Government Printing Office.

Scribner, S., & M. Cole. 1981. *The psychology of literacy.* Cambridge, MA: Harvard University Press.

11 *Adults learning literacy: The role of private speech in reading comprehension*

JUAN DANIEL RAMIREZ

11.1 INTRODUCTION

Despite international efforts and educational investments by many second and third world countries, illiteracy continues to be a serious problem in the economic and cultural development of poor countries and for specific groups of the population of many other countries. Illiteracy represents an endemic situation that demands not only a decided intervention on the part of responsible politicians, but also a joint effort of the social sciences in order to discover its causes and to devise the programs most needed for its solution. In relationship to this problem, we have been able to observe the increasing interest the study of literacy has awakened in the different areas of social science and education in the last few years. Many articles and books have appeared on this subject, opening up a hopeful panorama (see Langer, 1987; Saljo, 1988). Almost all the published material has as its theme of investigation the learning of literacy in children or the learning of new forms of literacy (e.g., computer literacy). However, on only a few occasions has the study of the learning and the use of literacy in adults been approached. By taking on the study of adult learning in existing adult education programs, we can further comprehend why illiteracy continues to reproduce itself. Also, understanding the processes of learning through the uses of reading and writing can cast a new light on the ways that one internalizes a semiotic instrument and its influence on higher mental functions. Knowledge such as this may foster the development of new adult education programs and the training of teachers working in this difficult field of education.

In this study, I propose to analyze some of the daily work undertaken by a group of female students and their teacher in a school for adults in southern Spain (Andalusia). The adult education program that serves as this school and another center was developed by the government of this region. In 1987, this program received an award by UNESCO for its contribution toward adult education. Inspired by the ideas and methodology of Paulo Freire, it tries to adapt to the "interest and motivation of the adult." A special priority is given to the process of dialogue between the educator and the learner as a means of selecting the subjects and generating words that may serve as topics in the learning process (*Curricular Design of the Education of Adults,* 1986–1987, p. 30). A main characteristic of this program is its emphasis on an active and participatory education that is rooted in daily reality. This discussion will explore the predominant educational practices in the center for adults to evaluate their results and to improve their methodology.

The dialogic character of this program rests on several theoretical constructs: literacy as an instrument to attain new forms of dialogue; the relationship between private speech and dialogue; and the role of private speech in the process of reading comprehension. The Vygotskian hypotheses on the social origin of speech *for oneself* and its functions and, in general, Vygotsky's theories as a whole are, in my opinion, useful instruments to furnish a study of these characteristics. In addition to the focus furnished by Vygotsky, one needs to incorporate another complementary focus that permits a closer relationship of literacy with private speech. This is only possible through a perspective that allows for the dialogic origin of both processes. The dialogic perspective of Mikhail M. Bakhtin satisfies this need. During the last few years, the social sciences have discovered the contributions of this Soviet philosopher, a contemporary of Vygotsky, of whom little was known in the Western world. Authors coming from different sciences have drawn a picture concerning his fundamental ideas that leads us to think the interest in his work will increase considerably in the coming years (Clark & Holquist, 1984; Rommetveit, 1988; Wertsch, 1985a, 1985b, 1991). In my judgment, his ideas on inner speech, dialogue, voices, social languages and genres, and the process of comprehension, aside from being powerful instruments used to analyze the learning of literacy, present the enormous advantage of greatly complementing Vygotsky's theories. The parallelism between the two theorists allows us to elaborate a methodology of analysis devoid of eclecticism and gives us a global image of learning to read that ranges from the simplest processes to the most complex ones.

11.2. THE SCENE, THE ACTORS, AND THE SCRIPT: CHARACTERISTICS OF THE STUDENT GROUP AND ITS SCHOOL ACTIVITIES

The center for adult education that is the focus of these observations is located in Valencina, a small village of Seville, southwest Spain.

Most employment is on small agricultural farms, in seasonal agricultural jobs in large *haciendas,* and in public services (e.g., waiters) in the provincial capital located 10 kilometers away, also named Seville. Despite their closeness, contact between Valencina and the big city has been rather limited for many years. The reasons for this isolation seem to stem from the geographical location of the village, which is found on a high-altitude plain in relation to the valley where the capital is situated. For this reason, and others, of a political nature difficult to justify, communication by road was deficient and public transportation was almost nonexistent and of very poor quality. Conditions have noticeably improved over the past 10 years, although many of the social, cultural, and economic characteristics of the rural Mediterranean world still prevail.

The only center for adult education that exists in Valencina educates students between the ages of 22 and 65. There are three educational levels in the program. The lower level includes people who are categorized as total or functional illiterates. The upper level attends to people who could not finish secondary school, while the intermediate level includes those students who abandoned school in the beginning of their secondary education. The students from the upper level must pass a final examination of the academic year, which will grant them the *graduado escolar,* according to the educational laws in this country (the equivalent of an American junior high school degree). Students of the intermediate level need to spend a minimum of at least 2 years in the center for adults, the first of which serves as preparation for later access to the third and last level of the adult education program. Similar characteristics exist between these two levels. They are the continuation of the educational process that, for some reason or another, got cut off at some point during the final phases. The most noticeable differences are found between these two levels and the lower level. The level of teaching people to read and write is almost exclusively oriented to initial literacy learning. Since this lowest level is the one that has served as the basis of the observations of my study, I will describe it in detail.

The lowest group is made up of six women between 40 and 65 years old. The majority has had some schooling experience, which in no case went much further than a couple of years in the classroom. The years that elapsed between the time the women left school and the time this study was made have erased all signs of what school means. For the majority of this group, this is the second year in the adult education program. All of them express their desire to continue until they reach the school level that meets their expectations. However, none of them shows any interest in continuing the schooling process up to the last level of the program. Their wish is to master the literacy skills for practical uses – for example, to read signs and advertisements in the shops, to read and write letters to friends and relatives, to understand bills and receipts, to do simple mathematical operations for better control of their domestic economy. The only woman who said she had never attended school was, at age 65, at first happy just to learn how to write and sign her own name. But, as the year progressed and she was able to control the rudiments of literacy, her aspirations grew. Throughout the entire year, she demonstrated an enormous discipline in her work and showed such enthusiasm that she won the admiration of her fellow classmates.

Attendance was very irregular. Four, including the student just mentioned, attended class daily. The other two students tended to miss class frequently due to their business responsibilities, although they maintained the expressed desire to continue attending class so as to maintain the skills they had learned. The average mean attendance was around three days a week.

In this center, as well as in others that we are still observing, it is extremely rare to find males in class. There are various hypotheses concerning this phenomena: perhaps there is a certain machismo that prevents their display of educational limitations in front of these women; perhaps there is a fear of losing their prestige in front of the community; perhaps it is just that they have too much work. Whatever the cause may be, we can verify an almost total absence of men in the lower level (learning to read and write). In the upper level, however, male presence is quite frequent, which invites us to think that the hypothesis that refers to personal prestige of the subjects should be explored in the future. Adult education for those in its lower levels is a useful instrument for sociocultural change for those of low socioeconomic levels.

In addition to describing the actors, it is also necessary to describe the classroom experience. The center begins its activity every afternoon at four o'clock. In the meantime, the reading and writing group students arrive one by one as soon as their schedules permit. Each one begins to work on individual exercises, which I will describe later in further detail. The teacher attends to the questions individually, making suggestions or explaining new exercises. Once the group is assembled, the teacher initiates collective tasks, such as learning some new words. Later, the students begin to talk about their experiences and problems of everyday life, which can encompass a variety of subjects: community concerns (urban problems, unemployment, the organization of festivities for a local holiday), concrete experiences concerning one of the women, or talk about recipes, which they seem to exchange frequently. While these conversations last, the teacher takes notes of the many subjects they speak about, and frequently prepares a simple text, using one or more of the topics of discussion. This text later serves for dictation or other similar exercises. On one occasion, one of the students, whose small son had learning disabilities, commented on her preoccupation with her child's problems in school. All her classmates agreed to help her write a letter to the principal of the school with the object of asking for special help for her son. They all contributed ideas, and the teacher, with their help, made up the final draft of the letter. After making some changes, the group accepted the letter, which was used later for a dictation exercise.

The schooling tasks that are going to be analyzed involve reading and copying words. This activity consists of reading simple sentences individually, reading texts guided by the teacher and completing sentences, with a predominance of the reading process over the written. In the first task, each student tries to read simple texts, made up mostly of short sentences, without any help from the teacher. In this type of exercise the teacher's role is reduced to detecting and correcting the errors made, after asking the students to read their final versions out loud. In guided reading a more difficult text is read out loud and in the teacher's presence. Her conduct consists of pointing out each of the words that the student is reading, correcting the syllabic mistakes, and asking for an explanation of the meaning of each part of the text read. Sentence completion, contrary to the other two tasks, incorporates the use of writing. The student has to complete the last part of a series of incomplete sentences (e.g., "In Andalusia there is a lot of . . ."; "Valencina is a . . ."). After reading each sentence, students select from several written words on another part of the paper the word that fits the empty space (e.g., "unemployment"; "village").

11.3. SELF-REGULATION OF THE READING PROCESS

Vygotsky's studies on the social origin of inner speech were developed from the study of childhood language. The object was to show the functional role that inner speech as well as its genetic ancestor, private speech, plays in the self-regulation of actions. There is no doubt of the importance of private speech or *speech for oneself* in problem solving situations, as a wide number of investigations have already demonstrated (Frauenglass & Diaz, 1985; Berk & Garvin, 1984; Goudena, 1983, 1987; Kohlberg, Yaeger, & Hjerholm, 1968). Likewise, the social and dialogic origin of the self-regulation process has been amply developed by Wertsch and his colleagues (Wertsch, 1979, 1980; Wertsch et al., 1980; Wertsch & Stone, 1985). However, the study of this kind of speech activity has been limited to the field of childhood investigation and to the classic treatment of problem solving (such as puzzles, classifying tasks, story tasks). By incorporating the Vygotskian hypotheses in the learning of literacy, a double objective appears: on the one hand, to demonstrate that these hypotheses are equally valid in studying the self-regulation processes in the actions of an adult and, on the other hand, to demonstrate that certain tasks, such as reading or writing in the initial learning phase, pose "problems" in the better sense of the word, and therefore need to be verbally regulated.

11.3.1. Private speech and the articulating mechanism of reading

A question came to mind from the very first moment I began observing the students as they read: what role did private speech play in the process of articulation of the written word? We can say that its role in the learning phase of literacy is fundamental. Two of the three women studied presented between them qualitative differences in mastering reading, which could be verified just by testing the articulating differences. The students, whom I shall call **Pq** and **A,** in contrast to student **M,** could read or do certain exercises by themselves, consulting the teacher only about words they could not understand or parts of the task they could not comprehend. A difference in the intensity of the voice was observed between the two, which could correspond to a certain difference in reading comprehension. While **Pq** emitted whispers that at certain moments reached sufficient intensity so as to be recognized as the word being pronounced, **A** did her reading in silence and on a number of occasions uttered certain whispers with a lesser intensity. One could just barely recognize a slight movement of her lips indicative of the internal activity. What can we attribute this activity to? In my judgment, the answer is in the framework of the Vygotskian theory on speech *for oneself.* As we can see in the case of **Pq,** and to a lesser degree in that of **A,** private speech can be coded as such when there is articulation or sounding out of the syllables that compose a word. The reading act is also a motor act, above all in subjects with minimal reading ability. Such activity is illustrated by episode I performed by **M,** a student who shows lesser skills than her two fellow classmates. Her reading was always guided by the teacher. In a given moment of the reading the following sequence occurred between **M** and the teacher, learning the word *maestro* (teacher).

Episode I

1. M: ma-es-tro
   (tea-cher)
2. M: maestro
   (teacher)
   (She repeats the word right through.)
3. T: Leelo otra vez.
   (Let's read it again one more time.)

4. M: El ma-es-tro
   (the tea-cher)
   (The word is read faster than the last time.)

This episode shows that **M**'s reading capacity allows for only the pronunciation of each particular syllable. However, we find a sequence of utterances (1 and 2) that frequently presents itself when the reading is guided by the teacher. In comment 1 the reading is done syllable by syllable. **M** reads each syllable with difficulties normal for her limited reading ability. In comment 2 she repeats the word to herself, without looking up at the teacher, as if she were trying to find the significance. From my point of view, private speech acts in this and other similar situations in two ways: by identifying each syllable one by one by means of its corresponding articulation, and by articulating the word as a unit. In the beginning of the first phase, the word is nothing more than a graphic unit separated by small spaces between other units; in the second phase, the repetition of the word transforms the graphic unit into another unit of sound and significance. While at first we observed a subject centered in the operative plane of reading, the next moment the word was transformed into a sign whose sound is oriented toward the interior of the individual searching for the meaning of what he or she read. The combined action of emissions 1 and 2 shows that the second reading of the word was done much faster in 4. Using the language of the theories of information processing, we can say that while in comments 1 and 2 we observed a process whose direction is bottom-up, in 4 we see the combined effects of the bottom-up and top-down processes.

11.3.2. The control of reading sentences

Private speech may function not only in the double process of the syllable articulation of the word and in the recognition of the same (repetition in 2), but may be involved in other aspects of the self-regulation of the actions in this case. Someone like **M,** who has not yet achieved adequate reading ability to read a written text smoothly, has to make a greater effort to control all the mechanisms of the reading process. As shown in episode II, **M** introduces a series of comments with lower intensity than the reading intonation. These seem to indicate a certain conscious effort based on the difficulties that the written text presents. This text is taken from a school newspaper assembled by students from another adult education center. The author is a housewife who describes what her housework consists of during a normal weekday. The text goes like this:

Y luego dicen que no trabajo. Me levanto temprano, preparo el desayuno, llevo a los ninos al colegio, voy a comprar, limpio la casa, y preparo la comida. Pongo la mesa, como de pie mientras les sirvo la comida. Siempre voy con prisa. Solo hay un momento del dia en el que estoy tranquila: las horas que estoy en la escuela.

(And then they say I don't work. I get up early, fix breakfast, take the children to school, do the shopping, clean the house, and fix lunch. I set the table, and while I serve them lunch I eat standing up. I'm always in a hurry. There is only one time during the day when I can relax; the hours I spend at center.)

Episode II

1. M: Y un, *esperate, no? xxx esto que es?*
(And the, *wait a minute, okay? xxx what's this?*)
2. T: Y, y, y
(And, and, and)
3. M: su
(the)
4. T: lu
(then)
5. M: lu-e-go pi en le ti . . . *esperate* di ce=
(then the ss-ay . . . *wait* they sa-)
6. T: cen
(say)
7. M: cen que no tra-b:a-jo
(say I do-n't wo-rk)
8. T: Y luego dicen que no trabajo
(And then they say I don't work)
9. M: que no trabajo
(I don't work)
10. T: Vamos a ver!
(Let's see!)
11. M: me que de *xxx* me le-van-to te . . . tren . . . tem-pra-no pa *ay! no, esperate* pre-pa-ro el de-sa-yu-no el li=
(I that of *xxx* I ge-t up er eaqr ear-ly fe *not that. wait* fix break-fast te)
12. T: lle
(ta)
13. M: lle-vo lo ni-no a la es-cu:e-la vo-y a com-prar vi *a no, esta es la* lim-pi-o la ca-sa pre-pa-ro la co-mi-da. *Esto no hace falta ni leerlo.* (se rie)
(ta-ke the chil-dren to sch-ool, do the shop-ping slea *no, this is a c* clean the hou-se, fix lun-ch. *I don't need to read this.* (She laughs to herself.)

In this episode we can observe the difficulties that are contained in reading this simple text. The reading of the first sentence, "And then they say I don't work," is executed with such difficulty that **M** considerably lowers the volume of her voice to the point that utterances become simple whispers and are impossible to transcribe. Some of these utterances reflect difficulties of reading. We can observe quite frequently that an imperative expression is present, *esperate* (wait)- (1, 5, and 11), and less frequently the question "Esto que es?" (What is this?). These utterances oriented to a private plane can be considered from the following options: (1) as expressions or externalizations of inner speech that are necessary in order to recognize the mistake and find the correct syllable, or (2) as manifestations that are functionally very similar to the utterances of egocentric speech in children, which are at the same time speech *for other* (teacher) and speech *for oneself.* In terms of the first option, it is unquestionably the case that in expressions such as "wait," the subject recognizes the lack of a connection existing between the erroneously articulated syllable and any other known word included in the group of words of the sentence she read. The second interpretation is also possible in terms of the mutual understanding between the teacher and the student, who in that precise moment are readers of the same text, as they are paying attention to the same words and sentences. The close participation in this context breaks the limits between social speech and private speech that may exist in other forms of communication.

11.3.3. A problem-solving task

As we have been able to see up to now, the externalization of inner speech demonstrates the problematic nature that reading represents for an unskilled reader. The learning of literacy offers multiple occasions in which the teacher creates problem-solving situations by using the text as a puzzle in which certain words or sentences act as pieces that complement a whole global unit. A typical relationship of part-to-whole is established between two parts that characterize *the good form* as was described by Gestalt psychology. One of the tasks that describes these types of situations very well consists of presenting on a piece of paper a group of incomplete sentences (cues) and an equivalent number of words that allow for their completion (target). The following sentence and the words or nominal phrases that complete them represent examples of this type of exercise:

a) *El rio Guadalquivir desemboca en . . .*
   Sanlucar de Barrameda[1]
   (The mouth of the Guadalquivir River is at . . .
   Sanlucar de Barrameda.)

b) *En Andalucia hay mucho . . .*
   paro
   (In Andalusia there is a lot of . . .
   unemployment.)

Obviously, an exercise of this type presents more difficulties than the simple reading of a sentence. The word or nominal phrase that completes the sentence (target) should be looked for among a large group of words. Episode III reflects the difficulties that this task contains and also how private speech is manifested in the presence of such an exercise. The task was attempted by the student **Pq,** who has better reading and writing skills than **M,** whom I dealt with in previous episodes.

Pq is working on the completion of a series of sentences. After the initial instructions given by the teacher and the completion of a couple of examples by **Pq** with the help of the teacher to demonstrate the characteristics of the exercise, **Pq** begins to work on her own. During most of the time that **Pq** works on the tasks, she is reading by whispering. It is not possible to understand what she says, but it seems likely that these whispers refer to the words she is reading. At a given moment, she asks the teacher to help her with an example she does not understand. In this episode, **Pq** asks for the teacher's help after discovering difficulties that keep her from continuing.

Episode III

1. **Pq:** El ri-o Guadalquivir de . . . de Sanlucar, no? no, no, no.
(The mou-th of the Guadalquivir River in Sanlucar, no? no, no, no.)
2. **T:** Antes lo has hecho bien.
(You did it very well before.)
3. **Pq:** Y ahora no me sale. Veras!
(And now it won't come out. Let's see.)
El ri-o Guadalquivir de . . . desemboca
(The mou-th of the Guadalquivir River)
4. **Pq:** (escribe) desemboca en en San – Bueno, Y adonde pongo lo demas que no me cabe? (Se queja de que no tiene suficiente espacio en el papel para escribir "Sanlucar de Barremeda.")
(She writes) . . . is at San – Now, where do I put the rest? It won't all fit. (She complains that she doesn't have enough room on the paper to write "Sanlucar de Barremeda.")
5. **Pq:** (Despues de borrar empieza a escribir de nuevo.) El rio Guadalquivir desemboca en . . . Sanlucar (comienza a escribir tras haber leido la frase a completar) San . . . San
(After erasing she begins to write again.) The mouth of the Guadalquivir River is at . . . Sanlucar. (She begins to write after having read the sentence that needs to be completed.) San . . . San)
6. **T:** Sanlucar
7. **Pq:** lu . . . Sanlucar
8. **T:** (Empieza a hablar con otra professora y no va a atender a Pq durante un buen rato.)
(Begins to talk to another teacher and doesn't pay any attention to Pq for quite some time.)

9. **Pq:** (Baja intensidad de voz) lucar de . . . Ba ba rra me da. (Eleva la voz) **Sanlucar de Barremeda.** Ahora.
(In a low tone of voice) lujcar de . . . Ba ba rra me da. (She raises her voice) **Sanlucar de Barremeda.**
10. **Pq:** (Vuelve a bajar el tono de voz mientras lee la siguiente frase.) Muchos andaluces . . . En Andalucia . . . (Lee de corrido una vez leida.) en Andalucia ha . . . hay mucho **paro.** (Eleva ostentosamente el volumen de voz solo para la palabra final.)
(She lowers her voice again while she reads the following sentence.) A lot of Andalusians . . . In Andalusia . . . (She reads quickly once she has read it to herself.) in Andalusia the . . . there is a lot of **unemployment** (She raises her voice ostentatiously just at the last word.)

The most interesting comment to make about this episode is the modulation of voice that marks the different states in the resolution of the tasks. Earlier, **Pq** had read and written in such a quiet tone of voice that only the simplest whispers could be registered. From the moment she claimed the teacher's attention, however, the volume of her voice increased and one could clearly understand the rest of her utterances. It is important to point out two aspects of **Pq**'s utterances from the moment (8) the teacher addresses another person and she must continue on her own: the first is the low tone of voice used to emit each syllable she is writing (e.g., Sanlucar); the second, in clear contrast to the latter, the elevated tone of voice – indicated in boldface – that marks the end of the written word (Sanlucar) or the discovery of the word that completes the new sentence (unemployment). When working on copying texts, all of the students appeared to follow the same pattern: in the first place one reads the word; then one repeats each of the syllables while writing them down, with the motor act of writing coinciding with the articulatory verbal act. **Pq** writes and articulates each syllable of the nominal phrases that constitutes the target (e.g., Sanlucar de Barremeda) until the words have been written down. Once the copying is completed, she speaks the completed words in a louder voice, marking the end of the task. This same process is repeated in the completion of the next sentence (In Andalusia there is a lot of . . . unemployment). Once again, her voice increases when she discovers the word that solves the problem.

Despite the similarities between the two sentences (low intensity in the reading and elevation in the last part), it is necessary to state a certain difference between them. In the first case, the task is solved with the teacher's intervention. In the second one the elevation of the tone of voice accompanies her discovery of the word. The relationship between the cue and the target in this last example is explained by the relation that exists between the given information and the new information within the sentence. The penetrating analysis by Wertsch (1979, 1985b) concerning the predicativity of inner speech in Vygotsky's theory, employing the categories developed by Chafe (1982) (given-new) is very useful to explain this type of action. The incomplete phrase, a combination of the grammatical subject of the sentence and the verb, represents the given information, while the target is part of the predicate that the student must discover. The incomplete phrase is expressed using a low tone of voice (attenuation), whereas the discovery of the target, the new information, receives the maximum intonation.

If in other different learning situations of literacy we find moments where reading is similar to a typical situation of problem solving under laboratory conditions, here the similarity is complete, considering the manner in which the task has been assigned. The subject has to explore cognitively all the elements of the problem and express the sign or signs that make the resolution possible.

11.4. THE ROLE OF PRIVATE SPEECH IN THE READING COMPREHENSION PROCESS

One of the biggest challenges in the teaching of literacy, especially in adult education, is the problem of achieving good reading comprehension from the beginning of the learning process. It is easy for an adult to lose interest if he or she encounters obstacles that are too difficult to overcome. The motivation descends rapidly in adults, perhaps more so than in children, if they can't make any sense out of what they are trying to learn. When they acquire a new communicative instrument such as literacy, they find the sense in its usage. One should take into consideration these two closely related aspects with the idea in mind of reaching the maximum level of implication on the part of the student. On the one hand, it is necessary to maintain their interest in the new skills they are learning, as I have mentioned before; on the other hand, the student should understand the text as a new means of establishing communication and dialogue with others. A fundamental characteristic of written speech, which the reader must grasp from the beginning, is dialogism. Literacy is a new form of dialogue, which goes beyond the temporary boundaries of oral communication (Volosinov [Bakhtin], 1986). The dialogic character of the text represents a crucial point in order to explain the dynamic process of reading comprehension. It is in this last premise that one finds the key to scholastic activity, and therefore it is also where the most important part of my analysis will be directed. In Bakhtin's view, it is not possible to explain the process of comprehension (Volosinov [Bakhtin], 1986) if the mechanisms of inner speech are not known. As Bakhtin pointed out, "The understanding of a sign is, after all, an act of reference between the sign apprehended and other already known signs" (Volosinov [Bakhtin], 1987, p. 11). Only through the manipulation of these signs in the inner plane of thought, in their inner speech, can people establish a relationship between the written or the heard and idiosyncratic experiences.

Bakhtin, like Vygotsky and also Wittgenstein (1985), considered words and their significance to be inseparably related to the social intercourse from which they emerge. Words are an outlet of our inner experience that others can have access to. Using these suppositions, the Bakhtinian notion of consciousness is based on three crucial aspects: it is essentially semiotic; it is social in origin; and it is dialogic. This approach to consciousness allows us to observe that inner speech and social speech are as inextricably related in Bakhtin's theory as they are in Vygotsky's theory. This is what Volosinov [Bakhtin] has to say:

> The complex apparatus of verbal reactions functions in all its fundamental aspects also when the subject says nothing about his experiences but only undergoes them "in himself," since, if he is conscious of them, a process of *inner* (covert) speech occurs (we do, after all, think and feel and desire with the help of words; without inner speech we would not become conscious of anything in ourselves). This process of inner speech is just as material as is outward speech. (Volosinov [Bakhtin], 1987, p. 21)

Therefore, inner speech is a form of hidden activity that is as material in its semiotic structure as is social speech. People need the inner experiences of signs to communicate with others, but also these signs are necessary for the experiences to exist in the first place.

An inevitable question arises from this analysis: what relationship exists between the process of understanding and inner speech? The answer is quite clear for Bakhtin: to comprehend is a process that cannot exist outside of inner speech; understanding cannot be accomplished without the inner signs that speech *for oneself* emits and coordinates. Because of their social origin, these signs can be communicated. Even though Bakhtin did not sufficiently explain the distinction between inner and outer signs, it makes one think that the differences between the two are based on the type of significance the words acquire through their usage. In my judgment, there are not any great differences between Vygotsky and Bakhtin in this respect. When signs are used in an inner dialogue, they will be dominated by the sense. However, when the speaker directs himself to the listener or an audience, the signs are dominated by the significance. In both cases, inner speech is the fundamental instrument that gives us access to our experiences and the ability to communicate the experiences to others.

To understand is, above all, to be able to relate the object sign of our comprehension to a unit composed of inner signs. An utterance is understood when it generates some kind of response: when it can be paraphrased by the listener's inner speech or when, for example, it elicits an answer. This is, then, the inner face of the dialogue. While the more personal voice of the addresser (speaker or writer) can externalize the inner signs through utterances, the addressee can grasp them through the signs of inner speech. Everything that is inner may be externalized through dialogue; all kinds of semiotic material become internalized in the understanding process through inner speech. Following Bakhtin, we can say that some signs illuminate others. We are not in the presence of a mechanical transmission of information from an addresser to an addressee, but quite the contrary; we are in the presence of a dynamic process where for each utterance we grasp, we lay down a set of answering words of our own. "The greater their number and weight, the deeper and more substantial our understanding will be (Volosinov [Bakhtin], 1986, p. 102). Comprehension is the part of the dialogue that is performed by the addressee. What is said to us or what we read generates a new utterance, either internally or externally. We are faced with an activity that is characterized by the evaluative reception of the expression of another in the semiotic material of our inner speech. "After all," Volosinov [Bakhtin] wrote, "it is not a mute wordless creature that receives such an utterance, but a human being full of inner world" (Volosinov [Bakhtin], 1986, p. 118).

We can summarize the Bakhtinian notion by saying that active comprehension is performed using the following steps: (1) the addressee maintains a responsive attitude that is present in the plane of communication before the utterance of the addresser has been spoken; and (2) this attitude is followed by the evaluative reception of the emission once it has been spoken. Immediately afterward, the evaluation can be followed by one of these two alternatives: (a) the changing of the role of addressee to addresser and the resulting response, or (b) the producing of a new utterance that is a paraphrase, an answer, or a comment, but which does not surpass the boundaries of inner speech and remains internal. This process is part of the act of oral communication, which, in Bakhtin's judgment, is the kind of dialogue that originates all forms of communication. The basis of this explanation is situated in the interchange of roles between speaker and listeners, or its equivalent, in the alternating of the voices of the interlocutors. As Bakhtin has written, "The listener becomes the speaker" (Volosinov [Bakhtin], 1986, p. 68).

11.4.1. Comprehension of the written text

I have analyzed the relationship that exists between inner speech and the comprehension process, trying to emphasize its dialogic character. As the utterance performed in the observations could be heard, I find it is more adequate to use the term "private speech," as it has been used throughout this paper. It is important not to forget that this notion is composed of a group of speech events functioning in close relationship with the individual action (i.e., reading actions). For this reason, the Bakhtinian concept of inner speech is used more frequently in Western psychology.

I shall try to explain how the comprehension of a text is accomplished, keeping in mind that we have a written text before us, aimed at instructing goals, and with an inexperienced addressee-reader. For this reason, it may become necessary to ask for another person's assistance (the teacher's) in order to interpret the meaning of the text and to understand the voice[2] of its author. A study that approaches reading comprehension in a subject who is a late literacy learner should answer the following questions: what type of relationship should exist between the author's voice and the reader's inner speech, and what is the teacher's role in the reading comprehension process?

The referential plane of scholastic texts, predominant in elementary schools, prevails above the subjective aspects of the author's voice. Frequently, these texts are written to stimulate or initiate the child in the usage of social languages[3] where technical and scientific knowledge is expressed. Each and every one of these languages, be they physics or biology, history or sociology, have their own vocabulary and symbols (mathematics, chemistry, etc.), and they even have a peculiar narrative structure. Yet, they all have something in common – the search for objectivity that subordinates the subjectivity of the author. For this reason, the referential aspects of the text acquire an absolute importance that manifests, among other things, a precise and unambiguous vocabulary. Despite the fact that each area of scientific knowledge and each professional practice has developed its own social language, as Bakhtin has pointed out, all of them have something in common. They try to achieve the adequate transmission of their own knowledge, superimposing the referential aspects of information over the subjective aspects.

A question comes to mind when it is the adult instead of the child who initiates learning how to read: can this learning be based on the referential aspects of the text exclusively? The answer is negative. At the beginning of the review of the notion of comprehension and inner speech by Bakhtin, I briefly noted that the motivation for reading is inseparably related to the comprehension of written texts. I should like to add that the greater the identification between the voices of the author and the addressee, the deeper and more substantial the motivation. The cultural proximity between the two, the similarity of the problems of daily life that affects one or the other, and many other factors that complete the complex picture of daily existence are crucial elements that transform the text into an authentic dialogue for an adult literary learner.

The teacher's role is the other facet of the learning situation that should be analyzed in depth. We shouldn't forget that the reading of a text on the part of a student represents a type of social intercourse that goes beyond a dyadic relationship between the writer and the reader. It implies a triad formed by the writer, the reader, and the teacher that guides the latter. In the learning situation, the reading of the text is mediated by the teacher, who, in an interpsychological plane, regulates the reading process.

11.4.2. From the author's voice to the reader's private speech

A good example of identification between the writer and the reader can be found in episode II, in which we observed the action of private speech in the comprehension of the text. In turn 13, the reader makes an exclamation at the end, where we find the evaluative reception of the material read. Of the three students presented, **M** has the lowest level in reading ability. The text dealt with the daily chores of a housewife and how difficult her daily life is. After having spent much effort and after making many reading mistakes, **M**'s pronouncement in utterance 13 demonstrates that she has understood perfectly – "I don't need to read this!" How can we explain that this passage read with such difficulty could generate comprehension? The first aspect to take into consideration is the teacher's assistance in correcting **M**'s syllabic errors and, above all, the brief review that she makes, turn 8, serving as a base of knowledge for what will be read immediately afterward. It is very possible that the teacher's assistance wouldn't have made much difference if the text had referred to any other topic foreign to the reader's personal experiences. **M**'s last exclamation demonstrates a complete comprehension of the text and of the author's voice. A certain experience is transmitted through each written word that is paraphrased in her inner speech and is spontaneously externalized. Such an example suggests that the similarities between addresser and addressee exercise more influence in the understanding of the text than do the skills of the reader.

The responsive attitude that characterizes private speech when the author's voice and the reader's voice are joined together through the text can also be seen in episode IV. The student being observed in this case, **Pq,** reads a text written by a student from another adult education center called "La Illusion" (Dreams or Hopes). The author talks about the hopes she had to attend the center and to be able to learn how to read and write. The text is as follows:

Desde hace anos tenia ganas de apuntarme a la escuela para poder aprender a leer y escribir y no tener que firmar con el dedo. Lo que me hacia ilusion era poder yo misma leer las cartas que me llegaban y saber escribirlas. Ahora me hace ilucion todo: leer los carteles que hay por las calles, poner mi nombre; aunque todavia me pongo algo nerviosa cuando tengo que firmar delante de la gente.

(For years I have wanted to sign up at the center because I wanted to learn how to read and write and to write my signature without using an X. I dreamed of being able to read the letters I received all by myself and of knowing how to write them. Now everything I do is exciting; reading the posters you find on the streets and writing down my name, even though I get a little nervous when I have to sign my name in front of people.)

Episode IV contains reading as well as interaction between **Pq** and the teacher with regard to the first three sentences.

Episode IV

1. **Pq:** Desde hace anos tenemos gana . . . ganas de aportarme a la escuela.
(Se han cometido dos errores "tenemos" por "tenia" y "aportarme" por "apuntarme.")
(For years I has want . . . wanted to segn up at the center. (Two mistakes have been made: "has" for "have" and "segn" for "sign.")
2. **Pq:** *Hombre! Esto esta mejor.*
(*Hey! That's better.*)
3. **Pq:** para aprender a leer y escribir y no tener que firmar con el dedo.
(because I wanted to learn how to read and write and to write my signature without an X.)
4. **T:** Muy bien.
(Very good.)
5. **Pq:** los
6. **T:** esperate, cuentame lo que primero.
(wait, tell me what the first part is about.)
7. **Pq:** que *quiero* aprender a leer y a escribir para no firmar con el dedo. *Yo gracias a Dios . . . por lo menos eso . . .*
(I *want* to learn how to read and write so I won't have to sign with an X. *I thank God . . . for that much at least . . .*)
8. **T:** de acuerdo
(all right – continue reading)
9. **Pq:** lo que me hacia ilusion era po . . . poder yo misma le leer, no? las cartas que me lle . . . llegaban y saber escribirla.
(I dreamed of being able to re . . . read, right? the letters I re . . . received all by myself and of knowing how to write them.)
10. **T:** Por que tenias tu ilusion hija? Venga, cuentame.
(What did you dream about, dear? Come on, you can tell me.)
11. **Pq:** *pa poder mandar a la gente las cartas, que no escribo a nadie,* no? y pa mas o menos xxx xxx, no?

(*to be able to send letters to people, because I do not write to anybody,* right? and to more or less xxx xxx, right?

12. **Pq:** Ahora me hace ilusion todas.
(Now everything is excitin'.)
13. **T:** todos
(everything)
14. **Pq:** leo los
(I read the)
15. **T:** esperate
(wait)
16. **Pq:** leer los carte . . . carteles que hay por las calles, po . . . poner mi nombre, aunque todavia no me pongo algo nerviosa cuando tengo que firmar delante de la . . . la gente.
(read the posters you find on the streets, writing down my name, even though I get very nervous when I have to sign my name in front of people.)

It is possible to observe various aspects related to the identification between the author's and the reader's voices. Likewise, it is also possible to observe the teacher's role in eliciting comments about the text when these do not occur spontaneously. When **Pq** discovers the central theme of the text (attending the center), she utters an exclamation 2, which demonstrates her responsive attitude toward it. The text has been positively evaluated and these data have not escaped the teacher's attention. When the teacher notices that **Pq** makes no exclamations about the author's motives for attending class (reading, writing, and signing with more than an X), she asks for her comments on what she has read (6). This happens again in turn 10 after reading a new part of the text. The teacher intervenes where the reader does not spontaneously externalize comments about the part she has read. It is important to point out here the confusion of voices that occurs from turns 7 on. In this utterance **Pq** responds in first person (perhaps because she is repeating from memory what she has read) as her comment "I thank God . . . for that much at least . . ." means that at least she doesn't need to sign with an X. In this way, **Pq** marks the difference between herself and the author's voice. Later, the teacher asks a question in second person (10) that confuses (we do not know if willingly or unwillingly) the reader with the author's utterance. What is curious in comment 11 is that the reader takes on the question and then answers it in a louder tone of voice and with a worried gesture, showing how concerned she is for her poor mastery of literacy, and the teacher does not correct her.

The identification of voices becomes so complete in this episode that the reader takes on the experiences reflected in the text as her own. More than the words contained in the text, what is really understood is the voice of the author who utters them. To comprehend is, in this case, more than just the result of the processing of the information contained in the text; to comprehend here is to assume as one's own the experiences that *another* communicates.

11.4.3. Social language and comprehension

I have referred to the reading of texts where the author's voice hints at problems and situations that are very similar to the reader's. Does this mean that the teacher should eliminate those texts where social languages characteristic of other areas of education (as in secondary school) are predominant? These, and the many other examples I could mention here, show the motivation toward the reading of certain subjects in which the subjectivity of the author is fundamental for comprehension. However, texts where the referential plane predominates over the subjective plane of discourse can also be used. It is possible to show, in the next two episodes, how some of the contents of the text are assimilated to the context of the reader's daily life. Therefore, the contents are expressed as a discourse that adjusts to the characteristics of the *colloquial genres* (Volosinov [Bakhtin], 1986; Bakhtin, 1986) that the subject uses inside and outside the center.

Episodes V and VI demonstrate guided reading by the teacher, performed by student **A**, apropos of a text whose central topic is the history and geography of Madrid, the capital of Spain. In simple language, it describes the political characteristics of this industrial city, founded in the times of Phillip II, and gives a brief description of paintings by renowned artists in the Prado Museum. It represents an example of a typical school text, written in a language oriented toward giving simple but complete information of the city. **A**, who intervenes in these next episodes, has reached a higher level of literacy skills than the other students I have observed. The majority of the interactions between **A** and the teacher take place at two different points: at the beginning of the text, and while reading the description of Madrid as an industrial city. The sentences that motivate the interaction between the two are the following:

> En Madrid viven los miembros del gobierno de la nacion, el presidente yh los ministros. (Members of government of the nation, the president, and the ministers live in Madrid.)
>
> Para trabajar en las fabricas fueron llegando gentes de todos los rincones de Espana. (People from all corners of Spain came to work in the factories. Galicians, Andalusians, and Extremadurans came.)

In order to analyze better the reading achieved by **A** and the interactions with her teacher, each episode will be analyzed separately.

Episode V

1. **T:** Vamos a leer.
   (Let's read.)
2. **A:** En Madrid viven los miembros del gobierno de la nacion. El pre . . . presidente y los ministros.
   (Members of government of the nation live in Madrid. The pre . . . president and the ministers.)
3. **T:** Que pasa en Madrid?
   (What happens in Madrid?)
4. **A:** Pues que vive el gobierno, el *principal* que somos el gobierno, no? y los que estan *al lado* de el.
   (Well, they live in the government, the *main body* of our government, right? and the people that are *next to* it.)
5. **T:** Los que estan *al lado* del presidente, como se llaman?
   (The people *next to* the president, what is their name?)
6. **A:** Pues se llaman los *concejales,* no?
   (They're called *town councilors,* right?)
7. **T:** Los concejales o ministros?
   (Town councilors or ministers?)
8. **A:** Los ministros.
   (Ministers.)
9. **T:** Los concejales son los que estan a *la vera* del alcalde.
   (The town councilors are the people *side by side* the mayor.)
10. **A:** Los ministros.
    (The ministers.)

The fundamental trait of this episode dwells on the error in interpretation consisting of substituting the terminology used in the context of political affairs, little known by this student (government), for another more familiar term (municipal). The word "minister" is substituted for town councilor, and even though they have two different meanings, they express a similar hierarchic relation (6). This and other mistakes occur later on in the reading, although I have not included them in the episode. After these errors, it is surprising that the teacher refrains from asking any further questions or making comments concerning the rest of the passage. This seems to indicate, in view of the difficulties the student has with the text, that the teacher decides to continue the reading without any further comments. Likewise, the use of colloquial expressions on the part of the student (el principal y al lado de – the main body and next to) catches my attention, as it helps me to understand the causes for the errors in the substitution of minister for town councilor. These expressions denote the distance that exists between the colloquial genre, which she uses to express her voice, and the social language used to express the text. In turn, the teacher does not explain the meaning of "minister," but she does assign the analogical relation that exists in both terms via the utterance "Los concejales estan a la **vera** del alcalde" (The town councilors are **side by side** the mayor). The rest of the analogy is not spoken by the teacher, but she does give the student the opportunity to complete the deductive process ("The town councilors are side by side the mayor" just like "the ministers are side by side the president"). In order to help understand the text, the teacher uses the same expressions as **A** does – al lado de (next to) – and she even introduces a new one, characteristic of the Andalusian dialect and used especially by low socio-cultural level speakers, a la vera (side by side). From the Bakhtinian point of view, we can describe the teacher's role in the following terms: her utterances incorporate ideological signs (political terminology) and the relationships that exist between them, by way of little genres that the speakers use in their daily life. Through this curious combination of social language and colloquial speech, these signs may be understood and incorporated into signs of private speech.

During the student's reading of the passage on which this episode is based, the number of questions and requests for comments uttered by the teacher descends considerably. The interactions continue when the reader reaches the part of the text that speaks about the industrialization of Madrid and the emigration of people from other parts of the country to work in the factories.

Episode VI

1. **A:** Para trabajar en las fabricas fueron llegua
   (For working in the factories, people from all corners of Spain come)
2. **T:** llegando
   (came)
3. **A:** llegando gentes de todos los rincones de Espana. *Claro! donde hay trabajo.*
   (came to work in the factories. *Sure! where jobs are.*)
4. **T:** Claro.
   (Sure.)
5. **A:** Llega
   (Come)
6. **T:** Quienes llegaron?
   (Who came?)
7. **A:** (She continues reading.) Gallegos, andaluces, extremm, extremenos. *Extremenos un monton.*
   (Galicians, Andalusians, Extremadurans. *A lot of Extremadurans.*)
8. **T:** Cuentame un poquito.
   (Tell me about it.)
9. **A:** Pues, Madrid, Madrid . . . Pusieron mucha fabricas. Claro cuando . . en aquellos tiempos pues no habia tanto trabajo no? Bueno, no habia tanta industria. Entonces Madrid, pos reprexxx, como er la capital pues alli pusieron las fabricas.

Well, Madrid, Madrid . . . They built a lot of factories. Of course when . . . in those days well there weren't many jobs, right? Well, there wasn't much industry. Then, Madrid, xxxx, as it was the capital, well, they built the factories there.)

10. **T:** Umm umm
11. **A:** Entonces se desplazaron gallegos (trata de recordar), andaluces y extremenos.
(Then the Galicians went [she tries to remember], and the Andalusians and the Extremadurans.)
12. **T:** y extremenos
(and Extremadurans)
13. **A:** *Extremenos un monton*
(*A lot of Extremadurans*)
14. **T:** que emigraron a Madrid a trabajar, no?
(they emigrated to Madrid to work, right?)
15. **A:** Claro. Y despues a Barcelona.
(Right. And then to Barcelona.)

The interaction between the teacher and the student begins when the latter exclaims, "Sure, where jobs are," which shows knowledge and comprehension of the subject (emigration). As Andalusia has traditionally been a land of people emigrating toward industrialized areas of the country, it is understandable that a certain interest arises in this part of the text. The knowledge that has activated the interest and comprehension of the text is apparent in comments 7 and 13. **A** knows that many emigrants were Extremadurans, and this knowledge is expressed spontaneously. In the first example, she emits an utterance that comments about the individuals from the different regions who emigrated to the industries in Madrid (extremenos un monton – A lot of Extremadurans). In the second example, this externalization does not arise from the reading itself but from the conversation with the teacher. In both cases it is evident, as demonstrated in comment 15 (comments about the emigration to Barcelona) that comprehension is the result of the interaction between the previous knowledge and the text. **A** shows she knows aspects related to the emigration toward the two most industrialized cities in Spain. In Bakhtinian terms, we can say the signs that constitute this part of the text have contacted the signs that operate in inner speech, and they shape the subject's knowledge, generating new utterances. These spontaneous comments indicate the text has been understood.

As shown, texts that express scholastic language characteristic of other areas of education should not be rejected as possible reading material in educating adults. However, one should not forget that comprehension of these texts is possible only when their content refers to known and potentially knowable aspects.

11.5. CONCLUSION

In this chapter I have tried to demonstrate the role private speech accomplishes in the different processes that underlie reading. The analysis of the form of speech *for oneself* is fundamental if we wish to know the process of comprehension in adults learning literacy. This analysis is also important if we consider how private speech acts in a text that has special characteristics. The program directed toward adult students places a special emphasis on the connection between daily reality and educational experiences. In a similar manner, the adult education program developed by the local government in Andalusia tries to establish a close relation with life at work, on the street, and in the house with life at the center. One of the program's objectives is to show the student, from the very beginning, social value and the usefulness of the cognitive and semiotic instruments that the center teaches. Naturally, literacy becomes the fundamental skill in this program. The texts used in teaching the students should connect with the subject matter that motivates them to continue their learning process.

The main conclusions on private speech and comprehension from the observations I made can be extracted as follows:

1. Private speech is manifested in the control of the basic processes of reading. It is possible to observe a close relationship between the level of reading skill and the articulation of the word being read. Of the three students I observed, the one who has a lesser reading and writing ability articulated the syllables in a higher tone of voice than the other two. Likewise, the most skilled reader was also the one who whispered the least.
2. Private speech acts in the identification of a word that has been read syllable by syllable. When a word is read with difficulty, the reader needs to repeat it to herself until she has achieved acknowledgment.
3. The subject gives orders to and/or questions herself when she makes reading mistakes or she does not know the syllable or word she has read (esperate!, esto que es?, etc. – wait!, just a minute!, what is this?, etc.). Speech *for oneself* is externalized through an utterance that is foreign to the text but is directed at the student herself so that she will pay more attention to the reading.
4. In tasks similar to problem-solving situations, the insight of the word that completes the sentence or text involves an exclamation. As what is expressed is the new information (like the piece that solves the puzzle), the intonation is higher than other words that constitute the given information.

I have considered the action of private speech in three basic levels of the reading process: in transforming the graphic sign into syllables, in recognizing the word that has been read, and in self-regulating the course of the reading and integrating the new information in the given context. In addition, private speech plays an important role in the comprehension process of the text read. It is manifested in the following ways:

5. Comprehension is favored when there is identification between the author's and the reader's voices. Comprehension is possible when the text reflects the aspects of daily life common in both the author and the reader. It makes one think that in order for there to be identification of voices, aside from a central theme, it is necessary for the author to express herself through the genres of conversation in informal contexts.
6. Once the prerequisite has been completed (identification of voices), speech *for oneself* externalizes answers and comments about the most significant part of the text. The utterances spoken by the reader show that her private speech maintains a responsive attitude toward and a constant evaluation of the text.
7. When the referential content of the information predominates over the subjectivity of the author (e.g., the geography and history of a city), the text is expressed in social language. The school text, which is used in the most formal education, has its own language, which acts as the key to understanding other social languages (e.g., history and geography). The comprehension of the school text is possible when the reader finds information that is familiar to her and when the signs of private speech are totally or partially identified with the theme to which the written sign refers. If this happens, the reader will make utterances (e.g., comments) that will demonstrate a responsive attitude and the evaluation of the submitted text.
8. The teacher's role is crucial in order to explain the comprehension process of reading in unskilled readers. What happens when the subject emits no spontaneous utterances? When the student does not respond to the information in the text, the teacher intervenes, asking her to explain what she has read. The answer, in the majority of cases, is not limited to a simple repetition of the utterance read but is accompanied by evaluating comments of information.

TRANSCRIPT NOTATION

(-) means separation between syllables when the student reads slowly, uttering each of them without connection with the rest of the syllables that compound the word.

(:) indicates an elongation of the syllable.

An italicized word or sentence (*esperate* – wait) is indicative of a comment or question in relation to the reading.

A **bold** word or sentence indicates that it has been uttered with a louder voice.

(xxx) represents a word that is whispered or uttered in a low volume of voice.

NOTES

This research was supported by a DGICYT grant of the Ministry of Education and Science (Spain). The paper was translated by Gail Elizabeth Smith. Address: Juan D. Ramirez. University of Sevilla. Laboratory of Human Activity. San Francisco Javier s/n. 41071 Sevilla (Spain).

1. Valencina is situated close to the Guadalquivir River. All the students are familiar with this river.
2. Voice could be defined as the idiosyncratic expression of the individual. It is the speaking personality or speaking consciousness (Emerson & Holquist, 1987; Wertsch, 1991). When I say that the author talks through his or her personal voice, I am referring to the fact that he or she talks about the themes in close relationship to personal situations.
3. Bakhtin defines social language as "generic styles of certain spheres of human activity and communication" (Bakhtin, 1986, p. 64). Social language has been developed in order to facilitate communication in specific areas of culture, scientific activities, and ideological fields.

REFERENCES

Bakhtin, M. M. (1986). The Problem of Speech Genres. In M. M. Bakhtin, *Speech Genres & Other Late Essays* (Edited by C. Emerson & M. Holquist). Austin: University of Texas Press.

Berk, L. E., & Garvin, R. A. (1984). Development of Private Speech among Low-Income Appalachian Children. *Developmental Psychology,* 20, 271–286.

Chafe, W. 1982. "Integration and Involvement in Speaking, Writing, and Oral Literature." In D. Tannen (Ed.), *Spoken and Written Language: Exploring Orality and Literacy.* Norwood, NJ: Ablex.

Clark, K., & Holquist, M. (1984). *M. M. Bakhtin: Life and Works.* Cambridge, MA: Harvard University Press.

Emerson, C., & Holquist, M. (Eds.). (1987). *Speech Genres & Other Late Essays* (By M. M. Bakhtin). Austin: University of Texas Press.

Frauenglass, M. H., & Diaz, R. M. (1985). Self-Regulatory Functions of Children's Private Speech: A Critical Analysis of Recent Challenges to Vygotsky's Theory. *Developmental Psychology* 21(2), 357–364.

Goudena, P. P. (1983). *Private Speech: An Analysis of Its Social and Self-Regulative Functions.* Diss.: University of Utrecht.

Goudena, P. P. (1987). The Social Nature of Private Speech of Preschoolers during Problem Solving. *International Journal of Behavior Development,* 10(2), 187–206.

Kohlberg, L., Yaeger, J., & Hjerholm, E. (1968). Private Speech: Four Studies and Review of Theories. *Child Development,* 39, 817–826.

Langer, J. A. (Ed.). (1987). *Language, Literacy and Culture: Issues of Society and Schooling.* Norwood, NJ: Ablex.

Rommetveit, R. (1988). On Literacy and the Myth of Literal Meaning. In R. Saljo.

Saljo, R. (Ed.). (1988). *The Written Word: Studies in Literate Thought and Action.* Heidelberg: Springer-Verlag.

Volosinov, V. N. (1986). *Marxism and the Philosophy of Language.* Cambridge, MA: Harvard University Press.

Volosinov, V. N. (1987). *Freudianism: A Critical Sketch.* Indianapolis: Indiana University Press.

Wertsch, J. V. (1979). The Role of Human Action and the Given-New Organization of Private Speech. G. Zivin (Ed.), *The Development of Self-Regulation through Private Speech.* New York: Wiley.

Wertsch, J. V. (1980). The Significance of Dialogue in Vygotsky's Account of Social, Egocentric, and Inner Speech. *Contemporary Educational Psychology,* 5, 150–162.

Wertsch, J. V. (1985a). The Semiotic Mediation of Mental Life: L. S. Vygotsky and M. M. Bakhtin. In E. Mertz & R. J. Parmentier (Eds.), *Semiotic Mediation.* Orlando, FL: Academic Press.

Wertsch, J. V. (1985b). *Vygotsky and the Social Formation Mind.* Cambridge, MA: Harvard University Press.

Wertsch, J. V. (1991). *Voices of the Mind: A Sociocultural Approach to Mediated Action.* Cambridge, MA: Harvard University Press.

Wertsch, J. V., McNamee, G. D., McLane, J. B., & Budwig, N. A. (1980). The Adult–Child Dyad as a Problem-Solving System. *Child Development,* 51, 1215–1221.

Wertsch, J. V., & Stone, C. A. (1985). The Concept of Internalization in Vygotsky's Account of Genesis of Higher Mental Functions. J. V. Wertsch (Ed.), *Culture, Communication, and Cognition: Vygotskian Perspectives.* Cambridge: Cambridge University Press.

Wittgenstein, L. (1985). *Philosophical Investigations.* New York: Macmillan.

12 *From "Paj Ntaub" to paragraphs: Perspectives on Hmong processes of composing*

FRANCINE FILIPEK COLLIGNON

INTRODUCTION

"Women learn like animals. Men study in their heads." Dia Xiong Vang, a Hmong refugee from Laos, protested her placement in a class of men and women studying English language and literacy in 1979. The recently resettled men and women from southeast Asia had been assigned to the same class in a community-based program in Providence, Rhode Island. In explaining this distinction between men and women, Dia confided to me, her teacher, that studying alongside men terrified her. Her perception of men's superior intelligence eroded the little self-confidence she had. Variations of her fear and argument recur often in my conversations with Hmong women concerning their apprehensions about studying literacy.

These remarks about learning and gender differences provoked my curiosity and added a new dimension to my inquiry into Hmong culture. The need to address the issue of a culturally appropriate pedagogy engaged me in an ongoing pursuit, supported by my belief that educators need to examine the historical and social sources of learners' attitudes toward reading, writing, and thinking processes.

This ongoing study is a collaborative effort with participants as informants rather than as subjects (Heath, 1983; McNiff, 1988). It originates in the field, in homes and in classrooms where adults learn rather than in more traditional academic settings. The approach is strengthened by "creative dialogue between members of a community which includes teachers, academics, parents, students, etc." (Whitehead, 1988, p. x).

Models for this kind of research come from several sources. "Action research," originating in the 1950s and 1960s, is research conducted by a practitioner with the aim of improving the effectiveness of one's own practice, rather than establishing generalizations for a community of researchers (Lytle & Cochran-Smith, 1989). In the wake of desegregation in southern schools, for example, teachers were confronted with educating students whose home and community experiences differed significantly from their own. Shirley Brice Heath (1983) has documented the way in which teachers in her graduate-level teacher education courses began conducting action research to learn about their new students as well as to analyze their own unconscious cultural practices in order to develop more effective ways of working with their students. Similarly, Laurence Stenhouse, whose work has been widely influential in Great Britain, has encouraged teachers to become researchers in their own classrooms and institutions, both "to demystify and democratize research, which was seen as failing to contribute effectively to the growth of professional understanding and to the improvement of professional practice" (Rudduck & Hopkins, 1985, p. 1).

My action research with adult Hmong learners focuses on two concerns: one probes how Hmong women learned in their villages in Laos. It grows from a recognition of their "composing" in textile arts and traditional celebrations. As will be explained, the "composing" in Hmong village life provides a bridge to approaches to the reading and writing that Hmong people need in countries where they have resettled. The other concern explores the implications of "the functional system" – a theoretical concept developed by the Soviet psychologist L. S. Vygotsky. This work attempts to locate his theory in an application to Hmong women engaged in the study of literacy.

Functional systems, as described by Vygotsky and Luria, emphasize the dynamic connections between different functions and processes. Vygotsky argued that "the key to understanding psychological development is the study of the changing 'interfunctional relationships' among the mental functions, the study of the emergence and development of new 'psychological systems,' " as Minick (1987) has written. In contrast to earlier theories that preceded his own work, Vygotsky argued that "These interfunctional connections and relationships are neither constant nor inessential. . . . Change in these interfunctional connections – *change in the functional structure of consciousness – is the main and central content of the entire process of mental development*" (Vygotsky, 1987, p. 188, emphasis in original). Ultimately, as Luria (1987, p. 370) writes, the changes in these interfunctional connections mean "that development involves the formation of new functional systems." For exploring the development of adults, this theory suggests that the investigator look to pre-existing functions as offering a point of departure, a prior way of functioning on which a new function may build or from which it may emerge. In working with Hmong women, I found that my students were seeking – and in that way suggesting to me – a way to connect literacy with a pre-existing function when they wanted to learn to write in the way that in their youth they had learned to sew.

The learning activities of Hmong women will be analyzed with reliance upon these notions, particularly by looking at emerging psychological systems that unite earlier and later learned functions. Both the attitudes and the strategies of these adult learners evidence the legacy of their childhood experiences. By applying the concept of functional systems to new learning, we can clarify the way in which elements in their early socialization are linked to their acquisition of literacy in adulthood. Frequently, these different strands are hard to distinguish from each other. A brief overview of Hmong social and cultural history will help us to identify the emergent functional systems and the components that these women learners bring to their literacy tasks.

Background: Getting to know the Hmong

Most of the 5 million Hmong, an ethnic hill-tribe, still live in their ancestral homeland in southwestern China (Johnson, 1985). Several hundred thousand also live in the highlands of Laos, Thailand, Burma, and northern Vietnam. The native life-ways of the Hmong in Laos, on whom this study focuses, remained largely intact, relatively untouched by contact with the institutions of modernized societies, prior to the time that they were forced to flee Laos as a result of events surrounding the Vietnam conflict.[1] Historically in Hmong culture, a patrilineal clan system "serves as the primary integrating factor in Hmong life as a whole" (Barney 1981, p. 22), with a headman governing each village through the authority of householders, the men responsible for one or more households. A specialized role such as that of the shaman is considered governance in a different realm. Because the household is the basic unit of Hmong society, most functions necessary for life are provided for in each household, with a largely gender-based division of labor. At an early age, for example, virtually all females begin learning to sew "paj ntaub," the traditional Hmong textile art. The sewing of "paj ntaub" would be a frequent, even a daily, activity, engaged in for hours at a time. Villages organized in the traditional ways continue to exist in China and Southeast Asia, while in refugee camps in Thailand or in settlements that are vastly different from their traditional villages, contemporary Hmong preserve vestiges of their social structure in the midst of profound change.

By the early 1980s, almost 3,000 Hmong of Laos, along with other Southeast Asian refugess from Cambodia, Vietnam, and Laos had been resettled in Providence, Rhode Island. Although the Hmong have traditionally relied on subsistence agriculture in their native villages, agencies sponsoring them and other agrarian peoples of the region to the United States often have been forced by economic necessity to resettle refugees in proximity to jobs in urban areas. Jewelry factories and other existing industries in greater Providence provide a kind of employment that requires little or no English.

In the mid 1970s when Hmong refugees first began arriving in the United States, very little information was available about them, and the only known source, written in 1924, was available only in the French original (Savina, 1924). The fact that no complete or up-to-date history or ethnography of the Hmong existed has been explained by native informants on the basis of two key points: the relative isolation of the Hmong in their native highlands and the lack of native language literacy among the Hmong people in their traditional environment. Villages had been sufficient unto themselves except for bartering a few scarce commodities, such as salt, with neighboring peoples or for selling their cash crop, the opium poppy, to outsiders. Most existing writing about the Hmong was the work of missionaries and military personnel whose experiences of Hmong language and culture came from contact with Hmong cultural life while attempting to engage Hmong people in the writers' respective institutional agendas. In particular, knowledge of Hmong language was scarce and an accessible form of written representation was not available.[2] Even for those in possession of a copy of the only Hmong-English dictionary (Heimbach, 1979), language conventions such as tone markers and the lengthy initial consonant clusters – such as "ntxh" – beginning so many Hmong words prevented Americans from matching the pronunciations of Hmong students' words with spelling in the dictionary. Thus, communication with the Hmong during the early phases of their resettlement, along with unfamiliarity with their way of life and the absence of written sources about them, compounded practitioners' efforts in supporting Hmong educational goals.

Literacy

The history of written language among the Hmong is somewhat controversial. While some speculate that an ancient script existed, some Hmong minimize its significance, considering this writing more "legendary, hiding in the mysterious past" (Thao, 1988). Others research remnants of scripts of a more recent time. Some women consider the designs that are batiked on the indigo-dyed cloth of the Blue Hmong native dress to be reminiscent of an ancient script (Hmong-Lao Unity Association, 1991).

Awareness of native literacy and definitions of it differ among individuals of Hmong ethnicity, depending on variables such as their age, location, and gender. Yang See Koumarn (1981) writes about education and language training emerging only during the most recent fifty years of

Hmong life as a result of wars and the consequent relocations of Hmong. He describes how, prior to the periods of French colonialism and American presence in Southeast Asia, Hmong children "learned orally from their parents or from the wise men in the village." He differentiates between different tasks children learned: "Girls learned to do household tasks" while boys were prepared to assume future leadership roles (ibid., p. 9).

Elderly men in the Hmong community recount varied introductions to foreign languages and literacies (English and French). The teaching of English during the 1950s was linked to military objectives in some of the mountain villages. One man remembers learning a controlled vocabulary of fifty-two English words needed to guide American helicopter pilots to remote areas of Laos (Kha, 1988). Others describe attending formal classes in English and French in the Laotian capital of Vientiane during the same era. Hmong informants concur that only a very few tribal women ever studied a language other than Hmong (ibid.). Regardless of the context in which they encountered literacy, male and female informants agree that language study and literacy were identified principally with men in Hmong consciousness (T. Kha, 1988; P. Khang, 1989; Thao, 1988; Vang, 1980).

Although these gender differences were clearly drawn in traditional Hmong society, changes started to take place with relocation. Shifting attitudes originated early in the processes connected with forced migration. Many Hmong informants identify the same event as the precipitating factor in this shift. The fall of Saigon on April 30, 1975, and the changing political situation that ensued signaled for many Hmong tribespeople the need to escape from impending genocide – and to enter a new world that would require a new language and the development of literacy.

Except for the comparatively few who had been exposed to writing or to other languages, most Hmong had no familiarity with either literacy or the institution of schooling on which it frequently depends. Most men and women of older generations and most women of all ages lacked any previous schooling or native language literacy – let alone any knowledge of English. Even before they had departed from refugee camps in Southeast Asia, however, refugees who had neither studied foreign languages previously nor learned to read and write their own dialect had to deal with English literacy. Letters read to them or cassette tapes they listened to from relatives in the United States underscored the critical nature of literacy. Those pursuing resettlement in the United States heeded reports that literacy in English is an imminent survival need. One young man, in describing his sense of urgency about learning to read and write in English, recalls selling a few prized possessions in order to pay for private tutoring in English as a second language (ESL) in a refugee camp (Chang, 1980). Another refugee describes having studied outside an overcrowded ESL classroom in a refugee camp. Rain or shine, he crouched behind a hole in the wall and peered through it at the instructor and the chalkboard. It was his only opportunity for ESL instruction.

The anticipation of their passage to another country, with its attendant anxieties about survival, intensified the role of literacy in the consciousness of many Southeast Asians who awaited resettlement. Once in the United States, the study of literacy assumed a crucial role in discussions among Hmong men and women. In attempting to make sense of their current life situations, Hmong people attribute everything from bad dreams to the unemployment status of many Hmong people to their minimal experience with literacy. Whether needing literacy skills to find a job or to negotiate daily activities like grocery shopping, almost every resettled Hmong person confronts the challenge posed by literacy in a print-dense society like the United States.

The changes faced by the Hmong are similar to challenges faced by other groups. The ethnographic research of Scollon and Scollon (1986) based on their work with Athabaskans in Alberta and pedagogical writings of Freire (1970) based on his literacy work with Brazilian peasants are two sources that can provide perspective on the challenges facing the Hmong. As the work of the Scollons and Freire shows, acquisition of literacy must be conceptualized as not simply a matter of learning the technical skills of writing and reading as ways to represent spoken sounds in written form, but as a transformational process that is characterized by a change in consciousness. Written language – like oral language – is not simply a neutral or value-free system but is an integral part of the cultural system in which it is used. Scollon and Scollon document dramatic differences in ways of speaking between their native Athabaskan informants and the native English speakers with whom they interact in order to understand the interethnic communication conflicts between the members of these two groups. As Gee (1990, p. xix) has also recently argued, one does not simply speak a language; one uses language in a way that is a unique discourse of a given group of language users: "Discourses are ways of behaving, interacting, valuing, thinking, believing, speaking, and often reading and writing that are accepted as instantiations of particular roles by specific *groups of people*. . . . They are always and everywhere *social.* Language, as well as literacy, is always and everywhere integrated with and relative to *social practices* constituting particular discourses" (emphasis in original).

In their work among the Athabaskans, the Scollons discovered a consciousness unique to that group, which reflected the group's social practices and which both contrasted and conflicted with the consciousness of the dominant society, which reflected values and practices of modern bureaucratic life. Writing about the difficulties in interethnic communication between the two groups, Scollon and Scollon (1986) contrast oral and literate traditions and suggest that even a reliance upon literate expression in discussing cultural changes, such as the move toward literacy, casts oral traditions into a subordinate position. Their point highlights the difficulty for teachers and researchers alike of finding ways to understand and work with people whose traditions differ from one's own.

In addition to differing modes of consciousness, the Scollons also have written about the implications of contrasting modes of communication. The indigenous people of North America are akin to the Hmong in their traditional reliance upon oral narratives. With modernization and migration, tribal people all over the world are faced with the new challenges of literacy. The work of the Brazilian educator, Paolo Freire broke ground in literacy theory when he wrote about "the program content of education" (1970, p. 86) in terms of consciousness. His commitment to literacy among Brazilian peasants was to empower the people, to go beyond teaching the technical skills involved in reading and writing. Freire intended that the members of the literacy circles be equipped for "reading the word and the world" (Freire & Macedo, 1987). In order to accomplish this goal, Freire developed a pedagogy of "conscientization." It consists of a dialogic process affording "the opportunity both to discover generative themes and to stimulate people's awareness in regard to these themes" (Freire, 1970, p. 86). The use of generative themes provided opportunities for verbal dialogues as well as for the acquisition of literary forms.

The "conscientization" that Freire champions involves people's awareness of the challenges and contradictions of their existence and how these relate to similar challenges faced by their kin and neighbors. He imagines that in the course of conscientization, learners move in circles of meaning expanding their thematic universes beyond the generative themes they originally explored. Freire considers teaching a political process. He advocates constructing pedagogies to free people from prior limits in their knowledge and consciousness. He has had an important impact upon literacy workers in the United States and in developing countries on several continents. The work among the Hmong reported in this chapter also reflects his influence.

Functional systems

Studying literacy development in the lives of Hmong adults in a cultural environment sharply at variance from their culture of origin requires a theoretical framework. In examining the continuities and changes in their learning strategies, I have chosen to rely upon Vygotsky and Luria's notions of functional systems. Vygotsky identified the most fundamental characteristic of developmental change as "the manner in which previously separate and elementary functions are integrated into new functional systems" (John-Steiner & Souberman, 1978, p. 124). In order to understand the integration of the components of such a system it is necessary to look at the development of learning strategies over the life-span. Vygotsky suggested that "the functional systems of an adult . . . are shaped essentially by her prior experiences as a child" (ibid.).

Two themes emerge from the developmental histories of Hmong women: the cultural practice of sewing as a central activity for women and the differential gender expectations concerning learning and thinking that characterized traditional village life. The implications of these themes for the way in which Hmong women acquire literacy in a very different environment will be examined with the aid of Vygotskian concepts.

"Paj ntaub" – which means cloth flower in English – is the textile art practiced by women. (Although a few Hmong men also engage in the activity, it is a social practice strongly identified with female roles and integral to the learning of girls and young women.) The term describes sewing that employs a variety of techniques: reverse appliqué, cross-stitch and other stitches embroidered on solid colored or batik-dyed cloth. "Paj ntaub" originally served communicative needs in Hmong traditional life and a decorative function for Hmong clothes. The term describes both the process of sewing with a number of techniques that every Hmong woman learns and some of the items this sewing produces, such as small hanging ornaments and pieces of cloth used in animist rituals.

Mothers passed the very precise art of Hmong embroidery to every daughter. At an early age, Ploua Lee Khang remembers sitting across from her mother: "I sew the Hmong dress, Hmong skirt. . . . My mother. When she do it, she told me to watch it, I watch her, watch she. . . . She do the other and I do the other, half and half. She taught me what to sew" (Collignon, 1990, p. I-69). Conversing further with Ploua about sewing with her mother, I learn that she sat across from her mother; the cloth they were sewing rested on their laps between them. Ploua watched, copied, pulled out a lot of stitches – any that did not match her mother's. Then Ploua tried again. She described that, eventually, she could sew "paj ntaub" on her own. Her recollections illustrate the importance of transforming joint activities into personal knowledge, a central concept in Vygotskian accounts of learning.

The symbolic representation on a "paj ntaub" could describe social data, such as what clan subdivision a person belonged to and his or her eligibility for marriage. "Paj ntaub" could also indicate one's economic status, such as the degree of wealth of a person's clan or health status, such as a person's soul loss/return.

Sewing "paj ntaub" can be considered a leading activity among the "composing" experiences of Hmong women. A leading activity (Griffin & Cole, 1984) is one that plays a central role in development. In Hmong villages, every female child learns to sew "paj ntaub," passes her acquired skill to others, and continues to perfect her ability throughout life. A woman's skill at "paj ntaub" is one criterion for her selection for marriage.

As a leading activity, "paj ntaub" provides a recognizable link between the early learning activities of Hmong women and their later adaptive strategies. One of the ways I have identified the connections between the socialization of Hmong women in childhood with their approaches to literacy is by joint reflection on interview materials. Ploua Lee Khang, whose recollection of learning from her mother was just cited, recounted in a cross-cultural, reflective interview (Spindler, 1987) how her favorite ESL teacher proceeds. In conversing about the transcript of her earlier interview, Ploua realized that she preferred teachers who employ the same process her mother used in teaching her: sew a stitch, wait for Ploua to copy, instruct her to change the stitch if it did not match, do another until it matches, and then encourage her to try alone. Ploua had described her language instructor's sequence in a similar way: his supplying students with a text to study, giving dictation from it, correcting the misspelled words, and having everyone try on one's own. "I liked to do dictation. . . . Helped me to remember what's the word spelling (Collignon, 1990, p. I-77). Ploua, somewhat orally fluent in English, explains more than her own learning process in that excerpt. She demonstrates how the socially facilitated learning approaches of her childhood serve as a component of her current strategies in addressing ESL literacy.

Within the socio-cultural tradition, functional systems are linked to distinctive forms of cultural practice. The strategy that Ploua cites as helpful in her current learning is connected to earlier, culturally patterned modes of learning, effectively reorganizing her functional system: "Higher psychological functions are not superimposed as a second story over elementary processes; they represent new psychological systems" (John-Steiner & Souberman, 1978, p. 124).

The similarities between the processes Ploua employs for sewing and for studying English are unrecognized by her until they emerge in the collaborative reflections on the transcript of an interview. Collaborative action research, such as the ongoing dialogue between an adult female Hmong learner and her teacher, provides data valuable to both parties.

Ploua Lee Khang realizes the benefits of her own reflection on her previous successful learnings. Attention to the connections between her past and current learnings make explicit to her potential sources of new strategies for learning. Other Hmong women, too, have written of similarities between learning sewing and language. Describing the process of sewing "paj ntaub," a Hmong woman explains that "There are hundreds of patterns which are used to design the art. All the patterns must be kept well known in the Needle Art person. These patterns are being slowly learned one by one. As if you were learning a foreign language you would have to slowly build up your vocabulary" (Catlin & Swift, 1987, p. 7). Interviews with Ploua Lee Khang and follow-up conversations with her have been a turning point in my pursuit of a culturally appropriate pedagogy with Hmong women. Such action research has supplied a key to hidden continuities between early learning and current productive strategies of Hmong women students.

Another piece of evidence pointing to the inherent connections between early learning practices and future approaches to be explored comes from my experience of instructing a recently arrived 58-year-old woman who had been one month in the United States. Her son had requested a home tutorial session for his mother. She waited for the instructor at a table set up where she and the instructor would sit across from each other. On the table, she had placed the composition book her son had bought her. With the son's bilingual assistance, I, the tutor, realized that I was expected to write Shoua's first name on the first line of the notebook. She attempted to copy it on the line beneath before passing it across the table and gesturing for me to write it again. It was awkward for us to keep passing the notebook across the table. Shoua kept copying her name again, no matter what other content was introduced.

When I arrived to tutor her the next week, Shoua proudly produced an entire notebook filled with her copying! Her name was lettered on 30 pages. Not until Ploua's remarks provoked my awareness of a connection between early learning experiences and their later applications did Shoua's action make sense to me. Shoua was replicating the learning process she knew best – the repetition of "paj ntaub" stitches for her teacher. Monotonous to me, repetition to her meant learning.

Both Shoua's use of copying and Ploua's preference for dictation fly in the face of current pedagogical trends toward meaning-based rather than grammar-based approaches to literacy. They also run counter to emphasizing communication rather than technical production in literacy education. Practices – such as dictation or copying – are not distasteful to people who have integrated them as part of well-developed functional systems for learning. Strategies that connect with one's early cultural patterns need to be utilized as bases for learning and perhaps even expanded, rather than discarded in favor of current popular practice.

Repetition was a way of life for the Hmong. Before the introduction of outside influences to Hmong life, the tales, ritualistic incantations, "kwv txhiaj" (extemporized sung poetry) (Catlin, 1980), and the instrumental music reminiscent of their favorite animistic themes served significant purposes of reinforcement and support. Similarly, "paj ntaub" were used to recreate traditional ways of representing reality, which had been repeated for countless generations – rather than serving to entertain or financially support as they sometimes do now. This traditional function of the textile art of the Hmong is both similar to and different from the literacy-influenced expression to which modernizing Hmong now adapt "paj ntaub" (to be explained).

The remarks of Dia Xiong Vang, the woman whose quote begins this chapter, also reflect the reality of Hmong early experience. Her recollections capture for the reader another level of village life. Culturally transmitted attitudes about male and female activities led her to specific conclusions about intellectual potential. She remembered closely circumscribed gender expectations. Whereas women sewed "paj ntaub," farmed, cooked, and breast-fed their children, men met, talked, told stories, strategized about their future plans, and worked with ideas. She assumed that women's activity was external, imitative. They only copied, mimicked. In contrast, men's activity was occurring internally. It was invisible. Dia concluded that men learn with their head, women with their hands. Men create; women copy.

Without careful examination, Dia's prior beliefs could remain an unanalyzed hindrance to her attempts at new learning. But the process of attempting to explain these beliefs helps Dia to objectify and thus detach this idea from her sense of herself as a learner. In this way, the process of self-exploration contributes to the reorganization of the functional system in ways that, as Freire has suggested, are essential for the power of literacy to become available to a learner. From her own experience of walking her children to American schools, Dia knows that male and female children go to school together. She never knew that before. Although reluctantly, she nevertheless registers for a coeducational literacy class. Only her disclaimers – "tsis paub" (I don't know) and "tsis saum" (I don't write) – before every task she attempts in class connect with her prior overwhelming consciousness of intellectual inferiority. The analysis of her new experiences and insights has enabled her to reconsider her former assumptions about intelligence and adapt to the cultural necessity of school and ESL literacy in a new culture.

The functional system becomes visible from the interlacement of elements like the observable ones described in the developing literacies of these three Hmong women. Elements of these women's prior experiences, such as meticulous attention to copying symbols, are retained, whereas other unnecessary ones, such as former assumptions about limits of gender, are discarded. In this way, the functional system undergoes reorganization.

But not only the functional systems of individuals are changed by their experiences in a new culture and homeland. Traditional cultural practices have also been modified in the process of their practitioners' cultural adaptation. Now, the Vietnam War's devastating effects are captured in Hmong performance and craft. The sung poetry resumes in the aftermath of war, old forms laced with new tales of horror and devastation. The design of "paj ntaub" now includes new content – linear picture stories within the traditional border of animist symbols incorporate helicopters, guns, and camouflage-colored figures, pursuing Hmong through the jungle; these pictorial representations now often replace the abstract geometric shapes of stylized flowers in the center of many Hmong art works. Interestingly, this reconceptualization also reflects a change in the function of "paj ntaub," which are now produced for sale to non-Hmong in addition to their traditional use within the culture. These compositions comprise a "continuum of meaning" (Berthoff, 1981, p. 36) and present evidence of the processive nature of literacy. The communicative forms are altered. Words are introduced on story cloths women sew. In the Vygotskian sense, words, which are symbols of speech, become tools of thinking. Hmong women study literacy.

Educational implications

The same Hmong women who study ESL literacy, who use new signs (words) and new tools (print, writing) have been chanting their grief and stitching the complexity of their lives for years. Literacy educators informed of current literacy and developmental theory would benefit from reflection on implications of this processive view of literacy. In addition, an understanding of the concept of the functional system suggests new perspectives on some accepted current practices in the areas of assessment, instruction, curriculum, and materials.

The issue of initial assessment, especially using diagnostic testing as an objective instrument, makes no sense in a framework that acknowledges the complexity and individuality of adult students' functional systems. More holistic ways of initial assessment need to be utilized, developed, and acted upon. For example, work on assessment of low-literate adults (Lytle et al., 1986) suggests building on existing models of adult assessment (Cross, 1981) that ascertain dispositional, situational, and institutional factors to be considered in pedagogy. Many of these factors have cultural bases.

The old ESL assessment categories of non-literate, semi-literate, preliterate, and literate in a non-Roman alphabet (Haverson & Haynes, 1982) to describe unschooled refugee adults need to give way to new descriptions.[3] More positive ways of talking about and relating to adults of other cultural backgrounds can serve to dignify their own educational efforts in a new culture to demonstrate a true valuing of what they already know. The old categories tend to highlight the assumed deficits of those not previously schooled rather than to identify strengths of their highly developed functional systems.

Curricula must ideally utilize the current strategies of adults accomplished in their own cultures and proceed with topics that expand the literacies and cultural consciousness of learners. Materials that codify meaning for learners (Freire, 1970) must be introduced by teachers, generated from learners, and produced collaboratively in educational settings. Prescribed syllabi and textbooks are not enough. For example, Hmong women have abstracted from experience and composed in song and in cloth for centuries. "Abstraction is not the opposite of reality but our means of making sense of reality in perception and in all we do with symbolic form" (Berthoff, 1981, p. 66). Hmong socio-history calls for educators to accompany Hmong women in the extension into writing of what they have already composed in song or in cloth, a journey from "paj ntaub to paragraphs."

Conclusion

Studying how Hmong (especially women) learn by using action research around their pursuit of ESL literacy contributes to an illustration of Vygotskian theory. Such an inquiry leads to a more processive understanding of the nature of literacy and the centrality of speech. When cultural adaptation necessitates reading and writing another language, as resettlement in the United States seems to require for the Hmong, then the Vygotskian emphasis on development and telescoping changes provides a methodology. Reciprocally, new insights into the elements of functional systems, as Vygotsky conceived them, suggest ways to proceed in exploring the roots of learners' strategies and processes. Examining the cultural roots of learners' consciousness of reading and writing in their lives reveals numerous pedagogical considerations. The issue of literacy is multi-dimensional. Collaborative action research provides a tool for linking theory and practice in the service of effective pedagogy. This inquiry demonstrates the centrality of any person's cultural context in her or his composing: thinking about, reading, and writing one's world.

NOTES

1. "All the Hmong who came to America were Laotian, part of the refugee remnant of the 300,000 pre-war Laotian Hmong, many of whom were recruited and trained in a 'secret army' supported by the American C.I.A. to fight against Communist Vietnamese and Pathet Lao insurgents in northern Laos" (Johnson, 1985, p. v). Hmong people themselves refer to the horrors of the war and the forced migration consequent to this political involvement as a "cruel drama" (Yang, 1981, p. 6) and in terms of a Hmong "diaspora" (Bliatout, 1982, p. ix).
2. Written Hmong using the Romanized Popular Alphabet has existed for less than half a century. Although William Smalley (1979) reports that work on the Hmong language (Meo/Miao as non-Hmong have identified it) had been done in China, he locates the origins of written Hmong in the 1950s and 1960s in Laos and Thailand in his work with G. L. Barney and also in the work of Bertrais (1964), Heimbach (1979) and Mottin (1978).
3. If these older categories are used for placement of adults in programs, this practice precludes more socially constructed classes with learners of different abilities working together and assisting one another. In the late 1970s Haverson (1980) invited reflection on new ways of addressing the needs of adult refugees. A Vygotskian perspective provides a theoretical framework for such a project.

REFERENCES

Barney, G. L. (1981). "The Hmong of Northern Laos." In *Refugee education guides: Glimpses of Hmong history and culture.* General Information Series, No. 16 (pp. 18–44). Alexandria, VA: Center for Applied Linguistics.

Berthoff, A. (1981). *The making of meaning.* Upper Montclair, NJ: Boynton/Cook.

Bertrais, Y. (1964). *Dictionnaire Hmong (meo blanc)–Français.* Vientiane: Mission Catholique.

Bliatout, B. T. (1982). *Hmong sudden unexpected nocturnal death syndrome: A cultural study.* Portland, OR: Sparkle Publishing Enterprises.

Catlin, A. (1980). *Music of the Hmong: Singing voices and talking reeds.* Providence: Rhode Island College.

Catlin, A, & Swift, D. (1987). *Textiles as texts: Arts of Hmong women from Laos.* Los Angeles: Woman's Building.

Chang, C. (1980). Personal interview.

Collignon, F. (1990). Finding words for new worlds: A collaborative model for adult literacy. A field project fulfilling requirements for a Certificate of Advanced Graduate Study. Rhode Island College. Unpublished.

Cross, K. P. (1981). *Adults as learners: Increasing participation and facilitating learning.* San Francisco: Jossey-Bass.

Freire, P. (1970). *Pedagogy of the oppressed.* New York: Continuum.

Freire, P., & Macedo, D. (1987). *Literacy: Reading the word and the world.* South Hadley, MA: Bergin & Garvey.

Gee, J. P. (1990). *Social linguistics and literacies: Ideology in discourses.* London: Falmer Press.

Griffin, P., & Cole, M. (1984). Current activity for the future: The zo-ped. In B. Rogoff & J. V. Wertsch (eds.), *Children's learning in the "Zone of Proximal Development."* New Directions for Child Development, No. 23 (pp. 45–63). San Francisco: Jossey-Bass.

Haverson, W. W. (1980). *Teaching ESL to illiterate adults.* Indo-Chinese Refugee Education Guides, No. 9. Washington, DC: Center for Applied Linguistics.

Haverson, W. W., & Haynes, J. L. (1982, May). *ESL/Literacy for adult learners.* Language in Education: Theory in Practice, No. 49. Washington, DC: Center for Applied Lingusitics.

Heath, S. B. (1983). *Ways with words: Language, life and work in communities and classrooms.* Cambridge: Cambridge University Press.

Heimbach, E. E. (1979). *White Hmong–English Dictionary.* Southeast Asia Program Data Paper No. 75. Ithaca, NY: Cornell University Press. (Originally published as *White Meo-English Dictionary,* 1969.)

Hmong-Lao Unity Association of Rhode Island (1991). Paj ntaub: Textile techniques of the Hmong. Video (Produced by Joyce Smith).

John-Steiner, V., & Souberman, E. (1978). Afterword. In L. S. Vygotsky, *Mind in society: The development of higher psychological processes.* Trans. M. Cole, V. John-Steiner, S. Scribner, & E. Souberman. Cambridge, MA: Harvard University Press.

Johnson, C. (Ed.). (1985). *Dab neeg Hmoob: Myths, legends and folk tales from the Hmong of Laos.* St. Paul, MN: Macalester College.

Kha, T. N. (1988). Personal interview.

Khang, P. L. (1989). Personal interview.

Koumarn, Y. S. (1981). The Hmong of Laos: 1896–1978. In *Refugee education guides: Glimpses of Hmong history and culture.* General Information Series, No. 16 (pp. 3–17). Alexandria, VA: Center for Applied Linguistics.

Luria, A. R. (1987). Afterword to the Russian edition. In R. W. Rieber & A. S. Carton (Eds.), *The collected works of L. S. Vygotsky,* trans. Norris Minick (Vol. 1, pp. 359–373). New York: Plenum.

Lytle, S. L., & Cochran-Smith, M. (1989). Teacher research: Toward clarifying the concept. *Quarterly of the National Writing Project and the Center for the Study of Writing, 11*(2), 1–3, 22–27.

Lytle, S. L., Marmor, T. W., & Penner, F. H. (1986, April). Literacy theory in practice: Assessing reading and writing of low-literate adults. Presentation at American Education Research Association, San Francisco.

McNiff, J. (1988). *Action research: Principles and practice.* London: Macmillan Education.

Minick, N. (1987). The development of Vygotsky's Thought: An introduction.

In R. W. Rieber & A. S. Carton (Eds.), *The collected works of L.S. Vygotsky,* trans. Norris Minick (Vol. 1, pp. 17–36). New York: Plenum.

Mottin, J. (1978). *Elements de grammaire Hmong Blanc.* Bangkok: Don Bosco Press.

Rudduck, J., & Hopkins, D. (1985). *Research as a basis for teaching: Readings from the work of Lawrence Stenhouse.* London: Heinemann Educational Books.

Savina, F. M. (1924). *Histoire des Miao.* Hong Kong: Imprimerie de la société des missions étrangères.

Scollon, R., & Scollon, B. K. (1986). *Narrative, literacy and face in interethnic communication.* Vol. VII of *Advances in discourse processes,* ed. Roy O. Freedle. Norwood, NJ: Ablex.

Smalley, W.A. (1979). Introduction. In E. E. Heimbach, *White Hmong-English Dictionary.* Rev. ed. Ithaca, NY: Cornell University Press.

Spindler, G. (Ed.). (1987). *Education and cultural process: Anthropological approaches* (2nd ed.). Prospect Heights, IL: Waveland Press.

Thao, X. (1981, 1988). Personal interviews.

Vang, D. X. (1980). Personal interview.

Vygotsky, L. S. (1987). *The collected works of L. S. Vygotsky, Volume I: Problems of general psychology.* R. Rieber & A. Carton (Eds.). New York: Plenum.

Whitehead, J. (1988). Preface. In J. McNiff, *Action research: Principles and practice.* London: Macmillan Education.

Yang, D. (1981). Why did the Hmong leave Laos? Trans. Sylvianne Downing. In B. T. Downing & D. P. Olney (Eds.), *The Hmong in the West* (pp. 3–18). Minneapolis: University of Minnesota, 1982.

13 *Toward a definition of law school readiness*

MICHELE MINNIS

PREFACE

Professions, like many other institutions, can be said to constitute distinct subcultures in society. That is, members of a profession share beliefs, values, norms, and special language concerning the world of experience the profession has made its domain. This chapter considers the legal profession in the context of an issue critical to the maintenance of any culture, namely, how its unique, defining properties are transmitted from one generation to the next. Specifically, the chapter examines current methods of socializing novices into the community of lawyers.

In the past, aspirants to a career in law learned their craft by apprenticing with practicing attorneys. Since approximately the turn of the century, however, schools of law have assumed an increasingly greater role in the education of lawyers. Moreover, the legal education process has become more formal and impersonal. Because law schools are now the primary transmitters of the culture of the legal profession, the inquiry here focuses on the content and pedagogy of law school programs.

Contemporary legal education provides a good medium in which to study the transmission of a professional culture, because contemporary legal education exhibits so dramatically the tension between change and stasis characteristic of intergenerational dynamics. Over the last 30 years, as women and members of ethnic minorities have been admitted to law schools in increasing numbers, the composition of the law student population has changed profoundly. In the face of these changes, law schools have retained traditional methods of teaching and performance expectations more appropriate to the exclusively white male student body of earlier years.

In the following pages, I argue that, in holding on to these traditions, legal education ignores the instructional needs of many law students and, thereby, forecloses the chances that these students will realize their learning potential in law school or afterward. Although the critique focuses on the law school experience of minority students, in some respects it applies to the experience of all law students.

The first year of law school is fundamentally concerned with the critique of written language and cognitive manipulation of alternative interpretations of texts. For that reason, the chapter analyzes cognitive and linguistic behavior underlying the specialized literacy skills expected of beginning law students. Because law schools do not teach these skills, and because many minority students enter law school without having learned either the skills or the means to teach themselves the skills, the chapter highlights what needs to be taught if minority students are to be appropriately, fairly educated in law school. This approach is Vygotskian in that it considers both the socio-cultural context and the cognitive operations necessary to mastery of a domain.

INTRODUCTION

Historically, legal education was reserved to middle- and upper-class white men. In the 1960s, prodded by civil rights legislation and the women's movement, law schools began actively recruiting women and minority applicants. Between 1963 and 1990, women's representation in the nation's law student population grew from 4 to 43 percent (American Bar Association, 1991). Of equal if not greater significance, in the past 20 years the proportion of minority students enrolled in law schools has more than tripled. In 1971, members of ethnic minorities accounted for only 4 percent of the total law student population. By the fall of 1990, that figure had climbed to 13.6 percent (American Bar Association, 1975, 1991).

Among minority applicants admitted to law schools during the past three decades, some have met traditional entrance standards based on undergraduate grade point averages (GPAs) and Law School Admissions Test (LSAT) scores (Dawson, 1984). Others, those having GPAs and LSAT scores below these standards, were admitted under affirmative action standards; that is, their marginal academic credentials were counterbalanced with evidence of their resourcefulness or accomplishment in nonacademic endeavors (O'Neill, 1970; Rosen, 1970; Romero, 1984). Many minority law students in both these categories have since graduated from law school, been admitted to the bar, and established themselves in positions of responsibility and respect in the legal profession (Skillman, 1986). Even so, every year, in numbers disproportionate to their representation in the law student population, there are minority students who either quit law school before they graduate or graduate with poor academic records and repeatedly fail bar examinations.[1]

Why does this happen? If minority students do not fare well in law school, is it because they are unprepared for legal education? Or, is it because legal education is unprepared for them, not attuned to them as learners? These explanations differ only in emphasis and may seem to say the same thing. Emphasis is critical here, however, for it identifies the locus of the problem. This chapter explores and attempts to clarify the second explanation.

The thesis of the chapter is that success in law school depends on specialized literacy skills, which law professors do not teach and which many minority students do not acquire before coming to law school and do not know how to acquire on their own. This thesis will be developed by examining and comparing four literacy tasks that are fundamental to American legal education. The tasks are as follows:

1. Reading and briefing judicial opinions.
2. Analyzing opinions in classroom dialogue.
3. Analyzing hypothetical stories in legal memoranda.
4. Analyzing hypothetical stories in law school examinations.

All four tasks are introduced in the first semester of law school, the most academically critical semester of any law program. In describing the tasks, I will identify cognitive and linguistic processes they seem to imply. Task 3, which covers the entire production of a legal memorandum, will be treated in greatest detail because, from the standpoint of cognitive and linguistic requirements, it is the most difficult. In Task 3, unlike the other tasks, students must communicate the analysis of a legal problem, in writing, to an imagined reader who is presumed to be unfamiliar with the specific situation and issues under discussion. Because it engages all the skills required in the other literacy tasks, as well as several additional skills, the task of composing a legal memorandum can be considered the crux of the learning assignment in first-year law. In the final section of the chapter, having analyzed the four tasks, I will consider how students who lack the needed skills might be assisted in acquiring them.

Other authors have identified skills necessary to law school work: focused reading (Delaney, 1983; Hamburger, 1984; Lundeburg, 1987), analytic reasoning (Benson, 1984–1985a; Bryden, 1984; Burton, 1985; Rissland, 1990; Stratman, 1990), oral argument (Philips, 1982), and expository writing (Diggs, 1970; Gale, 1980; White, 1984; Gopen, 1984a, 1984b, 1987). To my knowledge, however, no one has attempted to describe the cognitive operations implicit in the skills or to show how students must adapt those operations to the purposes of the various literacy tasks assigned during the first year of law school. Before turning to those tasks, it is well to consider the setting in which they figure so prominently.

OVERVIEW OF FIRST-YEAR LAW

Academic environment

American legal education is a remarkably uniform institution. From law school to law school across the country, curriculum, methods of instruction, and expectations of students are basically the same. Still, because law schools tend to be physically and in other ways isolated on university campuses, their internal workings are largely unknown to outsiders, even those within the university community (Philips, 1982).

Legal education has no undergraduate counterpart. It developed independently of and in a different pedagogical tradition than other academic disciplines (see, generally, Johnson, 1978; Stevens, 1983). Law school admissions requirements, unlike those for medical school and other graduate programs, specify no particular undergraduate major or prerequisite courses (Gopen, 1984a). Indeed, law professors seem almost to prefer that entering students be *tabula rasa* with respect to knowledge of the law and its institutions. "What you've studied before won't count much here; we'll teach you all you need to know" is the message frequently conveyed. When asked to explain what they teach, professors are apt to give the stock response, "how to *think like a lawyer*" (Llewellyn, 1951; Mudd, 1983; Bryden, 1984; Calhoun, 1984; McKay, 1985; Boyer, 1985).

If law professors are not more forthcoming about their teaching objectives, it is somewhat understandable. Legal education concerns and embodies opposition. As will be explained more fully in a subsequent section, students' previous experiences determine how the tension generated by that essential contrariety is perceived and dealt with.

The law school experience can be characterized as both structured and unstructured. Generally speaking, certainly in the first year, legal education is regimented. Most law schools accept only full-time students and admit students once annually, in the fall term. Entering cohorts proceed en masse through a three-year program.[2] The first year of the program is devoted to required courses,[3] which ordinarily are taught in sections of 50 or more students. Students choose elective courses in the second and third year, but, with a few exceptions,[4] the format and teacher–student ratios in these courses are much the same as in first-year courses.

Semester to semester and year to year, then, the pace and overall design of legal education is largely fixed. From the perspective of an individual student's day-to-day experience of legal education, however, there is little external structure. Class attendance is not mandatory and, in most courses, learning is evaluated only once, at the end of the semester. Moreover, in contrast with the practice in most graduate programs, law students are not paired with faculty advisors. Students are encouraged to seek their professors' advice, but, unless they are on academic probation, it is not customary for them to select or be assigned to personal mentors on the law faculty. Thus, although the law school program is highly structured overall, it is impersonal and demands initiative of students. That is, it demands self-directed, self-monitored habits of study. On their own, students must learn to recognize and make use of resources within the school setting. And, because direct feedback is delayed for months, they also must learn to discern and respond to *indirect* feedback on their daily efforts.

Classroom instruction

Instruction in first-year law courses involves total immersion in the course material. The lecture format common in undergraduate and other graduate programs is used infrequently if at all. Instead, from the beginning of each course, students are expected to participate in defining the course subject and to match wits with the professor in the process. That process is adversarial. As Philips (1982) has observed, teacher–student interactions in the law school classroom are patterned after those of judge and lawyer in the courtroom, particularly the appellate courtroom. Judicial opinions in appellate court cases are the currency of classroom exchanges.[5]

The preeminent instructional approach in first-year law courses is the case method (Gopen, 1984a; Stevens, 1985). The method consists in parsing and comparing appellate opinions through an inductive inquiry, a question-and-answer routine sometimes called Socratic dialogue. Before every class meeting, students are expected to have read and briefed, or summarized in writing, several appellate opinions from a book containing pivotal case law[6] on the course topic. When called on in class, students must be prepared to review and analyze specific opinions, compare the details of several opinions, and explain how the opinions might have been rendered differently.

The burden of divining pattern in the entire body of cases is on the students. Typically the professor's role is to expose, in the students' presentations, the hazards of ignoring alternative interpretations of the case material. Students are advised to be alert and ready to duck or strike lest their adversary, the professor, catch them off guard. In other words, law school classes, much like those in the martial arts, are run as a kind of contest between opponents. Always, discussion in such classes is exegetical; it is anchored in *texts,* in written accounts and judgments of past events.

At some point in the first semester of law school, students are introduced to legal writing. Sometimes legal writing assignments are incorporated into one of the substantive courses taught by the regular faculty. More often, legal writing is taught by faculty adjuncts as part of a legal methods course that includes exercises in law library research and the use of legal citation forms. Law schools vary in the emphasis they give legal writing and in whether the students' work in this subject is graded (see, e.g., Diggs, 1970; Gale, 1980; Boyer, 1985; Gopen, 1987; and Stratman, 1990).

However it is woven into the curriculum, basic instruction in legal writing almost always begins with repeated practice in composing a legal memorandum. A legal memorandum is a comprehensive report usually addressed to a fictitious senior partner in a law firm. The purpose of the memorandum is to explain the possible legal implications of a factual situation described by a client of the firm who has sought expert advice about that situation.

Student evaluation

Grades in all first-year courses, as well as many second- and third-year courses, are determined by a single, timed, written examination at the end of the semester. These examinations usually consist of one or more "hypotheticals," stories invented by the professor and designed to cover the spectrum of issues addressed in the course. Responding to the examination, students must identify the legal issues, explain the applicable rule of law, the legally important facts of the story covered by that rule, and various ways in which the facts might be interpreted in applying the rule.

Because examinations are the only formal assessments of students' academic work and because the number of A's awarded in each course section is arbitrarily limited, grades assume tremendous importance as progress reports. First-year grades are considered particularly telling, for first-year courses concern what have come to be accepted as basic subjects in law. Prospective employers of law students and graduates read first-year grades as critical indicators of one's mettle and potential as a lawyer (Kissam, 1989, p. 480).

In sum, although law professors say that they teach lawyerly *thinking,* communication skills are all-important in their evaluation of student performance. That is, success in law school depends on one's ability to participate effectively in legal discourse. To pass law school courses and the bar examination, one must be able to *read* the literature of law and to *speak* and *write* within the tradition that informs that literature. With these imperatives in mind, we will consider the role of each of the four previously mentioned tasks in developing the specialized literacy skills that distinguish lawyers from other professionals.

TASK 1: READING AND BRIEFING JUDICIAL OPINIONS

Appellate court opinions

The judicial opinions students read in their casebooks concern disputes that were adjudicated by a trial court and appealed to a higher court. Cases come before an appellate court when one of the parties to the dispute, claiming a legal error in the trial court proceedings, has petitioned the higher court's review of that claim. Cases on appeal are heard by a panel of judges.

Reviewing a case on appeal, appellate judges concentrate on the merits of the petitioner's claim and, ordinarily, accept as given the facts of the dispute established at trial. There are neither witnesses nor juries at appellate reviews, only attorneys and judges. Before the date scheduled for a review, each of the attorneys representing the parties submits to the court a brief, an extended written argument addressing the allegation of error in the appeal petition. At the review, having read the two briefs, the judges sometimes hear oral presentations of the arguments by each of the attorneys and question the attorneys to clarify their written or oral statements. Later, after deliberating about the case, the judges present and explain their decision in a written opinion composed by one of them. Where the decision is not unanimous, one of the judges holding the minority view composes a summary of the dissenting position. Unless the case is appealed again to a yet higher court, the appellate court decision is final.

For the parties in a case that has been decided on appeal, the judicial opinion is the last chapter in the story of their lawsuit. For attorneys, judges, and law professors, however, the individual case is but an episode that has been integrated into a longer, continuing story. That other story, the development of the common law, is organized by the principle of *stare decisis:*[7] like cases are to be treated in like manner.[8] Every case in common law is connected to similar cases that have already been heard. In deciding a case, judges look to these previous cases as precedent and may refer to them in their opinions. Some related prior cases will have more weight as precedent than others: some will provide binding precedent, others only persuasive precedent.[9]

The case addressed in an opinion can also *establish* precedent, or result in a new rule of law. For example, the new rule might revise the old by incorporating additional or clarifying details.

Briefing cases

Briefing cases is a formal, disciplined method of extracting the essence of a judicial opinion and, presumably, the essence of the case behind it. To brief a case is to analyze an opinion, specify its parts. This may sound like a straightforward assignment, but it is not. In the legal education literature, the contents of an opinion part vary, as do the names by which the parts are known. Delaney (1983), for example, names the parts as follows: procedural history, issue, facts, holding, judgment, and reasoning. Dernbach and Singleton (1981) present a slightly different taxonomy: issue, facts, rule, holding, and policies and reasons.

Beginning law students' errors in analyzing opinions may be due to general difficulty in decoding them. Traditional legal writing is dense and abstruse, characterized by vocabulary and constructions unfamiliar to most lay readers (see Gopen, 1987, p. 334; Benson, 1984–1985b, p. 531). Distinguishing the parts of an opinion presents additional challenges to the uninitiated, however, in that the parts are not labeled and, often, are implicit and cannot be pointed to in the text. Where the author of the opinion has not identified *as such* the legally significant facts in the case, the previously established legal rules used to decide the case, or the relationship perceived between the facts and the rules, this information must be *deduced* from what has been stated.

Translation and reduction of a text. To read a judicial opinion expertly, one must know, however subliminally, that the meaning of a piece of writing does not reside only in its words or in its author's intentions but must be constructed by readers as they interact with the text (Gopen, 1984a, pp. 334–335). Before considering the particular skills involved in analyzing an opinion, we will consider first the implications of this basic idea about the reader's role in, as Iser puts it, "performance of meaning under the guidance of the text" (Iser, 1976, p. 16).

VIRTUAL TEXT. Practiced readers of judicial opinions have techniques that permit them both to enter into a legal text, that is, to inhabit the world it creates through written language, and stand outside that text, that is, to scrutinize it critically and examine its possible meanings. To help explain how a reader enters into and stands outside a text, we will use a model of the reading process. The model is based on Bruner's (1986, p. 25) discussion of the mechanisms by which narrative literature recruits a reader's imagination and "make[s] it possible for the reader to 'write' his own *virtual text*" (emphasis added). Bruner's discussion of "virtual text" indicates that it refers to a familiar if ordinarily unnoticed experience, one's cognitive reconstitution of an actual text, words on page, as one reads.

Figure 13.1 is a diagram that uses the concept of virtual text to describe case briefing. In the diagram, the rectangle on the left (Actual Text) represents the judicial opinion to be briefed. The shaded rectangle on the right (Virtual Text) represents the residual of a reader's interaction with the opinion or, more precisely, the meanings the reader has produced in reading the opinion and incorporated into his own preexisting cognitive schemata. The rectangle for the virtual text is smaller than the one for the actual text because the former is a reduction of the latter. That is, readers attend closely to and remember only those elements of a text that they perceive to convey important information. Step 1, the reader's interaction with the actual text in forming the virtual text, is represented as arrows indicating shifts in attention back and forth between the two texts. The smallest rectangle, located beneath the virtual text, represents the case brief, a new actual text. The case brief is produced by the reader's extracting from his virtual text and expressing in his own words the legally important parts of the opinion. In the diagram, this process is labeled Step 2.

Simplified as it may be in comparison with what it is meant to depict, Figure 13.1 highlights what is most critical in case briefing: translating the gist of an opinion into one's own vocabulary and idiom. For beginning law students, the effectiveness of such translations will depend on the correspondence between the virtual texts they produce in reading opinions and the virtual texts their professors produce. Some degree of correspondence between a student's and a professor's virtual texts is achieved when both readers perceive identical features of an opinion as salient and identical features of an opinion as inconsequential. The rate at which beginning law students acquire this shared perception will be determined only partly by their ability to familiarize themselves with terms and constructions peculiar to legal writing. More fundamentally, that acquisition rate will depend on the student's awareness of the structures in written exposition and practice in using cognitive strategies to discern those structures.

PERCEIVING STRUCTURES. Obviously, perceiving structure in writing depends on familiarity with the structural forms used in written discourse. Readers who apprehend the formal properties of prose come to reading with templates, conceptual models of possibilities for ordering written communication. At the level of form, for example, even the sentence, perhaps the most readily discriminable prose unit, can be richly nuanced. As Gopen shows in his structural analyses of legal and

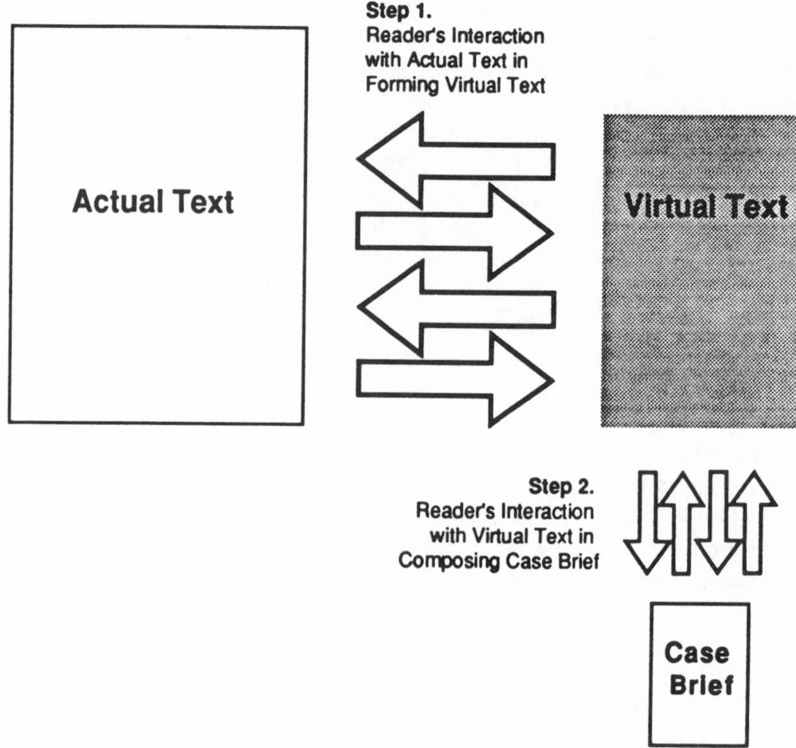

Figure 13.1. Schematic model of the case briefing process.

scientific writing (Gopen 1984a, 1984b, 1987; Gopen and Swan, 1990), knowledge of sentence form potentially includes far more than recognizing the grammatical necessity of certain sentence components (e.g., subject, predicate, object). A sentence template might incorporate, as well, awareness of the locations within sentences where readers expect to find emphatic material and appreciation for the communicative effects of alternative arrangements of sentence components.

Perception of the overall structure of written discourse requires other kinds of templates, most notably a template for the hierarchical outline. Beyond simply knowing the form of a hierarchical outline, though, one must be able to engage that knowledge while reading. Readers who have internalized the concept of hierarchical structure will perceive the ladder of abstraction in a text (Shaughnessy, 1977). They will see some statements as relatively general (or relatively specific) renderings of others, some ideas and discussions as subparts of others, and the whole of an exposition as integrated by an organizing idea.

To read a judicial opinion with the objective of discerning legal issues and issue-relevant rules, facts, and reasoning is to read seeking the opinion's rhetorical structure, the argument it propounds. Usually, the argument is woven into the opinion's larger, compositional structure.[10] Experienced readers of legal writing will distinguish rhetorical structure from compositional structure. Perceiving compositional structure entails observing *how* the author insinuates the argument in the text through various literary devices such as topic sentences, comparison and contrast, and recapitulation of major points.

Students who read judicial opinions without having learned the components of formal argument may fail to notice logical inconsistencies, implied assertions, and counterarguments that might have been raised but were not. Similarly, students who have not been taught literary conventions may fail to notice when the author of an opinion uses parallelism to mark similarities in apparently unrelated subjects or may fail to distinguish passages in which the author speaks from her own perspective and passages in which, for sake of discussion, she speaks from the perspective of another person. Readers are unlikely to be handicapped if oversights of this kind occur infrequently. Where such oversights characterize a person's reading habit, however, they will substantially diminish the quality and precision of that person's virtual texts.

Assuming that one is well acquainted with possibilities for structuring texts, by what means does one bring those possibilities into play while reading a particular text? Lundeburg (1987, p. 408) refers to such skills as "metacognitive strategies." As examples, she notes "planning," "monitoring," "checking one's thinking processes," and, at a step removed, "thinking about [one's] thinking." When Lundeburg compared the reading behavior of expert and novice readers of judicial opinions, she found that the experts used more metacognitive strategies and used them more consistently than did the novices. If such strategies are necessary to competent case briefing, it is reasonable to ask whether they are taught in law school.

Case briefing skills taught in law school

In the beginning weeks of the first semester in law school, professors in every class devote time to case briefing and usually prescribe routines and formats. The writing that students do in briefing cases is writing to be read only by themselves; briefs are not turned in to professors to be evaluated. The feedback students receive on their briefs is provided indirectly and to everyone at once, through analysis of the briefed cases in class. That indirect feedback is unlikely to concern structural patterns and writing conventions employed in the opinions.

Although the professors may recommend the reading strategies listed earlier, they do not teach students these strategies. Once first-semester classes are underway, students are presumed to be progressing on their own in the development of case-briefing skill.

The work of researchers, scholars, and professionals other than lawyers often requires interpretation of complex texts and metacognitive strategies such as those briefly considered here. Rarely, however, in these other pursuits, are beginning graduate students expected to master these sophisticated abilities at the rate beginning law students are expected to master them, or with the knowledge that one's grades and, in turn, career opportunities, depend on one's rate of mastery.

TASK 2: ANALYZING JUDICIAL OPINIONS IN CLASSROOM DIALOGUE

The character of oral case analysis

In all first-year law courses, regardless of subject, students are occupied primarily with learning legal language and legal analysis. The substantive law addressed in these courses provides a medium through which students can develop proficiency in legal reasoning and acquire vocabulary and diction proper to legal speech and writing. Briefing cases is instrumental in this learning, but face-to-face communication is required to perfect it.

In a seminal ethonographic study of legal education, Philips (1982, p. 182) notes that classroom interactions provide opportunities for students: (1) to hear teachers use new words and constructions in various contexts; (2) to use these words and constructions themselves in answering teachers' questions; and (3) to hear each other's usage, meaningful or not. Students are coached in legal analysis through these same interactions – that is, students practice legal analysis *while* practicing the use of new terms and phraseology.

The traditional format for instruction in legal analysis is the Socratic method, briefly described by Philips as follows:

> The teacher would call on a student, by title and last name (e.g., Ms. Smith), whether or not she or he had volunteered to speak, and ask that student a series of questions. Each question was structurally and topically dependent on the student's last answer or response, rather than having been planned out beforehand as part of a predetermined sequence. . . . The teacher might ask one student one or several questions before moving to the next student. When the teachers took up new cases, the first student asked to speak on such a case was often required to present information quite directly from [his or her case]

> brief. Thus that student might be asked to present the facts of the case or the reasons for the Court's holding. As the questioning proceeded, it was more likely to depart from the focus of the brief. (p. 182)

Philips acknowledges that law professors differ widely in classroom style and that these differences are not reflected in this account. Still, her description captures the open-ended, probing quality that is the hallmark of Socratic dialogue. In the last sentence quoted, Philips mentions the tendency for teachers to lead conversation *away* from the student's brief. This practice often gives students the false impression that their briefs are unimportant and merely set the occasion for extended discussions.

Regarding the general character of these discussions, White (1984) notes their intensely *legal* focus, that is, the professors' indifference to economic, social, or other contexts in which the events described in judicial opinions might be viewed. In addition, both White and Gopen (Gopen, 1984a) see close similarity between case analysis in the law classroom and the formalistic study of poetry. As attributes common to textual analysis in both poetry and law, Gopen mentions (1) consideration of multiple possible meanings, (2) recognition of the nonfungible nature of certain words, (3) appreciation for the effects of ambiguity of individual words and phrases, and (4) preoccupation with contextuality. Illustrating this last point, Gopen states that, in law, "the rule derived from one case is put in the different context of the facts from the next case, and as a result either the rule must change or the interpretation of it must change" (1984a, p. 344).

Although the students' case briefs may seem to serve only as points of departure for classroom discussion, they are actually the central subjects of discussion. Through the dialogue, the students' briefs of a case, their interpretations of the relevant legal text, are being critiqued. In questioning students on matters seemingly far afield of a case, professors *model* the kinds of questions the students themselves might have raised in briefing the case before class. Let us consider, then, the nature of the skills being modeled.

Skills involved in oral case analysis

The pattern of questioning typical of Socratic methodology suggests the turning of a kaleidoscope. For example, building on the case data presented initially by the student, the teacher might propose first one then another substitution in the data base and, with each substitution, ask whether the new situation would produce a legal result identical to that of the preceding one. Interjected material might be based on previously discussed cases or on related pending cases and policy issues. Often, however, substitute scenarios introduce apparently irrelevant information.

To get a rough idea of how interrogation in the law school classroom works, imagine the student who has been called on as someone who is planning a dinner party for luminaries and is being questioned about the seating arrangements by a more experienced host. Assume the student has stated that she wants to set the conditions for spirited, just short of openly hostile, table conversation. With this aim in mind, she proposes seating Carl Sagan, Oprah Winfrey, and Jesse Helms across from Martina Navratalova, Nelson Mandela, and Barbra Streisand. Having heard this scenario, the teacher might ask, "What would happen if you moved Barbra Streisand to another table and put Barbara Jordan in her place?" (substitution based on nominal similarity). Hearing the student's reply, the teacher might continue, "Now, maintaining that arrangement, what would be the result if you then replaced Nelson Mandela with Boris Yeltsin?" (substitution based on functional similarity).

Although this example differs in many ways from oral case analysis, it requires similar cognitive skills; namely, the ability to imagine the characteristics of each element in a configuration both separately and in relation to neighboring elements, to imagine each whole configuration separately, and to retrieve for imaginative comparison configurations previously considered. The difficulty in processing so much information would be reduced considerably if respondents were given plenty of time and the chance to chart the data on paper. As Philips points out, however, in the law school classroom as in the appellate courtroom, a premium is placed on the ability to answer quickly and coherently, "in clear English, with as few incomplete, rephrased, or awkward utterances as possible" (1982, p. 188).

A student speaker's success in keeping pace with the discussion will depend on his anticipating, or at least recognizing, the dimensions in which the professor is stretching the case and the legal implications of exploring these dimensions. Students who are not being directly questioned profit from observing those who are by participating vicariously as if they were. Not surprisingly, being called on in class is welcomed only by students who perceive themselves as junior colleagues of the professors rather than their intellectual inferiors, are confident in their preparation, and are secure enough or reckless enough to risk losing what Philips calls "verbal cool" in front of teachers and classmates.

Oral case analysis skills taught in law school

It is hard to say precisely what skills professors *teach* in first-year law classrooms, although, certainly, students who are psychologically, socially, and academically primed for law school might acquire and refine any number of skills in these classrooms. For the most part, as has been pointed out, the traditional instruction method is a matter of *employing* a procedure rather than, say, describing the procedure and illustrating how it is used to achieve a particular learning objective. That is, instruction occurs *inside* the procedure; it is not *about* the procedure, its rationale, its powers, or its limitations.

Many first-year students, traditional students as well as minority students, are bewildered and intimidated by this instructional approach. They feel they have been engaged in a game without knowing its object or rules of play. When they "swing on a curve ball" and miss, the next batter is called and the game continues. There is no replay in which, for example, the professor debriefs them, saying, "Notice how I set you up. I threw a straight pitch, then a curve. You weren't expecting the curve, so let's try it again. And, this time . . ." Instead, those duped by the pitcher's shrewdness are left to ponder their foolishness and devise their own strategies for avoiding humiliation during their next turns at the plate.

If law professors seem to relish being considered inscrutable, they are only following tradition. As Stevens (1983) explains in his history of legal education, the professors' concern to preserve mystery in the classroom has its roots in turn-of-the-century reforms at Harvard Law School. Introduction of the case method was the centerpiece of these reforms. They were inspired, in part, by Darwinian ideas of natural selection, or survival of the fittest, which were prevalent in the thinking of the day. Commenting on what was at the time a new pedagogical approach, Stevens writes:

> [The] machismo view of the case method was neatly caught in *The Centennial History of the Harvard Law School.* The student, it suggested, "is the invitee upon the case-system premise, who, like the invitee in the reported cases, soon finds himself fallen into a pit. He is given no map carefully charting and laying out all the byways and corners of the legal field, but is left, to a certain extent, to find his way by himself. His scramble out of difficulties, if successful, leaves him feeling that he has built up a knowledge of law for himself. The legal content of his mind has a personal nature; he has made it himself."(1983, p. 54)

The assumption that putting students into an ambiguous situation spurs them to teach themselves the way out persists in legal education today. But that assumption is not and never was unconditional. Its validity rests on a prior assumption that, in their previous schooling and social experience, the students will have been exposed to, if not coached in, competitive academic behavior and other survival skills appropriate to the situation encountered in the law school classroom. The latter assumption was valid only as long as law school admissions policies were designed to make it so, that is, designed to create student populations comprised of well-educated young men from families in corporate business and the professions. Thoughtful reappraisal of both these assumptions and their implications, although surely called for, did not occur when law schools began to admit first-generation college graduates from economically and educationally disadvantaged groups.

TASK 3. ANALYZE HYPOTHETICAL STORIES IN LEGAL MEMORANDA

In view of its cognitive and linguistic demands, Task 3 is the most challenging of the four literacy tasks discussed in this chapter. The end product of Task 3 is a memorandum that is similar in function to a judicial opinion. Here, after considering the form and purposes of a legal memorandum, we will concentrate on analytic and composing processes required in Task 3 but not required in the other three literacy tasks. Specifically, we will examine (1) the process by which, in analyzing a memorandum assignment, one abstracts a legal rule from material distributed across several judicial opinions and (2) the process by which, in composing a memorandum, one *contextualizes* analysis of the legal problem for readers.

The legal memorandum

The typical memorandum assignment casts students as junior associates in a law firm and presents them with a summary of a consultation interview with a prospective client and a packet of reference material. The reference material consists of appellate opinions in relevant cases and, where they exist, relevant statutes. The students are asked to use the references to scrutinize the client's story for its potential legal significance and to report their findings in a paper, eight to ten pages long, addressed to one of the firm's partners.

The format for a legal memorandum usually consists of an abstract, a body, and a conclusion. The abstract is divided into Questions Presented and Brief Answers. Each one of the Questions Presented should note a legal issue, the applicable rule of law, and the facts in the client's story that give rise to the issue. Each one of the Brief Answers should forecast the probable result of submitting its corresponding question to a trial court judge for resolution. The body of the memorandum is divided into the Statement of Facts and the Discussion. The Statement of Facts should succinctly narrate the client's story, including every fact to be considered in the discussion. The Discussion should provide a systematic analysis of each issue introduced in the abstract. The Conclusion should recapitulate the main points of the Discussion in terms of recommendations for action.

The production of a legal memorandum is both an exercise in legal analysis and an exercise in expository writing to communicate the context, process, and outcome of that analysis. In both the analysis and the writing, one must work within the constraints of multiple purposes. For example, were the memorandum actually to be used by a senior partner, it would be regarded as a preliminary assessment of the client's situation. Thus, students are encouraged to disclose weaknesses as well as strengths in the client's position vis-à-vis potential opponents in a lawsuit. At the same time, mindful that the client's position eventually may be argued in court, students must strive to construe as favorable to the client's position information that an opponent could construe as unfavorable to the client's position. In other words, the students have to turn potential weaknesses into strengths.

Although all the reference material must be considered, some will have more weight than others – namely, cases heard in courts that would have jurisdiction in the client's case, and cases most like the client's case. Often, similarities between the client's case and earlier cases will lie less in identical facts than in analogous relationships among facts or in other patterns of correspondence that must be discerned by the writer and explained to the reader.

When analytic considerations such as those just mentioned are added to the ordinary difficulties of communicating in writing, the complexity of a memorandum assignment becomes clear. In the following discussion, analytic and composing processes are treated separately. For the person actually producing a memorandum, however, these processes are interactive and iterative. Inevitably, that is, the memorandum writer's attempt to express his initial, conceptual, formulation of the analysis in prose brings to light previously overlooked features of the client's situation, thereby generating tension that can be relieved only by revising the analysis or revising the prose.

Overview of the analytic task. In analyzing a memorandum assignment, one of the central objectives is to arrive at a complete statement of each *legal issue* posed by the client's story (Hamburger, 1984, p. 81). Disputes, as described by clients to their attorneys, often include matters of contention not addressed by the law. The job of the memorandum writer is to extract, from all the issues that might be considered in the client's story, those in which the law takes an interest.

Although legal issues appear at the beginning of a memorandum, identifying the legal issues is not the first step in analyzing the assignment. To identify an issue is to state an uncertainty about the applicability of a rule to one or more of the facts. The first step in analyzing the assignment is to identify the appropriate legal rule. Without a rule of law as a guide, there is no way to appreciate the possible legal significance of the facts in the client's story. The rule serves as a filter for the facts, a tool for trapping possibly relevant facts and allowing others to drop out of consideration.

Where a memorandum assignment includes a statute among the references, the statute serves as a general statement of the relevant rule. In these instances, the facts in the accompanying cases can be used to clarify interpretation of the statute and pinpoint the issues in the client's situation. Often, however, memorandum assignments concern legal issues not covered by statutes. In these instances, case law alone will govern. The memorandum writer must review the reference cases and, on the basis of rule–fact relationships observed in each of them, synthesize a net rule that takes account of all of them.

Once the writer has either identified or synthesized the rule of law to use, he can attend to the following steps in the analysis: applying the rule to the facts in the client's story to determine the legal issues; identifying nonissues (rule–fact relationships that are self-evident but must be noted as immaterial in the dispute); developing arguments and counterarguments for interpreting the issues (using factual material from the client's story and the reference cases to support or illustrate argumentative points); and, evaluating the relative persuasiveness of each argument.

The reasoning processes involved in the steps just listed are no less important and no less complex than rule synthesis, but are routinely and thoroughly addressed in law school classes. Because it is the least explored part of legal reasoning, rule synthesis will be discussed in detail here.

SYNTHESIZING A RULE. Synthesizing a rule of law for a memorandum problem is not a matter of simply plucking the rule from each reference case and stringing all the rules together willy-nilly. Rather, the process is one of constructing an original formulation, a multipart rule that reflects the contributions of expressed or implied rules in all the reference cases. Many beginning law students have difficulty not only in accomplishing this constructive act but in appreciating the need for it. Their misunderstanding is revealed in memoranda discussion sections in which the main structural elements are the individual reference cases rather than issues that can be illustrated in several reference cases. A discussion section organized around reference cases indicates that the

Table 13.1 *Topical order in case-based and issue-based discussions*

Case-based organization	Issue-based organization
Topic 1: Reference Case 1	*Topic 1: Issue 1*
• Summary of case 1 (issue, rules, facts, reasoning, holding)	• Statement of issue 1, relevant rule, and relevant facts from client's situation
• Comparison and contrast of facts in case 1 with client's fact situation to identify and analyze pertinent issues	• Analysis of issue 1 through application of rule to facts in client's situation – analysis includes comparison and contrast of court's treatment of related facts in *all* reference cases
Topic 2: Reference Case 2	*Topic 2: Issue 2*
• Summary of case 2 (repeats above)	• Statement of issue 2 (repeats above)
• Comparison and contrast of facts in case 2 (repeats above)	• Analysis of issue 2 (repeats above)

author has not constructed a net rule and, consequently, does not perceive the legal issues in general terms, that is, apart from their embodiment in specific cases. Where the *cases* are the focus of discussion, the reader is obliged to accompany the writer in a search for the issues. The differences in case-based and issue-based organization are highlighted in Table 13.1, which shows topical order in the two approaches.

For beginning law students, the tendency to organize memoranda discussions around cases is strong, for the cases are prefabricated structural units. Attempts to steer students toward the issue-based alternative are complicated by the difficulty of explaining what it means to synthesize a rule. Ordinarily, the process takes place internally. Hence, it is not fully articulated in words or easily described as a sequence of objective acts. Moreover, the process is highly idiosyncratic. It varies from one person to another and, within the same person, varies depending on the material being considered. Despite these limitations, it is possible to convey some understanding of the rule synthesis process through illustration. Table 13.2 provides such an illustration in the form of a self-directed Socratic dialogue between a law student and herself. Although such a dialogue normally would occur silently through highly condensed inner speech,[11] Table 13.2 presents it as if it were an audible, comprehensible, conversation.

Table 13.2 is based on a rudimentary memorandum assignment, the kind that might be used to introduce the memorandum. The assignment

Table 13.2 *Student's self-interrogation to synthesize a rule of law in the Ferguson Memorandum Assignment*

The son says that his deceased father, Colonel Ferguson, was unduly influenced in executing his second will. What do the cases have to say about "undue influence"?

Steffans, the earlier case, presents a four-part test. The fourth part is linked to the others with "and," which suggests that all four conditions must be met to find undue influence.

But the four parts omit key words. Who is being referred to in each part?

Part 1, "susceptibility to undue influence," undoubtedly refers to the testator. The other parts probably refer to the alleged influencer. That is, the alleged influencer would have to have "opportunity to influence" and "be disposed to influence" the testator, and would have to "covet the result" achieved when the will was signed.

Although *Kendall* refers to the *four-part* test, it also mentions a two-part test: (1) "a confidential relationship between the testator and the one alleged to have exercised undue influence" and (2) "suspicious circumstances surrounding the making of the will."

How might these two tests be related?

The Kendall opinion suggests a relationship. In stating that the four-part test "need not be considered here . . . ," the judge implies that, where the conditions of the two-part test are met, the four-part test becomes irrelevant.

Why? Why would the court regard the four-part test as irrelevant if the facts of the case met the conditions of the two-part test?

Well, the two-part test is more to the point. It focuses on evidence directly related to the events alleged to have occurred. The four-part test, on the other hand, focuses on evidence that might be used to *infer* undue influence where the events surrounding the execution of the will are unknown. Indeed, in *Steffans* (four-part), in contrast with *Kendall* (two-part), there is no mention of the events directly surrounding the drafting of the will. This is only a theory, of course, but it fits the information I've been given.

How are the tests alike?

Part 1 of *Kendall*'s two-part test, "existence of a confidential relationship," offers a *specific example* of the kind of evidence needed to meet the more general second part of *Steffans*' four-part test, "opportunity to influence." And, part 2 of *Kendall*'s two-part test, "suspicious circumstances," is accompanied by a couple of specific examples; namely, "sudden and unexplained change in the attitude of the testator" and "activity by the beneficiary in procuring the drafting and execution of the will." Similarly, parts 1, 3, and 4 of *Steffans*' four-part test seem to offer *additional* examples of "suspicious circumstances": the testator's "susceptibility," and the alleged influencer's "disposition to influence" and "coveting the result."

I can use all this information to draft an outline that combines the two rules:

1. Opportunity to Influence (part 2 of four-part test)
   a. confidential relationship between testator and alleged influencer (part 1 of two-part test)

Table 13.2 (*cont.*)

2. Suspicious circumstances (part 2 of two-part test)
   a. sudden and unexplained behavior by testator (*Kendall*)
   b. activity by alleged influencer in procuring drafting and execution of will (*Kendall*)
   c. evidence testator was susceptible to influence (part 1 of four-part test)
   d. evidence alleged influencer was disposed to influence testator (part 3 of four-part test)
   e. evidence alleged influencer coveted the result of influencing testator (part 4 of four-part test).

What else do these cases tell me?

In *Kendall,* all the evidence considered is *affirmative* evidence; it met the conditions of the test: Kendall's relationship with her sister and the sister's attorney was considered a "confidential" relationship. And the behavior of the sister and her attorney related to the signing of the will was considered "suspicious." In *Steffans,* however, the evidence was *negative* evidence; none of it passed the test.

Perhaps Steffans' *examples of what doesn't meet its test suggest their opposites, that is, what would meet its tests. Okay, I'll start at the top of the outline. What facts did the* Steffans *judge consider in deciding that the alleged influencer, the paperboy, did* not *have an opportunity to influence Steffans?*

Steffans' contacts with the paperboy were limited to brief meetings in which she paid what she owed for the paper. And, often, she avoided even this contact by putting the money for the paper in an envelope under the doormat.

If the court considered such interactions "insufficient opportunity to influence," would it consider more frequent and longer interactions "sufficient?"

Maybe.

As for the next item in the outline, "confidential relationship," Kendall *already provides two positive examples: member of immediate family or personal attorney. So, I'll move on to "suspicious circumstances." Here, too,* Kendall *provides two positive examples, items a. and b., so I'll go to item c., "susceptibility to influence." What facts did the judge consider in determining that Steffans was* not *susceptible to outside influence in executing her will?*

Steffans was a real estate broker; she had a reputation as an eccentric; she told a neighbor that she intended to leave her entire estate to the paperboy; and she told the neighbor why she chose the paperboy as her heir.

More generally, what do each of these facts indicate?

That Steffans was familiar with financial transactions; that she was independent and self-directed or, at least, known to make decisions that others considered odd; that she was fully aware of the terms of her will; and that she had expressed her own reasons for disposing of her possessions as she did.

If the court considered facts such as these to be evidence of "no susceptibility," would it not consider as evidence of "susceptibility" the following testator characteristics and behavior: unfamiliarity with financial transactions, reputation as an

Table 13.2 (*cont.*)

indecisive person, lack of awareness of the terms of the will, and no expressed reasons for choosing the heir?

Maybe.

Now, as for the last two items under "suspicious circumstances," "disposition to influence" and "coveted result," Steffans presents no evidence concerning these parts. So, *what does this tell me?*

That probably I was right when I concluded that *Steffans'* four-part test was an all-or-nothing test.

But, what would I consider evidence that one person was disposed to influence another and coveted the result of such influence?

That the first person stood to gain something through the influence and needed that thing and couldn't get it otherwise.

Does what I think matter?

Sure it does. So, I'll add those items to the rule outline. Now, then, I have specific events and behavior to look for when I study the Colonel Ferguson fact pattern:

1. Did the Arizona Properties attorney have opportunity to influence Colonel Ferguson? Specifically, did the attorney have a confidential relationship with Ferguson?
   a. Was he Ferguson's relative or his personal attorney?
   b. Were his contacts with Ferguson frequent or infrequent?
   c. Were these contacts brief or lengthy?
2. Are the circumstances of the drafting and signing of the contested will known? If so, were they suspicious?
   a. Was there anything sudden or unexplained about Ferguson's behavior before or after he signed the contested will?
   b. Is there evidence the attorney was active in drafting the will or having it executed?
   c. Is there evidence Ferguson was susceptible to the attorney's influence? Specifically, is there evidence that Ferguson:
      1) was either familiar or unfamiliar with financial transactions?
      2) was considered either a self-directed and decisive person or a dependent and indecisive person?
      3) had full knowledge of the terms of the contested will?
      4) had his own reasons for disposing of his estate according to the terms of the contested will?
   d. Is there evidence that the attorney was disposed to influence Ferguson? Specifically, is there evidence that he stood to gain something through such influence?
   e. Is there evidence that the attorney coveted the result of influencing Ferguson? Specifically, is there evidence that he needed the thing he might gain through such influence and could not get it otherwise?

concerns a client whose 87-year-old father recently died, leaving an estate of over one million dollars to the land development company of which he was vice-president. The father, Colonel Ferguson, was a decorated World War I veteran. He had worked for the development company less than five years, having been hired shortly after the death of his wife. During his tenure with the company, the father made business trips to three foreign capitals at the company's expense and went fishing two or three weekends a month with the company's attorney. This attorney drafted the father's will that was in effect when he died. The son questions the validity of this will, claiming that his father executed it under pressure, or undue influence, from the attorney. The son maintains that his father's earlier will, which would have made the son the beneficiary of his father's fortune, should be reinstated by the court. The son admits that his father, from whom he was estranged since his mother's death, was "not at all senile."

The reference cases for this assignment, which are extremely abbreviated versions of the original, are presented in the appendix to this chapter. Both cases concern undue influence. In the earlier case, *Steffans,* the court rejected the claim of undue influence; in the later case, *Kendall,* the court upheld the claim.

In reading Table 13.2, assume that the student has studied the details of the client's story carefully and has just begun to analyze the two reference cases. The questions and directions the student puts to herself are set in italic, the answers in regular type face.

SKILLS INVOLVED IN SYNTHESIZING A LEGAL RULE. The imaginary student behind the Table 13.2 dialogue did not hit upon *the* correct method of synthesizing a legal rule, for, as was mentioned earlier, there is no one correct method. Nonetheless, most law professors probably would accept this student's approach as a lawyerly one, because it is systematic and grounded in the words of the reference texts. As a recipe for synthesizing a legal rule, that approach might be summarized as follows:

1. Build the rule (or rules) on the scaffolding of a hierarchical outline.
2. Divide the cases by jurisdiction and begin with those that would have jurisdiction in the client's situation.
3. Proceeding chronologically through the cases (earliest to latest case or vice versa), search the text of each for signals that a rule is being invoked.
4. As you identify statements that appear to be rules, articulate them, classify them, and compare and contrast them in detail.
5. Use the rules that are stated most generally as main headings in the outline; fit the more specifically stated rules under these headings.

6. For each rule or rule-part identified, locate the particular facts hooked by that rule.
7. For each fact, determine its nature as evidence: that is, whether it is affirmative or negative; where the evidence is affirmative, ask what would constitute negative evidence (and vice versa).
8. Notice the judge's disposition toward the evidence; that is, which facts were deemed convincing and why, which were not and why.
9. Ask what was left out. Among the rules and facts that might have been considered, which were not considered? Why?

Overview of the composing task. Table 13.2 shows only part of the analytic task but enough to indicate that its demands for cognitive agility and attention to detail can be exhausting. Indeed, many beginning law students are fairly consumed by the analysis of a memorandum problem and arrive with relief at the point of writing the memorandum. Having through great effort found a resolution to the client's situation, the students assume that reporting their findings will be relatively easy.

Far from being easier than the analytic task, the composing task brings into play an important *additional* consideration, the perspective of a reader who is unacquainted with the client's story. In other words, composing a memorandum requires contextualizing the legal analysis of the client's story, presenting it in a way that respects the reader's ignorance of the characters and issues involved.

ESTABLISHING CONTEXT. The need to establish context for readers distinguishes the memorandum assignment from the other three literacy tasks. Performance of the other three tasks can be compared with conversations in which the context for the exchange is known to the participants and not necessary to explain. When a student briefs a judicial opinion, for example, she communicates with herself, within the discourse framework established by the author of the opinion, about what she understands the author to have said. As both author and reader of the brief, the student has no reason to consider the perspectives of other persons who have not read the opinion. Similarly, when a student analyzes a case orally in class, her statements, as well as those of other students and the teacher, are contextualized by discussions in previous class sessions and by the cases read and briefed for that particular session. Someone who has not attended previous meetings of the class might have difficulty following the discussion, but that is of no concern to the discussants; they converse with each other within a frame of reference built by their common experience in the course. That frame of reference is assumed during the examination at the end of the course. When a student takes a law examination, she converses with her teacher, within doctrinal and methodological contexts developed throughout the course and within specific factual contexts provided by the examination questions. Thus, writing an answer, a student can refer to material in the question or in the course without having first to present the material to readers who have not taken the course and read the examination question. When a law student writes a legal memorandum, however, and in this task alone among the four, she must communicate comprehensibly, in writing, to persons who have little if any knowledge of the specific information on which the communication is based.

To a large extent, the need to orient readers to the subject and scope of a memorandum is addressed by the memorandum format. Readers can see at a glance, from the headings, where to look for particular contents. Moreover, because it has built-in redundancy, the format allows readers repeated opportunities to grasp the theme of the memorandum and the option of reading short parts, the abstract and conclusion, for capsule statements of the theme. Thus, format reveals the memorandum's overall assembly, and thereby provides readers important contextual information. But format cannot carry the entire burden of communicating context. In the end, that responsibility rests with the author. And it weighs most heavily over the discussion section.

A memorandum's discussion is its vital core, the measure of its cogency as legal discourse. If the discussion is incoherent, or analytically flimsy, or fails to separate issues sharply, the whole piece collapses. Here, it is not enough that the author see for herself the nature of the client's legal problem and how the court is likely to approach it. She must show readers how to see the problem as she does. To do that, she must frame the discussion, that is, specify the problem it addresses, the parts she perceives to comprise the problem, and the logical connections among the parts.

The need for writers to establish context for readers – to signal, for example, the direction in which a discussion is headed and why it is headed in that direction – is apparent in prose that lacks contextual cues. Table 13.3 presents a sample of such prose. The left column of Table 13.3 contains the first four paragraphs in the discussion section of a memorandum. The memorandum was written by a first-year law student in response to the Colonel Ferguson assignment. The right column shows a professor's questions in response to the student's text.

On a quick first reading, perhaps because its sentences are fairly well written, the discussion section excerpt in Table 13.3 appears comprehensible. On a close reading, however, the excerpt is maddeningly cryptic. The writer has not explained the logical relationships among her assertions. There are numerous possible relationships among the terms and ideas contained in the four paragraphs. But the writer has not acknowl-

Table 13.3 *First four paragraphs of discussion section in student's memorandum and professor's questions*

Student's Discussion Section	Professor's Questions
A. P. Ferguson, Jr., a beneficiary of a first will, has asked us to challenge the validity of the testator's second will in probate court. The first will should be reinstated because the second will is invalid. "Undue influence can occur when there is a confidential relationship between the testator and the one alleged to have exercised undue influence, and there are suspicious circumstances surrounding the making of the will." *In re Will of Kendall*	How are the ideas in these three sentences connected? What is "undue influence?" Is it the only ground for invalidating a will? Why is the *Kendall* rule cited? Is it *the* rule for determining "undue influence?" Is "undue influence" the main issue here? Is it the basis for your assertion that the second will is invalid?
In the case at bar the beneficiary of the second will, a corporation, financed trips for Colonel A. P. Ferguson, the testator, "allegedly for purposes of learning foreign land development strategies," to Hong Kong and other foreign lands. It seems unlikely that an eighty-seven year old man with probably few years of life left be interested in the development of lands (*sic*).	What do the trips and their alleged purposes have to do with the *Kendall* rule? Are they evidence of a "confidential relationship" or of "suspicious circumstances?" Is the colonel's age the only fact relevant to questions about his foreign trips?
Further, these trips before the colonel revoked the will which was executed was executed to his surviving child, A. P. Ferguson, Jr. (*sic*). These foreign land trips seem to have influenced the colonel's revoking of the first will.	Is your conclusion about the effect of these trips on the colonel based solely on the fact that they occurred *before* he revoked his first will? If so, why? Do you have any contrary evidence?
The contention that there was undue influence is fair because suspicious circumstances exist. The trial court in Kendall admitted the second will to probate. The court found that the attorney who drafted the second will was not the testator's personal attorney, but rather the beneficiary's.	

Table 13.3 (*cont.*)

The court also determined that the testator had been propped up to mark the will with an "C" (*sic*). The court concluded that undue influence had occurred.	Why are you telling me these facts from *Kendall?* Are they somehow analogous to the colonel's foreign trips?
In the case at bar, however, the corporation may argue that the trips to foreign lands were part of the vice-president's duties and that as vice-president the colonel helped make decisions as to who would travel and why that person would travel.	It is well to explain *what* the corporation will argue about the trips, but not until you have explained *why* it will argue about them.
The beneficiary of the second will could also argue that because he was chosen to make these travels was reason enough to indicate that the colonel was vastly interested in foreign land development and is why he willed his $1.3 million estate to the corporation (*sic*).	

edged these possible relationships by indicating the particular relationships that she perceives and that are guiding her from one statement to the next. In neglecting to announce her rhetorical intentions at the outset, the writer handicaps the reader through the entire piece. When basic, orienting, questions are not answered in the opening sentences of the discussion and additional questions are raised by each succeeding sentence, the reader's "attention costs" are compounded. Uncertainty about how to construe the text does not diminish as the reader proceeds; it grows.

The deficiencies in the Table 13.3 discussion excerpt are reminiscent of those in writing protocols examined by Mina Shaughnessy in *Errors and expectations* (1977), a landmark work on the essays of inexperienced undergraduate writers. Commenting on these writers and their difficulties in composing, Shaughnessy states:

> One of the most notable differences between experienced and inexperienced writers is the rate at which they reach closure on a point. The experienced writer characteristically reveals a much greater tolerance

> for what Dewey called "an attitude of suspended conclusion," than the inexperienced writer, whose thought often seems to halt at the boundary of each sentence rather than move on, by gradations of subsequent comments, to an elaboration of the sentence. The [essays of the inexperienced writer tend], as a result, to be made up of "sentences of thought" rather than "passages of thought," and although the essays are not always short, they tend to be so because of the difficulty the writer has in staying with his point beyond its initial formulation. (p. 227)

The author of the paragraphs in Table 13.3 is considerably more advanced as a writer than were Shaughnessy's students. Like them, however, she is handicapped by inexperience in the discourse skills expected of students in her educational setting.

SKILLS INVOLVED IN ESTABLISHING CONTEXT. In reading a judicial opinion, as was noted in a preceding section, comprehension depends on the ability to perceive structure in the text. In writing a legal memorandum, comprehensibility depends on the ability to create structure in text and mark that structure for readers. To create structure is to create boundaries that limit the meaning of assertions. Context is the conceptual domain enclosed by the boundaries. Marking structure is, thus, a way of establishing context.

At the level of form, for example, grammar and punctuation, the sentences in Table 13.3 are well marked for readers. At the level of meaning, for example, logical relationships among assertions, the Table 13.3 excerpt as a whole is poorly marked or, more exactly, inconsistently marked. Some statements promise information that is not subsequently provided. Some statements answer questions that have not been raised.

To establish rhetorical context for readers, memorandum writers must, at minimum, (1) introduce the components of the discussion (specific issues, rules, and facts to be addressed), (2) articulate logical connections among the components, and (3) explain how these connections imply a particular course of action with respect to the client's situation.

Few writers succeed in fully contextualizing their assertions in a first draft. Rather, the process is an iterative one that engages the same skills used in critically reading texts by other authors. The trick is in being able to read one's own composition and question it as if someone else had written it. Achieving the perspective of the other is the first, most basic, meaning of revision. The reader's column in Table 13.3 makes the perspective of the other concrete and, thereby, models for the writer the first step in revising. The second step is a matter of reworking the text to answer the questions.[12]

Over time, students who regularly seek and receive criticism of their writing internalize the critic's perspective. As a result, they produce first drafts that are more reader-sensitive and that can be subjected to more refined, penetrating critique. Students who do not have opportunities for regular feedback from interested readers do not develop as writers. Unaware of how their writing might be improved, they persist in turning in papers characterized by what Flower (1979) and Flower and Hayes (1981, 1984) term "writer-based" rather than "reader-based" prose.

Memorandum skills taught in law school

The legal memorandum assignment is the place in the first-year law curriculum where everything comes together: interpretation of legal texts, synthesis of rules from several texts, explication of legal issues, organization of an argument, and written communication of legal reasoning in a self-explanatory exposition. Oddly enough, however, considering the centrality of the memorandum assignment as an integrating task, legal writing is treated as a marginal subject in legal education.[13] At many law schools, the teaching of legal writing is disdained by the faculty and willingly delegated to faculty adjuncts or, in some instances, upper-level law students (see Boyer, 1985; Gale, 1980; Stratman, 1990).[14]

Gopen (1987) notes that, in recent years, bowing to pressure from within and outside the legal community, a few law schools have begun to commit substantial resources to the development of legal writing programs. These programs offer students individualized coaching in the memorandum skills described here and, for Gopen, represent a wave of the future. Meanwhile, at the majority of law schools, students do not receive the kind of individual feedback that writers need to appreciate their readers' perspectives on their work.

TASK 4. ANALYZING HYPOTHETICAL STORIES IN LAW SCHOOL EXAMINATIONS

The law school examination

In traditional law school courses, students' grades are based entirely on their performance on one written examination, administered at the end of the semester. Although short-answer and multiple-choice examination questions are used occasionally, essay questions are most common, particularly in first-year courses.

The typical essay question tells a story. As in the memorandum assignment, the story may be presented from the point of view of one of its characters. More often, it is told from the perspective of a disinterested observer. For example, the story might recount a series of related events in which the characters involved in events in one part of the series are unaware of characters and events in other parts. In this example, the last line in the question might be a general directive, such as, "Discuss the rights and liabilities of all the parties."

Ordinarily, these essay questions touch the major doctrinal topics covered in a course but, as Kissam (1989, pp. 439–440) notes, approach these topics from a different angle:

> Classroom work . . . is primarily concerned with the analysis of pivotal or test cases and the use of basic legal theory to understand, interpret, and evaluate legal doctrine.
>
> On . . . exams, however, the student typically is expected to employ legal doctrine taught throughout the course to resolve or argue about "*borderline*"cases that tend to sit, as David Chambers has put it, "in nervous juxtaposition between the situations in cases discussed in class." (emphasis added)

In answering an essay question, the student's task is to identify all legal issues and, with respect to each issue, to invoke the appropriate legal rule and apply the rule to the relevant facts, showing how alternative readings of the facts might lead to different results.

Because law school examinations are meant to differentiate students, they are strictly timed and, almost invariably, contain more legal issues than can be dealt with thoroughly in the time available. Often, too, examination problems contain little tricks designed to foil students who do not question seemingly logical initial reactions to the facts presented. Thus, if one is to perform well on a law examination, one must be both quick and cautious in answering.[15]

Skills involved in writing an examination answer

Most of the skills needed to answer an essay question are exercised in the other tasks discussed in this chapter. In the essay examination, as in the memorandum assignment, students use rules to screen a hypothetical story. For the examination, however, the rules are derived, not from a few reference cases, but from all the cases discussed in a course.

To be able to cite readily the rules during an examination, one must have prepared an outline of the course ahead of time. Such outlines will be most useful if they are organized around issues, tightly phrased statements of relevant rules, and numerous examples of facts that would trigger each rule. The more diverse the examples, the more helpful they will be, for the critical skill in issue spotting is recognizing instances of the general in various specifics (Kissam, 1989, p. 440).

Students are expected to produce their own course outlines and are strongly discouraged by their professors from using commercially prepared briefs and law course outlines in doing so. Despite the professors' advice, as Philips (1982, p. 186) observes, students do resort to forbidden sources of information:

> Virtually all of the students use these study aids, and the further on they are in a semester, the more they rely on them. The students learn from their fellow students that these aids exist, and they also learn from their peers which aids are thought to be the best ones for particular courses.

Thus, in preparing for a law examination, it is possible to avoid the tedious but enlightening task of synthesizing the rules on one's own.

In the examination situation, in addition to having the course material organized and committed to memory in outline form, students must be able to recall quickly terms and phrases from their outlines and weave them into their answers as needed. This retrieval and application process is aided considerably by what Kissam (1989) refers to as the implicit paradigm in successful examination answers – "good paragraph thinking":

> A good answer may (and sometimes does) consist of nothing more than a series of paragraphs in which each paragraph identifies a specific issue or subissue, identifies an appropriate authority in sufficiently precise terms, and applies this authority to the problem, often showing how to arrive first at one result and then the other. (p. 443)

Regarding the preceding statement, Kissam adds:

> In this paradigm it is not necessary that the paragraphs be well written as a formal matter, or that the paragraphs be carefully or coherently related to each other, or that any paragraph display sound practical judgment about which matters are more important, or that any paragraph show how a conflict between competing arguments might be resolved in a reasonable manner. Indeed, the best evidence for these latter claims may be that the paradigm of good paragraph thinking is equally useful in answering well-constructed short-answer questions that test for the same qualities as . . . essay questions. Nonetheless, the graders of [essay examinations] written in the style of good paragraph thinking . . . are likely to believe that these essays represent relatively successful constructive thought or writing ability. These are the answers, after all, that appear to reflect our success as teachers, and it would be surprising if law professors did not think that successful . . . answers represent the many complex qualities of successful legal thought. (p. 443)

Table 13.4 *Summary of literacy tasks and teaching methods*

Literacy task	Component skills	Typical method of instruction	Typical feedback on performance	Formal evaluation
read and brief judicial opinions	recognize and summarize the rhetorical structure of a written legal argument	professor prescribes format and guidelines	indirect, through class discussion of cases briefed	course grade at end of semester
analyze judicial opinions orally	respond quickly and coherently to questions about legal texts and hypothetical scenarios	professor directs Socratic dialogue with individual student speakers	direct to student speakers, indirect to vicariously participating students	course grade at end of semester
analyze hypothetical fact patterns in legal memoranda	analytic: synthesize multipart rule from reference cases; apply rule to facts to identify legal issues. composing: state legal issues and organize the analysis of each in light of the rule and the reference cases; establish context for readers through background, orienting, transition, and summary statements.	professor prescribes reliance on legal analysis demonstrated in class, gives little attention to synthesis, expects students to know how to organize compositions	feedback tends to focus on legal analysis	course grade at end of semester
analyze hypothetical fact patterns in law school examinations	before examination: organize a course outline around representative issues, rules, and facts in the subject area. during examination: identify and analyze legal issues in formulaic paragraphs	some professors suggest guidelines for good answers and/or give a practice exam at mid-term	grades on practice examinations (where given)	course grade at end of semester

If we assume Kissam's assessments are accurate, law students who are hip to the "good paragraph formula" have a decided advantage over students who do not know the formula or that they are expected to use it on examinations.

Examination skills taught in law school

The skills involved in analyzing an essay examination question are practiced in law class discussions. In most law schools, however, the skills involved in outlining course material in preparation for an examination and in composing rapidly under time constraints are not taught.

Some law professors advise students about how to construct course outlines. Rarely, though, do professors actually walk students through the production of these outlines. Similarly, some professors encourage students to practice examination taking with questions from previous examinations or may even schedule a practice examination. Even where practiced examinations are part of the first-semester routine, however, feedback to students is minimal. The professors' written comments on practice examination papers, as on real examination papers, usually are limited to marginal jots indicating the number of issues the student author considered out of the total the professor considered in constructing the examination.

REVIEW OF THE FOUR LITERACY TASKS

The preceding four sections have described the skills and underlying cognitive and linguistic behavior required in four specialized literacy tasks introduced in the first semester of law school. Table 13.4 summarizes key points about the kind and amount of pertinent instruction students receive in each task.

As should be clear from the instruction column in Table 13.4, on-line coaching by professors in the performance of a task is limited to Task 2, oral analysis of judicial opinions. By and large, in acquiring the skills required by the other three tasks, students are expected to depend on previous learning, general prescriptions, indirect feedback, and ingenuity in adapting to new situations techniques practiced in class.

Most law students get the picture early on. They see that their success in law school will be determined by their ability to apply creatively to every task they are assigned the process of inquiry demonstrated in their classes. Students who excel in law school excel because they know *how to do* what they see they are expected to do. Such students do not require step-by-step demonstrations of critical reading. In briefing cases, without being told to do so, they search for continuities and discontinuities *among the cases* and articulate the patterns they discern. In writing legal memoranda and examination answers, these students do not need to be shown how to move up the ladder of abstraction (derive general principles from specific instances), or how to move down (illustrate general principles with specific instances), or how to organize a composition with one's reader in mind. "Good" law students require no demonstrations because they have acquired these skills before coming to law school.

Contemporary legal education is designed for the good students, those who can understand what the professors mean but never explicitly say in law classes. Not surprisingly, given that mutual unspoken understanding between teachers and students requires common prior experiences, most good law students are traditional law students. They are students whose economic, social, and educational backgrounds are much like those of traditional law professors. These students, that is, are members of middle- and upper-class society, the dominant culture, the culture that has shaped the law. Accordingly, they are inclined to accept without question beliefs that are characteristic of that culture and that give them an advantage in law school. In short, their personal histories have taught them to confront the world aggressively; they esteem reasoning over other ways of knowing, individual accomplishment over collective accomplishment, and competition over cooperation.

But what of the other law students, those who see what they are expected to do but do not know how to do it? The following, final, section explores *their* perspectives on legal education and proposes how it might be changed to meet their needs as learners.

EDUCATIONAL IMPLICATIONS OF THE TASK ANALYSIS

At every law school, there are a number of law students who are not good students in the sense described in the preceding section. Because minority students are disproportionately represented in this group, we will concentrate on their situation.

Due largely to circumstances outside their control, relatively few minority students begin law school practiced in the skills one learns in private schools and well-financed public schools, that is, the skills of literary criticism, oral disputation, and expository writing. In addition to contending with the stress that is programmed into legal education, then, these students must attempt to overcome deficiencies in the requisite reading, public speaking, and writing skills.

Often, when minority students (or, for that matter, traditional students) fail to teach themselves the skills, law professors conclude that the students are incapable of learning the skills. Given the professors' penchant for generating multiple interpretations of any and all situations, it is surprising that they have not considered alternative explanations of this situation. One obvious, testable explanation is that (1) traditional law school instruction is pitched above the skill development level at which many minority law students are currently functioning, and (2) the gap between these students' performance levels and the level of instruction cannot be closed without the professors' assistance, that is, without additional instruction.

The research of Russian psychologist Lev Vygotsky (1978, 1987) describes a developmental phenomenon that is helpful in elaborating this hypothesis. Vygotsky's research in the dynamics of learning led him to observe that, in determining how to teach a problem-solving task, one must take account of two levels of cognitive development in the student: the level at which the student can perform the task unassisted and the level at which the student can perform with expert assistance or in collaboration with peers. The "zone of proximal development" (ZPD) is Vygotsky's term for the distance between these two levels (Vygotsky, 1978, p. 86; 1987, p. 187).

In explaining the ZPD concept, Vygotsky notes widespread misunderstanding regarding individual learning capacities:

> In studies of children's mental development it is generally assumed that only those things that children can do on their own are indicative of mental abilities. We give children a battery of tests or a variety of tasks of varying degrees of difficulty, and we judge the extent of their mental development on the basis of how they solve them and at what level of difficulty. On the other hand, if we offer leading questions or show how the problem is to be solved and the child then learns to solve it, or if the teacher initiates the solution and the child completes it or solves it in collaboration with other children – in short, if the child barely misses an independent solution of the problem – the solution is not regarded as indicative of his mental development. This "truth" was familiar and reinforced by common sense. Over a decade even the profoundest thinkers never questioned the assumption; they never entertained the notion that *what children can do with the assistance of others might be in some sense even more indicative of their mental development than what they can do alone.* (Vygotsky, 1978, p. 85, emphasis added)

For the most part, legal education operates on the assumption Vygotsky criticizes. Again, that is, when students do not learn what law schools teach *in the manner and at the level they teach it,* the professors conclude that the students lack the ability to learn it. At the same time, legal education disparages social learning and, thereby, effectively closes one avenue through which students might improve academic performance without the professors' direct intervention. Moreover, in pitting students against each other in a contest for class ranking – in fact, in making every learning activity a contest – law schools forfeit opportunities to teach the skills needed to work productively in groups. If Vygotsky's observations are correct – and any mother can attest to their validity – *exclusive* reliance on competition as a goad to learning is a counterproductive approach to education.

Consider law school from the point of view of students who have been admitted under affirmative action policies. Such students, *by definition,* are culturally different from traditional law students. Affirmative action is for students who are members of ethnic minorities, who are poor, and who have had the kind of education our society provides the poor. These students' experience of the dominant culture and their confidence in its institutions is bound to be qualitatively different from that of traditional law students. Instead of respecting these differences by exploring them as educators and acknowledging them in their discourse on the law, most law professors ignore them. They pretend it is inconsequential that members of minority groups have not been socialized from birth into the values and norms of the dominant culture. Worse, the professors fail to recognize how thoroughly the teaching methodology of legal education is predicated on that socialization. Despite everything that suggests otherwise, they behave as if students who have not had that socialization and the formal education that cements it have an equal opportunity to succeed in law school.

For many minority students, nothing in law school is more tangible than this inequality. It is so woven into the fabric of legal education that it seems inextricable from it. In a paper written shortly before her graduation from law school, Gauna (1985) describes her struggle with this realization. Addressing fellow minority students in the incoming law class, attempting to prepare them for the experience of legal education, she writes:

> I had always imagined the universe [to be] orderly . . . at least until I entered law school. I am a Chicana from a small . . . town. My father and mother worked but did not earn enough to keep a family of nine above poverty income level. Your background may be similar. . . . As you enter law school you may think none of this matters. I didn't. . . .
>
> In law school most of your colleagues will be white, well educated, and aggressive. Badges of wealth and prestige will surround you. You will meet the sons and daughters of prominent people and people educated at the best schools. They will show you their competence and expertise as correct answers easily roll off their tongues, as provocative questions spill out of their mouths and leave you in awe. You will become painfully aware you are an unskilled player in a game that is the legacy of the privileged. The game is alien to your upbringing. It is

> a manipulation of words in a foreign tongue – words which mystify, manipulation which obscures your search for justice. You will feel as if you don't belong. . . . You will feel stupid and ignorant. Bear in mind this is the game, it is not education. (p. 2)

Like many black, Hispanic, and traditional Native American law students, Gauna was a first-generation college gràduate who grew up in an extended family. In her social environment, respect for elders was the norm. For her, the idea of sparring with a teacher in intellectual debate was not only foreign but distasteful. Recalling her childhood, she mentions that she was expected to answer equally to parents, grandparents, aunts, and uncles. "Cooperativeness, not competitiveness, was essential to this way of life," she explains (p. 5). Elsewhere, noting how deference learned at home extended to other authorities, she states that "teachers were within the class of 'prominent persons' I dared not interact with. . . . [I'd] been taught to 'stick with my own kind' and remain as invisible as possible" (p. 10).

The rearing Gauna describes reflects values opposite to those promoted by legal education. One of her own law professors, a third-generation lawyer, said that engaging in heated policy debates at the family table was one of the most enduring memories of his youth. The differences between his and Gauna's early-childhood recollections help explain differences in their receptivity to legal education. Where, for him, succeeding in law school meant carrying on family tradition, for her, it meant learning behavior at odds with family tradition. As she comments in her paper, rules of play accepted in law school were not acceptable to her:

> Group learning was almost impossible. Most of my classmates were heartlessly competitive. . . . Knowledge and understanding were coveted, to be secreted away to gain an edge. They were not to be shared. Ambition justified rudeness, disrespect, and perhaps even underhandedness. In white society, ambition is respected. If I were to call someone ambitious in English, it would be a compliment. If I were to say the same in Spanish, it would be an insult. (p. 5)

The professors' combative style, adopted, perhaps, to steel students for courtroom confrontations, was perceived by Gauna as wrongheaded and demeaning:

> [Another obstacle you will encounter] is the traditional method of teaching law. My first mistake was to ask a question because I didn't know the answer. My question was skillfully transformed into a weapon and turned against me. As I attempted to answer what I didn't know, I was made a wonderful example of what legal thinking isn't. . . . And so I learned: never ask a question unless you can

> impress your professor with an insightful answer. I suppose there's a perverse logic to it all – much like training an animal through fear. [But,] there is a better way of training animals, and of teaching law. (p. 5)

As it happens, Gauna was an outstanding law student and is today a law professor. She was exceptional. She had the language skills to speak her mind clearly and, more important, the self-assurance to recognize that "the system," not she, was fundamentally flawed. Many minority law students lack her kind of confidence, are disabled by their experiences in law school, and leave it, whether before or after graduating, feeling less capable than when they entered.

Legal education has not been entirely insensitive to the predicament of minority students. Many law schools sponsor support programs for them.[16] These programs are crash courses designed to help students adjust quickly to the tempo and demands of law school. They do not straightforwardly address the cultural values behind the tempo and demands. That is, they do not present legal education as socialization into a new cultural reality. Well intentioned as they may be, such programs make participating students feel stigmatized as remedial students and, at the same time, breed resentment in nonparticipating students who are not given the extra help. That the academic performance of minority students remains a concern in legal education is testimony to the limited effectiveness of these programs.

If nothing else, the task analyses in this paper suggest the kinds of instruction that could improve these programs. But there is another way to read the message of this chapter. In that reading, the message is that the existing law program does not deserve to be supplemented, but, rather, should be rebuilt to serve the needs of *all* the students law schools have committed themselves to educate. This interpretation recognizes the reality that the law student population has changed in a way that demands revising instructional priorities.

It would not be easy for law faculties to revise their instructional priorities. The existing pedagogical model has been in place for nearly a century and has come to be regarded as necessary to achieving the goals of legal education. Should legal educators brave the challenge of overhauling that model, however, they could begin by dusting off those goals and comparing them against their teaching practices.

One goal all law schools share is that of graduating students who are imaginative problem solvers – people who can use their powers of reasoning, understanding, and communication to help resolve disputes. Were law professors to decide wholeheartedly to achieve this goal with all law students, they would question seriously whether that goal is well served by large classes, infrequent tests, indirect feedback, minimal instruction in writing, and lack of personal mentoring. In addition, the professors would examine their own cognitive processes. They would endeavor to become conscious of and share with students critical steps in analysis and writing that, through familiarity and repeated exercise, have slipped from their awareness. In sum, they would make their assumptions their values, the culture of the legal community – everything that comprises "thinking like a lawyer" – concrete and accessible. Difficult as this task would be, it would repay the effort and benefit every law student. It would lead legal education to high ground and, perhaps, to a new realization of what equal opportunity, indeed the law itself, is most deeply about.

APPENDIX: REFERENCE CASES FOR COLONEL FERGUSON MEMORANDUM ASSIGNMENT

(From Dernbach, John C., and Singleton, Richard V., III. 1981. *A practical guide to legal writing and legal method.* Littleton, CO: Fred B. Rothman, 86–88.)

In re estate of Steffans (1962)

This case involves the validity of the will of real estate broker Maxine Steffans. Steffans left her entire $385,000 estate to Rodney Prentice, a young man who has been her paperboy for eight years. The court has recently required those challenging a will for undue influence to show (1) susceptibility to undue influence, (2) opportunity to influence, (3) disposition to influence, and (4) coveted result. The court below concluded that no such influence occurred, and we agree.

Mr. Prentice testified without contradiction, and the trial court found as fact, that Steffans spoke to Prentice only when he came to collect his biweekly payment for the paper, and that she frequently paid him by putting a small envelope under her doormat to avoid this contact. A neighbor also testified that Steffans, who had a reputation as an eccentric, told her that she, Steffans, was willing Prentice her entire estate because he brought the paper on time. Under the circumstances, the claim of undue influence is speculative at best, particularly when the neighbor did not pass this information on to Prentice or anyone else.

In re Will of Kendall (1969)

Harriet Kendall's first will, executed when she was fifty-two, left her entire estate to her husband, Ralph. She entered a nursing home in 1965, when she was eight-one. Shortly thereafter, she called an attorney to ask some questions about her will. Harriet was bedridden at the time, unable to carry on a conversation for more than several minutes, and prone to forgetfulness.

The attorney made his first visit to the nursing home with Harriet's sister, Mabel. Mabel suggested that Harriet think about writing a new will. On their second visit, about one week later, the attorney and Mabel brought a new will for Harriet to sign. Although she was too weak to sit up and sign it, she was able to mark it with an "X" after Mabel propped her up with some pillows. When Harriet died in early 1966, her husband learned that the second will left her estate to Mabel's only son, Edmund. He also learned that the attorney who drafted the second will was not Harriet's personal attorney, but rather was Mabel's attorney. The trial court nonetheless admitted the second will to probate. We reverse.

There are two tests for determining whether there was undue influence in the execution of a will. The first test, described in *re Estate of Steffans (1962),* need not be considered here because we find the trial court erred under the second test. Undue influence can occur when there is a confidential relationship between the testator and the one alleged to have exercised undue influence, and there are suspicious circumstances surrounding the making of the will. The existence of a confidential relationship depends on the ease with which the confidant controlled or influenced the drafting of the will. Suspicious circumstances exist when there is a sudden and unexplained change in the attitude of the testator, activity by the beneficiary in procuring the drafting and execution of the will, or similar circumstances. The activity of the attorney and the beneficiary's mother in procuring a will from an elderly woman in this situation meets both requirements.

NOTES

This chapter owes much to thoughtful criticism and commentary on earlier drafts by Vera John-Steiner, Patricia D. Irvine, Karl E. Johnson, Jennifer Davis Hall, Eileen Gauna, Robert J. Desiderio, Pamela B. Minzner, Susan Christopher Nunn, Larry W. Smith, Frederick M. Hart, and Suedeen G. Kelly.

1. It is difficult to produce hard numbers supporting this statement, partly, no doubt, because law schools are reluctant to publicize student outcome data that may discourage minority applications. But, for a discussion of the difficulties minority students commonly face in legal education, see Holley and Kleven (1987).
2. The three-year course of study offered by law schools is completed with the award of the Juris Doctor, or J.D., degree. The J.D. degree does not confer eligibility to practice law. That is acquired on a state-by-state basis, by

passing a bar examination conducted by the state board of bar examiners. Law school graduates who intend to practice law usually take a bar examination within a year of graduation.

3. Makeup of the core curriculum varies somewhat among schools but almost always includes introductory courses in the law of property, contracts, torts, and civil procedure, as well as criminal law, constitutional law, legislative and administrative procedure, legal research, legal method, and legal writing.
4. Second- and third-year students take a few smaller, seminar and legal practice courses.
5. The judicial opinion, the species of legal writing students encounter first in law school, becomes through its centrality in legal education the exemplar of legal discourse. Concerning his own law school experience, James Boyd White (1984) writes that "our reading was not wholly confined to the judicial opinion, but the judicial opinion provided the context in which other things were read, if they were read at all, and it was the model by which we measured everything else" (p. 1670).
6. Case law is sometimes also called "common law" or "judge-made law" to distinguish it from law "on the books" – statutes, regulations, ordinances, and the like – which is enacted by legislatures and other entities authorized to make law.
7. "Stand by the decision."
8. *Stare decisis* is practical, economic, and flexible. It saves judicial time and energy that otherwise might be spent rehearing disputes that have been decided already. And, when previous decisions are outmoded or otherwise no longer helpful in solving a newer dispute, *stare decisis* gives judges the freedom, albeit limited, to change the law.
9. Generally speaking, courts are bound to follow precedents of higher courts in their jurisdiction. Sometimes courts look to settled law in other jurisdictions for guidance. In these situations, precedent is considered only persuasive; the judge is not bound by it.
10. Concerning the perception of legal issues and argument in an opinion, one law professor said that the activity reminded her of that involved in "finding the hidden pictures" in kindergarten worksheets. In such worksheets, for example, the most immediately noticeable picture might be of a family with small children, gathered at a picnic. If one looks at the picture just so, however, one can see monkeys and tigers in the trees, and, from that perspective, the picture is of a jungle scene.
11. For a discussion of the characteristics of inner speech, see Elsasser and John-Steiner (1977, p. 359).
12. Witte (1983) describes an empirical investigation of this reworking process.
13. Stratman (1990, p. 154) brings home this point by citing a 1988 resolution by the American Bar Association Section on Legal Education and Admission to the Bar that "writing skill could not be classified as a lawyering professional skill."
14. Commenting on the use of adjuncts and students as teachers of legal writing and research, Gale (1980, p. 322) observes that "the message students

receive from the assignment of sub-faculty teachers is that legal writing and research are low-level, non-academic skills adequately taught by those who have barely learned them or by those who are too intellectually inept to handle the conceptual intricacies of subject matter law."

15. Concerning time limitations on law examinations, Kissam (1987, p. 438) remarks that "time constraints, it is believed, are necessary if one is to test comprehensively while limiting the number of words a faculty member must read. Many commentators also deem time constraints necessary to provide a 'fair' distribution of grades between students and to differentiate between 'the good student and the very good student.' "
16. See, for example, Romero, Delgado, and Reynoso (1975) and the spring–summer 1970 issue of the *University of Toledo Law Review.*

REFERENCES

American Bar Association. 1975. *Law schools and bar admission requirements: A review of legal education in the United States – fall, 1974.* Published by the American Bar Association Section of Legal Education and Admissions to the Bar, 1155 East Sixtieth Street, Chicago, IL 60637.

American Bar Association. 1991. *Law schools and bar admission requirements: A review of legal education in the United States – fall, 1990.* Published by the American Bar Association Section of Legal Education and Admissions to the Bar, 1155 East Sixtieth Street, Chicago, IL 60637.

Benson, Robert W. 1984–1985a. Up a statute with gun and camera: Isolating linguistic and logical structures in the analysis of legislative language. *Seton Hall Legislative Journal* 8(2):279–305.

Benson, Robert W. 1984–1985b. The end of legalese: The game is over. *New York University Review of Law and Social Change* 13:519–531.

Boyer, Allen. 1985. Legal writing programs reviewed: Merits, flaws, costs, and essentials. *Chicago Kent Law Review* 23:23–51.

Bruner, Jerome. 1986. *Actual minds, possible worlds.* Cambridge, MA: Harvard University Press.

Bryden, David P. 1984. What do law students learn? A pilot study. *Journal of Legal Education* 34:479–506.

Burton, Steven J. 1985. *An introduction to law and legal reasoning.* Boston: Little, Brown.

Calhoun, Emily, 1984. Thinking like a lawyer. *Journal of Legal Education,* 34:507–514.

Dawson, George L. 1984. The Law School Admission Test battery: A different selection concept for the 1980s and beyond. *Journal of Legal Education* 34:388–406.

Delaney, John. 1983. *How to brief a case.* New York: John Delaney Publications.

Dernbach, John C., and Singleton, Richard V., III. 1981. *A practical guide to legal writing and legal method.* Littleton, CO: Fred B. Rothman.

Diggs, Paul C. 1970. Communication skills in legal materials: The Howard Law School program. *University of Toledo Law Review* (2 & 3):763–789.

Elsasser, N., and John-Steiner, Vera. 1977. An interactionist approach to advancing literacy. *Harvard Educational Review* 47:355–369.

Flower, Linda. 1979. Writer-based prose: A cognitive basis for problems in writing. *College English* 41:19–37.

Flower, Linda, and Hayes, John R. 1981. A cognitive process theory of writing. *College Composition and Communication* 34(4):365–387.

Flower, Linda, and Hayes, John R. 1984. Images, plans, and prose: The representation of meaning in writing. *Written Communication* 1(1):120–160.

Gale, Mary Ellen. 1980. Legal writing: The impossible takes a little longer. *Albany Law Review* 44:298–343.

Gauna, Eileen. 1985. Everything I've always wanted to say about law school. Unpublished manuscript.

Gopen, George D. 1984a. Rhyme and reason: Why the study of poetry is the best preparation for the study of law. *College English* 46(4):333–347.

Gopen, George D. 1984b. Perceiving structure. *Harvard Law School Bulletin* 35(Summer/Fall):27–29.

Gopen, George D. 1987. The state of legal writing: *Res ipsa loquitur. Michigan Law Review* 86:333–380.

Gopen, George D., and Swan, Judith A. 1990. The science of scientific writing. *American Scientist* 78:550–558.

Hamburger, Max J. Analysis and synthesis: The law student's nemesis. *Northrup University Law Journal of Aerospace, Energy and the Environment* 5:79–96.

Holley, Dannye, and Kleven, Thomas. 1987. Minorities and the legal profession: Current platitudes, current barriers. *Thurgood Marshall Law Review* 12(2):299–345.

Iser, Wolfgang. 1976. *The act of reading.* Baltimore: Johns Hopkins University Press.

Johnson, William R. 1978. *Schooled lawyers: A study in the clash of professional cultures.* New York: New York University Press.

Kissam, Philip C. 1989. Law School examinations. *Vanderbilt Law Review* 42:433–504.

Llewellyn, Karl N. 1951. *The bramble bush: On our law and its study.* New York: Oceana Publications.

Lundeberg, Mary A. 1987. Metacognitive aspects of reading comprehension: Studying understanding in legal case analysis. *Reading Research Quarterly* (22)4:407–432.

McKay, Robert B. 1985. What law schools can and should do (and sometimes do). *New York Law School Law Review* 30:491–515.

Mudd, John O. 1983. Thinking critically about "thinking like a lawyer." *Journal of Legal Education* 33:704–711.

O'Neill, Robert M. 1970. Preferential admissions: Equalizing access to legal education. *University of Toledo Law Review* (2 & 3):281–320.

Philips, Susan Urmston. 1982. The language socialization of lawyers: Acquiring the 'cant.' In George Spindler, ed., *Doing the ethnography of schooling: Educational anthropology in action.* New York: Holt, Rinehart and Winston.

Rissland, Edwina L. 1990. Artificial intelligence and law: Stepping stones to a model of legal reasoning. *Yale Law Journal* 99:1957–1981.

Romero, Leo M. 1984. An assessment of affirmative action in law school admissions after fifteen years: A need for recommitment. *Journal of Legal Education* 34(3):430–436.

Romero, Leo M., Delgado, Richard, and Reynoso, C. 1975. The legal education of chicano students: A study in mutual accommodation and cultural conflict. *New Mexico Law Review* 5:177–231.

Rosen, Sanford J. 1970. Equalizing access to legal education: Special programs for law students who are not admissible by traditional criteria. *University of Toledo Law Review* (2 & 3):321–376.

Shaughnessy, Mina P. 1977. *Errors and expectations: A guide for the teacher of basic writing.* New York: Oxford University Press.

Skillman, Nerissa Bailey-Scott (Ed.). 1986. A report on the NBA/ABA legal education conference: An assessment of minority students' performance in law school: Implication for admission, placement, and bar passage. *University of San Francisco Law Review* 20:525–552.

Stevens, Robert. 1983. *Law school: Legal education in America from the 1850s to the 1980s.* Chapel Hill: University of North Carolina Press.

Stevens, Robert. 1985. Legal education: The challenge of the past. *New York Law School Law Review* 30:475–490.

Stratman, James F. 1990. The emergence of legal composition as a field of inquiry: Evaluating the prospects. *Review of Educational Research* 60(2):153–235.

Vygotsky, Lev. 1978. *Mind in society: The development of higher psychological processes,* ed. M. Cole, V. John-Steiner, S. Scribner, and E. Souberman. Cambridge, MA: Harvard University Press.

Vygotsky, Lev. 1986. *Thought and language.* Cambridge, MA: MIT Press.

White, James Boyd. 1984. The Judicial opinion and the poem: Ways of reading, ways of life. *Michigan Law Review* 82:1669–1699.

Witte, Stephen P. 1983. Topical Structure and Revision: An Exploratory Study. *College Composition and Communication* 34(3):313–341.

Author index

Subject index